D1600841

ENEMIES UNDER HIS FEET

ENEMIES UNDER HIS FEET

Radicals and Nonconformists in Britain, 1664–1677

Richard L. Greaves

Stanford University Press • *Stanford, California* • *1990*

Stanford University Press
Stanford, California
© 1990 by the Board of Trustees of the
Leland Stanford Junior University
Printed in the United States of America

CiP data are at the end of the book

To
Sears and Marni McGee
and
Paul and Kirsten Seaver

Preface

This volume builds on my earlier study, *Deliver Us from Evil: The Radical Underground in Britain, 1660–1663* (New York and Oxford: Oxford University Press, 1986), which analyzed militant activity in England, Ireland, and to a lesser degree Scotland, from the revolts of John Lambert and Thomas Venner to the Dublin conspiracy and the northern rebellion in 1663. The present volume examines radical and more general nonconformist activity from the period of the Second Dutch War to the temporary implementation of a policy of religious toleration in 1672 and its effect on radical activity in the period prior to the Popish Plot and exclusion controversy. As in the case of *Deliver Us from Evil*, I have again borrowed a biblical phrase, "enemies under his feet" (1 Cor. 15:25), for part of the title.

I have used the anachronistic term "radical" rather than such contemporary terms as "phanatick" or "godly," each of which is heavily biased. In his presidential address to the Royal Historical Society in 1987, G.E. Aylmer not only justified the use of "radical" and "radicalism" on pragmatic grounds, but expressed amazement at the range, eloquence, and vitality of seventeenth-century radical thought and propaganda.[1] J.C.D. Clark has recently argued that the radical cause was "initially and chiefly a religious, not a secular phenomenon,"[2] a thesis I would generally endorse. His assertion that "the conceptual framework of disaffection continued for many decades to be provided by theology," though made primarily in reference to the eighteenth century,[3] is generally true of the seventeenth. Like Dr. Clark[4] and Colin Davis, I would contend that the term "radical," though indisputably anachronistic, is a useful tool of communication when referring to the more extreme forms of dissent. In attempting to explore the activities of radicals in the period 1660 to 1688, I am thus examining a segment of what Dr. Clark has called "an endless thread,"[5] but in so doing it is essential not to confuse radical activity in the late seventeenth century with that of our own day, nor to attempt to read back modern notions of "radicalism" into the age of Charles II and James II. Radical activity must always be judged in historical context. The mere act of opposing a regime is not enough to make one a radical; the advocacy or implementation of revolutionary goals is the determining factor. Perhaps the first writer to refer to these dissidents as an "underground" movement was Francis North, Baron Guilford (1637–85), who noted that in the 1660s "there was at work underground, other partys of Republican Atheists, who were for overturning all, & restoring their fancyed Comonwealth, & their titles to Crowne—& church—lands."[6]

Delineating the boundaries of radical activity will always be a subject on which historians and social scientists disagree. I have chosen not to equate radicals with all Protestant nonconformists, but have instead limited the term "radical" to those who espoused active disobedience of the law, particularly in the form of such activities as rebellion, assassination, the publication of allegedly seditious literature, and the use of violence to prevent legally constituted authorities from enforcing the law. Although virtually all radicals were Protestant nonconformists, not all nonconformists were radicals. That nonconformity should be potentially so militant is hardly surprising, given its intellectual heritage of a doctrine of armed resistance developed by such men as John Ponet, Christopher Goodman, and John Knox. Not all those who embraced the distinctive tenets of nonconformist theology and ecclesiology, however, were willing to endorse a militant posture *vis-à-vis* the Stuart regime; hence the term "radical" is most appropriate when not used synonymously with the entire Protestant nonconformist community. The latter in any event was not neatly divided into two groups, but was more akin to a continuum, with advocates of passive disobedience flanked by militant radicals on the one hand and those who essentially made their peace with the regime on the other.

With its predecessor, this book underscores the extent to which organized opposition to the restored Stuart regime was present in the 1660s and 1670s. Much of the material analyzed in these pages will be new to many readers, but it was familiar enough to Charles II and his advisers, who were repeatedly faced with the challenge of evaluating the reports of alleged conspiracy and dealing with such militant activity as the Galloway (Pentland) rebellion and the attempted assassination of the duke of Ormond and the archbishop of St. Andrews. Contrary to common assumptions, militancy was not confined to a handful of lunatics, nor was it solely the creation of the imaginative minds of informers determined to retain their employment.

Charles's government faced widespread defiance of the laws by those who worshipped in conventicles or published illegal writings, many of which were allegedly seditious. This pervasive spirit of will-ful disobedience, which was rampant among nonconformists, pro-vided the context in which militants justified violent action as a means to achieve their ends. I have, therefore, deemed it essential to discuss the radicals in the wider context of nonconformity. In so doing, I have offered a rather different and broader perspective of the 1672 Declaration of Indulgence and its ramifications.

Moreover, I have continued to deal with dissident activity in all three kingdoms and among the exile communities on the Continent, seeking to determine not only what the radicals were doing but what connections may have existed between them. There were, to be sure, links extending from Ulster through Galloway and Edinburgh to Rotterdam, and from Vevey through Amsterdam to London and Somerset. Ties also existed between the Scots and the English along the borders, and extended from there to London. What emerges from this study is an account of the tangled web of conspiracy, ide-alism, frustration, resiliency, and ineptitude in the radical commu-nity, as well as the place of that community in the broader world of nonconformity. The government had a difficult time understanding this world, but considerable effort was spent to develop and imple-ment policies to deal with the militants. To overlook this fact is to omit a fundamental aspect of Charles II's reign, and thus distort our understanding of it.

For biographical information on many of the figures referred to in this study, the reader may consult the *Biographical Dictionary of British Radicals in the Seventeenth Century*, 3 vols., ed. Richard L. Greaves and Robert Zaller (Brighton: Harvester Press, 1982–84), and A.G. Matthews, *Calamy Revised* (Oxford: Clarendon Press, 1934).

I am delighted to have the opportunity to acknowledge some of the debts incurred in writing this book. A fellowship from the American Council of Learned Societies under a program funded by the National Endowment for the Humanities enabled me to do much of the research for both volumes; the present work was also made possible by a grant from the American Philosophical Society. Robert Zaller and Paul Seaver read the manuscript with meticulous care and offered numerous helpful suggestions; any errors that remain are, of course, my own responsibility. For assistance with matters pertaining to the Dutch and the Irish, I owe special gratitude to Keith Sprunger and Paul Hardacre, respectively. Among many others to whom I owe thanks, I would like to single out Leland Carlson, Ian Gentles, Janelle Greenberg, Christopher Hill, J. Sears McGee, Michael Perceval-Maxwell, Mary Robertson, Lois Schwoerer, Leo Solt, Ted Underwood, and Dewey Wallace. For their valuable studies of the Fifth Monarchists and Scottish church history, I am indebted to B.S. Capp and Julia Buckroyd, respectively. Richard Schlatter, to whom I owe an abiding debt, died before this book was finished; he would, I hope, have been pleased to see the work come to fruition. The staffs of the following libraries have been exceptionally helpful: the Public Record Office (Chancery Lane), the Bodleian Library, the Department of Manuscripts at the British Library, Dr. Williams's Library, the Nottingham University Library, the National Library of Scotland, the Edinburgh University Library, the Huntington Library, and the Rijksarchief in Zuid-Holland (which provided microfilm). A British historian in his own right, Norris Pope, Associate Director and Editor-in-Chief of Stanford University Press, has been very helpful. I am also grateful to Nancy Atkinson for her masterful copyediting. To my two daughters, to my wife, and to my parents I am especially grateful for their abiding support and love.

R. L. G.

Contents

1. "Trumpet in Sion": Radical Conspiracies and the Second
   Dutch War   1

   Radicals on the Eve of the Dutch War, 3; The Exile
   Community on the Eve of the War, 12; The Second Dutch
   War and the Radicals, 15.

2. "For God and the Covenant": The Scots and the Galloway
   Rising   49

   The Troubled Search for a Religious Settlement, 49;
   Smoldering Embers, 54; The Troubled Southwest, 59;
   The Galloway Rising, 64; Insurgents in Flight, 76.

3. "Factious and Seditious Spirits": Scotland and Ireland,
   c. 1666–1672   85

   Scottish Conventicles: "Hot, Fiery, Young Teachers," 86;
   Physical Assaults on Scottish Clergy, 96; Radical Political
   Activity in Scotland, 101; Ireland: Radical Schemes, 103;
   Irish Security, 109; Nonconformists in Ireland, 112.

4. "The Present Distresses": The Nonconformist Challenge in
   England, 1664–1672   121

   Assessing Resistance: Passive Disobedience or Sedition?,
   121; Coping with Dissent: The 1664 Conventicle Act, 129;
   Fighting "the Lords Battale": The Quakers and "Anti-
   christs Servants," 134; Conflicting Courses: The Toleration
   Dispute, 142; A Nation in Turmoil: From the Second
   Conventicle Act to the Declaration of Indulgence, 151.

5. "The True Englishmen's Complaints": The Radical Press, 1664–1672   167

    The Radical Press in England, 167; Scotland, the Covenanters, and the Press, 184.

6. "The Militant Christian": Kidnappers and Crown Jewels   191

    Restless Radicals, 192; To Kill a Duke: The Ormond Kidnapping, 204; The Theft of the Crown Jewels, 209; The Search for an Accommodation, 215.

Conclusion: Radicalism and the Policy of Indulgence   224

    The Impact of the Indulgence in England, 224; Scotland: The Flawed Compromise, 235; De Facto Toleration in Ireland, 241; A Retrospect, 243.

Notes   253

Index   307

ENEMIES UNDER HIS FEET

"Trumpet in Sion"

ONE

Radical Conspiracies and the Second Dutch War

In the early 1660s, the government of Charles II quickly discovered that the restoration of monarchy and the episcopalian state church had not eradicated the revolutionary fervor of the previous two decades. The sheer numbers of potential dissidents posed a severe challenge to the regime: nearly 70,000 men had been in arms in July 1652, while the nonconformists must have numbered well over 100,000 in the aftermath of the great ejection of August 1662. Many of the ex-soldiers were, of course, nonconformists, yet by no means could all nonconformists be regarded as radicals. There were, however, enough militants to cause the government serious concern, even after their schemes failed, as in the case of Major-General John Lambert's insurrection on the eve of Charles's return, Thomas Venner's Fifth Monarchist uprising in January 1661, the abortive Tong plot in 1662, and the equally unsuccessful Dublin conspiracy in the spring of 1663. The government's problems were compounded by the need to evaluate a virtual torrent of information about alleged plotting, much of it spurious, and some of it even incited by the state's own agents provocateurs. Defiance of the law in the nonconformist community was nevertheless both pervasive and persistent, making it difficult for magistrates—and informers—to determine which dissenters were genuinely a threat to the regime.

The radical "community" was coextensive with neither nonconformity nor specific nonconformist groups. In fact, the Presbyterians, Congregationalists, Baptists, and Quakers all had radicals in their midst, and these militants demonstrated a willingness to suppress their religious differences in order to make common cause against the Stuarts. Yet the radicals never formed an effective, cohesive group united by strong leaders and a common vision of a new order. They were only loosely unified, primarily by common animosities, including dislike of the Stuart monarchy, opposition to popery and prelacy, resentment over the execution of leading regicides, and hatred of General George Monck. Persecution of the godly angered them, and some were concerned about the security or recovery of their estates.

In the early 1660s, the militants hoped to launch a general insurrection, but such an effort required leadership and organization skills that they lacked. This was vividly manifested in the northern rebellion of 1663. The key figure among the northern radicals was the Congregationalist minister Edward Richardson, whose group was in touch with a revolutionary council in London that had also been involved with the Tong conspiracy. The declaration that Richardson drafted for the insurrection, *A Door of Hope Opened in the Valley of Achor for the Mourners in Sion out of the North,* endorsed the use of violence to topple an ungodly regime and proclaimed a global crusade to destroy the papacy and the Turks. The conspirators had ties to Scottish Covenanters as well as exiles in the Netherlands, but the government was able to monitor their plans through informers strategically placed within the rebel ranks. Undeterred by Richardson's flight to the Netherlands and preemptive arrests by the state, the conspirators proceeded with their rebellion on the night of 12–13 October. Units gathered in Yorkshire, Durham, and Westmorland, but their numbers were woefully short of what had been expected, partly because of inclement weather, and the insurrection collapsed before godly rule or religious freedom for all Protestants could be established.

The ignominious failure of the northern rebellion laid bare the massive organizational problems of the English radicals, forced some of their leaders into exile, underscored the improbability of obtaining significant assistance from dissidents in Scotland and Ireland, and undermined radical claims of a certain and swift victory over the Stuart regime. On the contrary, it was Charles II's government that won a crucial propaganda victory, both by demonstrating rebel impotence and by treating most of the insurgents with relative leniency. Although the radicals' defeat did not destroy their determination to overthrow the monarchy and the episcopalian state church, it forced them to reassess their means.

Previous conspiracies had tended to focus, conceptually at least, on coordinated uprisings in the three kingdoms, although never in the early 1660s did the dissidents come close to mounting such a rebellion. The defeats of the early years did not persuade them to relinquish these schemes, but they did prompt the radicals to think of domestic insurrection as part of a broader plan that entailed Dutch financial and military assistance and, ideally, coordination with a Dutch invasion. Henceforth many of the leading dissidents looked increasingly for support from the Netherlands and to some degree from France. In addition to providing a sanctuary for the exiles, the Netherlands was a useful source of weapons and ammunition.

As the English and the Dutch moved toward war in 1664, the radicals began to think in terms of coordinating a Dutch invasion with a rebel insurrection as the means to topple the Stuart regime. To be effective, such a plan necessitated both strong leadership from a radical such as Edmund Ludlow and the full commitment of Jan De Witt and the Dutch government. The danger was apparent to Charles and his advisers, who stepped up intelligence activity in the Netherlands in order to counter radical conspiracies. The militants also faced a formidable problem in building a cohesive community in wartime conditions, when patriotism tended to outweigh dissatisfaction with the government. If the radicals were to succeed, they could not afford to have significant elements of the nonconformist community throw their support to the king against the Dutch. Nor, for that matter, could the Dutch commit themselves to the militants unless the dissenters agreed to place religious freedom above patriotic loyalty. In the end, many nonconformists preferred the constraints of their position to an English defeat at the hands of the Dutch, and that choice doomed the hopes of the militants.

Radicals on the Eve of the Dutch War

Numerous manifestations of popular discontent with the Stuart regime were present throughout the mid-1660s. Some of it was undoubtedly typical of the resentment expressed by those dissatisfied with virtually any government, but the depth of hostility and the nature of a good deal of the discontent suggest that it originated with committed dissidents. The principal objects of attack were the king and his court, the established church, and the level of taxes,[1] though there was also lingering resentment against the duke of Albemarle for his betrayal of the Good Old Cause, and a rising tide of antipopish sentiment. Although reduced, the expectation of imminent deliverance, whether political or religious, was still widespread. A radical doggerel of 1667 warned:

> For Fate is turning now her wheele about,
> And in revenge will roote the bloody out:
> The time of which Catastrophe will bee,
> Within the 4: yeare after 63:
> For May that yeare doth captivate a king;
> November after death to him doth bring.
> But if not then, in 72 September
> Lett all, the dyeing captives, remember.[2]

Some were convinced that the government could not stand long and would shortly be overthrown either by force of arms or by Christ's apocalyptic return.[3]

Personal hostility to the king was expressed with little abatement. Among the more frequent epithets applied to him were "rogue," "tyrant," and "whoremaster."[4] Sensitivity to his immorality, which even troubled some of the royalists, was often acute. Thomas Povey, treasurer of the Tangier Committee, remarked to Samuel Pepys a-propos the royal mistresses: "The King doth spend most of his time in feeling and kissing them naked all over their bodies in bed—and contents himself, without doing the other thing but as he finds himself inclined; but this lechery will never leave him." One of those who accused Charles of an illicit relationship with the countess of Castlemaine was Mary Roe, daughter of the regicide John Alured. To many, such behavior was not only morally reprehensible but inimical to good government. Thus a London barber-surgeon remarked sarcastically in 1666 "that ther was like to be good goverment when the King keepeth other mens wyfes and makes them his Concubynes."[5] Accusations of moral laxity extended to the court as a whole, which was denounced by one dissident as nothing more than "a Company of Whores & Rogues." Charles was castigated by one former Cromwellian soldier for allowing the profanation of the Sabbath and a general climate of wickedness.[6]

Revulsion against the king and his court as well as disgust with the government's apparent incompetence prompted frequent comparisons between Oliver Cromwell and Charles, to the latter's detriment. At Hull the people formulated their contrast in largely economic terms, convinced that "in Ollivers time there was better Care to secure the Coast trade then is now."[7] Although much of the complaining amounted to nothing more than customary grumbling, the depth of radical hostility was manifested in recurring threats against the king's life and the fervently expressed yearnings for his imminent execution or natural death. After condemning Monck as a traitor, a Northumberland man longed "to see his Majestye goe the Same way that his father went before him," while a Cumberland dissident forthrightly declaimed: "Hang the King. He is a knave, and a whoremaisterly rouge." Others expressed a willingness to return to arms in order to overthrow the monarchy.[8]

The hostility of the dissidents to the established church was an extreme manifestation of the more pervasive tendency to disparage the clergy. Pepys, for instance, referred caustically to "the pride and debauchery of the present clergy," while his friend Robert Blackborne, secretary to the Admiralty Commissioners in the 1650s, observed that the clerics were widely detested and mocked, especially for their excessive use of excommunication. Prelates attracted particular hostility; one Middlesex yeoman, pleading insanity, was fortunate to escape punishment for deprecating the bishops as "murdering rogues." A former Cromwellian soldier predicted in 1666 that the prelates would be ousted within a year, and there was indeed concern at year's end that the attacks on the bishops and the church might incite a rebellion in England akin to that which erupted in Galloway in the autumn.[9] The year 1666 was, in any event, important among those devoted to apocalyptic considerations, particularly because 666 was the "number of the Beast." As B.S. Capp has demonstrated, the interest in 1666 was widespread, extending even to the German states and Russia, and including Jews as well as Protestants.[10]

Animosity to the Church of England was periodically manifested in crude acts of irreverence. At Wollaston, Northamptonshire, dissidents "bedaub'd" the vicar's Book of Common Prayer with tar and grease, and referred to the baptismal font as a swilling tub. Bristol fanatics used long poles to break windows in four churches in July 1664. At Newcastle and Dover dissidents openly ridiculed and disrupted burial services, and a man was hanged at Oxford in 1664 for stealing the surplice and other church ornaments.[11]

Religious convictions and fears were also responsible for the continuation of antipopish sentiments, the most serious form of which was the accusation that the king himself countenanced Catholicism. Fears of a popish uprising were fanned by dissidents to suit their own ends. In April 1667, for instance, Peter Crabb warned Henry Bennet, Lord Arlington, a secretary of state, that the western counties had armed themselves because of rumors of a Catholic insurrection, and he blamed the nonconformist clergy for spreading such stories in the hope of facilitating their own rebellion. Three years earlier there had been concern because a letter, allegedly from a Jesuit in Ireland to a London colleague, hinted at a Catholic plot; the letter may have been fabricated to foment anti-Catholic feelings.[12]

Passage of the Conventicle Act in May 1664 caused substantial unrest. As passage of the bill approached, a correspondent of Sir William Blakeston, a deputy lieutenant in Durham, reported that "the Phanaticks looke with a Rebellious spiritt, and their Language smell[s] much of dissatisfaction; and [they] begin againe [after the northern risings] to meet with much confidence, which is much to bee feared will bee an oportunity for them to hatch their Rebellion."[13] Blakeston, afraid for his life at the hands of northern radicals, in April reported to Joseph Williamson with undoubted exaggeration that there had been a dramatic change in people's outlook, and that affairs were "far out of order." Resentment also ran high owing to the repeal of the 1641 Triennial Act; the weaker 1664 version, which lacked enforcement provisions, was unsatisfactory to dissidents. Ensign Benjamin Walsh probably reflected the views of many radicals when he yearned for the return of the Long Parliament, esteemed because it refused to stoop to the monarchy.[14] Thus the hard core of discontent present in the 1660s was reinforced by the weakening of the Triennial Act and imposition of the Conventicle Act, both of which steps struck at principles dear to the dissident community.

Throughout 1664 the government labored to unravel the full story of the northern conspiracy and to apprehend prominent malcontents. Among those for whom warrants were issued in February and March were the regicide William Say (who was at Vevey with Ludlow), and the Fifth Monarchists Anthony Palmer, John Vernon, Nathaniel Strange, and Thomas Glasse. Three men who had robbed the exchequer at Taunton of £500 to raise money for the northern rebellion were executed in September 1664.[15] Although Sir Thomas Gower and Sir Thomas Osborne continued to interrogate suspected northern rebels, they complained that the sectaries met more frequently than ever and that "the rebells in Yorkshire do still prosecute theire intended treasonable designes."[16] Indeed, Captain Edward Shepperdson, who had been involved in the Derwentdale plot, confessed in April that a new conspiracy was under way. In Durham dissidents were reportedly circulating papers "to excite the relations of those that have suffered, & all others of there interest, to kill . . . all those Who have bene active against them." The failure of the northern uprising notwithstanding, Sir Philip Musgrave was concerned because the disaffected in Westmorland were "numerous & dangerous."[17]

Rather than being cowed into submission by the collapse of the northern revolt, the radicals continued to scheme. Quakers who came to Yorkshire from London told John Atkinson, who turned informer after his arrest in the northern conspiracy, that radicals were considering putting the City to the torch. He recommended that the duke of Buckingham keep the Baptists and Fifth Monarchists under close surveillance. Recurring but apparently unsubstantiated reports suggested that a revolutionary council was still meeting in London and was in contact with unspecified foreign enemies. Information of dubious veracity obtained by Sir Brian Broughton in March indicated that the council had dispatched orders to Irish extremists to rise, though the latter reportedly declined to do so without assurances of substantial support from English rebels, which could not be given. Thus the council was forced to await "word of the Irish contest, which its thought will be in May." Broughton's information noted that reinforcements for the Irish rebels intended to sneak into Ireland by way of the Scottish Highlands. Thirty-two dissidents in Ireland, according to an intelligence report, had invited Ludlow to lead an assault on Kinsale and Limerick. Among them were Sir Henry Ingoldsby, whose name had been linked to the Dublin plot, William Allen, and John Nelson, like Ingoldsby a former governor of Limerick. The government was sufficiently alarmed by these reports to order the lords lieutenant and their deputies to take appropriate precautions.[18]

In April Sir William Blakeston likewise heard that the meetings of the revolutionary council were continuing in London with the encouragement of ministers on the Continent. Other radicals met in the City, among them the "Counsell of old Parliament Rumping members" that reportedly convened at the home of a Mr. Speers in Lothbury. The imminent passage of the Conventicle Act disturbed dissidents, who were not only holding secret meetings in the City and at Hackney in May, but also purchasing suspicious quantities of horses and gunpowder.[19]

The recurrent plotting necessitated regular attention to matters of security. Because one source of the agitation was the ability of dissidents to maintain contact with radicals incarcerated in the Tower, the government on 4 January 1664 ordered Sir John Robinson to prohibit prisoners from enjoying its liberty. A number of inmates were subsequently transferred to more inaccessible locations. Orders were issued to send Sir Henry Mildmay and the regicides George Fleetwood and Augustine Garland to Tangier, though Mildmay died en route at Antwerp. Robert Overton and the regicides James Temple, Gilbert Millington, and Thomas Waite were moved to Jersey, Paul Hobson to Chepstow Castle, Robert Danvers (alias Villiers) to the Isle of Wight, and George Elton to Carlisle. Others were sent to Tynemouth, Hull, Scarborough, and Southsea.[20]

The condition of the militia, which had caused so much consternation in the aftermath of the northern revolt, was improved as a result of a special levy of £70,000 per year for three years. The money was first raised in all lieutenancies except London in 1663, and Charles ordered that the funds be levied again in 1664 because of the continuing conspiracies. To his lords lieutenant he wrote: "The notoriety & apparency of the same danger, is infinitely multiplied by the restlesse & never to be satisfied mindes of those, upon whom the pardon of past offences hath had no other effect then to give them a Confidence to comitt new ones."[21] Nevertheless, in Herefordshire, where the militia was still unsettled, there was grumbling that the county could not afford the tax. The £70,000 was levied again in 1665.[22]

Officials were particularly interested in apprehending the elusive Henry Danvers, a warrant for whose arrest had been issued on 30 December 1663, but efforts to seize him failed. In June he reportedly met in the Midlands with an agent who had allegedly informed radicals in Ireland that a scheme to rebel was complete and had the support of the revolutionary council in London. Danvers then went to the City to confer with dissident leaders. The date for the rebellion in England was 31 July, and the Irish contingent purportedly hoped to rise as soon as possible.[23]

Corroboration that another rebellion was in the works came in scattered reports throughout the first half of 1664. Captain Nicholas Cordy (or Cordey), who had served in the regiment of Colonel George Twisleton, was arrested in January for alleged involvement in a conspiracy on behalf of the Good Old Cause, and documentary evidence of a plot was found at Oxford the same month. Rumors and allegations multiplied in the spring from as far afield as Westmorland, Dorset, Hampshire, and Wales.[24] One informer reported increased activity by women, some of whose husbands were prisoners: "Women are now almost wholy employed" as rebel agents, he stated, especially to convey intelligence. In June, female couriers brought messages to Yorkshire radicals from Ireland and western England, and Westmorland authorities seized a letter in cipher conveying intelligence from Margaret Tomlinson to dissidents in the south.[25]

Much of the radical activity centered in the north. Rebels who had fled when the northern rising collapsed returned to their homes, fueling fears of renewed violence. Dissidents from Ireland were also arriving in the north with tales of oppression. "The continewed designes of our restles Enimies" were a source of genuine concern

among northern magistrates. They were especially disturbed by reports that a new insurrection was being planned by radicals in the
Gildersome and Northallerton areas, both strongholds of the 1663
northern rebels.[26] In county Durham a government spy was instructed "to procure the subscription of the disaffected pertie to such
engagements as may bring them within the compas of the law." The
zealots "are in so great a readines," Sir Roger Langley wrote to Secretary Bennet, "that they want little, but to attend there intended
tyme for rising." Langley was worried that the militia would not act
if the rebels struck at harvest time, and he pressed Bennet to find a
secure place to detain malcontents such as Captain Robert Hutton,
one of the alleged northern plotters. His concern was well-founded,
for Captain John Mason, another northern conspirator, had escaped
in July from York Tower. Expectations of an insurrection the last
week in July prompted officials in Durham to postpone a general
rendezvous of militia and volunteers, though guards of horse and
foot were posted. Companies of militia were also dispatched to York
"to rescue the country from the dangerous attempts of seditious conventicles, &c."[27]

Despite the ominous warnings, July passed without a new rebellion. One of Bennet's correspondents, who had found "very few that
doe not wish well to the blackest designe," nevertheless observed
that disaffection was ebbing in late July. He also noted, however,
that dissidents were encouraged by visions and prophecies that focused on the death of the king and the overthrow of episcopacy. The
continued suspicious meetings of radicals as well as the forthcoming
anniversary of the battles of Dunbar and Worcester on 3 September
were goads to further surveillance. Information from Dorset noted
dissident hopes of a change of government by Michaelmas.[28]

In 1664 the radicals began to look to the possibility of an Anglo-
Dutch war as the means to attain either religious toleration or support for a rebellion. As early as the spring a group of London malcontents, who met at a tavern near the Exchange and in a Lothbury
coffee house, expected the Dutch to provide them with weapons in
the event of war. Among the leaders of this group were two former
officers, Lieutenant-Colonel Abraham Holmes and Major Jordan.
For his involvement, Holmes was imprisoned in Windsor Castle
without a trial.[29]

Although the leading northern conspirators who remained at large were similarly hoping for war, they resolved to press ahead with their scheming even in the event of peace. In September, according to Bennet's informer Leonard Williams, they accumulated funds—which they "managed verry warrily"—and planned an attack on the Tower and Whitehall. Entry to the former, they judged, could be obtained by a small group armed with pistols on the pretext of viewing the armory.[30] Among those who met at a widow's house in Petty France were such hard-core radicals as Roger Jones, author of *Mene Tekel*, the inveterate rebel Thomas Blood, Timothy Butler, the one-handed Major Lee, and Hobson's friend Thomas Gower. The Fifth Monarchists were represented by Jeremiah Marsden, Nathaniel Strange, Edward Cary, and either Anthony or (more likely) Thomas Palmer. Three of the group—the northern rebels John Mason, Christopher Dawson, and Reginald Faucett—had recently escaped from prison in the north. Although Williams was apparently unaware of it, the government had another informer, John Atkinson, placed among the dissidents.[31] The attempt of magistrates to arrest these men about 21 September failed when the latter were forewarned, but Williams continued to provide Bennet with information, including the fact that they were acquiring arms and money. They were, moreover, in contact with Scottish dissidents, whom they encouraged to rebel.[32] Corroboration of this came from the dean of Durham, who informed Bennet in October that John Joplin of Durham, though in prison, was corresponding in code with exiles in the Netherlands, using a woman as courier.[33]

In Staffordshire Sir Brian Broughton continued to monitor radical movements. From one of his agents he learned in November that a messenger had been sent from Staffordshire to the Irish dissidents with instructions "to bee redie with speede," for there were allegedly 1,300 men at sea and a like number in England ready to act. Instructions were expected in Warwickshire, Leicestershire, and Staffordshire in the coming week, although nothing of substance materialized. The government, however, was unwilling to take a chance and issued a proclamation ordering all ex-Cromwellian officers to leave London and Westminster, exempting only those with a special license.[34]

In January 1665 Captain Roger Jones (alias Rogers), disguised as a carter, worked with Captain Harris and others to enlist and arm recruits in Buckinghamshire and Hertfordshire. The authorities considered arresting Jones, but initially declined lest the radicals learn that their movements were being monitored. When an attempt was finally made at the end of January, Jones escaped. Efforts to apprehend Captain Edward Cary (alias Carew), Jeremiah Marsden, and other prominent London malcontents were equally unsuccessful.[35]

Reports of seditious schemes were widespread on the eve of the war. The government learned in January that "the most sober fanatiks" were planning "to surprise Bristoll and there to beginne upon the first oportunity[,] they haveing a suffitient party thereabout" to defeat the royalists.[36] One of Sir Thomas Gower's informers, John Ironmonger, reported that dissidents in the west anticipated assistance from France. More ominously, Colonel Fulthorp and various northern conspirators, including Captains Robert Hutton and Thomas Lascelles, met for two days at Northallerton with two agents from Scotland. One of the latter was an unnamed former ministerial associate of James Guthry, who had been executed in 1661. One of the Scottish agents was dispatched to London, and letters were sent to Nuthall, near Nottingham. The purpose of the meeting was to establish reliable means of correspondence and arrange for places where agents could acquire fresh horses and funds. There was also a meeting at Cowton in the North Riding at which Captains Best and (William?) Carter were present.[37] According to Ironmonger's information, however, the disaffected did not intend to rise until the Dutch navy was at sea.[38]

The Exile Community on the Eve of the War

In the year preceding the outbreak of war, exiles in the Netherlands were divided in their plans for the future. Some were quiescent in the expectation that Charles would honor the promise of liberty of conscience made in the Declaration of Breda. Joseph Hill, a minister at Middelburg, indicated that the Presbyterians were willing to emulate the Huguenots by serving the king and hoping for an indulgence, though this group was also being courted by radicals.[39] Militant exiles were under the surveillance of royalist agents, es-

pecially Colonel Joseph Bampfield, who had begun reporting to Sir
George Downing in October 1662, and Edward Riggs, who practiced medicine in Rotterdam and utilized a host of aliases to cover
his work as a spy. The latter disclosed to Bennet in January 1664 that
the militants were preparing for a summer rebellion, buoyed by the
deteriorating relations between London and Amsterdam. John Desborough and Thomas White were meeting with other radicals at
Arnhem. In the meantime Richard Tyler continued to purchase arms
and smuggle them into England, until in May 1664 he was arrested
and imprisoned in the Tower.[40] To Bennet he insisted that his weapons were intended only "for the Royall Companies use," although
he acknowledged contact in the preceding nine months with Dr.
Edward Richardson, Thomas Cole, now "a Burger in Roterdam, &
a considerable man there," and Captain Mead.[41] In the autumn dissidents in Derbyshire, Nottinghamshire, and Lincolnshire sent two
agents—James Washington and a Mr. Lunn, the latter presumably
the former Tong plotter—to the Netherlands to share information
on radical plans.[42]

　　The Dutch encouraged English and Scottish dissidents in the
hope of fostering fears at Whitehall of Dutch support for the militants in the event of war. In July there was a report from Bergen op
Zoom that "the States knowe how to Master England whensoever
they shall have dispute with it, by sending Moneye into Scotland for
them to Rebell, & alsoe to doe the like into England, to the discontented there." According to one of Bennet's informants, Dutch assistance was predicated on the direction of the rebellion by "joynt
counsells of a select party in both Nations," England and Scotland,
who in turn were to correspond with militants in the Netherlands
under the supervision of Edmund Ludlow and Algernon Sidney.[43]
In January 1665 there was a report that Jan De Witt, the Grand Pensionary and de facto head of the Dutch government, had enlisted
"severall discontented English, privatly," to scheme against the Stuart regime.[44] In response to such pressure, Whitehall insisted that
Englishmen would stand together in the event of war. When the
Dutch ambassador cited the hopes of the zealots to profit by an
Anglo-Dutch conflict, the duke of York retorted that "the English
have ever united all this private differences to attend [to a] Forraigne

[threat]." Nevertheless, intelligence accounts continued to underscore the fact that radicals throughout the country looked expec-
tantly for the outbreak of hostilities with the Netherlands.[45]

As the war drew closer, speculation increased about the intentions
of Ludlow and Sidney. In contrast, Richard Cromwell, who was living in Paris under an assumed name, posed no serious threat to the
government, and in fact considered moving to Italy in the autumn
of 1664 to escape involvement in the hostilities. Sidney, who had
gone to Rome, was forced to leave in 1663 when he was dogged by
assassins. He spent three weeks with Ludlow at Vevey before going
to Bern and then Germany. At Augsburg in the autumn of 1664 he
narrowly escaped assassination by a royalist agent.[46]

In the meantime, Ludlow and John Lisle were concerned for their
own safety.[47] As early as November 1663, a group of "ruffian like
fellows, desperadoes with long Cloakes & Carbines under them,"
attempted to ambush Ludlow. The group, which was led by Major
Germaine Riordan, an Irishman who had served in the duke of
York's regiment, included Frenchmen, Savoyards, and at least one
other person from England or Ireland. Ludlow subsequently traveled in the company of an armed escort, and when in Lausanne
was provided with a dozen guards by the magistrates.[48] An Irish
assassin murdered Lisle in Lausanne on 11 August 1664, which
prompted William Say and Colonel John Biscoe to flee to Germany.
Ludlow, however, declined to accompany them, convinced that it
was "much better to be in a condition of making opposition against
my enemies, than to live in the perpetual fear of being discovered."[49]
Prior to his move to Germany, Say—at Sidney's request—went to
Holland to ascertain potential Dutch support for the "honest party"
in England.[50]

Ludlow's intentions continued to interest Whitehall, and Downing kept the earl of Clarendon apprised of his purported movements
as well as those of Sidney, Colonel Thomas Wogan, and Captain
John Phelps. If for no other reason, Ludlow was an irritant because
his name inspired malcontents who longed for the Good Old Cause,
and thus sparked repeated but false reports of his presence in England
and Ireland. In January 1665, as a case in point, there was a story that
Ludlow had gone to the Netherlands to organize recruits for an ex-

pedition to Scotland, Bridlington ("Burlington"), and Kent, where "the Castells are commanded by insignificant negligent persons." This was apparently to be coordinated with a rising in Bristol. Moreover, among remnants of the old northern conspirators, Ludlow was "much made of," and there was concern that his allies had the unofficial backing of the French.[51]

To compound matters, Colonel Gilby Carr, who was in the Netherlands, maintained contact with dissident Presbyterians in Scotland. By February 1665, the exiles claimed to have some 3,000 men in the Netherlands. The informer John Ironmonger put the number at closer to 800, but they were reported to be "good soldiers . . . who are spirited with zeale to hazard any thing." Another source indicated that no less than four regiments of disaffected Scots and English were forming in the Netherlands, but this was clearly an exaggeration. The estimate of Sir William Davidson, who put the number of exiles at just over 160, was probably an understatement.[52] In early 1665 the English government continued to hope that the war would unify the English and Scots, and thus deprive the militants of any chance to capitalize on the hostilities.

The Second Dutch War and the Radicals

If the war were to become the means to restore the Commonwealth, the radicals had to persuade the English and Scots that the Dutch were spearheading a crusade either to save Protestantism or to restore the political rights that only a republic could guarantee. Even if the Dutch had had the power to invade England and impose a puppet regime of republicans, its ability to survive would have been doomed without popular backing. In the end the monarchy retained its support not only because of patriotism and economics but also because of division among the dissidents themselves as to the propriety of assaulting the government in the midst of a foreign war. There was no unified radical front, no organized propaganda campaign on behalf of the Dutch, no master strategy of opposition to the regime, no forceful radical leadership, no effective cooperation between Scottish and English dissidents, even in exile. Ludlow remained in Switzerland, Desborough finally surrendered to the Stuart regime, and Sidney could persuade neither the Dutch nor the French to provide solid assistance.

Mixed Expectations

Initially the Dutch were unsure as to what support they might offer to the English militants. Although De Witt was unwilling to back an invasion, discussions with the dissidents continued. In February the Dutch naval commander, Jacob van Wassenaer, lord of Obdam, dined with the regicide Valentine Walton, "one of the Scarlet die who is received into Counsell with the Dutch," and a merchant from King's Lynn.[53] De Witt himself was inquiring "after any who can make stirs" in England or Scotland, but his task was rendered difficult by the number of royalist agents in the Netherlands. Downing did not trust a Mr. Prescott, who also offered his services to De Witt as an envoy to radicals in England. The principal reason for the Dutch reluctance to render substantive assistance to the militants was the latter's failure to provide an organized front to oppose Charles II. As one of Arlington's agents in London observed in July, the Dutch would not commit themselves to the rebels "because noe person appears to them that can satisfy them that there is any united Intrest here which they can rationally depend uppon as sufficient to make any considerable disturbance."[54]

For the Dutch there was also the more fundamental question of whether the reestablishment of an English republic was in their best interests. The Commonwealth had proved to be no friend in the early 1650s, yet the same trading interests that had provoked enmity between the two nations then now helped push England into renewed hostilities. Although Charles and Clarendon did not want this war, they acquiesced, convinced that the Dutch would make economic concessions rather than fight. Once the fighting was under way, the Dutch had to assess not only the feasibility of supporting the exiles and their domestic allies from a military standpoint, but the foreign policy implications if the radicals succeeded in reestablishing a republic. The anti-Dutch policy of the Commonwealth had, after all, been succeeded by the friendly attitude of the Protectorate. Unfortunately for the Dutch, the leading supporter of that government among the exiles, John Desborough, returned to England in

1666. Nevertheless, a restored republic guided by the likes of Sidney and Ludlow must have seemed less of a threat than a monarchy that could, by miscalculation and pressure, renew hostilities against the Netherlands. Moreover, in the 1660s the Dutch were increasingly aware that the greater threat to their well-being came from France, whose expansionist tendencies menaced the Spanish Netherlands. No wonder De Witt was frustrated in 1664 by the vicissitudes of English foreign policy, which he attributed to greed and capriciousness; England, he judged, was oblivious not only to justice but to its own self-interest. Once war broke out, the possibility of helping establish a thoroughly Protestant republic had to be considered, especially because of its potential as a useful ally against Catholic and monarchical France.[55]

For their part, radicals in England and Scotland were confused by their inability to obtain reliable information on Dutch intentions. This exacerbated the difficulties they experienced because of turncoats, such as William Scott and Colonel Joseph Bampfield, within their ranks. Ostensibly one of them was the "fiery zealot" John Atkinson, the former northern conspirator, who was purportedly planning to go to the Netherlands in February or March to spy on the exiles. But Atkinson had now become a double agent, having once again pledged his ultimate loyalty to the radicals.[56] Instead of going to Holland, he stayed in London, where he associated with Jeremiah Marsden, Captain John Mason, and a number of other militants who hoped for Dutch assistance. Atkinson was responsible for shipping copies of *Mene Tekel; or the Downfal of Tyranny* to the north. The anonymous author, Captain Roger Jones, was allegedly a "bedfellow" of Atkinson's.[57] It was apparently Atkinson's link to the radical press that betrayed his role as a double agent to the government, for he was arrested at the beginning of April and interned in the Tower. His apprehension, according to the informer Leonard Williams, caused consternation among the radicals, who assumed Atkinson had been betrayed. "How they disoblige each other, how unfitt they are, to carry on any designe," he concluded. A discourse setting forth the case against the Stuarts, which is now in the Public Record Office, includes the names of Atkinson, the Quaker Christopher Eyon, Mrs. Thomas Gower, and others, and was probably found in Atkinson's possession.[58] The discourse contains a litany of radical complaints against the tyranny of Charles I and the greater evils of his son, episcopal oppression and "Prelatique encroachments," the persecution of nonconformists, the execution of regicides, and burdensome taxes and unjust exactions. Accordingly it was the duty and honor of saints to take "a two edged sword in theyre hands to execute thy [God's] judgments written upon wicked Kings, as well as others: yea the people may & are bound to punish him . . . according to the nature of his crime, depriving him of his Crowne & life."[59]

Interrogated by Arlington, Atkinson offered to betray the location of the dissidents' meetings and arms caches in return for his liberty, but the government showed no interest. Atkinson did confess that Captains John Lockyer and Roger Jones had money, presumably to finance radical activity, and that they had some hope of Dutch assistance. Jones, Atkinson opined, was already thinking of throwing himself on the king's mercy and would confess if arrested. Leonard Williams thought Atkinson might divulge more information if he confronted Atkinson, but nothing seems to have come of this.[60]

Atkinson's father-in-law, George Bateman (alias Grisley Pate) of Durham, was himself involved with elements of the radical underground that extended from London into the north. Bateman and Eyon claimed to have word in early 1665 that the Dutch were organizing as many as eight to sixteen regiments of horse and foot comprising Scots and English soldiers to invade northern Scotland. The information was false, but on the basis of it an effort was undertaken to prepare zealots in England to join the invaders, who would allegedly supply arms provided by the Dutch. There was hope too of taking Newcastle with 600 or 700 men.[61] According to Ironmonger, details of these plans were conveyed by women, the chief of whom were Lady Frances Vane and Anne Danvers, wife of Henry Danvers. Raby Castle, which belonged to the Vane family, was one of the centers of radical activity in Durham. The conspirators were supposedly in touch with the discontented in Ireland. Ironmonger reported that they planned diversionary actions in Durham, the west, and the Isle of Wight, but the heart of their scheme was an uprising in London. According to John Ward, one of the northern conspirators, those of his confederates who were still at large were well armed, ready to rise, and full of hope because of the Dutch War.[62]

The more militant Fifth Monarchists in London, led by Nathaniel Strange, wanted to launch an attack on Whitehall in early 1665. However, the "soberer Fanatiques" prevailed on Strange, "a rash heady person," to postpone the attempt until they knew what "advantages they might have by the war with Holland."[63] Another zealot, Timothy Roberts, the ejected vicar of Barton, Westmorland, reported that dissidents in that county and the Borders were ready to rise. The Fifth Monarchists also urged Captain Owen Cox, who had fought against the Dutch in the 1650s, to take command of a frigate and transport the exiles back to England or free John Lambert from his incarceration on Guernsey. Cox, however, died in a shipwreck later in 1665.[64]

Beyond London, radicals looked to the war as an opportunity to advance their cause. From Staffordshire Sir Brian Broughton apprised Williamson in February that the militants in the north, Leicestershire, and London were prepared to rise when the fleets engaged, presumably in May. Reports from Newcastle confirmed that a scheme was under way, bolstered by expectations of a Dutch invasion. So too in Yorkshire, militants—undeterred by the failure of 1663—found new hope in the Dutch. Their prospects were buoyed as well by prodigies observed in both Yorkshire and Devonshire that seemingly pointed to momentous events.[65] This anticipation was tempered, however, by a growing skittishness occasioned by fear of informants. Leonard Williams, himself a turncoat, observed to Bennet in March that the alarmed dissidents were "fitter at present, to treppan one another, then to carry on any designs." Nevertheless, at the king's behest Clarendon ordered the justices of the peace in late March to detain suspicious persons and be vigilant in discovering zealot machinations.[66]

The Radical Response to the War

In general, the militants' lack of organization and popular support reduced them to little more than observers of the fighting. As the fortunes of the naval war ebbed and flowed, the mood of the dissidents rose and fell accordingly. The mood of the radical community perceptibly darkened at the news of the Dutch defeat off Lowestoft on 3 June 1665. In Newcastle the dissidents were reported to "hange doune their heads" in dismay at the English victory. It was, said one royalist, "a perfect Antidote to gratifie those Spirits who thirsted for a change." But while hope of Dutch relief dwindled, others began to "buildd much upon what may be done if the plauge [sic] encrease."[67]

Radical spirits were lifted by news in late July that the Dutch had repulsed an English attack on their ships at the Norwegian port of Bergen. When an unidentified fleet was sighted east of the Isle of Wight the following month, the Welsh Fifth Monarchist Vavasor Powell, who was still in prison, prophesied that the Dutch would emerge victorious in the next encounter.[68] There was, however, no further fighting between the two fleets in 1665, although the English successfully captured nine ships engaged in the East India trade.

The first major engagement of the new season with the Dutch— the Four Days Battle—commenced on 1 June 1666 off North Foreland. Only a heavy fog on the final day prevented the Dutch from achieving a decisive victory. The emboldened exile community, it was reported, "flatters themselvs that if Ingland . . . lose one other fightt ther Captivitie wil be neer Expired." Their church services were filled with prayers for more Dutch triumphs. There was some suspicion that the Dutch owed their superiority to intelligence about the English fleet provided by Maurice Thompson, the influential London merchant, and his brother. Further concern was aroused by Captain Andrew Yarrington, a prime suspect in the fictitious Yarrington plot, who was "known to have been on board most of the English fleet, before the last engagement."[69] News of the battle was sent to Scotland in terms that implied that the Dutch were now masters of the sea and could blockade the Thames. Gilby Carr dispatched one of his men to Scotland to prepare dissidents for an invasion, but they were reported "soe broken . . . by the last ill successe they had, and so distrustfull of each other, that there are no generall meetings, but the matter is kept among few." One of Arlington's correspondents reported that the Scots were expecting a landing by the French and Dutch, and that Presbyterians were preparing to rise in defense of the Covenant. "They doubt not uppon that intrest to carry that whole Kingdome before them."[70]

In the aftermath of the Four Days Battle and the accompanying surge in radical spirits, the government ordered the militia to prepare for an invasion. The lords lieutenant were directed to keep suspicious persons under surveillance and to detain the most dangerous, especially those in possession of unusual quantities of horses or arms, which were to be seized.[71] Secretary Bennet, however, believed that the Dutch would not invade unless the dissidents rebelled in one of the three kingdoms or unless the Dutch fleet established superiority at sea. The French too, he thought, wanted to spark an insurrection in one of the three kingdoms and hoped for Lambert or one of similar stature to lead it. The French, he concluded, would probably strike at Ireland, the Dutch in Scotland. The state of English coastal defenses was nevertheless a cause of worry, particularly at Portland and Weymouth.[72]

Instead of benefiting the radicals, the Dutch success dealt their cause a severe blow. Fears of a Dutch or French invasion galvanized all but hard-core militants behind the government and thereby undercut radical hopes to profit by the war. From around the country reports flowed in of the enthusiastic response to the plea for military preparedness. At Oxford the Baptists professed their willingness to fight the Dutch as well as the French, while from Lancashire Sir Roger Bradshaigh noted that the Presbyterians and "fanatics" were as ready to accept commissions as any.[73]

The sectary Katherine Johnson urged the king to save his crown by dismissing Albemarle, who was "not fitt to be a Generall in your Fleet." Better, she argued, that he should pray with his people and repent with the Privy Council. Ultimate responsibility, she insisted, was Charles's, for he thirsted after conquest rather than peace. It was apparently the same woman who told Charles that the people cursed him and longed for Cromwell. She asserted that "the nation ar redie with every puf of wind to rise up in armes because of the opression that is Laid upon them," and that some threatened to stop fighting the Dutch because "when the wars is over we ar slited sik [i.e., like] dogs."[74]

In late July the defeat of the Dutch in St. James's Fight off Sheerness temporarily dampened radical expectations. After the Four Days Battle, some militants had looked with confidence to the overthrow of the Stuarts early in the summer, but in mid-July the mood generally shifted to one of cautious patience.[75] When Admiral De Ruyter and many of his men became ill, most of the Dutch fleet had to be recalled. On 15 September (O.S.) De Witt, learning of the "miraculous accident" of the fire in London, ordered De Ruyter to keep the fleet together. The next day the States General directed him to join De Ruyter at sea, but the latter became so sick that he had to return on the 23rd. Two days later De Witt challenged the English fleet, but the latter retreated into the Thames and refused to give battle, leaving the Dutch with little recourse other than to sail home.[76]

Distracted by domestic problems, the Privy Council committed a crucial blunder the following spring by not readying the fleet. Despite domestic dissension, the Dutch were far from beaten and now had Denmark as their ally. As early as December 1666 the Venetian resident had reported to his government that the Danes were willing to invade Scotland if the Hague would provide 4,000 to 5,000 troops. The Dutch declined. The following month, however, Arlington's agents informed him that 20,000 arms would be sent to Scotland by the end of February as a prelude to a Franco-Dutch invasion. In April a Dutch squadron actually sailed into the Firth of Forth, and Whitehall feared that the Dutch intended to land on the Yorkshire coast.[77]

Still, the English were woefully unprepared when a Dutch fleet commanded by De Ruyter sailed into the Thames in early June. With the fleet were 4,000 troops under Colonel Doleman, who helped take Sheerness Fort, which commanded entrance to the Medway, on the 10th. Two days later the main fleet sailed up the Medway, captured the *Royal Charles*, and burned other warships. Subsequent attacks were made on Landguard Fort opposite Harwich by Doleman's men (3 July), and on Plymouth, Portsmouth, and Torbay, where two merchant vessels were burned on 8 July. The Dutch had hoped for an uprising by English dissidents, and their forces were even directed to offer religious toleration to the inhabitants of the Isle of Sheppey.[78]

The stunning attack was followed by inevitable recriminations and rumors, including one—attributed to dissidents—that places of trust were being given to Catholics. Others grumbled that such a debacle could not have happened in Oliver's day, when state funds were spent on the navy and the military instead of the theater and women. In general the radicals were buoyed by the Dutch success, and some reportedly bragged that "the Dutch would not acquiesce till they were suffred to preach agayne publickly."[79] Some attributed the English disgrace to the prominence of "the popish & profane party" at court, while others were dismayed that the attack did not bring an immediate cessation of "the debauchery & drunkennes of the great ones." In the Netherlands the exiles held a service of thanksgiving in Rotterdam, while that city's *Gazette* published a baseless story about the people of London crying out for the replacement of the monarchy with a commonwealth.[80]

The Dutch attack in June and July did not provoke a radical uprising, though some certainly feared that they would "have their throats cutt here by some insurrection or riseing, the more encouraged by the power of an Enemy at sea." Maintenance of domestic order was largely achieved by the government's prompt decision to call up the militia, to levy 10,000 foot and 2,500 horse, and to summon Parliament. Although militarily prudent, such actions brought criticism, especially by those who suspected that the duke of York was intent upon creating a professional army and making "the government like that of France."[81] The war itself had sparked antimilitary sentiment by failing to bring either economic advantages or naval glory in return for the high taxes. Concern regarding Charles's military intentions was by no means a radical monopoly, for as early as 25 July the House of Commons refused to adjourn until it passed a resolution—which carried unanimously—that the troops be disbanded as soon as peace was concluded. The disquietude in the country may have been due in part to warnings from the disaffected. In Devon, for example, the Presbyterians asserted that soldiers would soon be taken to the Continent and placed under the command of Catholic officers.[82]

The Role of the Exiles

If the radicals were to receive any meaningful assistance from the Dutch or the French, it would have to come through negotiations with the exile leaders, particularly John Desborough, Edmund Ludlow, and Algernon Sidney. But Desborough was persuaded to return quietly to England by Charles's government, Ludlow was deeply distrustful of the Dutch, and Sidney alone was unable to inspire Dutch and French confidence.

Moreover, political differences among the exiles undoubtedly made their adoption of a common policy against the Stuart regime more difficult. Ludlow, Sidney, Say, Robert Phaire, and William Cawley were committed republicans, whereas Desborough and Thomas Kelsey, though no monarchists, had supported and served the Protectorate. Nevertheless, differences of this nature seem to have had relatively little impact in exile. More important were disputes over strategy, particularly how far the Dutch and later the French governments could be trusted. On this issue Ludlow was profoundly suspicious, whereas Sidney, Cawley, and others were not. There was yet another group of exiles who were content to live in peace, eschewing plotting. But perhaps the greatest problem among the exiled radicals was the failure of the English and the Scots to develop a strong alliance. The religious and political differences between the two groups were simply too extensive and deep-seated to bridge, even in the context of exile.

When war was declared in February 1665, Sidney went to the Netherlands in an attempt to persuade De Witt to sign a treaty with the exiles promising to invade England and support the restoration of a republican government. Sidney assured him that most Englishmen did not want war, that the dissidents were strong and willing to fight, and that a number of former officers would come to Holland to join an invasion force. Unpersuaded, De Witt opposed the plan when it was presented to the States General. Sidney's case would have been stronger had Ludlow accepted his invitation to join him in Holland, but "the bone of contention betweene us," Ludlow observed, "was touching the Tearmes on which to Engage with the Hollanders." As a matter of conscience, Ludlow was troubled by the earlier Dutch perfidy in surrendering Sir John Barkstead, Miles Corbet, and John Okey, and he had also been warned by a prominent person in Bern that involvement in the Dutch War would jeopardize his sanctuary.[83]

Although the Dutch were originally cool to the idea of supporting the radicals, there was some change of opinion in the early months of the war, as Say indicated to Ludlow in a letter from Rotterdam.

Reflecting the latter's concern that the radicals might be left without adequate support, Say wrote: "Invitations and incouragements are not only offered, but pressed upon you; and there is no ground to fear their retreat, of which you seem to doubt." The States General had begun to realize, he argued, that the safety of their own republic depended upon the restoration of a sister regime in England. Say expected substantial support for the radical cause in England, Scotland, and Ireland, but acknowledged that the real weakness was inadequate leadership: "Nothing seems now so much wanting as fixed councils both here and in England, and no one can be more serviceable than your self in this important matter."[84] A second letter indicated that "the present most Considerable person at the Hague"—presumably De Witt—"did lately very much Enquire after you," and that the Dutch hoped to put either Ludlow or Lambert (if he could be freed) at the head of a "Number of men." Ludlow agreed only to send his wife, who had "a heart full of weight with Love & Zeale for the publique Cause," to London. Thomas Cole had already returned to England for discussions with City dissidents.[85]

Pressure began to mount on Ludlow to go to the Netherlands to explore possible collaboration with the Dutch. This was the message from Ludlow's friends in London, who were in contact with the exiles in the Netherlands by means of Edward Dendy's wife. There was some communication too with malcontents in Scotland, who "made use of" Major-General Robert Montgomery "to agitate" for the overthrow of the Stuart regime. According to Say, dissidents in Scotland and England had coordinated their planning, and a rising in northern and western England was possible with as little as five days' notice.[86]

In the Netherlands Say and Sidney met with William Nieupoort, the Dutch ambassador to England in the 1650s, to discuss an alliance. Say subsequently reported to Ludlow in May that the Dutch had given him £2,000 to help further the scheme, with the promise of an additional £8,000. In return the Dutch expected the militants to raise 4,000 foot for an attack on Newcastle, which Say thought could be managed. Sidney likewise pressed Ludlow to hurry to the Netherlands before the Dutch changed their minds. In his judgment

time was too short even for Colonel John Biscoe to travel to Switzerland for talks with Ludlow. The latter's reluctance strongly displeased his friends and prompted Slingsby Bethel to suggest that
Ludlow categorically state that he had no intention of participating
in a rebel-Dutch alliance. Ludlow, however, refused to go this far,
but did agree to write on behalf of the importance of unity among
the saints in the war against their common enemy, Charles II.[87]

In Leyden, meanwhile, a group of exiles met after the battle of
Lowestoft in June 1665. The leaders, according to one of Sir William
Davidson's informers, included Desborough, Colonel Robert Phaire
(or Faire), Major (or Colonel) Thomas White, Major William Bur-
ton, and Captain (Benjamin?) Groome. Phaire was dispatched to
England for consultations with radicals there, and Captain John
Phelps followed. By the end of the month the leading militants had
congregated at Rotterdam, among them Desborough and the regicides Thomas Wogan, Sir Michael Livesey, and Daniel Blagrave.
From Downing's informant, William Scott, son of the regicide
Thomas Scott, came the additional news that militants were "at
work" in western England, especially around Poole in Dorset. This
group must have maintained contact with Desborough and Wogan's
party.[88]

The threat of an alliance between the radicals and the Dutch
coupled with fresh conspiracies at home (particularly the Liverpool
and Dover plots) persuaded the government to issue a proclamation
demanding that exile leaders return to England. Richard Cromwell
was considered for the list, not least because his name was periodically linked to purported conspiracies. His wife, Dorothy, twice dispatched her servant, William Mumford, to London to ask Dr. John
Wilkins to persuade Clarendon to omit Cromwell's name on the
grounds that his creditors would destroy him if he returned. Cromwell was still residing in Paris under assumed names and pondering
a move to Italy or Spain, away from his fellow exiles. According to
Mumford, he had no contact with the militants and never intended
to command an invasion by a Scottish regiment from a base in
France, as had been alleged. A preliminary list (dated 26 March) included Cromwell, but his name did not appear when the proclamation was issued on 9 April. Ironically, at this time the authorities

received word that rebels were going to act as soon as the fleet sailed, and that some of them wanted Cromwell to rule, though others preferred a commonwealth. The rising was supposed to commence in London, where the password would be "tumble downe Dick." The key figure in this alleged and probably spurious plot was John Cowborne, former major of foot to Colonel Buffett. Despite the new allegations, however, Cromwell's name was not added to the proclamation, undoubtedly because the government realized the discredited and inept Richard was not a serious threat.[89]

The proclamation contained thirteen names, including those of the exile leaders John Desborough and Thomas Kelsey. Three of the men were wanted principally for their role in the Tong plot: Captain Humphrey Spurway, Edward Radden, and Thomas Cole. On the list too was Dr. Edward Richardson, architect of the northern revolt.[90] For unexplained reasons the government struck the names of other radicals, including Sidney, James Harrington, and Oliver St. John. The proclamation ordered the thirteen to return and stand trial or be attainted of high treason. All were accused of having "treasonably engaged themselves in actuall service in the said Warre."[91]

One of the names on the proclamation was that of William Scott, son of the regicide Thomas Scott. While a trooper in Colonel Joseph Bampfield's regiment, William betrayed the English spy Thomas Corney and Nicholas Oudart to the Dutch authorities; both had been in the employ of Sir William Temple. Arlington, however, was ignorant of this and recruited Scott to spy on the exiles beginning in 1666. Scott's brother-in-law, Richard Sykes, was a contact between the exiles and dissidents in northern England, while Sykes's brother William, a merchant, was close to Kelsey and Gilby Carr, and was allegedly "of their secrit Councill." Sir Thomas Gower had information in October 1665 that William Sykes wanted to return to England, where he planned to gather intelligence for the Dutch and the exiles.[92]

A government agent—possibly Philip Alden—provided Albemarle with a document detailing the activities of spies working for the dissidents. They had been instructed to procure information concerning troop movements, the construction of naval vessels, merchant convoys, and the size and supply of military units. Orders were also given to communicate with one of the Sykes brothers. According to this document, Ludlow, Desborough, and "all the old officers in the States service will come to head the Dutch, & bring a Declaration & show it then."[93] Rather than lead an invasion, Desborough obeyed the proclamation and in July returned to England, where he was imprisoned.[94]

The distrustful and pragmatic Ludlow still refused to become actively involved in any scheme to invade his homeland, notwithstanding Sidney's insistence that he was neglecting his duty and a personal plea from William Cawley. Shortly after France declared war on England in January 1666, Brigadier Stouppe, a Swiss-born officer in the service of the French, visited Ludlow at Vevey with the encouragement of the Dutch ambassador in Paris, Conrad van Beuningen. His mission was to ascertain the possibility of a radical alliance with the Dutch and French, for which substantial funds were reportedly available. Ludlow responded "that if any just and honourable way should be proposed for the restitution of the republick in England, I would readily use the best of my endeavours, and hazard my life in that service." From Count von Dohna's chaplain Ludlow learned that De Witt, Nieupoort, and others of "the honest party" wanted him to go to Paris with Sidney to conclude a formal treaty, to which Louis XIV had reportedly agreed in principle. De Witt sent the French sovereign a letter of introduction on behalf of Sidney; subsequently Louis himself contacted Ludlow.[95]

The pressure on Ludlow to act was intensified with letters from dissidents in London, exiles in Rotterdam, and Phelps. The Rotterdam group tried to persuade him that this was "the Lords Call to a glorious worke, wherein the Interest of the Lords people throughout the World was concerned," while from England came an admonition that "the Clowd & the Piller was moving, & the Lords Servants [are] called to follow it." He should not, they added, be discouraged by the failure of the northern rebellion, "this being better managed." Additional pleas came from Say, Biscoe, and Sidney, the latter urging Ludlow to meet him in Basle for direct discussions preparatory to a joint trip to Paris. Say was perhaps prescient in observing that if Ludlow refused to act, no one would "stirr." Ludlow, however, was convinced that Sidney was better suited to command, and he was unwilling to work with the French government, "that king being no less a montayne in Christes way."[96] Ludlow's refusal to seek aid from the French is a poignant reminder that there was nothing of the politique in his character. He was probably also shrewd enough to realize the impossibility of restoring an English republic with the aid of an absolutist and Catholic state.

Late in 1666 Ludlow agreed to meet with Phelps and Thomas Blood in Lausanne. There he argued that the French could not be trusted, that involvement in the war jeopardized sanctuary in Switzerland, and that in any event he was better placed where he was to help raise recruits. Nevertheless he agreed to an alliance with the Dutch if certain conditions were met: (1) The States General must publish a declaration admitting its error in surrendering the regicides Barkstead, Corbet, and Okey; (2) it must "owne the Interest of the Long Parlament" and pledge to help restore a republic in England; (3) it must furnish troops of the Reformed faith as well as funds and artillery; and (4) it must undertake not to leave the dissidents in a worse condition than they currently experienced. The conditions were never agreed to by the Dutch.[97]

The militant exiles were now unsure of their next move. According to Ludlow's information, a Dutch secret committee composed of De Witt and seven others still held out the possibility of an alliance with the radicals, but the attitude of France was an enigma, particularly because the French did so little to assist their own ally, the Netherlands. Some of the militants, including Phelps, were unwilling to trust Louis XIV, but Sidney, Nicholas Lockyer, and Major Thomas White were prepared to negotiate in Paris. Sidney's price for a French alliance was 100,000 crowns, but Louis's government was willing to offer only 20,000, with the promise of an additional 40,000 later, in addition to troops. Even this was contingent upon the ability of the radicals to demonstrate that such an expenditure would be "advantageous"; this could be shown, Ludlow was told, by his participation. Because the offer included French Catholic troops, it was intolerable to exiles in the Netherlands. Moreover, Sidney's offer to head an invasion force was not acceptable to leading militants in England as well as to some of the Dutch, undoubtedly because of his relatively inconsiderable military experience. Soldiers, ministers, and merchants in the exile community thereupon appealed to Ludlow to take command, and De Witt and Nieupoort sought his participation. Until his conditions were met, however, Ludlow refused.[98]

Despairing of Ludlow's help, Sidney contrived a scheme with various Frenchmen to liberate Lambert from Guernsey in July 1666. A letter to Lambert was intercepted, however, and Charles's agents were able to arrest Jean François de Briselone, Sieur de Vancourt, governor of the Isle of Chanzy, as well as a ship master involved in the plot. As early as 3 July, Arlington had been able to inform Ormond that the French hoped to free Lambert and "kindle a flame" in the three kingdoms.[99] During the course of the ensuing eight months, there was a good deal of concern at Whitehall that the Dutch would invade Scotland and the French Ireland, possibly in conjunction with radical uprisings.[100] It was therefore deemed imperative to monitor radical activities at home and abroad as closely as possible.

The exiles were observed by a network of English spies that provided a steady flow of intelligence to Whitehall. Much of it came from Aphra Behn and William Scott, who sought a royal pardon and monetary remuneration in return for his espionage work. Behn learned of a radical agent in London who recruited informers in English ports to provide data on the movement of merchant vessels that the Dutch could seize. Although the exiles were essentially unperturbed by the results of the St. James's Fight in July 1666, they were, according to Behn, increasingly dissatisfied with Bampfield and threatened to place themselves directly in Dutch service. Bampfield himself discovered that a new recruit, Captain Sands Temple, hoped to acquire command of an English ship and place it at the disposal of the Dutch navy.[101]

Exile leaders discussed war plans with the Dutch. Captain Thomas Woodman, who had served the English republic in the 1650s, was engaged with De Witt and Colonel Thomas Doleman in a plan to block the Thames with sunken vessels. Doleman had been in the employ of the Dutch government during the 1650s. According to Scott, De Witt was also in contact with Sidney, whom he held "in great esteem." Sidney in turn was reportedly involved in consultations with the Quaker Benjamin Furly, "being resolved to shape som designe for Ingland." Although Bampfield was dubious about the value of Furly's information concerning English affairs, Behn observed that Furly was "the most trusted person amongst us." Furly was also in contact with John Phelps and Major Radwell, while Sidney met with Major Thomas White and prepared a tract espousing republican government. Phelps was staying in Rotterdam with a Mr. Raven (or Ravens), in whom the Dutch displayed interest because of his plan for a landing in England.[102]

In the end, not even the wartime experience was sufficient to unite the exiles. Ludlow, Sidney, and Desborough went their different ways, depriving English radicals of a potentially potent triumvirate. Nor did the English and Scottish exiles join forces to plan concerted action against Charles's government. Moreover, some exiles had lost their will to fight, perhaps chief among them Dr. Edward Richardson, who professed to have turned his back on political activism: "Publiq affairs I meddle little in." Grateful for the hospitality and religious freedom provided by the Dutch, he nevertheless was unwilling to see the ruin of England and its monarchy. Once a cornerstone of the northern conspiracy, he proclaimed in August 1666 that "I am of no party but that of righteousnes against unrighteousnes, for Jesus Christ against every way of wickednes among whomsoever it is practised." In sharp contrast, a group of zealots who met at Antwerp in September infuriated Behn by their flagrantly treasonous speech against Charles's government.[103] The divisions within the exile community were undoubtedly among the factors that persuaded the Dutch not to provide substantive support to the militants.

Although negotiations for peace commenced in January 1667, the Dutch continued with their war plans, hoping to mount an attack on England or Scotland with Ludlow's assistance. Although once again pressed by associates in the Netherlands and England, he demurred, judging his principles unsuitable for an alliance with the Scottish Presbyterians and still holding out for Dutch acceptance of his conditions. In April the Dutch sailed into the Firth of Forth and attacked Burntisland, and in June the main fleet launched its brilliant assault on the Medway, with Doleman taking the place that would have been Ludlow's. In the end the latter had agreed to come to

Holland, but only if his status at Bern was assured. He was in any case still distrustful of the Dutch, fearing a sudden withdrawal of their support that would leave the militants dangerously exposed. Justifying his own inaction, he concluded that "it's most cleare that the Dutch had never any reall Intention to doo the honnest party of England any good, but that they sought their Goods rather then their Wellfare." [104]

Wartime Plotting

Although the radicals failed to coordinate their activities with the Dutch, they took advantage of the war to sustain their disruptive endeavors in England. In this respect, the war gave them new life in the aftermath of the failed northern insurrection in 1663. Because their hopes were really pinned on the Dutch, however, the scheming of the war years was poorly organized and largely ineffectual. Moreover, most of the leading English radicals were now in exile, where their inability to develop a concerted plan of action with the Dutch left dissidents in England without a clear sense of direction. Whether in the end the Dutch would have gambled on aiding a *united* republican cause can only be a matter of conjecture. When they finally did intervene, in 1688, it was not on behalf of a republic but on behalf of a monarchy ruled by law and opposed to France. Nevertheless, for the radicals, the Dutch War was to a degree the story of missed opportunity.

Although faced with both the war and the plague, the government decided to strike at the zealots in the late summer of 1665. One of the first to be arrested was Henry Danvers, who had been accused of high treason, but on 3 August he was rescued in Cheapside as he was being taken to the Tower. When magistrates interrogated his servant at Moddershall, Staffordshire, they discovered that Danvers's brother Charles, of Soper Lane in London, had been shipping books—presumably publications of the radical press—into the shires. Henry Danvers, however, continued to elude arrest. [105]

The government was more successful with a series of arrests that commenced in August when Albemarle announced the discovery of a new conspiracy. The government's edginess, exacerbated by the war, had been reflected in May when the king complained to the lord lieutenant of Lancashire about the plotters.[106] The conspiracy that triggered the new arrests—the Dale-Buffett plot—was uncovered in August and was a revival of a similar scheme conceived in 1662. One of the Buffett brothers, Colonel Francis or Colonel Richard, was in Cornwall promoting a conspiracy to seize the Tower and Whitehall Palace. With the usual exaggeration, the Buffett group claimed to have 2,000 men for the attack on the Tower and another 10,000 men in the west. Major (Daniel?) Dale (alias White), who had escaped from the Tower, visited Bristol, Taunton, Glastonbury, and Cornwall in connection with the plot, and then left for London, reportedly to determine when (unnamed) rebels in the City would be prepared to revolt. Another plotter, Richard Edwards, who had been indicted at Wells for treasonable words, went to Ireland to promote the conspiracy.[107] The king responded by ordering the lords lieutenant to imprison suspicious persons, to require security of others, and to assemble volunteer or militia units so long as the people were not overly burdened at harvest time, which would exacerbate discontent.[108]

In connection with the Dale-Buffett plot, the magistrates compiled a list of thirty likely insurrectionaries in Devon and Somerset, of whom no less than twenty-five were former officers. Among them were such radical stalwarts as Edward Radden, described as Desborough's secretary, and his associate Captain Humphrey Spurway, both of whom had been involved in the Tong plot and had spent some time as exiles in the Netherlands. The list also included the names of men allegedly involved with the Buffetts in a July 1662 conspiracy: Captain John Barker, Major Colbourne, and Captain (John?) Pyne.[109]

The flurry of arrests that followed Albemarle's announcement of the plot extended as far as the northern shires. Claiming to have information concerning ongoing conspiracies, the duke of York directed officials in the north to secure suspicious persons.[110] Among those targeted for detention were Captains Thomas Lascelles and Matthew Beckwith, both of whom had been arrested in connection with the Lascelles plot in December 1662. As far as the north was concerned, all of this was purely precautionary, for the region proved to be quiet. On 20 August Sir William Coventry reported to Arlington from York that "ther is noe signes of any intention of rising heere." The south too was generally calm, though twenty barrels of powder were seized by authorities as they were being transported to Malmesbury, Wiltshire, via Reading. Weapons were also being shipped to Malmesbury hidden in hogsheads (large casks).[111]

In late August the government discovered yet another conspiracy—this one real enough—under the direction of Colonel John Rathbone and Lieutenant-Colonel Ralph Alexander.[112] Their plan called for a party of men to cross the Tower moat in boats, scale the walls, and surprise the defenders. Simultaneously another squad was to assault the Horse Guards at the inn where they were quartered. The plotters allegedly intended to burn the City and execute the king, Albemarle, Sir Richard Browne, and Sir John Robinson, governor of the Tower. The day chosen for the rising was 3 September—the anniversary of Cromwell's death and of the battles of Dunbar and Worcester—a date described in William Lilly's almanac as one when a planet "then ruling . . . Prognosticated the downfal of Monarchy." The planning was allegedly undertaken by a revolutionary council in London in conjunction with a sister body in the Netherlands. The conspirators purportedly intended to establish a republic and redistribute property equally. Alexander escaped and eventually fought with Monmouth in 1685, but Rathbone and seven other ex-officers were condemned to death at the Old Bailey and executed on 30 April 1666.[113]

Further investigation turned up the names of a dozen radical leaders believed to be "engagd in this businesse." Henry Danvers, though "very warrie since his greate fright" in London,[114] was reputedly "the Head of a considerable partie" in Staffordshire, while the leaders in neighboring Leicestershire were three captains, one of whom appears to have been Henry or Timothy Clare. Both had been involved in Lambert's insurrection of April 1660.[115] Cheshire was supposed to be the responsibility of Colonels Thomas Croxton and Robert Duckenfield, both of whom had been secured on the eve of the northern revolt, and Derbyshire of Colonel Thomas Saunders, Major Nathaniel Barton, and Captain Robert Hope, who had been arrested in late 1661 as a suspected plotter.[116] Although Vavasor Powell was in prison from 1660 to 1667, he was accused of having "a great partie" ready to revolt in Wales. Colonel Peter Stubber, who had commanded the guard of halberdiers during part of Charles I's trial and had lost his Irish estate at the Restoration, reportedly went to Ireland to enlist the support of their "many friends" in Ulster. Command of the rebels was supposedly given to Desborough, though he was still in the Netherlands.[117] Although the government could not prove these allegations, the possibility of a widespread conspiracy provided an opportunity for extending the security measures instigated in the wake of the Dale-Buffett plot, and for passage of the Five-Mile Act. Not even the opposition of Clarendon, the earls of Manchester and Southampton, and Philip Lord Wharton could prevent this penal legislation against nonconformists. The new act, however, was not only a fresh example of the narrow religious interests of the Cavalier gentry but a product of renewed militant activity and wartime concerns.

In September and October the government cracked down on suspected militants, arresting hundreds and requiring many others to provide security. Some escaped by fleeing to Ireland. No fewer than fifty persons were committed to Lincoln Castle, including Colonel Edward King, the former governor of Lincoln, and Captain John Pym, who had served in Colonel Pride's regiment.[118] At Worcester the list of prisoners included Captain Andrew Yarrington, Captain (Thomas?) Wells, and Lieutenant Osland, all of whom had been named in the alleged Yarrington plot in 1661. In addition to ex-military men, many nonconformist ministers were detained, among them the Presbyterian Philip Henry, whose diary describes the impact of the crackdown on the nonconformist clergy. Officials were particularly pleased by the arrest of Captain Thomas Gower, who had returned to county Durham, where the dissidents hoped that Dutch ships would disrupt commerce enough to provoke a rebellion.[119] Another influential rebel caught in the net was Captain Roger Jones, the author of *Mene Tekel* (though Albemarle questioned this). Jones was imprisoned at Hertford, but intelligence of a plot to rescue him prompted authorities to transfer him to the Tower. Clarendon thought that if Albemarle had not made the arrests, particularly of some of the principal Rathbone conspirators on 1 September, there would have been an insurrection two days later.[120] The crackdown was the result of wartime conditions, especially the expectation of an alliance between the Dutch and the radicals, and not simply a pretext invented by the government.

Despite the heightened security, the country remained restless under the burden of war and continued dissident activity. From Leeds one of Arlington's correspondents observed in October 1665 that radical action was imminent because the war had seriously disrupted trade. He also noted that the zealots were encouraged by the appearance of Dutch ships, and that they expected "a partie to be landed for a bodie for them to goe to."[121] Orders were issued for Colonel John Russell "to prevent any fanaticques from secureing the Isle of Ely," to seize and disarm malcontents, and to prevent enemies from landing. Moreover, two companies of militia were dispatched to secure Yarmouth. Unrest was exacerbated by hostility stemming from the collection of the hearth tax. In December a series of arrests in the West Riding headed off an alleged rising by "inconsiderable people."[122]

In addition to its military concerns, the government had to cope with the inexorable spread of the plague, which reached its peak in September, when more than 30,000 deaths were recorded. Although the plague aroused fears that militants would rebel when people fled London, such concerns proved groundless. Some nonconformists, however, took advantage of the disaster to preach their message of judgment and redemption in deserted pulpits, but not to incite revolt. From the north came a loyalist report, probably spurious, that dissidents "exceedingly rejoyce . . . that the plague Increaseth, hopeing that itt will goe throw the kingdome"; however, they reportedly refused to rebel until their friends in the south acted.[123]

Against this background, the government began receiving reports in November of an insurrection scheduled for 1 January 1666. The plot, Albemarle soon discovered, had been instigated by "some people come out of Holland lately," including Robert Goodall, who was sent to the Tower on 8 December.[124] The focal point of the conspiracy was to be Lancashire, Cheshire, and the West Riding. The principal informant, one A.S., provided the state with detailed accounts of the conspirators' meetings that covered a period from 24 September to 9 December 1665. Two of the primary agents in the plot were John Wilson, probably the same Cheshire man arrested in 1662 for seditious correspondence, and Joseph Flather, father-in-law of Henry Bradshaw. The latter had recently been released from York Castle to practice medicine after promising not to conspire, although he allegedly agreed to provide funds to the conspirators. Some of those reportedly involved were still prisoners in York Castle, including Captain John Hodgson, arrested in connection with the northern revolt in 1663 and rearrested in August 1665. David Lumbey, at whose house near Leeds the council of northern rebels had met, was also allegedly part of this conspiracy.[125]

The plotters were enjoying some success recruiting men, raising money, and acquiring weapons when one of them discussed their plans with Joshua Greathead, unaware that he had informed on the northern rebels. Greathead passed the intelligence to Joseph Crowder, who had been pardoned for his involvement in the northern revolt and apparently now served as Greathead's channel to the government. By early December the leaders thought they had raised enough money to provide each captain with £100 and each soldier with 20s. As one of the conspirators said, they were determined to "fight it out and resolve rather then yield to dye all of us upon open feilds." The plan called for rebels in Lancashire, Cheshire, and Derbyshire to convene at Littlebrook, while the Yorkshire men were to meet at Morley, and then march to Halifax via Leeds in order to rendezvous with the first contingent. The Lancashire party, however, did not think it would be ready until Candlemas in February.[126]

By mid-December 1665 the authorities were prepared to strike. A dozen men were committed to York Castle on 16 and 17 December. The list does not include Wilson, who was also arrested. Yet others were to be apprehended. On the 19th Albemarle ordered the deputy lieutenants in the north to secure the malcontents, and on the 23rd the earl of Derby directed the militia captains to prepare for action. The north, however, remained quiet. When the prisoners were interrogated in January, Wilson acknowledged the veracity of most of what A.S. had said, but in general Arlington thought the results of the examinations were unsuccessful. Those arrested were, as the earl of Orrery remarked, "inconsiderable persons," but "considerable enough to do mischief, if embodied."[127]

Although the government survived 1665 with neither insurrection nor invasion, in January 1666 there was a fresh threat when the French declared war. Militants were encouraged; it was reported that they "have lifted upp theire heades very high, and are greatly encouraged in theire expectations of some suddaine troubles." Dissidents were spreading the word that the French were sending "vast summes" to Scotland in order to undermine Stuart sovereignty.[128] But Charles's government was keeping a wary eye on Scotland, and had already detained Major-Generals Robert Monro and Robert Montgomery as early as the spring of 1665.[129] It was, of course, no secret that the Dutch hoped Whitehall would be distracted by unrest among the Scots; accusations that rebellion was being promoted from the Hague were even made. According to Downing, De Witt was inquiring in March 1665 "after any who can make stirs in England or Scotland," and there was a report two months later that Colonel Gilby Carr, a veteran of the Dublin conspiracy, had been commissioned by the Dutch to levy men in Scotland. Unsuccessful attempts were made to line up the support of the earl of Cassillis and William Lockhart, both of whom had sat with Lord Wariston in Richard Cromwell's Parliament.[130] On 27 December 1665, the government declared twelve Scottish officers fugitives for serving with the Dutch during the war, and two Glasgow merchants—George Porterfield and John Graham—were similarly condemned for spreading seditious materials in the Netherlands.[131]

The Fifth Monarchists, it was feared, were preparing to capitalize on the government's preoccupation with the war and the plague. In January 1666 Hugh Courtney and Walter Thimbleton were reportedly scheming with other Fifth Monarchy Men in Essex and Hertfordshire. Thimbleton, moreover, was allegedly a contact between the exiles and militants in England, while Courtney was regarded as "the cheef Champion of their Cause." However, one of Arlington's associates commented that the Fifth Monarchists were divided over the anticipated advent of the millennium: The "most rigid" of them "expect deliverance in some extraordinarie way without the voice of reason." One Fifth Monarchist, Captain Harris, had spent the previous two years seeking to enlist the saints to revolt.[132]

In February 1666 allegations of a plot by assorted militants in

Somerset to assassinate the king, burn London, and give no quarter to Cavaliers were brought to the government's attention. A letter from one of the suspects, Robert Bennet (or Bennett) of Taunton, claimed, with gross exaggeration, that over 40,000 had taken a revolutionary oath. Their banners, it was said, were emblazoned with the words "Charles shall done & lose his crowne." Another of the suspected plotters, John Pitman of Bradford, boasted that he would just as soon thrust "my sword in the blood of the king, as in the blood of a dog." The conspirators were watched so closely that they had difficulty meeting in Somerset, and a letter to an associate in London was intercepted. Authorities issued an order for Pitman's arrest, a search of the houses of conventiclers, and the detention of three non-conformist ministers in Taunton.[133]

The government was also monitoring a conspiracy based in Liverpool. Schemers had met there in mid-October 1665, at which time they dispatched agents into Scotland "to revive their party there and to settle a strict correspondence with their . . . Brethren of that kingdom." Irish malcontents were represented at Liverpool by Lieutenant-Colonel William More, Philip Alden, and Thomas Blood, each of whom had been linked to the Dublin plot. Alden, of course, was now a government agent reporting to Albemarle. More returned to Ireland disguised in a "Great Busshy Perawig" to recruit in Munster and Ulster. Dissidents met in Dublin, where they railed against royal authority, as well as at Ormond and Orrery. Some even bragged that though Albemarle had discovered their plot in England (presumably the Rathbone conspiracy), the root of it was still alive and would grow. Once again Ludlow's name surfaced, as he was expected to arrive in Ireland with funds to support the radicals. There was also an expectation among Irish dissidents that the French and Dutch would assist them by distracting the English.[134]

Claiming—probably falsely—to take their orders from Ludlow and Desborough, the plotters scheduled a meeting at Coventry on 1 January 1666, but moved to the Liverpool home of Captain Browne, another former Dublin conspirator, to avoid surveillance. There they allegedly decided to act after the next major naval engagement in the spring. Blood and George Ayres, who apparently had been engaged in the Dublin plot, were sent to Ireland to apprise supporters of their plan. In Dublin the conspirators reportedly planned an assault on the castle as well as an attempt on Ormond's life by John Chambers (alias Thomas Mills), who lived near Stone, Staffordshire. Simultaneously English dissidents, who with great exaggeration claimed 10,000 horse, supposedly were going to march in small bands to Scotland and rendezvous with Ludlow and Desborough. The magistrates had considerable difficulty trying to locate the principals, not knowing, for example, whether Blood was with his wife near Dublin or in northern Ireland with Gilby Carr. Ormond was troubled, fearing that the dissidents would strike in conjunction with an invasion of Ireland. For that, he insisted, he was unprepared.[135]

The government's problems were further complicated by reports of yet another plot allegedly under way in Dover. This, however, was of import only because Whitehall could not afford to ignore any cabal with purported ties to the exiles or the Dutch government. The previous November, one of the dissidents, the porter and ex-soldier Thomas Lord of Dover, carelessly expressed his hope that the Dutch would land up to 2,000 men and join forces with local rebels. Two of the suspected conspirators, Captain Not (or Nod), a Quaker of good estate, and Thomas Collins (alias Cullen), formerly governor of Dover Castle, received weekly communications from the exiles. The Dover group, which claimed it could count on 200 men in the town to rise with them, allegedly expected Richard Cromwell or Ludlow to head an invasion force before May 1666.[136] For their part the Dover cabal was reportedly convinced they could take the castle with as few as a hundred men, and that the time to act was imminent because of the large supply of salted ox meat, beer, and bread stored at Dover. One of the conspirators, William Sylvester, a tailor and former ensign, had known the plotter Thomas Tong. The others allegedly included Lieutenant Hopkins, who had served under Thomas Kelsey, and Captain Samuel Taverner of Deal, a Baptist minister whose name had been linked to the Tong plot. Sylvester claimed to have the support of the Dover garrison, which reportedly asked him "when their condition shall be mended by a change of Government, for that they are now but as slaves."[137]

The dissidents spent a relatively quiet spring in 1666 as they waited for the war to resume. From Salisbury came word that radicals would rebel in June throughout northern and western England, at Bristol and Taunton, and in northern Ireland. There was also a report that a group of ex-soldiers was preparing to assassinate the king and burn London. In the northeast Christopher Eyon, who had contacts in the Netherlands as well as London, was predicting an invasion before August and proclaiming that the future would bring "either a State & no King, or else a King & no State."[138] One of Arlington's informers was on the trail of a suspected cabal in Southwark, but the parties concerned were highly secretive. Some excitement was provided in May when the Fifth Monarchist John Patshall, who had participated in Venner's insurrection, escaped from the Gatehouse at Westminster. It had been hoped that he would provide information leading to the arrest of Thomas Blood and Roger Jones.[139]

Unsettling rumors of rebel schemes continued, though royalists were uncertain as to their accuracy. An alleged plot to assassinate the king with poniards the size of a knife or by poison was discovered on 28 July. One of the principals was reportedly Captain Cressey of London. Rumors of a similar plot involving the king's fruiter and confectioner reached the government in August. Whatever validity such allegations had, at most these schemers were but tiny cabals of fringe malcontents.[140]

Such radical activity as there was in England after the St. James's Fight was mostly in the west, where dissidents reportedly tried to foment discord with charges that the king and his mother were scheming to introduce popery. Former officers such as Colonel John Blackmore and one of the Buffetts maintained their hope that the Good Old Cause could triumph within a year. They still had the ability, according to the informer Peter Crabb, to raise as many as 2,000 recruits in a few hours—an allegation undoubtedly exaggerated in order to retain his employment as a government agent. In the northwest Sir Philip Musgrave discovered a plot among the Quakers, though the earl of Carlisle thought it of little consequence "unles our foes abroed should land men upon us." There was concern in the northeast that the appointment of Sir Edward Charlton as governor of Hartlepool was a prelude to the introduction of Catholicism, but no substantive evidence of plotting. To be safe, magistrates continued to detain suspicious persons and seize caches of weapons.[141]

Contacts between militant exiles and their associates in England suggested the imminence of a fresh insurrection or an invasion. Some of the suspicion focused on the Fifth Monarchist George Cokayne, who corresponded from London with the Congregationalist Nicholas Lockyer in Rotterdam. One of Arlington's correspondents told him on 1 October that rebels in Yorkshire, Derbyshire, Nottinghamshire, and Lincolnshire were waiting for the return of James Washington and Lunn from the Netherlands before rebelling.[142]

In England tensions were heightened throughout the autumn of 1666 by recurring reports of suspicious troops of horse. A party of 120 to 140 armed horsemen was seen near Chippenham, Wiltshire, in October, and Colonel James Long, who conducted an investigation, initially thought they might have been a muster to repress an insurrection. Further inquiry, however, persuaded him that the men were indeed rebels who were planning an uprising. Among those arrested was an ex-officer from Yorkshire named Hardy, who claimed that he only wanted the peaceful unification of Baptists and Quakers, though the latter disavowed him.[143] In November bands of horsemen ranging in size from 50 to 500 were reported in Gloucestershire, and groups of 50 in Staffordshire and 80 in Cheshire (where Sir Geoffrey Shakerley discounted the sightings as the mischief of fanatics). The next month there were accounts of armed men riding in the night. When a party of horse was spotted heading for Bristol, the mayor and deputy lieutenants ordered a search for suspicious persons. Contemporaneous with the Galloway uprising in Scotland in November, the dissidents in Wiltshire had "many clandestine rendevous, . . . cunningly enough fathering thos meetings on the Papists." These reports were almost certainly not the result of mistaking musters for suspicious riders, since musters normally produced little comment. If these armed parties were disaffected men, their actions were not part of an insurrection, though they may have met secretly for religious or political purposes. In any case, the frequency and nature of the reports contributed to the tension already present because of the war.[144]

The accounts of mysterious armed bands were closely related to the rash of false stories deliberately circulated by dissidents in the autumn of 1666 to create discord. In October rumors circulated that Albemarle had either resigned or been dismissed, and that Sir John Robinson had been replaced as lieutenant of the Tower of London by a papist. One of the more common tales was the old canard that Charles intended to impose Catholicism on the country. One variation of this was a rumor that Catholics on the Isle of Wight had a secret plan to destroy the Protestants.[145] A royal proclamation directed against Catholics alleviated some of the anxiety among the populace, but a few magistrates pressed Joseph Williamson to find the source of the rumors by inspecting the mails.[146] Thus what modern politicians euphemistically call "disinformation" was circulated by the dissidents as well as by informers who tended to exaggerate radical activity, and on occasion by the government itself when reports of plotting could justify increased security.

Such may have been the case at this time, for the government took additional security precautions by requiring that all members of Parliament, the military, and the royal household subscribe to the oaths of allegiance and supremacy. The oaths were also to be tendered to all suspicious persons, including Catholics, and those who refused were to be disarmed. The administration of the oaths to the garrisons proceeded quietly, though at Hull ten men (most of them Irish) refused them.[147] It was probably in connection with these efforts that officials compiled a new list of 580 ex-officers, including their religious affiliations where known.[148] Yet such action was probably the result of growing government concern about the militant threat rather than a contrived scheme made possible by spurious threats.

Dissidents in the north continued to be a source of disquietude. At Chester Sir Geoffrey Shakerley undertook a search for concealed weapons and threatened ex-Cromwellian officers with detention if they continued to refuse the oaths. His castle was full of prisoners, most of them zealots. When the Privy Council ordered the release of Colonel Robert Duckenfield, Shakerley protested to Albemarle and Arlington on the grounds that Duckenfield and Zachary Crofton (recently deceased) had been the leaders of a plot in 1665. Duckenfield, however, got his freedom after providing security.[149] Shakerley also monitored persons going to and from Ireland by posting agents at Liverpool and Holyhead. Because of the unusual number of persons coming into Chester en route to or from Ireland, he ordered innkeepers to provide an account of their guests. Thomas Blood was back in the north by January, sometimes disguised in a wig and using aliases as he operated in the Warrington and Manchester region. In the spring he was spotted at "a rigid Anabaptist's."[150]

Reports of plotting continued to surface as the war entered its final phase in 1667. In January the authorities intercepted a letter from John Hase to a Mr. Horne at Westminster outlining a conspiracy to burn London and to assault Charles and the dukes of York and Albemarle. Hase himself procured thirty-one barrels of gunpowder, a hundred muskets, and forty pairs of pistols, while his brother acquired additional weapons. However, the projected dates for the uprising, 6 or 20 January, passed without event.[151] The same month there were rumblings of an intended rising in Leicestershire, Nottinghamshire, and Derbyshire involving numerous well-armed ex-soldiers. All of this was enough to prompt the king to order the lords lieutenant to ready the militia to preserve order. In April a deputy lieutenant in Oxfordshire obtained intelligence pertaining to an alleged conspiracy to attack Whitehall as soon as the Catholics revolted or the French appeared. Clarendon was warned the same month that the Fifth Monarchists were scheming again, although the charge was unsubstantiated. One allegation centered on a German physician, Dr. Albertus Faber, who was incarcerated in Oxford Castle for participating in a supposed plot with Fifth Monarchists and other nonconformists. In May disclosures were made of plotting in Norfolk, London, and Leeds, the latter involving the Baptist preacher Edward Wilkinson, who had been engaged in the northern revolt.[152]

Assessing the radical threat was complicated in the late winter and spring of 1667 by charges that linked the duke of Buckingham to the dissidents. Arlington, his political rival, learned from one of the duke's servants that the duke had asked the astrologer John Heydon to cast the king's horoscope, a treasonable offense. Heydon and Buckingham's steward, Henry North, were committed to the Tower, but the duke himself eluded arrest. If anything, the attempt to discredit Buckingham increased his popularity in dissident circles.[153] Although Viscount Conway overstated the case when he suggested that the duke considered himself to be another Cromwell, Buckingham clearly retained his links to the nonconformists and to John Wildman, who served him as a secretary and legal adviser. Buckingham's reputation in radical circles is reflected in Ludlow's praise of him as one who had "lately asserted the peoples Interest against Tiranny, & Popery." The government interrogated prisoners in the Tower and York Castle but failed to procure incriminating evidence against him. The fact that the two chief witnesses, John Gryce and George Middleton, died mysteriously (possibly by poison) may have saved the duke. A third witness, the ex-radical William Leeving, was found dead in York Castle on 5 August, with a note on his body asking to be excused from testifying against Roger Jones, John Atkinson, and John Joplin. Professing his innocence, Buckingham had surrendered on 27 June and was released the following month. There had been some consideration in radical circles to recruit sailors for an attack on the Tower in order to liberate him.[154]

Throughout the war years, then, English radicals did not instigate a single rebellion, though Scottish Covenanters tried without success to take advantage of the Galloway uprising in their own country. The activities of the radicals clearly concerned the government, perhaps even to the point of preventing a more effective prosecution of the war because of the distractions and the need to enhance domestic security against internal enemies. But the domestic plotting was ineffective, lacking popular backing, adequate organization, and Dutch support. Militants in England waited in vain for leadership and a viable plan of action from the exiles, but the latter were rendered ineffectual by Ludlow's refusal to cooperate with the Dutch, Sidney's inability to establish his own claim to leadership, and the obvious impossibility of accepting French aid if such support involved the participation of Catholic troops.

The Fire of London

Although a number of radical conspiracies had included plans to burn London, militants made no attempt to profit from the catastrophic fire that broke out in September 1666. Because it generally coincided with the anniversary of the battles of Dunbar and Worces-

ter as well as Cromwell's death, some government loyalists and common folk were quick to blame the dissidents. These suspicions were
reinforced by the earlier threats to burn the City, and by the sectarian
proclivity to see the hand of providence in virtually everything.[155]
Among those whose names were linked to the fire were Captain John
Mason, Ralph Rymer junior, who had been convicted of misprision
of treason in the northern rebellion, and Apolonia De Brill, who was
accused of having concealed Ludlow.[156] Remarks by dissidents such
as the London grocer George Greenwood, who hoped Westminster
Abbey would burn like St. Paul's, intensified suspicion of radical involvement. Although such mistrust was groundless, it made officials
take prophecies more seriously in the ensuing two years. The parliamentary committee that investigated the fire even examined William
Lilly in October 1666 because he had predicted both the fire and the
plague in *Monarchy or No Monarchy* (1651).[157]

In general there was a tendency on the part of the English to see
"more of villainye then chance" in the fire, though some attributed
it to the French or Dutch rather than the dissidents. A great many
also blamed the Catholics, which circumstance gave credence to radical claims of a papist threat to the country.[158] Several pamphlets were
published that purported to document Catholic responsibility. *Londons Flames Discovered* (1667), an unauthorized version of testimony
taken by the House of Commons committee that investigated the
fire, blamed Jesuits and French Catholics. The pamphlet was burned
at Westminster by the hangman in September 1667.[159] *A True and
Faithful Account of the Several Informations* likewise included parliamentary testimony, and concluded with a confession from an ex-
Catholic who said that French, Irish, and English papists were all
involved in the fire, "thinking thereby to destroy the Heads of your
Religion." The fire, according to this witness, was supposed to have
been the prelude to a French invasion at Dover.[160] Dissidents were
responsible for these pamphlets, as well as a later work, *Trap ad Crucem: or, the Papists Watch-word* (1670), sometimes attributed to the
radical bookseller Francis Smith. It contained testimony before justices of the peace accusing Catholics of starting several fires in London.[161] There is, however, no evidence to suggest that radicals deliberately vilified the Catholics in order to draw blame from themselves.

Almost from the beginning, responsible voices doubted the existence of a conspiracy to burn the City. As early as 8 September Sir Heneage Finch concluded that there was "nothing of plot or design in all this," and that investigations of the numerous stories of fireballs proved them to be fictitious. There was, he observed, no attempt on the life of the king or the duke of York, nor any insurrection or foreign invasion. Arlington noted "the little cause we had to suspect that there was anything more than the heavy hand of God in it." After its own investigation, the Privy Council concluded that the fire was the work of "the hand of God upon us," compounded by dry and windy weather.[162] The government thus chose not to use the fire as a pretext for discrediting the dissidents, undoubtedly because it had no credible evidence to accuse them of arson.

Although Whitehall was convinced that the radicals were not responsible for the conflagration, care was used throughout the kingdom to prevent zealots from taking advantage of the disaster. Of immediate relevance to the war was the king's recall of Albemarle from the fleet. The militia was called up in many places and guards were posted in the towns and on the ships in the harbor at Hull. Suspicious persons were once again detained. Fireballs the size of tennis balls were confiscated near Lutterworth, and at Bristol instruments of arson were found in the house of a quondam alderman who refused to abjure the Covenant. Seven or eight persons were arrested and the city gates shut up.[163] Yet despite the dislocation and the fire's economic ramifications, which extended far beyond London, the kingdom was unusually quiet.[164] The public exposure of both the king and the duke of York during the tragedy left them open to assassins, but no attempt was made on their lives. This may have been in part attributable to the fact that the fire's damage was particularly extensive in that part of the City where the radicals were most numerous.[165]

For the militants, the Dutch War was less of a missed opportunity than at first appears. The sympathy of many nonconformists was with their country rather than the zealots, and even a widespread insurrection coordinated with the Dutch attack in June and July 1667 would probably have failed for lack of popular support. The inability of the exiles to arrange an uprising at the appropriate time was a clear manifestation of their organizational impotence and ample justification for the lack of confidence that the Dutch government demonstrated in them. When the peace treaty was signed at Breda in late July, the Stuart regime had survived not only a war but also a violent outbreak of the plague, a fire that devastated much of London, and a rebellion in Scotland. The radicals failed to capitalize on any of these crises. Yet in their turn the men at Whitehall, preoccupied with these events, neglected to take advantage of the division fostered by the war within the ranks of the discontented to crush the militants. If the zealots failed to advance their cause during the war years, neither did the government succeed in substantially depleting their strength. Like the war itself, the struggle between the Stuart regime and the dissidents in this period was indecisive.

"For God and the Covenant"

TWO

The Scots and the Galloway Rising

Although radical political ideas had less appeal in Scotland than in England, pronounced religious disaffection was common in staunchly Presbyterian circles. Loyalty to the Covenant ran deep, fostering enmity toward Charles II when he repudiated his earlier commitment to it. His imposition of prelacy only exacerbated matters, and as the government deprived the more recalcitrant Presbyterian ministers, particularly in the southwest, it unwittingly fanned the embers of discontent. When rebellion spontaneously erupted in November 1666 as the country was preoccupied with the Dutch War, the radicals had an excellent opportunity to strike. In the absence, however, of meaningful support from friends in England and Ireland, or from the Dutch, the rebellion collapsed.

The Troubled Search for a Religious Settlement

The weak support for episcopacy in Scotland made Restoration religious policy more difficult to implement than in England. Only the absence of a strong radical political tradition made it feasible at all, for most militant Presbyterians were at least monarchists, though firmly committed to upholding the Covenant. Unlike their English counterparts, militant Scottish Presbyterians had less incentive to pursue a more moderate course because they faced no serious challenge from radical religious groups. Ironically the absence of such groups made the threat from Presbyterians to a peaceful settlement substantially greater in Scotland than in England.

The government struck against the leading Protesters and their supporters in the summer of 1660. On 23 August the Committee of Estates ordered the arrest of James Guthry of Stirling, Robert Trail of Edinburgh, and eight other ministers, and on 15 September another Protester leader, Patrick Gillespie, principal of Glasgow College, was apprehended. Guthry was tried before Parliament and executed for treason on 1 June 1661, proclaiming to the end his fidelity to the Remonstrance and the Solemn League and Covenant, but professing his willingness to accept monarchical government. Gillespie, however, threw himself on the mercy of Parliament and was acquitted of treason, though confined to Ormiston in East Lothian.[1] The other Protesters, including James Simpson of Airth, also escaped with their lives, although some of their lay supporters were less fortunate. The marquis of Argyll was beheaded on 27 May 1661, and Captain William Giffen, who had allegedly been on the scaffold when Charles I was executed, followed on 1 June.[2] Sir Archibald Johnston of Wariston, declared a fugitive and a rebel on 1 January 1661, fled to the Continent and escaped execution until July 1663. Other Cromwellian radicals were accused of treason, including John Hume of Kello; the former trustee William Dundas; Robert Andrew, an assessment collector in Perthshire; Colonel David Barclay, who had sat in the Cromwellian Parliaments; and Colonel Gilby Carr, a prominent Protester.[3]

The king was determined to restore modified episcopal polity in the Kirk of Scotland, for Presbyterian government was, in his view, unsuitable "to our monarchicall estate." The bishop of Galloway echoed the royal position in late 1661 when he insisted that "presbyterian governement as it is in this age professed and exercised in Scotland is directly inconsistant with Kingly power," not least because the Presbyterians believed that an ungodly ruler could be deposed. To permit such polity in Scotland, he warned, would encourage English dissidents.[4]

In the spring of 1661 the government ordered the Scottish clergy to take the oaths of allegiance and supremacy, and those who refused to subscribe, attend diocesan meetings, or observe the anniversary of Charles's restoration were threatened with deprivation. That August Charles directed the Scottish Privy Council to prohibit meetings of Presbyterian synods as well as sermons prejudicial to the peace of the kingdom. The following month the Council instructed local officials to incarcerate those whose preaching disturbed the peace or alienated the affections of the king's subjects.[5] A proclamation from the Council dated 9 January 1662 directed that synods, presbyteries, and sessions meet only by prelatical appointment, and warned that any disrespect to the bishops would be appropriately punished. The prelates, however, were occupied with parliamentary business until the autumn, so that some Presbyterians continued to gather in defiance of the proclamation. A new one was therefore issued on 10 September declaring such meetings seditious. Once Parliament was dissolved on 9 October, the bishops were ready to convene diocesan assemblies and impose their authority more effectively. The Council had helped set the stage for their work eight days earlier by giving ministers who had not been legally presented to their benefices and collated by a bishop one month to leave their presbyteries. Moreover their congregations were warned that they faced prosecution as conventiclers if they persisted in attending the services of such ministers.[6]

As the government began to implement its repressive program, some of the more outspoken clerics registered their anger. At Banchory, Alexander Cant thundered "that whoever would own or make use of a Service-Book, King, Nobleman or Minister, the curse of God should be upon him"; Cant was deprived. Robert MacWard (or MacGuire, McVaird, Macguaire) of Glasgow lashed out against the "glaring defections of the time," for which act he was charged with sedition.[7] Because the Wamphray minister John Brown castigated clerics who attended the archbishop of Glasgow's synod as Covenant-breakers, perjured knaves, and villains, he was imprisoned in the Edinburgh Tolbooth and released only after promising to leave Scotland.[8] Robert Blaire of St. Andrews offended by overzealously commending the Covenant and making "bold reflexions" upon Parliament, for which he was incarcerated in Edinburgh Castle.[9] The tenor of such comments boded ill for the government's hope of a peaceful ecclesiastical settlement.

The percentage of ministers deprived of their livings—more than a quarter—was higher than in England, where some 20 percent were ejected. Altogether, 262 of the approximately 952 clergymen were deprived in Scotland, a number higher than that at the Reformation. The southwest was hardest hit: 32 of the 37 ministers in the synod of Galloway were removed, 75 of 121 in the synod of Glasgow and Ayr. Dumfries lost more than half of its clergy, Fife and Lothian a third, whereas northern Scotland was almost entirely unaffected. In some areas, such as Kintyre in Argyll, every cleric was ejected.[10] The list of those who refused to conform includes some of the most influential ministerial leaders, such as John Carstares and Donald Cargill of Glasgow, and Robert Trail of Edinburgh.[11] Because of his reputation, the government was particularly anxious to persuade Carstares to conform, but neither a brief period in prison nor an appearance before the Council changed his mind. The number of ministers who refused to conform so alarmed the Council that it extended the deadline from 1 November 1662 to 1 February 1663, but to little effect.[12]

Clerics who refused the oaths of allegiance and supremacy faced not only ejection but exile. One observer noted in January 1662 that the Councillors "never sit but they have a great many ministers before them," some of whom refused to subscribe and were thereupon banished.[13] Among those so sentenced in 1662, most of whom were from the southwest, were Robert Trail, James Naesmith of Hamilton, Matthew Mowatt and James Ruatt of Kilmarnock, James Veitch (or Veatch) of Mauchline, Alexander Blair of Galston, John Livingston of Ancrum, James Garner of Kintyre, and John Neave of Newmilns. In the eyes of the Council, their preaching had been "seditious and factitious," undoubtedly because they refused to recognize royal authority in spiritual matters.[14]

As the number of deprivations mounted, the government faced a growing problem with conventicles. A 1662 Conventicle Act and conciliar directives that prohibited ejected clergy from preaching and commanded them to leave their former parishes had only minimal impact.[15] In March 1663 the Council instructed the lord chancellor to obtain information on conventicles from Sir James Turner and others, and a month later the bishop of Edinburgh and his synod ordered their presbyteries to bring charges against unlicensed ministers. Parliament further addressed the problem by passing the Act against Separation and Disobedience to Ecclesiastical Authority on

10 July, imposing heavy fines on recusants and branding their meetings "seditious and of dangerous example."[16] A month later the Council, acknowledging that "many subjects doe countenance and joine in these unlaufull meitinges," gave all ministers who preached "seditiously" or improperly held their livings a period of twenty days to leave their parishes or suffer the penalties for sedition. Moreover, they were prohibited from residing within twenty miles of Edinburgh or three miles of any royal burgh.[17]

Although the Council prosecuted a number of offending clerics during the summer and fall of 1663, as late as mid-November it complained about the number of ministers who "openly and avowedly disobeyed" the January 1663 act requiring post-1649 clergy to be episcopally collated. Problems of enforcement undoubtedly were influential in the government's decision to reinstitute the High Commission on 16 January 1664 at the urging of Archbishop James Sharp.[18] The Commission began prosecuting offenders, both lay and clerical, including William Tallidafe (or Tillidaff) of Dunbog, Fife, who, in a celebrated act of defiance with John Carstares, had persuaded the St. Andrews minister James Wood to renounce a declaration in support of episcopacy that the archbishop had elicited from him.[19] Yet neither the Council nor the Commission could stem the rising tide of conventicles, even in Edinburgh. Complaining of the number of deprived clergy who flocked to the capital and other towns to "hold their meitinges and keip seditious correspondences," on 17 November the Council gave these ministers forty-eight hours to leave or face prosecution for sedition.[20]

These efforts were to no avail. Ministers such as Gabriel Semple, Robert Paton (or Patoun), and Thomas Thomson preached in the woods and fields as well as in private homes. In December 1664 the earl of Rothes reported to the earl of Lauderdale that the "fanatics" had become much bolder and were now meeting in the fields by the hundreds despite the efforts of his men to stop them.[21] The Council found it necessary in December 1665 again to order unlawful clergy to cease their ministry or to leave their parishes within forty days; those who attended conventicles were to be treated as seditious persons. By this time, the center of illegal activity was clearly in the southwest, and the king was convinced that these conventicles, meeting "under pretence and colour of religion," were in fact "the ordinary seminaries of separation and rebellion" as well as a reproach to his authority.[22] As the conventiclers began arming themselves, the battlelines were drawn.

Smoldering Embers

If one were to judge only from the newspapers of the early 1660s, Scotland was a country largely at peace, kept so by the government's diligence in curtailing the activities of nonconforming clergy. In June 1661 Henry Muddiman's *Kingdomes Intelligencer* reported that two or three ministers—"snakes"—at Dumfries refused to celebrate the anniversary of Charles' restoration, but they pleaded ignorance and promised to obey. A story from Edinburgh at year's end reassuringly noted that all but one or two ministers celebrated Christmas with proper solemnity. In June 1662 a news item acknowledged the persistence of trouble, but assured readers that the Scots were loyal and that conditions were peaceful. Two years later the *Intelligencer* reported that the leaders of the dissidents were on the move in order to "help the Old Cause forward again," but insisted that strict care was being exercised to discover their schemes. By August 1665 the *Newes* boasted that there were no longer enough persons of rank who "retain the *Old Leaven*" to create further disturbances, and in October it opined that Scotland "is at present in perfect peace and quietness."[23]

For propaganda purposes, however, the newspapers, with their pronounced government bias, presented an inaccurate depiction of conditions in Scotland. Samuel Pepys observed this in the spring of 1663, when he noted the prevalence of religious nonconformity and an attack on the bishop of Galloway. Reports of Scottish affairs, mostly by English observers, were far from rosy. One of James Hickes's correspondents apprised him in January 1661 that several Englishmen had been murdered, and Hickes in turn warned Secretary Nicholas that many "false hearted servants & pretending subjects"—possibly English—remained in Scotland and were potential threats to the king. In October of the same year Hickes cautioned Joseph Williamson that Scotland would remain quiet only as long as

English troops were present, after which "Rebellion will appeare."[24] Writing from Ayrshire the next month, Colonel William Daniel notified Albemarle that the local magistrates had been no help when the return to episcopal polity was proclaimed, and that copies of the proclamation had been torn down "by rude hands." "They all pretend zeal to the King but not in a way consistent to his authority," he grumbled.[25]

In the spring of 1663 there were indications that something was "A Brewing . . . it goes on very egerly, the persons hyly ingaged."[26] About the same time another observer warned that "the Presbyterian Party are in a good posture both for money & armes and are now endevoring to ingage severall places." In October 1664 Secretary Bennet was told that there was no reason to believe that "considerable persons" in Scotland were plotting, though there was "a generall discontent and dissatisfaction amongst the ministers and people," who encouraged each other at their meetings to expect a revolution to uphold their principles. Yet unless the Dutch invaded, he concluded, "I cannot see the least probability of any suddaine disturbance nor any preparation towards it."[27]

The general thrust of these reports from government loyalists was accurate. The principal reason for the widespread discontent—Presbyterian hostility to prelacy—was manifested in various forms, of which the refusal of ministers to take the prescribed oaths was only the most obvious. The Venetian resident was seemingly shocked by the fact that the bishops were greeted with "hisses and murmers." In the presbytery of Linlithgow, twenty-five women prevented John Mowbray from preaching, broke the bridle on his horse, and "refused to let him go back or forwards," while at Ancrum four young men harassed the minister James Scott, for which they were banished to Barbados. At the West Kirk in Edinburgh the people not only castigated William Gordon but denied him entry to the church because he observed the traditional festival days and was believed responsible for the deprivation of David Williamson.[28]

Seditious and inflammatory speech was a recurring problem, sometimes emanating from Presbyterian pulpits. In the fall of 1662, for instance, Hugh McKell (or Mackail), chaplain to Sir James Stewart, used an Edinburgh pulpit to inveigh against the king as well as the government of church and state. Stewart's son Walter, an Edinburgh merchant, was cited before the Council for allegedly speaking seditiously, but he quietly submitted. In April 1663 the lord chancellor reported that several ministers had been preaching against the government, even to the point of calling the king an apostate and perjurer. Such sentiments were expressed in lay circles too, as in the case of a Glasgow weaver who hoped to see Charles and his supporters hanged.[29] The Council took such reports seriously enough to investigate them. So many disaffected persons were going to Edinburgh that in September 1662 the Council ordered all burgesses, innkeepers, and other inhabitants of the city to report those who sought lodging each evening. The same month groups of twelve to twenty English dissidents reputedly entered the country, and the government received reports of suspicious correspondence between radicals in Newcastle and Scotland through the agents "Pattison and Johnson," the latter probably Captain Robert Johnston, who was involved in the Tong plot.[30] Middleton, however, did not expect dissident Presbyterians to revolt unless they received foreign assistance. This was still basically the view of Archbishop Alexander Burnet in February 1666, although he was concerned that "the least commotion in England or Ireland or encouragement from foreigners abroad would certainly engage us in a new rebellion." If an uprising came, the earl of Rothes concluded, "the goverment off the church will be maid the pretext," though grievances over polity alone "are not much considerable."[31]

Feelings of hostility toward the regime were intensified by the return of militant Presbyterians from Ireland. Recognizing the danger, in February 1661 the Scottish Parliament ordered all persons coming from Ireland to possess written evidence from a magistrate documenting their peaceful deportment. In September of the same year the Council directed the sheriff of Clydesdale to apprehend two suspicious ministers who had come from Ireland. As Irish officials rounded up the Dublin conspirators in the spring of 1663, the king instructed his Scottish Council to detain and interrogate all persons coming from Ireland, "for we conceave it more safe that tuentie innocent should be secured and kept for some few dayes then that one guilty person should escape."[32] He was especially anxious for the arrest of Gilby Carr and Thomas Blood, but to no avail. Four months later, on 7 October, the Council revived the February 1661 act, giving persons from Ireland without acceptable papers fifteen days to leave Scotland, and requiring those with testimony of sound character to provide security for their good behavior. In the aftermath of the northern rebellion, the king instructed the Scottish Council to undertake a diligent search for the leading conspirators. John Crookshanks and Michael Bruce, both wanted for questioning in connection with the Dublin plot, had fled to Scotland and were illegally preaching in 1664; the Council put them to the horn in August. Crookshanks not only eluded arrest but frequently preached to large conventicles right up to the eve of the Galloway rebellion, as local authorities declined to arrest him out of either sympathy or fear.[33]

Officials had to contend too with the Quakers, although in retrospect they posed little threat to the government. The Council took a special interest in Anthony Hague and Andrew Robinson (or Robeson), who had been active in the border region, and John Swinton, laird of Swinton, all of whom were thought to be communicating with English Quakers "to the prejudice of the Church and State." Because "many" Quakers met in Edinburgh, in June 1663 the Council directed the city's magistrates to prohibit landlords from renting houses to them. There was trouble too in Aberdeen, where the shoemaker Richard Rae of Dumfries was arrested the same month "for keiping conventicles," and where some magistrates' wives were attending Quaker meetings.[34] As in England, incarceration failed to deter the Friends. Prior to his arrest in Aberdeen, Rae had served twenty months in the Edinburgh Tolbooth, while Hague and Robinson, after spending a year and a half in the same jail, resumed their meetings; less than three months after their release the Council ordered their apprehension. The government was clearly frustrated by the "great multitudes" of Quakers who persisted in meeting in Edinburgh, and by the continuing efforts of English Friends in Scotland. The latter were returned to Berwick for incarceration because Scottish magistrates had insufficient space to detain them.[35] In November 1665 Arlington complained that Quakers and other sectaries had of late been "more then ordinarily insolent in their unlawfull

Meetings" in the border area; many were from England. The Councillors finally decided to proceed against the Quakers under the terms of the act for excommunicated persons, by which they would charge them "with horning, denuncing and taking the gift of their escheit," that is, proclaiming them outlaws and subjecting their property to forfeiture.[36]

The outbreak of war with the Dutch in 1665 intensified concerns about security and dissident activity. Intelligence reports from the Netherlands indicated that the exiles were unusually busy, and that the Dutch might furnish Scottish malcontents with money and weapons. Because of its adverse economic impact, the war was in any case unpopular with the Scots, so that the government was forced to take the precaution of confiscating weapons in the south and west. Feelings ran so high that Archbishop Burnet warned Archbishop Sheldon on 22 May that "the first news of any disaster at sea will dispose us to a new rebellion."[37] In June Mrs. Robert Trail was incarcerated for writing to her husband in the Netherlands; suspicion was intensified because she used an alias for him.[38]

By 17 June 1665 one of Arlington's correspondents was convinced that "the business in Scotland is now shrunck to nothinge," but he was nevertheless concerned that a change in Dutch military fortunes might encourage Scottish dissidents "to resume thiere tumultuous counsells and resolutions." As a preventive measure, in September 1665 suspicious authorities ordered the arrest of leading Scottish dissidents, including the earl of Eglinton's brother, Major-General Robert Montgomery, Colonel Robert Halket (or Hacket), Major-General Holburn of Menstri, Sir George Maxwell of Nether Pollock, Sir Hugh Campbell of Cessnock, Sir William Cunningham of Cunninghamhead, Sir George Munro, Sir William Muir of Rowallan, the prominent Protester Sir John Chiesley of Carswell, and the former Edinburgh provost Sir James Stewart, also a Protester. Lieutenant-Colonel James Wallace, however, escaped the dragnet by taking refuge with his wife's relatives near Carrickfergus in Ireland.[39] There was in fact a conspiracy the next year to seize the fortresses of Edinburgh, Stirling, and Dunbarton. Robert MacWard and John Brown seem to have known of the plans. The plotters sought Dutch assistance, but on 15 July 1666 the States General secretly resolved that at least one of the forts first be captured. Only then would they provide a subsidy of 150,000 gulden, 10 cannons, 2,000 brace of pistols, 1,000 carbines, 3,000 muskets, 1,000 matchlocks, 1,500 pikes, and side arms for musketeers and pikemen.[40]

When France too declared war in January 1666, there was reason for further concern about affairs in Scotland. On 26 February one of Arlington's correspondents reported that news of French involvement had "greatly encouraged" the disaffected "in theire expectations of some suddaine troubles here," not least because "vast summes" were reputedly being sent to Scottish nobles by the French government. But the same informer also accurately observed that the exile community in the Netherlands was "broken all to peaces" and would probably never work closely with the French or the Dutch. Nevertheless there was concern in the spring that the French might land troops in Scotland or Ireland. On the eve of the Galloway rebellion Archbishop Burnet cautioned Williamson that if the English lost at sea, the ejected ministers in Scotland would usurp their former charges and inflame the people "to a new rebellion." To substantiate his case he pointed to the growth in conventicling during the war years, even in Edinburgh while the courts were sitting. Many of the illegal meetings were, of course, in the southwest, but others were in the southeast as well. In a war setting, with fears of a Dutch or French invasion a recurring concern, the growth of conventicles at which worshippers increasingly appeared with swords and pistols was a serious threat to security.[41]

The Troubled Southwest

During the early 1660s southwestern Scotland became a festering sore in the side of the government. Disgruntled lairds and tenant farmers were increasingly unhappy with the repression of their staunchly Presbyterian clergy, although the majority of the Lowlands population generally accepted the new regime. The rest could refuse to attend their parish churches, migrate to Ulster, or actively oppose the government. By the fall of 1662, so many parishioners in Glasgow were refusing to attend church that collections declined sharply. Presbyterian clerics who refused the oaths and were imprisoned became ready symbols of state persecution.[42] The 1662 Act of Indemnity, which subjected approximately 700 persons, mostly in the west, to fines ranging from £200 to £18,000 Scots, also contributed to the growth of hostility. "We have here provoked the phanaticke party to the last extremity,"[43] admitted the earl of Newburgh in September 1662.

By February 1663 the Privy Council had become alarmed with the number of ministers in the diocese of Galloway who refused to relinquish their churches and endeavored "to keip the hearts of the people from the present government of Church and State by their pernicious doctrin." Twenty-six of them, including Robert Ferguson of Buittle, Kirkcudbright, William Maitland of Whithorn, and Alexander Peden (or Pedin, Pedden) of Glenluce, were cited on the 24th to appear before the Council and to remove themselves and their families from their respective presbyteries.[44] A month later the Councillors issued a similar directive in connection with fifteen clergymen in eastern Scotland, among whom were John Crookshanks of Redgorton, Patrick Campbell of Killin, and Andrew Donaldson of Dalgety. By this point there were already reports that conventiclers numbering in the thousands were meeting in the fields, especially in the west.[45]

An incident at Kirkcudbright in the spring of 1663 underscored the depth of popular hostility. When the bishop of Galloway appointed Bernard Sanderson as the new minister, a band of parishioners led by William Arnot, Janet Biglow, and the widows Jean Reany, Agnes Maxwell, Marian Brown, and Christian McCavies threatened to pull him from the pulpit, and likewise hindered John Wishett, who had been invited to preach the sermon of admission. During the ensuing tumult, Arnot, with a partially drawn sword, threatened to block the church door, while a sizable group of women prevented the service from continuing. The disruption had been planned in a series of meetings convened by Arnot and abetted by the refusal of various local men to accept the office of magistrate, which left the town with "no setled magistracy and government." To restore order the Council directed the earl of Linlithgow to secure Kirkcudbright with 100 horse and 200 foot, who were given free quarter in the town. The leaders of the disturbance, including five women, were incarcerated in the Edinburgh Tolbooth, while another thirteen women were jailed at Kirkcudbright. Lord Kirkcudbright, who had boasted that the new pastor would only be admitted "over his belly," and the former provosts John Carson and John Ewart were likewise imprisoned in Edinburgh for refusing to prevent the demonstration. Newly appointed magistrates were charged to protect both the Kirkcudbright minister and the bishop of Galloway. In retrospect this affair—and a similar disturbance at Irongray northwest of Dumfries—had no serious consequences, but it might have been, as one of Ormond's correspondents observed, "more than a spark, and amongst matter very combustible." On this occasion the government was fortunate.[46]

Although the *Kingdomes Intelligencer* reported in June 1663 that Scots in the west were becoming more submissive in ecclesiastical affairs, Lauderdale complained that summer about the "considerable" number of people, including gentlemen, who refused to attend services conducted by the new ministers. Despite the fact that "there be a great partie of disaffected persons to the establisht Church government in the West," he was confident that the authorities could compel obedience.[47] In response to reports of clerics whose behavior was "factitious and seditious" because of their conventicles, the Privy Councillors acted in July. Ten ejected pastors from southern and western Scotland, including Alexander Livingston of Biggar, Matthew McKell of Bothwell, John Shaw of Selkirk, and Archibald Hamilton of Wigtown, were commanded to appear before the Council by the 23rd. Five more western ministers received similar citations on the 30th. The government also attempted to enforce obedience by quartering troops in the homes of those who opposed the new clergy. This happened in 1663, for instance, at Anwoth, northwest of Kirkcudbright, after Alexander Robertson preached illegally in the parish church, and at Carsphairn and Balmaclellan in northern Kirkcudbrightshire. The bishop of Galloway himself requested that soldiers be dispatched to Stranraer in Wigtownshire to impose order. Billeting only exacerbated the discontent, and the hard-drinking Sir James Turner, whose troops were often involved, found himself forced to defend his actions as early as July 1663. Three years later his men provided the spark that ignited the Galloway rebellion.[48]

The use of military force to repress dissent had no stronger supporter than Archbishop Burnet of Glasgow, who complained bitterly throughout 1664 that not enough was being done to force dissidents into compliance. He credited the Commission with compelling seven or eight of the most influential dissidents to leave Glasgow for Amsterdam, yet he still grumbled that "of all our ministers who publikely affront authority not one is apprehended."[49]

When the Second Dutch War broke out in 1665, concerns about southwestern Scotland inevitably increased. In the Netherlands Colonel Gilby Carr reportedly "promiseth much" to the States with respect to potential rebellion among western Scots. Although Arlington discounted rumors of trouble, the government, as previously noted, arrested more than a dozen gentlemen in the west as a precautionary measure. In addition the Privy Council ordered malcontents in the west disarmed, though some persons refused to surrender their pistols and swords; expectedly, this policy increased dissatisfaction with the government.[50] The state made fresh efforts to stop the flow of intelligence and ministers between Ulster and western Scotland, and to monitor the activities of leading dissidents, especially Sir John Chiesley. In April approximately twenty seamen were arrested, two of whom were believed to have been in correspondence with the Dutch. Early the following year, exiled ministers in the Netherlands smuggled an antimonarchical pamphlet into Scotland; "it speakes," blustered Archbishop Burnet, "a Language, which is very consonant both with the practice and profession of many considerable persons in this countrey."[51]

Although there was relatively little plotting against the state by Scots during the war years, there was a notable increase in conventicles and in the militancy of those who attended them. Exiled ministers returned to the country and convened "great companies of disorderly persons whose spirits they embitter by their rebellious lectures and sermons." That assessment, voiced by the usually alarmist Archbishop Burnet, was reinforced by the earl of Rothes, who reported frequent conventicles led by ejected clergy often disguised by masks and gray clothing. "Thes roges stirs up the uimin [women] so as they are uors than deivils, yay I dear say if it uear not for the uimin uie should have litill trubell with conventickils."[52] One of the rene-gade clerics, Alexander Peden, held his services at night at Kilmar-nock and Craggie, armed with pistols and a sword. Worshippers too increasingly bore weapons, turning the conventicles into armed as-semblies. In addition to Peden, the most prominent conventiclers included John Crookshanks, Gabriel Semple, Robert Archibald of Dunscore, and Samuel Arnot of Kirkpatrick Durham. One of the most popular was John Blackader of Traquair, whose illegal meetings in the fields of Dumfriesshire and Galloway regularly drew more than a thousand persons. John Knox's great-grandson, John Welsh of Irongray, whose followers openly demonstrated against their new episcopally appointed cleric, held conventicles at least once a week in Dumfriesshire and Ayrshire.[53]

Inability to curb the conventicles frustrated the king's men, al-though some of the offenders were apprehended and whipped in Edinburgh or banished to the Shetland Isles or Barbados. Dissenters were aided by the fact that many justices of the peace and sheriffs were notably reluctant to apprehend them. In August 1666 the Council sought to make landlords responsible for the behavior of their tenants and servants, with the power to evict them for attend-ing conventicles, and holding borough magistrates accountable for the actions of townsfolk. Two months later the Councillors issued a proclamation intended to secure better obedience to ecclesiastical au-thorities. The earl of Kellie even proposed making all Presbyterian ministers wear special badges of identification, but by the mid-1660s the government had already committed itself to military force as the cornerstone of its conventicle policy.[54]

The responsibility for implementing the military policy to crush dissenters rested with the earl of Rothes, a staunch ally of Arch-bishop Sharp. His principal agent, the unscrupulous Sir James Turner, moved throughout the southwest, fining dissidents identi-fied by orthodox clerics, quartering his troops in the homes of those who were tardy in paying, and pocketing some of the fines for his personal use. At times he fined people without an appropriate hear-ing or reliable testimony from a minister, and he sometimes imposed penalties that exceeded the offense. Innocent persons were forced to pay, access to him was sometimes denied even to those who paid to see him, and extra soldiers were quartered in the homes of those who complained.[55] In the spring of 1665 Turner spent two months at Kirkcudbright, after which he was ordered to Ayr, Irvine, and Kilmarnock, all in Ayrshire. Renewed complaints from conforming clergy brought him back to Kirkcudbright as well as to Nithsdale in 1666 with 120 foot and 30 horse. Included in his orders was a command to arrest and fine those who attended conventicles or sheltered fugitive clergy. In July he was sent to Dumfries, but in the next three months his horse and nearly half his foot soldiers were recalled because of the Dutch War. Once the danger of a Dutch invasion was past for 1666, however, Rothes wanted to dispatch more troops into the western shires "to drau that stuberne pipiell to giff obedins to the laus."[56] The stage was set for the Galloway rebellion.

The Galloway Rising

Most modern historians believe that the rebellion in the southwest was unpremeditated, the result of "a chance occurrence, rather than concerted action."[57] There is some contemporary support for this view, which was advanced, for example, by Sir Robert Moray on 1 July 1667 as he investigated the causes of the insurrection. The more he inquired, he informed Lauderdale, "the lesse appearance I finde that there was a formed designe of rebellion, and that it might have been more easily quasht than it was." A good deal of blame was cast by contemporaries on the behavior of Sir James Turner and his men, though he protested that he had been less vigorous in punishing dissenters than his instructions mandated. Various rebels eventually confessed as much, but also attributed some responsibility to the preaching of dissident ministers.[58] This too was the judgment of Lieutenant-General William Drummond, who insisted to Lauderdale that "the preachers at many conventicles had disposed the people to be in radiness to ryse in armes when the opportunytie showld offer," although the actual spark that ignited the rebellion was only accidental. While the insurrection was still under way, Archbishop Burnet suspected a "design" and voiced suspicions that the rebels were in contact with dissidents in England and Ireland. Jeremy Taylor, bishop of Down, lent some credence to this theory by noting that John Crookshanks and Thomas Kennedy had been in Ireland on the eve of the uprising; hence he concluded that "the Scotch rebellion was either borne in Ireland or put to nurse here."[59]

The only modern authority who has given any credence to charges of a conspiracy is Julia Buckroyd, who suggests that an uprising had been tentatively planned but that no date had been set. The timing, she argues, was thus an accident, as was the form of the rebellion, with its unsettled plans, lack of supplies, and absence of a well-conceived manifesto detailing its aims. Nevertheless Buckroyd points to discussions between Scottish rebels and the Dutch, to the rapid recruiting of men (more than a thousand in the first week), and to the role of Captain Andrew Grey and Lieutenant-Colonel James Wallace as evidence that some planning had been under way.[60]

Although the event that triggered the revolt was demonstrably unplanned by dissident leaders, some form of action was being plotted. On the eve of the outbreak one of Turner's sources informed him that two agents from northern Scotland had come to the southwest to recruit discontented persons for an uprising, and that the scheme included the seizure of Ayr. These agents may have been Crookshanks and Kennedy. In any event, shortly before the insurrection, ministers from the southwest had gone to Edinburgh, where they not only preached secretly but consulted with other Covenanters, including Lieutenant-Colonel James Wallace. Out of these discussions came a decision to dispatch Gabriel Semple to dissidents in the southwest to ascertain "what they designed to do, and to report at Edinburgh." When he discovered that they "were longing for an opportunity of appearing together for their defence," he urged them not to act rashly. Within days after his return to Edinburgh, Semple was visited by the Galloway laird "Monrieff"—presumably William Maxwell of Monreith—who accepted an invitation to stay in the capital long enough to attend the next meeting of the informal Covenanters' council. The subject clearly would have been the question of retaliation against Turner. It was at this point that the council received word that action had been taken by John Maclellan, laird of Barscobe.[61]

Further evidence supports the strong probability of a conspiracy. In August 1666 John Welsh of Cornley in Galloway returned from Edinburgh, where he had reportedly learned that an uprising had been proposed for all three kingdoms the previous 29 or 30 May. In October Welsh and Cornet Robert Gordon of Knockbrex were dispatched by dissidents in Galloway to obtain the latest intelligence from the Edinburgh committee. Upon their return they reported to a group that met at the house of Andrew Dempster in Balmaclellan; in this group were a number of men who would shortly participate in the Galloway rebellion. Two or three days before the uprising commenced, Welsh told George Roome, who would also join the rebellion, that their group expected the arrival of two ships from the Netherlands carrying 2,000 exiled Scots and Englishmen. Interestingly, some three weeks after the uprising was crushed, the Scottish Council received information that the exiles had been shipping weapons to Scotland.[62] Thus it seems reasonably certain that on the eve of the revolt, a committee of militants in Edinburgh was planning an uprising, with the expectation of assistance from exiles in the Netherlands and perhaps from English militants as well, and that this committee was in contact with discontented elements in Galloway.

On 13 November, at Dalry in Kirkcudbrightshire, three or four of Turner's soldiers apprehended an elderly peasant accused of recusancy, threatening to strip off his clothes and broil him on a gridiron in his own house. Four local men, including Maclellan of Barscobe, came to his rescue, shooting a corporal in the stomach with "Tobacco Stapples" and forcing the other soldiers to surrender their weapons. News of the incident did not reach Turner at Dumfries until the following evening, at which time he dispatched orders to his scattered forces to join him and the thirteen soldiers who were with him. By this time Maclellan had gathered additional supporters, including John Nelson of Corsock, and had overrun the tiny garrison of sixteen at Balmaclellan.[63]

Maclellan and Nelson must have been part of a network—at least an informal one—of dissident lairds, for on the night of the 14th upwards of 150 armed men, including 50 horse, mustered at Irongray in response to their call; some sources put the number as high as 400 or 500. The experience of organizing large outdoor conventicles must have helped. One of the most zealous recruiters was the Irongray minister, John Welsh, one of the most active conventicle preachers before the rebellion. Command was given to Captain Andrew Grey (or Gray), who had been associated with the minister William Veitch at Newcastle, and who was possibly an Edinburgh merchant. On the morning of the 15th this band captured Turner—still dressed in his nightgown and feeling "indisposed"—and his men at Dumfries. For good measure they also seized the recusancy fines he had collected, which amounted to 6,600 or 6,700 Scots merks.[64] To the rebels Turner was a "Tyrant" who had "Laid ther families wast[e] . . . for not keeping of the Church." The soldiers were warned to expect no quarter if they insisted on defending prelates. At the town cross in Dumfries the rebels toasted the king's health before moving Turner to a secure house in neighboring Maxwelltown.[65]

By this point Maclellan had contacted Wallace and Semple's group in Edinburgh. Although Semple and Monreith were displeased by the news, "the most forward said, there had been talking enough upon that affair, that it was fit to take that opportunity to appear, which if they did not, Sir James Turner, that was at Dumfries, would come with all his men and destroy the country; and that it was best to prevent that by marching to Dumfries and securing of him." Among those present, only William Ferguson of Caitloch (or Kaitloch) was reluctant to sanction such action. Semple rode all night to apprise Maclellan of the council's support: "If that rising was general they would carry it; if it were but in that corner [of Scotland], they could not do it." Wallace, however, was firm in his resolution, convinced that it "was clear that it was our duty to own our brethren in Galloway, yea, and . . . share with them in what should be their lot." On the 18th he set off to join the rebels.[66]

Taking Turner with them, the insurgents reached Dalry on the 16th. Their numbers still grew; Turner now estimated their size at 250, up 100 from the previous day. Grey, claiming to act on behalf of a higher but unnamed authority, offered to relinquish command to Major Stewart of "Monwhill," but the latter refused. The insurgents pressed on to Carsphairn, from where Grey mysteriously left on the 17th for Newcastle.[67] According to Wallace, Grey, "having been the chief actor in the business," had become concerned for his safety and quit when many of the initial rebels returned to their homes. Wodrow, however, speculates that he left because Nelson of Corsock refused to let him kill Turner. Command in any case may have already shifted—temporarily—to Colonel Gilby Carr, for as early as the evening of the 16th a Dumfries bailie reported to the Privy Council that the rebels acknowledged Carr's presence.[68]

On the 16th the Privy Council directed the western earls to restore peace. The following day the Councillors ordered Lieutenant-General Thomas Dalziel (or Dalyell) to prepare his troops to march, and instructed "the heretours of the severall countyes, especially these of the southerne and westerne shyres and such others as his Majesties Councill shall think fitt, be presently requyred to signe the Declaration concerning the Covenant, and that such as shall delay or refuse be secured and looked upon as enemies to his Majesties authority and government." In Edinburgh the night watch was doubled, special precautions were taken to ensure the security of the gates, an oath of allegiance was imposed on the militia, and fresh efforts were made to monitor all temporary lodgers. Defensive measures were also implemented in Glasgow.[69] News of the rebellion at first greatly alarmed officials in London because of exaggerated accounts of 4,000 men-at-arms, and some consideration was given to dispatching troops from Ireland to Scotland. But more accurate reports soon arrived and Rothes promised that the uprising would "come to nothing." Henry Muddiman, a client of Albemarle, passed off the disturbance as "some such kind of feud as is frequent among" the Scots. Ormond, however, was cautioned to keep a close eye on northern Ireland.[70]

On the 18th the insurgents continued their march toward Ayr, enlisting six or seven more lairds at Dalmellington, including William Maxwell of Monreith and Robert Maclellan of Balmagechan. They were joined at Dalmellington by the minister John Welsh, who lectured Turner on the glories of the Covenant and the evils of prelacy. The same day the duke of Hamilton chased a band of armed rebels that had been spotted near Hamilton, but they eluded him by marching throughout the night. Other bands at Eaglesham and Kilbride, undoubtedly moving south to rendezvous at Ayr, also evaded him.[71]

The insurrectionists reached Tarbolton on the 19th, augmenting their strength with fresh recruits from Ayrshire and Clydesdale. They planned to march into Glasgow the next day, but word that Dalziel and Hamilton were in the city[72] persuaded them to retreat to Ayr instead. There they seized some 200 weapons from the tolbooth and searched the homes of gentlemen for horses and arms. By now the rebels claimed to have 1,100 men, with more on their way from the north; Turner put their number at less than 800, but he was probably in no position to see the full force, including scouting and foraging units. Majors Joseph Learmont (or Learmonth, Lermond), who had been enlisted by William Veitch, and John McCulloch were now involved. The Council impeded the movement of recruits from the northeast by halting the ferries between Leith and Stirling, checking passengers on other ferries, closing the bridge at Stirling to all but those with approved passes, and examining all persons traveling through Leith, which itself was secured with troops.[73]

On the 21st Charles issued a proclamation declaring the insurrection to be "ane oppen, manifest and horrid rebellion" and giving the mutineers twenty-four hours to surrender or face charges of high treason. Simultaneously the Council ordered a general levy in the counties of central and southern Scotland adjacent to the troubled shires, but at least some of the commissions to the nobles appear to have been intercepted by a rebel party headed by Robert Trail's son.[74]

At this juncture the insurgents, now under Wallace's command, apparently decided to march on Edinburgh. Turner indicates that Wallace first took command of the rebel forces on the night of the 24th, but in fact he had done so on the 21st at Bridge of Doon. He had come from Edinburgh with the Presbyterian firebrand James Mitchell, who in 1668 would attempt to assassinate Archbishop Sharp. Presumably delayed by strategy discussions and the search for supplies, the insurgents advanced that day only as far as Coylton. At Ochiltree on the 22nd they were joined by the minister John Guthry and approximately a hundred men recruited in Galloway by John Welsh. Expecting no further help from the southwest, the rebels decided that night to march eastward.[75]

Despite the onset of bad weather, which would dog them the rest of the way, their tempo increased, bringing them to Douglas by the evening of the 24th. The previous night, Andrew McCormack, who,

like Crookshanks, had come from Ireland, informed Wallace that
Captain Robert Lockhart had recommended that the troops be dismissed because they had no chance of success. But Wallace and his
compatriots refused on the 24th, convinced that their undertaking
was providentially ordained: "Our master whom we serve (we know
well, if ever there was a handful about whom he exercised a providence, it is about us) he needs no men, or if he will make use of men,
we will not want." Captain Andrew Arnot, brother of the laird of
Lochridge, had joined them, bringing some 40 men from Cunningham, though 200 had been expected.[76]

On the 25th the mutineers marched northwest to Lesmahagow, as
if they had altered their plans and now intended to strike Glasgow
from the southeast, though this may only have been a feint to confuse royalist commanders. A rebel party had in fact been sighted the
previous day in Fenwick, some ten miles southwest of Glasgow, but
they were probably new recruits en route to join the main force. At
this juncture Wallace restructured his officer corps: "We found great
want of officers, there not being, to the few number we had, half of
the officers requisite, not above four or five that ever had been soldiers before." With weapons, ammunition, and horses also in short
supply, the insurrectionists altered their course on the 25th and
moved into Lanark, hoping to find more of each. They had virtually
no success. By Turner's reckoning, there were now 440 horse and
more than 500 foot soldiers as the rebellion neared the two-week
mark, but their total strength was probably closer to 1,200; the Presbyterian historian Robert Wodrow, in fact, suggests 3,000.[77]

Although a party of thirty-six men organized by the earls of Glencairn and Hartfell and Lord Kenmore had skirmished with some of
the rebels as early as the 18th, government forces were still not in a
position for a major engagement, partly because Dalziel's men had
detoured on their march westward to suppress disturbances in the
north, where substantial looting was occurring. Dalziel himself had
seven troops of horse and 2,000 to 3,000 foot soldiers, while additional forces—said by some to number 400 horse—were raised by
the duke of Hamilton, the earls of Annandale and Nithsdale, Lord
Drumlanrig, and others.[78] In Edinburgh the Council continued to
issue instructions for the militia, the arrest of dissidents, and the

security of the capital and the castles of Edinburgh, Stirling, and Dumbarton.[79] Simultaneously the king directed the earl of Carlisle to call out the militia in Cumberland and Westmorland, and to prepare his own and Lord Freschville's troops, a company of foot from Hartlepool, and other forces to march to Rothes's aid if necessary.[80] Admitting that the rebellion was more serious than the government had originally surmised, Arlington directed Ormond to take precautions to ensure that northern Ireland did not also revolt. These measures included the use of ships to intercept radical correspondence between Scotland and Ireland. Muddiman similarly acknowledged that "the Scotch businesse is broke farther then . . . at first it was imagined it would have done[,] some discontented persons having laid hold on the occasion to joine themselves together & formally to declare for King & Covenant." There was some concern that the Dutch might take advantage of the insurrection to strike at Scotland; hence guns from several ships were mounted on the citadel at Leith and a ship was readied to sink at the river's mouth to prevent an assault by fireboats. Unidentified vessels were in fact sighted off Leith, but took no action.[81]

Dalziel finally left Glasgow in pursuit of the rebels on the 23rd. Two days later Annandale, having linked forces with Dalziel at Sanquhar, was concerned that the rebels, whose numbers had now reached between 1,500 and 2,000, would soon receive the support of "persons of quality or interest." According to his informants, the mutineers were "very resolute and speake of great expectations." At Lanark the rebels renewed their oaths to the Covenant in a ceremony conducted for the cavalry by Gabriel Semple and John Crookshanks and for the infantry by John Guthry. Their cry, "For God and Covenant," tied them to the old Covenanters, but they also declared in favor of liberty of conscience and freedom from taxes, and against apostacy, recusancy fines, and billeting.[82] They issued a formal manifesto replete with professions of loyalty to the king, complaints of oppression, and demands for the termination of episcopacy and the restoration of presbyterianism and the deprived ministers.[83] Because of the renewal of the Covenant, perhaps as many as 200 dissidents dropped out; these had probably enlisted only on account of economic grievances or hostility to Turner's actions. According to

Turner himself, one of those who quit was Alexander Peden, though other clerics, including Semple, Welsh, and John Fletcher, pressed on. The Hawick minister John Scot and Major Kilgour (or Gilgour) arrived from eastern Scotland, but left the insurgents by the 27th, apparently because of the poor organization.[84]

From Lanark the rebels marched north on the 26th to Bathgate and Torphichen. Their goal was now Edinburgh, for Welsh and Semple had received a letter from James Stewart promising men and supplies if the insurgents could reach the capital. Dalziel, who had hoped to force a battle at Mauchline or Douglas Castle, had still not caught up with them. The rebels destroyed bridges and ships to delay their pursuers and consumed most of the food on their route. They reportedly seized conforming ministers, transported them ten or twelve miles from their parishes, and stripped them before turning them loose. One preacher was allegedly pulled from his pulpit, dragged through the church by his gown, and wounded in the head; his reader was similarly treated.[85]

About midnight on the 26th the rebels launched their thrust toward Edinburgh despite inclement weather. It was, said Wallace, "a dreadfully dark . . . and foul night. . . . Except we had been tied together, it was impossible to keep together; and every little burn was a river." At 10:00 A.M. on the 27th they rallied at Kirkliston, five miles west of the capital, where a preacher exhorted them "to cary themselves not onlie pieouslie to God, bot civillie and discreetlie to man." From Kirkliston they marched toward the southeast to Colinton, from where they could see Edinburgh Castle. At this point Dalziel was still some eight miles behind them. Veitch was dispatched to Edinburgh to consult with Stewart, though he never reached him and was in fact briefly detained by loyalist troops. Captain Arnot, however, sent James Mitchell into the city.[86]

Expecting an imminent assault, the Councillors shored up the city's defenses. Their reports, greatly exaggerated, indicated that the insurgents might attack with as many as 3,000 horse. All available forces in the Tweeddale-Merse region were ordered to Edinburgh "with all convenient speed"; Lord Ramsay rounded up the horses in the capital; and the foot company of the College of Justice was armed with muskets. That night Dalziel dispatched two emissaries to the rebels with an offer of royal grace. When word arrived that a Dutch fleet had been spotted off the coast, one of Dalziel's men warned the rebels that whoever trusted the Dutch "leand on a broken reed." The rebel spokesman, Alexander Robertson, retorted that they too would fight to repel any Dutch invasion, but there was no promise to lay down their arms. On the contrary, the dissidents sent a messenger to the capital to ascertain what support they might expect, only to discover that the lord provost, Andrew Ramsay, had 2,000 citizens in arms ready to defend the city, with security so tight that the "many fanatics" in Edinburgh were unable to join or supply the insurgents. As the bulk of the rebel force slept at Dalkeith and Newbattle, there was a skirmish between 2:00 and 3:00 A.M. outside Colinton when a party of loyalists attacked.[87]

Aware now that Edinburgh would not rise, Wallace wrote to Dalziel, citing the proclamation of the 21st and seeking assurances of pardon if the mutineers laid down their weapons. The Council responded on the 28th with nothing more than a promise that the rebels could petition for mercy if they surrendered. Cognizant of an opportunity to encircle the insurrectionists, the Councillors ordered the troops in Teviotdale to march toward Edinburgh while Dalziel closed in from the west. Simultaneously the marquis of Montrose moved against Wallace's men with a party of armed gentlemen from Edinburgh.[88]

On the morning of the 28th Wallace's forces retreated through freshly fallen snow into the Pentland Hills. The confrontation with Dalziel's troops occurred late that afternoon at Rullion Green, seven miles from Edinburgh. Before the battle the rebels sang the Seventy-fourth Psalm. By Major-General William Drummond's estimate, they numbered 1,600, but Wallace put their number at only 800 or 900. However, they enjoyed a hilltop position and fought "desperatlie enough," urged on by Semple and Welsh's battle cry, "The God of Jacob, the God of Jacob."[89] One of Williamson's correspondents subsequently reported that "all of the Armye affirmes they never saw men fight more Gallantly and abyd better then they did." With the earls of Linlithgow and Argyll playing prominent roles, it took Dalziel's forces three charges to carry the day. "Wee fought obstinately a long time with swords," Drummond wrote, "until they mixed like chessmen in a bag." Approximately 50 insurgents were killed and some 120 captured, a number that would have been greater but for nightfall. Nevertheless, it was, the commissioners claimed, "a totall rout."[90]

Lairds sympathetic to the rebels, including William Muir of Caldwell, the laird of Ralston, and William Porterfield of Quarrelton, had been recruiting in Renfrewshire, where they had raised a party of forty to eighty cavalry. Three ministers—John Carstares, who was Porterfield's brother-in-law, Gabriel Maxwell of Dundonald, and George Ramsay of Kilmaurs—were part of this group. They dispersed, however, as soon as they learned of Dalziel's victory at Rullion Green.[91]

Of the factors that contributed to the rebel defeat, none was more crucial than their failure to spark an uprising in Edinburgh. The capital had not been subjected to the harsh treatment meted out to Presbyterian stalwarts, nor were the dissidents sufficiently prepared to strike before the magistrates implemented effective security measures. Whether a carefully crafted manifesto setting forth a popular program of reform would have offset the ill-preparedness of the insurrectionaries is doubtful, but it might have made the control of Edinburgh more difficult for loyalists. Gabriel Semple cast the principal blame for the rebels' defeat on the gentlemen and ministers of the west who refused to join them, but additional recruits would have made a significant difference only if a larger force would have inspired the capital to revolt.[92] The rain and snow are often cited as factors in the defeat, but the weather was no less a handicap to Dalziel, who probably suffered more from it because the mutineers destroyed bridges and boats and consumed much of the available food.

Undoubtedly the rebel cause was adversely affected by the inability of the leaders to meet the early expectations of their men. With most of their potential leaders already in preventive detention, it was critical to find replacements as rapidly as possible. Major-General Robert Montgomery and Wallace would have made a potent duumvirate, but the former, contrary to expectations, backed Dalziel, as did the laird of Gadgirth, another potential leader. Although early word that the rebels had the support of the earl of Annandale was unrealistic, expectations were nevertheless raised; when dissidents learned of his loyalty to the government "they then as heartily curst him & his company."[93] Rebel spokesmen such as Alexander Robertson similarly raised false hopes by telling recruits that the provost and people of Edinburgh supported their cause, reinforcing this with fictitious horror stories that Dalziel had hanged a hundred persons at Glasgow and would similarly execute all nonconformists. There was disillusionment too that anticipated assistance did not arrive from England and Ireland, where uprisings were also expected. The cumulative impact caused a substantial decline in morale that contributed to the insurgents' defeat. Spirits also waned as the confrontation with Dalziel's army neared, particularly among those who had been persuaded by the ministers to believe that God would "scatter their enymyes befor them" like the chaff in the wind, giving them victory without recourse to fighting.[94]

English radicals indeed watched the insurrection with interest, and some at least were disheartened by the events at Rullion Green, yet virtually no meaningful aid came from south of the Tweed. Had the insurrection not been prematurely triggered, English help might have been possible. At least one of the rebels who was executed, Ralph Shiells (or Shield), was an Englishman, although he was either a clothier or a collier living in Ayr and may have had no contact with radicals in England.[95]

More problematical is the possible involvement of Thomas Blood, one of the principal figures in the 1663 Dublin plot. The best evidence for his participation in the Galloway rising is Viscount Conway's statement that the king told him of Blood's role in late November 1666, and the earl of Orrery's remark to Ormond the following month, based on information from Arlington, that Blood was involved. If so, he went to Scotland from Ireland after first going to Cheshire, Liverpool, and Wales. In Ireland he and Colonel Gilby Carr were implicated in a conspiracy to seize Limerick, after which Blood reputedly went to Scotland. The government issued warrants for his arrest in February and March 1667, about which time he was reportedly associating with an unnamed Baptist in Westmorland. The absence, however, of Blood's name from the proclamations listing the principal Galloway rebels raises doubt about his participation.[96]

The evidence for Colonel Carr's involvement is stronger, not least because of the testimony already noted from the Dumfries bailie who cited rebel claims that Carr was with them. Another report placed him at the head of some 4,000 Covenanters in the rebellion, but the exaggeration of the numbers casts doubt on the report's accuracy. One of Williamson's correspondents also indicated that Carr was with the rebels. Rothes, who was in a position to know, indicated on 20 December 1666 only that "should anie fforiners send with gilbert car, or sum suthe rouge, ten thousand earms, in a verie fyou [few] day ther uold be pritie men to teack them in ther hands." Rothes implies that Carr was abroad seeking to find support among foreign governments for the insurrection. He could indeed have been with the rebels briefly in the earliest days of the uprising and then gone to the Continent in search of assistance, yet his name too is missing from government lists of the principal insurgents and from Wallace's account.[97]

Several of Blood's known associates, including the ministers Andrew McCormack (alias Goodman) and John Crookshanks, were definitely involved. Both had been implicated in the Dublin conspiracy, which fact provides an unmistakable link to radicals in Ireland and, through them, in England. Referring to the Galloway revolt, Wallace called them "two main instruments of the attempt." There is also indisputable evidence that dissidents in northern Ireland such as John Cuningham of Bedland joined the Galloway rebels; Cuningham was subsequently arrested in Ireland and returned to Scotland for punishment. Wallace himself may have been linked to the Dublin conspiracy. The rebels, however, never received substantive assistance from England despite expectations that they would "be seconded by disturbances" in that country.[98]

Insurgents in Flight

On the heels of the victory at Rullion Green, the Privy Council commanded the earls of Annandale and Nithsdale and Lords Drumlanrig and Herries to keep their forces together in order to apprehend the rebels, while the troops raised in Tweeddale secured Linton Bridge. The units raised in Fife, Angus, Perth, and the Mearns, however, were dismissed. Similar instructions were relayed to commanders in the Merse, Teviotdale, the Forrest, Dumbarton, and Stirling. The governor of Berwick and magistrates in neighboring counties kept a special watch for fleeing rebels. Three troops of the earl of Oxford's regiment as well as forty of the king's guard and sixty men of the dukes of York and Albemarle were already on their way north, and a 10:00 P.M. curfew had previously been imposed on York.[99]

The Council authorized Dalziel, who was scheduled to return to the west on 4 December, to quarter his troops in the homes of the insurgents and their supporters in the course of his campaign to arrest the fugitives. Hamilton too received orders to arrest the rebels and their abettors in Lanarkshire. A proclamation issued on the 4th decreed the apprehension of fifty-seven rebels, including Wallace, Learmont, Semple, and Guthry. The king simultaneously revised his directive of 27 November to his officials in northern England, seeking now not the arrest of all disaffected persons but only those believed to have been in league with the insurrectionaries. In Cumberland, certainly, the latter had well-wishers, although Sir Philip Musgrave reported that Carlisle was quiet.[100]

On 4 December Arlington directed Ormond to arrest any rebels who fled to Ireland as well as those who corresponded with them. Ormond already had two unnamed men under surveillance who had recently returned from Scotland and were allegedly preaching sedition. He subsequently asked the bishop of Down to provide him with a list of clergy who had gone to Scotland before the insurrection and had now returned, of the landed men who supported them financially, and of those who had provided hospitality to Crookshanks.[101] Although the ports were under surveillance, some fugitives reached Ireland, among them William Wallace, the commander's son.[102]

The depth of popular support for the rebels is repeatedly attested to in loyalist letters. Rothes, for instance, complained that the people were hiding the insurgents, and that few of the leaders, including the clergy, could be found. "The Common people in the West of Scotland," observed Musgrave, "have kyndnes enough for those that have been in rebellion & wil not be very redy to discover such as sculke at their owne homes."[103] Three weeks after the uprising, Dalziel had

seen enough of western Scotland to insist that the mutineers were
supported by most of the people, and he subsequently painted a
vivid picture to Lauderdale of a region festering with rebellious tendencies. If foreign forces invade, he said,

this Land wil all go in Rebelion and it seems this Last if it had not been
Mistymed had been Much Moir terible. And no peple heue with Moir
egernes sought after Marterdom then thir Rouges to karry thair desyn or
dyce. Mane of the wimen upbraden thair husbends and Children for not
deyen.

Drummond too attributed the rebel defeat to the fact that the insurrection had begun precipitantly, and that "the foolisher sort" had
proceeded "blindly and madly." The state had indeed expected more
support for the rebels from the Scottish aristocracy and the townsfolk than had materialized.[104]

Some of the rebels may have sought refuge in the Highlands, but
reports placing their number at 400 or 500 were surely exaggerated.
The difficulty in finding the insurgents is underscored by the fact
that the government spent years in the effort. Further proclamations
to this end were issued, for example, in May and June 1667. As late
as June 1670 the earl of Linlithgow, working in conjunction with the
provost of Edinburgh, searched the capital for rebels still at large.[105]

Although there was originally some talk of executing 10 percent
of the common mutineers as well as all officers and clerics, the state
chose to execute only thirty-six of the rebels, though more would
surely have died if all the leaders had been apprehended. The first to
die were hanged on 7 December. Ten in all, they included at least
three rebel officers—Major John McCulloch of Barholm, Captain
Andrew Arnot, and Cornet Robert Gordon, whose brother John, of
Knockbrex, was also in this group. On the scaffold Arnot prayed for
the condemned men, threw out a declaration proclaiming their allegiance to king and Covenant as well as their opposition to bishops
and the king's wicked advisers, and then "pluckt out a pockett bottle
of sack and with a roaring voyse uttered . . . that hee would drink
no more of the vyne till hee had it new in his fathers kingdome."[106]
Their heads were sent to Kirkcudbright, Kilmarnock, and the Wa-
tergate in Edinburgh for public display, and their right arms to Lan-

ark, where they had subscribed to the Covenant. "We hope," Arlington explained, "a little more than ordinary severity therein will deter others from the like undertakings."[107]

Because the prisoners were generally "stuborne in ther wicked and rebellious way, the most of them declaring ther willingness to dye for the Covenent," Rothes thought them undeserving of mercy, but the prospect of executing more than 120 prisoners was daunting.[108] Five more were tried and convicted on the 12th. Two of them, the minister Alexander Robertson and John Nelson, laird of Corsock, had been members of the party that kidnapped Turner, while a third, John Lindsay, was one of a number of rebels from Edinburgh. Robertson died unrepentant, insisting he had acted to preserve true religion and to extirpate idolatry; the faithful, he exhorted, should be resolute in "fighting the good fight." Nelson and Hugh McKell, a chaplain and ministerial candidate who had denounced Rothes and Sharp five years earlier as Haman and Judas, had been subjected to the boot, a form of torture in which the victim's leg was placed in a wooden frame, with wooden wedges driven between it and the leg, squeezing the calf or crushing the shin bone. "The extreametie of paine," Rothes cooly observed, "maid them roar and Cry," but neither confessed. McKell's trial as well as the execution of Lindsay had to be delayed because of their wounds, but the other four died in Edinburgh on the 14th.[109]

In Glasgow, where Rothes personally conducted the investigation, four more "Whigs," none of whom had been leaders, were hanged on the 19th as an object lesson. In the face of widespread sympathy for the rebels, the magistrates made certain that the scaffold speeches did not incite the crowd by using five drummers to drown them out.[110]

The executions resumed in Edinburgh on the 22nd when six more men were hanged, the most notable being McKell and Humphrey Colgwen (or Colhoune), a Glasgow merchant, both identified as leaders. Praying for the king's prosperity and asking forgiveness for their judges, they "declared their blood lay only at the prelats Door [and they] wold not be hindered to expresse them selfe[s] in such Maner which expressions had to[o] great Dipping in the hearts of the Commonality."[111] Twelve more prisoners were sentenced at Ayr on 24 December, all of them minor figures. Because local hangmen refused to perform the executions, one of the condemned men, the tailor Cornelius Anderson of Ayr, amply plied with brandy, saved his own life by hanging seven of his fellows. Two more died at Irvine on the 31st, and two at Dumfries on 2 January 1667.[112]

Instead of cowing the disaffected, the executions hardened their resolve. On 4 January, dissident women retrieved the heads of four executed rebels that had been on public display in Glasgow. Several days later an anonymous dissident issued a lengthy letter addressed to the king that castigated Rothes for "drinking the blood of the Saynts." Rumors that on his march through the west Dalziel would "hang everie mane at his owne Doar that had not Conformed" only heightened tension. Gilbert Burnet subsequently accused the general of acting "the Muscovite too grossly" by threatening to roast men on spits and killing others, and Sir William Ballantyne was accused of similar brutality, but the repression was normally confined to imprisonment, fines, the expropriation of goods, and the billeting of troops in homes. This continued until August 1668, when the army was finally disbanded.[113]

Because of the important role of ministers in the insurrection, the Council pondered the feasibility of forcing all deprived clergymen to live in one place, but in the end took no action. At the Councillors' suggestion, however, in March the king ordered them to tender the oath of allegiance and the declaration against the Covenants to all suspicious persons, imprisoning those who refused. A proclamation required all people in those areas where discontent was strongest to surrender their weapons, with the exception of gentlemen's swords. The affected areas were the counties of Ayr, Lanark, Renfrew, and Wigtown, and the stewartry of Kirkcudbright. The ban on arms remained in force until 9 October, at which time subscribers to the oath of allegiance and the declaration against the Covenants were allowed to possess weapons again. Magistrates were also authorized to seize the horses of dissidents in the same areas if they were worth more than 100 Scots merks. In March parishes were instructed to make certain that conforming ministers were protected, and two months later Charles directed the Council to see that any affronts to the clergy were severely punished. Nevertheless violence to orthodox clerics continued unabated, ranging from assaults on their persons to the plundering of their goods. In June the king, manifestly irate, ordered parishioners to take a more active role in defending their pastors, made those who abetted such attackers equally responsible for the crime, and required parishioners to assume financial liability for losses sustained by their ministers.[114]

Despite extensive efforts the state failed to apprehend most of the leading insurgents, including the two principal officers, Lieutenant-Colonel Wallace and Major Learmont. Wallace had escaped the preventive dragnet in the spring of 1666 by fleeing to Ireland, but this time he sought refuge in the Netherlands, where he eventually became an elder in the Scottish church at Rotterdam and died in 1678. James Mitchell had seen him on the German border in 1670. Learmont went underground and was subsequently implicated in the 1668 plot to assassinate Archbishop Sharp. John Nelson of Corsock, one of those responsible for kidnapping Turner, was executed, but John Maclellan of Barscobe, an instigator of the rebellion, eluded arrest, as did most of his fellow lairds. So too did Captain John Paton, who had fought with Gustavus Adolphus as well as with Cromwell at Marston Moor and Charles II at Worcester. Only two ministers—Hugh McKell and Alexander Robertson—were hanged. The two men who preached with Crookshanks at Lanark when the Covenant was renewed—Gabriel Semple and John Guthry—both escaped, the latter with the aid of Gilbert Burnet's mother. Semple was finally arrested in 1681, by which time the state was no longer interested in imposing a harsh sentence.[115] Altogether at least eighteen clerics had participated in the insurrection, with the fugitives including John Carstares, Samuel Arnot, Alexander Peden, John Welsh, and William Veitch.

By July 1667 the Privy Council had completed its examination of prisoners in the tolbooths of Edinburgh and Cannongate. Those who were "clearly guilty" and refused the oath of allegiance and the declaration against the Covenants were, as the king wished, destined for banishment to Barbados and Virginia, but a pardon was obtained for two commoners who agreed to subscribe. Those who denied participating in the rebellion were released if they subscribed, but otherwise continued in prison. The lairds and clerics, however, were excluded from these provisions and held accountable for charges of high treason.[116]

On 15 August 1667 fifty-six of the rebels still at large, most of whom had fought in the Pentland Hills, were indicted for high treason *in absentia* and declared fugitives. The list included Maclellan of Barscobe and most of the preachers. An assize was thereupon sworn and six of the fifty-six, including Maclellan and the clerics John Welsh and James Smith, were found guilty, as were Wallace and Learmont (though not named on the list of fifty-six). The following day the court found fifteen more guilty, among them the western lairds who were unable to reach Wallace before the defeat at Rullion Green. They included William Muir of Caldwell, Robert Ker of Kersland, and John Cuningham of Bedland as well as the ministers Gabriel Semple, John Guthry, Alexander Peden, William Veitch, and John Crookshanks. As late as December 1671, Gabriel Maxwell, the former pastor at Dundonald, was indicted and sentenced to death *in absentia* for high treason in connection with the insurrection.[117]

In September 1667 the Council completed and sent to the king a set of five proposals designed to restore order to the kingdom. The key was an offer of indemnity to all but a select list of principal rebels and assaulters of conforming ministers on the condition that they provide security for their behavior. In the ensuing proclamation of 1 October, fifty-six persons were excepted from the offer, of whom sixteen were ministers. The second proposal, also approved, directed the landed classes to require bonds from their tenants assuring their peaceful deportment, with power to disarm and evict those who refused. The king also accepted the Council's proposals to settle the militia, exempt those who took a bond to maintain the peace from subscribing to the declaration against the Covenants, and permit those who subscribed to the oath of allegiance and the declaration to retain their horses and weapons. The intent of the policy was to discriminate between quiescent dissenters and hard-core militants. Thus Lauderdale explained to Sharp that "as wilfull opposers and Contemners must be severlie punished, So peaceable dissenters may be endeavoured to be reclaimed."[118]

The offer of indemnity was only partially successful. On 9 October a number of imprisoned rebels in Edinburgh provided security and were released, but in the west some 300 refused to sign a bond while 218 complied. Opposition to the indemnity was especially pronounced in Kirkcudbright and Dumfriesshire, where only 14 accepted and 128 refused. In Lanarkshire, on the other hand, 147 signed bonds and 100 did not. Most of the 300 who declined the offer of indemnity were poor men, primarily servants, subtenants, and artisans. At the Council's request, on 9 May 1668 Charles issued a proclamation ordering the arrest of 235 of those who rejected the indemnity. Some of these were subsequently banished, in 1668 and 1669, to Barbados, Virginia, and Tangier. Most of those who refused to sign a bond, however, seem to have eluded the magistrates as successfully as their leaders, at least in part because sympathizers offered them refuge. In July 1668 the Edinburgh magistrates threatened any who harbored the fugitives with a fine of £100 sterling, or of £50 sterling for aiding those who rejected the indemnity.[119]

Despite the state's inability to apprehend most of the leaders and their recruits, the failure of the insurrection destroyed the ability of the dissidents to mount effective political opposition for a decade. The disaster in the Pentland Hills made it readily apparent that radicals in England and even in Ireland, while generally sympathetic to the rebels, were unwilling to commit themselves to a Presbyterian crusade whose ideals were ultimately incompatible with their own principles of republicanism and religious toleration—the rebel call for the latter notwithstanding. But neither Wallace's defeat nor the absence of meaningful assistance from sympathizers in England and Ireland broke the spirit of the Scottish dissidents, whose devotion to the conventicle movement continued unabated. Their resolve is reflected in two letters written on 26 December 1666 by "W. Mack.," almost certainly a rebel fugitive, to his wife and father in Galloway. At the time of writing he was in Carlisle en route to Whitehaven, Cumberland. He urged his spouse to "forget not Zioans afflicktions and the troubled seas of gods peopl," and suggested that Bible reading was more beneficial than church attendance, which entailed "submiting to the prelaticall power." Worried that his father might cooperate with officials investigating the rebellion, he warned him not to do or say anything "against the troubled frinds of christ for if you do it sal be the greatest of your conflicks at your death[,] and [beware] of keping to[o] much fellowship with the episcopal partie . . . for if christ be king in Zioan there wilbe a change therefor."[120] It was the hope of such a change that sustained Scottish dissidents and prevented the government from imposing religious uniformity on Scotland.

"Factious and Seditious Spirits"

THREE

Scotland and Ireland, c. 1666–1672

Despite the failure of the Galloway rebellion, the Covenanting tradition remained strong in Scotland, where it was primarily manifested in the perpetuation of conventicles. The Scottish conventicling experience, which was exported to Ulster, tended to differ in degree from that south of the Tweed. Scottish convocations could be astonishingly large, sometimes in excess of a thousand persons. More and more of them came armed with swords and pistols, prepared to defy the government by force if necessary. Some militants went so far as to assault conforming ministers, a practice that also eventually spread to Ulster. The dissident tradition in Scotland—almost wholly motivated by religious considerations—was thus different from that in England with respect to its nature and its manifestations. Yet despite these differences, English and Scottish dissidents maintained some contact, particularly concerning religious matters.

The Irish situation differed from that in Scotland because of the continued presence of English radicals generally hostile toward monarchy, prelacy, religious conformity, and the Restoration land settlement. They maintained regular contact with dissidents in England and, to some degree, in Scotland, in the latter case primarily through the movements of Covenanters who traveled between Ulster and southwestern Scotland. Ireland played a key role in the continuation of a radical tradition in the late 1660s and early 1670s, although most of the Ulster ministers opted for moderation.

Scottish Conventicles: "Hot, Fiery, Young Teachers"

The Galloway insurrection left the government badly divided as to its causes as well as the most prudent course to deal with dissenters in the future. Hard-liners such as the earl of Rothes, James Sharp, and Alexander Burnet saw the rebellion as proof of their earlier warnings that the nonconformists endangered the security of the state and should be ruthlessly suppressed. "If we make a right use of our late victory and improve it," Burnet insisted, "it will conduce much to the King and kingdomes advantage and help to settle this unquiet and tottering kingdome[;] if not our remissenes in pursuing this will lay the foundation for a new and worse rebellion." Complaining that the disaffected had been treated too leniently before the uprising, Sharp urged that all Scots be required to sign the declaration abjuring the Covenant. But Lauderdale, who had generally favored more lenient treatment of the nonconformists, relied increasingly on moderates such as the earl of Tweeddale and Sir Robert Moray, the first president of the Royal Society, both of whom favored a policy of religious toleration and opposed the use of troops to impose punitive measures on recusants. Such measures, in their minds, had incited the Galloway rebels.[1]

The problem of the dissenters was compounded by the reluctance of the Scottish nobility to disband the troops raised to quell the insurrection, for command of those forces provided them with additional revenue and power. Professional soldiers such as Dalziel and Drummond similarly urged the king to maintain a strong standing army, warning that another rebellion was imminent. "The people," Drummond cautioned Lauderdale, "ar unsetled and generally fearfull of a revolutione." Tweeddale and Moray countered such arguments by stressing that the western shires were peaceful, that Dalziel had no hard evidence for his predictions of an imminent insurrection, and that such talk was no more than a pretense to continue the old policy of using an army to extort funds from dissenters.[2] As long as the war continued, Lauderdale was unwilling to risk disbanding the standing forces, but once peace was made he had the backing of Tweeddale, Moray, and Sharp to reduce the number of troops and raise a militia. The latter was not ready until August 1668, at which time it numbered 18,000 and was specifically intended to thwart "factious and seditious spirits."[3]

Despite occasional reports of scheming for a new insurrection, dissidents were generally quiescent throughout most of 1667. Although there had been substantial sympathy for the rebels, there was also a realization that, in the words of a royalist observer, "their lait Madness & rebellione" had been futile. For a time the number of conventicles seems to have dropped off, but the government, cognizant of the connection between illegal assemblies and the Galloway rising, nevertheless actively explored ways to reduce the illegal meetings. Consideration was given by the Scottish Council to punishing an entire parish in which a conventicle was held, but this idea was dropped because many residents were unaware of such assemblies. The king himself attributed some of the blame for unchecked conventicles to Councillors and Commissioners who permitted offenders with influential friends to escape punishment. Nor was the law that required deprived ministers to live at least twenty miles from their former parishes effectively enforced, this laxity making it easier for them to hold conventicles.[4]

The offer of indemnity to Galloway rebels in October 1667 had the unintended effect of encouraging dissenters by implying the possibility of greater leniency. A new wave of conventicle activity in the autumn persuaded Lauderdale to take a firmer stand against active dissidents. He hoped to drive a wedge between them and the moderate nonconformists by leaving the latter alone, and eventually by giving official recognition to peaceful dissent. Thus in January 1668 the Council ordered the provost of Edinburgh to implement the November 1664 act decreeing the expulsion from that city of all ministers who had already been ejected from their pulpits unless they had a special license. The Council also called for special efforts to ensure that no illegal religious meetings were held in the capital, and instructed magistrates throughout the country to enforce the twenty-mile provision. Apart from these measures, the earl of Linlithgow argued, there was no need for more laws, for the "acts of councill [are] so many and so full already . . . as nothing can be added thereto."[5]

The problem was one of enforcement. Reports mounted of illegal religious gatherings—and rumored insurrections—in regions as scattered as Fife, Ayrshire, and Lanarkshire, and at least one nonconformist minister came from Ireland to hold conventicles. The Council accordingly ordered the arrest and imprisonment of clergymen convening or preaching at conventicles as well as of "the principall persons" attending them. When magistrates at Anstruther and Largo in Fife were negligent in suppressing illegal meetings, the Council dispatched its own agents to investigate, and some of the offenders were eventually fined £100 and imprisoned. In July 1668 the Councillors not only made all principal Edinburgh magistrates subscribe a bond requiring them to enforce the laws against illegal meetings but empowered them to search the houses of residents suspected of holding conventicles or harboring Galloway fugitives. Again, the connection between conventicles and rebels was made explicit. Under the terms of the bond the magistrates had to pay the royal treasury £50 sterling for each conventicle that met in the city or its suburbs, although the money could be taken from fines imposed on those who were arrested. Had the provost rejected the terms of the bond, Charles was prepared to quarter troops in Edinburgh to ensure its security. Almost immediately a search turned up forty offenders, some of whom were fined or banished to Virginia.[6]

For a time in mid-1668 the authorities enjoyed some success in their campaign against conventicles. The arrest of Michael Bruce near Stirling in early June was a blow to the nonconformists. Suspected of complicity in the Dublin conspiracy, he had been preaching illegally in both fields and homes, allegedly "infuseing into . . . [the people] the principalls of sedition and rebellion." He was apprehended only after a struggle in which he seriously wounded one of his captors, and was incarcerated in Stirling Castle before his transfer to Edinburgh two weeks later. A plot by Scottish women to rescue him was foiled. Although the Council found him guilty of sedition and ordered him banished to Tangier, Bruce was instead taken to London in September, presumably for further interrogation—another instance of the government's willingness to reduce punishment in the hope of acquiring useful information about dissident activities. Whatever transpired in London, Bruce was allowed to settle at Killinchy in county Down rather than Tangier.[7] The authorities also apprehended Thomas Hogg and Thomas Urquhart, who had been preaching to conventicles in the northern shire of Moray; Robert Home, the deprived minister of Crawfordjohn, Lanark; and George Forbes, the former pastor of Portpatrick, Wigtown.[8] But among those who eluded the dragnet were the Galloway insurgent John Welsh and John Blackader. While the latter operated in Edinburgh, Fife, Renfrewshire, and Ayrshire, Welsh convened illegal gatherings in Clydesdale, usually in homes; he once held a midnight service in the "Camnethine" church (Cambusnethan, Lanarkshire?) with more than 200 in attendance as he christened over twenty children.[9]

Lauderdale's attempt to split the dissenters was frustrated when moderates such as Robert Douglas defied the law by preaching at homes in parishes that had no conforming clerics. According to the earl of Tweeddale, the moderates justified such activity by citing the similar practice of English nonconformists. To punish all dissenters, thus forging a greater unity among them and increasing the possibility of militant retaliation, was a risk Lauderdale and Tweeddale hoped to avoid. Instead they considered allowing moderate dissenters to preach in parish churches without conforming to episcopal polity. The provost of Edinburgh, Sir Andrew Ramsay, thought this might be done in part by transferring the six assistant ministers in Edinburgh churches to country parishes and replacing them with two or three "of the ablest preachers of sound principalls, prudent and pieus and of vog[ue] with the multitude."[10]

Although Tweeddale could report to Lauderdale from August to October 1668 that there were no longer any conventicles in Edinburgh or the open fields, the respite was short-lived. In the capital itself David Home preached to a small conventicle gathered at a widow's house in late February 1669. In the west, dissenters, encouraged by reports of conventicles in England and Ireland, held illegal meetings on a daily basis. Most of the ministers were itinerants who traveled in disguise.[11] On 4 March the Council reacted by directing the militia commissioners in Ayrshire, Renfrewshire, Lanarkshire, and Kirkcudbright to investigate all illegal assemblies held in their districts since 1 November 1668, and to arrange for the appearance before the Council of the clergy and principal persons who attended. A month later the Councillors further decreed that a heritor (or land-owner) on whose property a conventicle was held would be fined £50 sterling. In May provisions were made to put to the horn (out-law) those who left their parish churches, attended illegal assemblies, or had their children baptized illegally. Because the greatest threat, in the Council's judgment, was still in the western shires, in June it summoned the archbishops of St. Andrews and Glasgow, the duke of Hamilton, and the earls of Dumfries and Callander to meet with it to discuss western affairs. There was also a special request to the provost of Ayr seeking information not only about conventicles but also concerning "the designes and practices of the disaffected partie there." The Councillors hoped personally to examine the ministers and key lay persons involved in the western conventicles. The mini-mum punishment for offenders, they determined, would be impris-onment until adequate assurances of lawful behavior were provided, although Sharp protested that this was not stringent enough.[12]

The list of arrested clerics grew, but the campaign against conven-ticles had only checkered success. In June 1669, the earl of Kincardine told Lauderdale that only two illegal meetings had been reported in Ayrshire, but the number of conventicles in Renfrewshire continued to grow.[13] Two months earlier the Council had heard the confessions of eleven ministers charged with conducting illegal religious services. Nearly all of them had been ejected from Ayrshire livings, and two of them—Alexander Blair of Galston and James Veitch of Mauch-line—had been in trouble in 1662 for "seditious" preaching.[14] In June the Council ordered the arrest of James Hamilton of Blantyre and Andrew Morton of Carmunnock for conducting illegal services in Glasgow, and summoned James Curry of Shotts and Gilbert Ham-ilton of Crawford for holding meetings at Hamilton.[15]

While these stepped-up efforts against conventicles went forward in the first half of 1669, a renewed effort was made to split the non-conformists by offering moderates an indulgence. The royal letter setting forth the terms, dated 7 June and recorded by the Scottish Council a month later, offered to restore ejected clergy to their for-mer parishes, if vacant, or to other parishes if presented by patrons or the Council. In return the ministers had to accept episcopal collation and attend their local presbyteries and synods. Those who refused collation could still resume pastoral responsibilities and receive a manse and glebe as well as a small allowance, but they were denied the normal stipend. Indulged ministers could not permit persons from other parishes to attend their services or be married or baptized by them without the approval of their pastors. Charles instructed his officers to proceed with severity against those who refused these terms and persisted in conducting illegal services.[16]

The nonconformist response to the indulgence was decidedly mixed. In the ensuing nine months more than forty moderates accepted the king's terms and were appointed to parishes, while dozens of others were allowed to exercise limited ministerial functions in assigned parishes.[17] From the beginning, however, there were problems, in no small measure because some of the indulged clerics "doe use before they begin their sermons to lectur upon part of scriptur," a practice that in the past had increased the preachers' opportunity to criticize contemporary ecclesiastical and political practices as unscriptural. The Council prohibited this practice in January 1670. Some of the indulged clerics even continued to hold conventicles. Moreover, lay dissenters in the southwestern shires, to which most of the indulged ministers were assigned, often left their parishes in order to listen to these preachers. With the support of dissenters in England and Ireland, militants, including the exiles in the Netherlands, opposed the indulgence. Reportedly, plans existed to send ministerial candidates to England and Ireland for Presbyterian ordination. Some militants, according to Kincardine, intended to step up the pace of conventicles in order to force the Council to adopt severe measures, which would give the militants the opportunity to "fish in troubled watters" by taking advantage of an upsurge in discontent. Illegal services did, in fact, continue. One of the largest occurred near Berwick in late August, when more than 500 persons, including the countess of Angus and her son, received the sacrament.[18]

In keeping with the royal directive to deal firmly with hard-line dissenters, the Council stepped up its efforts to quash conventicles. On 3 August all heritors were ordered to apprise magistrates of any illegal meetings held on their lands, and on 13 January 1670 instructions were again issued for the arrest of ministers and principal persons attending conventicles retroactive to 15 November 1669. "We shal," said Tweeddale, "fill prisons as fast with them as we doe pulpits & what a wild way will that be." A new proclamation, dated 3 February, directed magistrates and militia commissioners to see that all preachers who conducted illegal services after 9 October 1669 and all heritors and substantial tenants who attended them or had their children baptized by deprived ministers appeared before the Council. Thus began a new attempt to dissuade such persons from future conventicling by intimidation, fines, and imprisonment in the capital. But the illegal services continued. James Hamilton and one of the Mitchells held two meetings at Kirkintilloch, Dunbarton, and the itinerant John Rae conducted an illegal service in a house owned by the earl of Glencairn at Finlayston, Renfrew. Violations were especially frequent in Edinburgh and the shires of Stirling, Linlithgow (now West Lothian), Dunbarton, Lanark, Ayr, and Renfrew.[19] The Council responded in April 1670 by appointing a special seven-man commission headed by the duke of Hamilton to ensure that the laws were enforced in these counties, in part by convening special sessions in the affected areas and by committing offenders to prison. Simultaneously the Councillors directed the Edinburgh magistrates to arrest all ejected clergy in the capital who lacked a warrant to preach from the Council, and to imprison those with warrants who persisted in holding conventicles.[20]

Two illegal meetings in the late spring of 1670 were of particular interest to the Council. The one convened at Livingseat in the Lanarkshire parish of Carnwath in May or June may have been extraordinarily large, for on 16 June Rothes reported to Lauderdale that a recent conventicle had been attended by 1,500 or 1,600 persons, mostly men. The second unlawful assembly, convened on the Hill of Beath near Dunfermline, Fife, on 19 June, may have included as many as 2,000 persons, some of them armed with swords and pistols. When soldiers appeared, they were blindfolded and detained until the service was concluded. Most of those in attendance were undoubtedly local folk from such places as Dunfermline, Culross, Inverkeithing, and Kirkcaldy, but others had come from as far afield as Glasgow, Edinburgh, and Galloway, perhaps in the course of business travels. Some may have belonged to a small band that traveled with the ministers to provide protection. John Maclellan of Barscobe, one of the early leaders of the 1666 insurrection, was there. The preachers, John Blackader and John Dickson, took as their texts 1 Corinthians 9:16 and 15:25, the latter having ominous overtones because of its apocalyptic implications: "He must reign, till he hath put all enemies under his feet." Relatively few of those who were involved were ever arrested, but some of those who were caught and refused to testify were sentenced to exile in America. For clergy who held conventicles, however, Tweeddale and Lauderdale generally rejected harsh punishment, preferring instead that offenders sign bonds pledging to hold no more illegal assemblies.[21]

In response to the Carnwath and Hill of Beath conventicles, as well as to one in the west on 26 June reportedly attended by 3,000 persons, the Council ordered the earl of Newburgh's troop to march through the shires of Stirling and Linlithgow (West Lothian) as far as Carnwath, Lanark, in search of conventiclers, apprehending them by force of arms if they resisted. Similar commands were given to the lord chancellor's troop, which was dispatched to Clydesdale and Ayrshire. With Hamilton urging that a standing army be raised to quell the conventicles, and with Sharp in favor of stringent action, Lauderdale and Charles were forced to acquiesce, particularly because loyalists in England and Scotland increasingly favored the suppression of illegal assemblies. Fresh reports of numerous public conventicles at Torwood and other places in the shires of Stirling and Linlithgow and at Kirkintilloch, Dunbarton, reinforced the demands for tougher action.[22]

Despite his personal proclivity to toleration, the king informed Lauderdale on 7 July 1670 of his desire that the Scottish Parliament enact new legislation to suppress illegal assemblies and punish recusants. The intent was not to crush dissent, which was obviously impossible, but to underscore the government's determination to repress the unbridled conventicling. In his speech to Parliament three weeks later, Rothes underscored the point that the rash of recent conventicles "look liker endeavours to rendezvous for Rebellion, then any pretence of Religious Worship." The resulting legislation—the Clanking Act—prescribed the death penalty for preachers at field conventicles, and either the provision of surety of 5,000 merks or exile for those who held illegal indoor services. Those who attended indoor conventicles risked fines fixed at a quarter of their annual income; attendance at outdoor assemblies required twice that amount. Intended as a warning to militant dissenters as well as a means to satisfy the demands of hard-liners such as Archbishop Sharp, the act was temporarily effective.[23] For the remainder of the year no new cases pertaining to conventicles came before the Council. It did, however, put five of the most prominent conventicle ministers to the horn on 11 August: the Hill of Beath preachers Blackader and Dickson, James Hamilton, James Mitchell, and James Porter. The same month the Councillors examined two other conventicling ministers, Alexander Strange, who promised to behave, and Hugh Peebles of Lochwinnoch, Renfrew, who refused and was confined to Dunbarton town.[24]

Early in 1671 the dissenters gradually began to hold illegal meetings again, particularly once preachers who had fled to Ireland after passage of the Clanking Act began to return. There was a conventicle in the Glasgow area in January, but in the ensuing six months, reports of illegal meetings were more frequent in the province of St. Andrews than Glasgow. In March the Council instructed the justices to enforce the laws against nonconformists, and specifically directed the sheriffs of Lanark, Ayr, and Renfrew to do the same. Informed that a number of ejected ministers living in those shires failed to attend the parish churches, the Councillors ordered the sheriffs to imprison those who persisted in their recusancy. An attempt was also made to hold indulged ministers to their terms: In January the Council confined those who refused to attend presbyteries to their parishes, and in July it directed sheriffs to inform the Council of preachers who ignored the ban on lecturing. But local magistrates were often less than enthusiastic in implementing the conciliar directives; such recalcitrance was a major factor in allowing dissent to thrive. In October 1671, for instance, the Councillors complained that the sheriffs of Lanark, Ayr, and Renfrew had not submitted the report called for in the March directive. As the number of illegal assemblies grew in the Glasgow area, magistrates were ordered to enforce the laws in February 1672, and the same month the Council sentenced Alexander Carmichael to exile for holding conventicles.[25]

When Parliament convened in June 1672 it renewed the 1670 acts against conventicles and recusancy, and enacted a law that imposed fines on those who had not had their children legally baptized. It also made illegal ordination punishable by imprisonment, confiscation of goods, and exile. In July and August the state proceeded against numerous conventiclers—mostly lay persons—for their participation in illegal meetings extending as far back as November 1670. Some were prosecuted for recent conventicles at Boghall, Lanark, where "diverse outed ministers" participated, and where the countess of Wigtown was present; at the Bridge of Earn, near Perth; and at Glendinning, Dumfries. Despite the possibility of harsh fines and imprisonment, the conventiclers continued to draw people from sizable distances.[26]

The attraction of the conventicles was enhanced by the fact that many parishes had no approved pastor. The province of Glasgow had twenty-five vacancies in January 1671, probably due at least in part to the resistance of dissenting patrons to appointing conforming clerics as well as to the reluctance of such ministers to serve where parishioners threatened them physically. When Archbishop Robert Leighton appealed to Gilbert Burnet for assistance, the latter proposed a new indulgence, the intent of which was both to fill vacant livings and to pacify dissenters or at least split their ranks by obtaining the cooperation of as many moderates as possible. Lauderdale, Tweeddale, and Moray supported the plan, which the Scottish Council sanctioned in September. The new indulgence thus had little meaningful connection with the Declaration of Indulgence promulgated in England the previous March. Under the terms of the Scottish Act, two nonconforming ministers would normally be appointed to a single living and share its stipend. A parish that already had an indulged minister could have two dissenters assigned to it, in which case the original incumbent would retain half the stipend, leaving the newcomers to split the remainder. In return the newly indulged pastors had to agree not to leave their assigned parishes, to marry or baptize only their own parishioners or those in adjoining parishes without clergy, and to preach only in the parish churches. Unlike the first indulgence, on this occasion the authorities seized the initiative by assigning 136 dissenters to parishes without consultation, perhaps in the expectation of providing an air of finality to their proceedings. But rumors of the terms of the new indulgence had been enough to spark protest meetings in August, and more dissenters were troubled in September once the conditions had been officially announced. In the end more than fifty of the dissenters assigned to churches rejected the conditions.[27]

To the extent that the new policy widened the rift among nonconformists, it was at least a partial success. Fewer ministers were now available to hold conventicles and more parishes had pastors. Ejected ministers who did not receive a post under the new indulgence were required to attend their local churches or face imprisonment. An indulged pastor, however, had the right to invite a deprived minister to share his pulpit if he lived in the same parish, an obvious attempt to undercut the lure of holding conventicles. But militant dissenters remained unconvinced that the compromise was conscionable, and not only circulated their objections throughout the country but deliberately held illegal assemblies adjacent to services conducted by the indulged clergy. Lauderdale responded to the new round of conventicling by advising Hamilton to implement the laws vigorously, incarcerating the preachers and fining the laity. Although Hamilton thought that the indulgence had "more broke ther party than anything formerly," in fact the dissenting cause was in some respects stronger than ever.[28] Those who remained constituted the hard core that was unwavering in its hostility to anything episcopal. In the ensuing years conventicles increased rapidly, the dissenters organized more effectively, and the state was left to respond with more repression.

Physical Assaults on Scottish Clergy

Nothing more clearly manifests the depth of nonconformist hostility toward the episcopalian regime in the Scottish church than the recurring attacks on conforming ministers. The problem became acute when, in the aftermath of the Galloway uprising, pastors reported the names of rebels to the magistrates. Convinced that the rebels were damned, the ministers, in Gilbert Burnet's words, "acted so ill a part, so unbecoming their characters, that the aversion of the country to them was increased to all possible degrees: they looked on them now as wolves, and not as shepherds." Rothes complained bitterly of the "creualtie of the ffanaticks aganst the pur ministirs." The government tried unsuccessfully to prevent further attacks by making heritors and parishioners liable to fines and responsible for compensation for assaults on conforming clergy in their parishes.[29]

Assaults occurred frequently in the summer of 1667. Archbishop Burnet complained that the Galloway fugitives were plundering and beating orthodox clerics at night, and had even murdered one of them. A gang of twenty or thirty operated in this fashion in the Dumfries area, nearly killing William Blake, an elderly pastor. Patrick Swinton was attacked at Borgue, Kirkcudbright, for which the heritors of the parish were called to account by the Council. These "Whigs," as loyalists called them, may have been part of a large gang of thirty or forty who operated in the Galloway-Nithsdale area, but it was unclear to officials whether this group comprised Galloway fugitives or "idle cuntrie fellowes." By summer's end these people were boasting that they would drive every minister who accepted episcopacy out of Galloway. In the stewartry of Kirdcudbright and in Nithsdale, complained Burnet, they "have dealt so severely with our ministers, that most of them are forced to flee." Not even Edinburgh was immune, for in October dissidents attacked clergymen attending an assembly, cutting holes in their garments; the trained bands had to be called out to restore order.[30]

Unlike the Galloway rebellion, which was mostly a male affair,[31] the assaults on orthodox clerics sometimes involved women. Such was the case in the attack on James Brown at East Calder in Midlothian, in which entire families took part, including children and servants. Several of those who participated had been involved in the Galloway rebellion.[32]

The most celebrated case was an attempt to assassinate Archbishop Sharp by James Mitchell (alias Small), a Presbyterian preacher who had been commended by Robert Trail to Galloway ministers in 1661 as capable of teaching school or tutoring gentlemen's children. A Galloway rebel, though he had left the insurgents on the eve of Rullion Green in order to consult with supporters in Edinburgh, he was excepted from the indemnity in 1667. As he later confessed, he made his attempt on Sharp because the archbishop "had a hand in trowbleing and prosecuting these that were in the rebellion." Although Robert Wodrow has called his assassination attempt a personal deed "without concert or approbation from presbyterians," there is evidence that there was a conspiracy plotted by Presbyterian radicals previously associated with the Galloway insurrection. Chief among these were Major Joseph Learmont, the second-in-command to James Wallace, and John Maclellan of Barscobe, the laird whose attack on Turner's soldiers incited the uprising. On the eve of the attempted assassination the three men stayed in the house of Robert Gray, an Edinburgh burgess, whose wife was "a great whigg."[33]

Between 4:00 and 5:00 P.M. on 11 July 1668, Sharp entered a coach, which was parked outside his lodgings at High Gate, Edinburgh, and began distributing alms. While Dr. Andrew Honeyman, bishop of Orkney, climbed into the coach, Mitchell, approaching from the rear, discharged five shots from his pistol. As he fired, Honeyman held out his arm to straighten his cloak, causing Mitchell to hit his arm rather than Sharp. Mitchell escaped down Blackfriars Wynd, then shed his disguise, including a wig, at a house in Steven Law's Close. Antiprelatical sentiment was so strong in the capital that instead of attempting to seize Mitchell, bystanders reportedly sneered, "It's but a Bishop."[34]

Charles issued a proclamation for the apprehension of the as-yet-unidentified assassin on the 14th, offering a reward of 5,000 merks to the person who caught him and 2,000 merks to any accomplice who identified him. The same day the Scottish Council instructed the provost of Edinburgh to undertake an immediate search for Galloway fugitives in the city and for persons who could not provide a satisfactory account of themselves. A maid's tip led to the arrest of Robert Gray on the night of the 16th, but not until the 18th did he and his wife begin to answer the interrogatories put to them. As the story slowly unfolded, the authorities learned that Learmont and Maclellan of Barscobe had stayed at Gray's house, and that Learmont had only escaped during the search for the assassin. Not until the 30th did Tweeddale discover Mitchell's identity, but in the meantime a number of conventiclers had been arrested, some of whom had been hiding Galloway fugitives in the capital. One of these was thought to have been Wallace himself, though the magistrates were unable to find him. If he was in the city in July, he was probably part of the plot against Sharp. Both Wallace, who had opposed the attempted assassination because it would discredit the Covenanters, and Learmont reportedly fled to Ireland.[35]

Among the others implicated by the Grays were John Welsh of Cornley, another Galloway fugitive, and Anna Ker, widow of John Duncan, former minister of Dundrennan, Kirkcudbright, who permitted conventicles to meet in her Edinburgh house. Both "much regraited" that Sharp had not been killed. On 29 July Mrs. Duncan was banished. At least two other women—Margaret Dury, widow of the Edinburgh merchant James Kello, and Janet Chalmers, wife of the messenger John Crawford—received the same sentence for refusing to testify.[36]

Because both Sharp and Tweeddale were aware that the attempted assassination was not the work of a lone gunman, there was concern that it might portend a new insurrection. Sharp, in fact, linked the attempt on his life to an alleged companion-scheme to assassinate Charles, and Tweeddale learned that the rebels had expected assistance from militants in Cumberland and Westmorland under the command of Colonel Hill, a "tub preacher" who had served under Cromwell in Ireland, and a Mr. Banagachan. Arrangements were therefore expedited for settling the militia in the shires of Dumfries, Ayr, Renfrew, Lanark, and Wigtown. In July the king also gave the Council the authority to banish or pardon Galloway fugitives who had not accepted the indemnity, and directed them to "rid the kingdom of such seditious preachers" as had been holding conventicles.[37] In the midst of increasing rumors that Galloway rebels were congregating, the Council dispatched the earl of Linlithgow to Glasgow in August to use troops to disperse them, but the reports proved to be baseless. Units of the earl of Newburgh's troop were sent into Galloway, Clydesdale, and Nithsdale in early September in order to seek out and arrest rebels. On 29 September instructions were issued to settle the militia in the shires of Bute, Dunbarton, Aberdeen, Banff, and Kincardine, with similar action to occur in the remainder of the northern shires the following spring. The crackdown led to the arrest of several Galloway rebels, including Cannon of Mordrogat and William Millar, a companion of Learmont and Maclellan of Barscobe. Mitchell eluded arrest until 1674, when he was recognized by Sharp. At his execution in January 1678 he defiantly proclaimed, "Blessed are all they that take the proud Prelates and dash their brains against the stones."[38]

The king's directive to the Scottish Council on 29 September 1668 had instructed it to impose exemplary punishment on any who treated orthodox clergy violently, but aggression continued. The previous month Archbishop Burnet had complained that ministers were being assaulted and forced at the point of a sword to swear never again to preach under the present government. After Gilbert Burnet was appointed to a professorship of divinity at the University of Glasgow in December 1669, he too submitted similar reports to the Council. One of those attacked in the fall of that year was John Row of Balmaclellan, in the very heart of the region that had given birth to the Galloway rebellion. Those responsible included the former minister of the parish, Thomas Vernour. At Kilmacolm, Renfrew, the people not only injured the pastor, John Irwing, but attacked another minister as he passed through the town in early 1670. Ugly attacks on ministers occurred at such places as Carmunnock and Glassford in Lanark, at Kirkcudbright and Dumfries, at Kilmarnock and Stewarton in Ayrshire, at Neilston in Renfrew, and at Towie, Aberdeenshire in 1669–70. Such actions were partly responsible for the king's decision to treat the dissenters with greater severity. In his speech to the Scottish Parliament on 28 July 1670, Rothes specifically noted Charles's anger over the treatment of orthodox clergy; the Clanking Act followed, imposing the death penalty and confiscation of goods on those who harmed conforming clergy. But offenses continued, including a riot at the Kirk of Shotts, Lanark, in September 1671, that prevented a newly appointed pastor, Henry Lindsay, from preaching. The following January, dissidents, including women, assaulted Alexander Ramsay, minister of Auchinleck in Ayrshire, wounding him, plundering his house, and committing "diverse other insolencies and outrages upon him and his family."[39] Robbing the houses of conforming ministers was an increasingly popular way of manifesting anger toward the religious tenets of such clerics.

Radical Political Activity in Scotland

Despite their steadfast determination to hold conventicles and their willingness to deal violently with conforming clergy, Scottish militants apparently engaged in little specifically political activity in this period, at least according to the surviving records. Those with anti-Stuart or republican tendencies were generally linked to English dissidents. There had been reports in the early 1660s of regular communications between English militants in such places as Berwick, Newcastle, and Wolverhampton with friends in Scotland, but some of this may have concerned only religious matters.[40] In 1662 Captain Robert Johnston admitted the existence of a network of radicals in Scotland, England, the Netherlands, and France. Although the 1663 northern rebels reportedly had accomplices in Scotland, including Captain Hume, the expected Scottish contingent failed to materialize when the insurrection commenced.[41]

In September 1666 a Scotsman named William Steward was arrested in Warwick on suspicion of being a dangerous person and apparently returned to Scotland; he may have been the William Stewart of the stewartry of Kirkcudbright who fought in the Galloway rebellion and subsequently rejected the indemnity. If so, was he on a mission as a dissident agent when he was apprehended in Warwick? About the same time the government intercepted a letter from a Scottish dissident who had been followed to conventicles at Edlingham and Norham in Northumberland, again possibly an agent. The virulency of his antiprelatical sentiments was unmistakable: "It is True, the Dumb Greedy Doggs, and the Pittyfull Puppy Priests have little to give you but what comes off the Popes Foul Fingers. . . . I will venture my Life to run the hazzard of a Bloudy Winding Sheet in the Quarrel."[42]

Fresh indications of radical activity surfaced in 1670, including an alleged scheme to assassinate Lauderdale. In July one of Joseph Williamson's correspondents reported from Carlisle that the dissidents were "very Brisk & Looke for a sudden alteration in these Countrys & to that purpose have imployed one to view the Gaurds [sic] & order of the Garrison of Carlisle." This spy then went to Kirkenberry in Scotland to confer with friends, and upon his return reported that the Scots "were resolved to pull downe the Bisshops & reestablish the Covenant." After again reconnoitering the Carlisle garrison he concluded that it would not be difficult to seize the town.[43] This indeed suggests some cooperation between English radicals and militant Scottish Presbyterians, perhaps for an incipient plot involving both kingdoms.

Reports throughout the period indicated that Scottish dissidents were secretly purchasing weapons in England; given the chronic shortage of arms in Scotland it would have been difficult to buy sufficient quantities there without attracting suspicion. In addition to reported shipments in 1661 and 1663, the Scots allegedly bought large numbers of weapons in London in the spring of 1669, although hardly enough to arm 100,000 men, as one gunsmith claimed. A year earlier, officials had found a cache of weapons in the Lanark house of Mr. Rae, a smith, although he eluded arrest; this may have been the Galloway rebel Robert Rae, already a wanted man for having refused the indemnity. Weapons were also being shipped to Scotland from the Netherlands in 1668.[44]

Occasional glimpses of militant speech and activity in Scotland are visible in the half-dozen years after the Galloway uprising. Support for the insurgents was manifested throughout these years by friends and supporters who offered them refuge and on occasion even rescued those who were caught. An instance of the latter occurred when William McArmick, who had been excepted from the indemnity, was rescued by a group of dissidents, among them women; they killed a loyalist in the process. By June 1672, speech highly critical of the government and malicious reports were so rampant that the king issued a proclamation prohibiting the Scots from uttering "any false, slanderous or untrue speeches to the disdain, reproach and contempt of his Majesty, his Councill and proceidinges."[45]

Radical political activity in Scotland was probably contained as well as it was because the principal leaders were either in prison or in exile. Sir John Chiesley and Sir James Stewart, arrested in 1660, refused to subscribe a bond of security in 1667 and were transferred from Edinburgh Castle to the Dundee Tolbooth in order to curtail frequent visits to them by other dissidents. Whether or not Colonel

Gilby Carr was involved in the Galloway uprising, there is no indication that in the ensuing years he engaged in radical activity in Scotland. In February 1671, in fact, Charles and the Scottish Council
granted him permission to return to Scotland for one year if he provided security for his behavior.[46] In the end, radicals in England and
Ireland received no substantial support from Scottish dissidents in
this period apart from the latter's willingness to provide sanctuary
for militant nonconformists periodically forced out of Ireland.

Ireland: Radical Schemes

In Ireland the Restoration had sown seeds of discontent in two
areas: a land settlement that dispossessed various Protestants, and
the return to a policy of episcopalian exclusivity in religion. With the
implementation of these policies, disaffection increased in the early
1660s, as reflected in allegations of plotting, the distribution of radical publications, and the illegal stockpiling of weapons and ammunition. Dissidents in Ireland were a diverse lot, varying from Ulster
Presbyterians with links to their compatriots in Scotland, to ex-
Cromwellians and sectaries centered primarily in Dublin and Munster. The latter were primarily interested in religious toleration and
the security or recovery of their estates, while the Ulster Presbyterians, some of whom were decidedly militant, insisted on fidelity to
the Solemn League and Covenant.

Despite such differences, militants in these groups periodically
made common cause to challenge the Stuart regime, as in May 1663,
when a cabal of ex-Cromwellian officers, Presbyterians, and Congregationalists plotted to seize Dublin, Cork, Limerick, Waterford, and
Clonmel, and to coordinate their efforts with an uprising in Ulster.
By radical standards their aims were modest: confirmation of Irish
estates held by Englishmen on 7 May 1659 and establishment of the
state church according to the principles of the Solemn League and
Covenant. The willingness of Congregationalists and Baptists to join
forces with Presbyterian militants suggests that the latter were probably willing to consider toleration for their nonconformist allies, although concern about the land settlement certainly facilitated cooperation among these groups.

In retrospect, the debilitating impact of the failed 1663 Dublin conspiracy on the radical community in Ireland is evident enough. Although the conspirators failed completely in their attempt to seize the castle, reimpose the Solemn League and Covenant, and recover lost lands, plotting nevertheless continued. Particularly in the context of the Dutch War, the government could not afford to ignore the radicals, with their ties to the disaffected in England. In April 1665 one of Ormond's informers outlined alleged schemes that loosely linked dissidents in England, Ireland, and Scotland. The previous month he had learned that English radicals, supposedly with a thousand men at their disposal and sufficient funds to pay them, had allegedly made an unsuccessful attempt to poison the king through agents at court, and would try again. Even if this failed they reportedly hoped to launch a general insurrection once the Dutch had defeated the English navy. They also expected the Dutch to supply Scottish dissenters with weapons, ammunition, money, officers, and even troops.[47] In Ireland the radicals allegedly hoped to capitalize on growing disenchantment with the terms of the Bill of Explanation, which, as finally passed in December 1665, sanctioned the confiscation of a third of the lands of soldiers and adventurers. Radicals in Ireland still built their plans around an assault on Dublin Castle and seizure of the city. Meetings were reportedly held on a regular basis in Dublin, with agents from Munster and the King's County in attendance. The leaders in turn sent weekly letters to dissidents—some of whom were identified as Baptists—in counties Down, Antrim, and Armagh. By September agents of the archbishop of Dublin had apparently intercepted some of this correspondence, although it seems not to have survived. Meetings of dissidents in the north were in any case increasing, and there was anticipation that in 1666, a year with apocalyptic overtones (666 being the "Number of the Beast"), "ther will be strange things done."[48]

The conspiracy uncovered by Ormond's informer was an early version of a scheme that evolved throughout 1665 and early 1666. The Rathbone plot, discovered in August 1665, may have been one version, and the Liverpool conspiracy, under way by October 1665, certainly was another.[49] The Dublin plotters Thomas Blood, Philip Alden, and William More went to Liverpool to meet with English radicals, and More subsequently sought recruits in Munster and Ulster. After another meeting at Liverpool in January 1666, Blood and George Ayres went to Ireland to enlist further support. Among the leaders of the conspiracy in Ireland were Colonel Robert Phaire, the former Protectoral governor of Cork, and Captain Thomas Walcott, a Baptist who had served under Ludlow in Ireland in the same period. Phaire had recently been in the Netherlands, where he had met with Desborough, Thomas White, Major William Burton, Captain (Benjamin?) Groome, and reportedly (but improbably) even Ludlow in June 1665.

The conspirators had hoped to coordinate an uprising in the three kingdoms for 1 January 1666, but this had to be postponed. The night of 24–25 March and the period immediately subsequent to the first major naval engagement of 1666 were proposed as alternate times. The plotters hoped to restore the Long Parliament, over forty of whose members they claimed had engaged with them, and to overthrow monarchy, the House of Lords, and episcopacy. The "old blades," as they called themselves, expected Ludlow to serve as their commander-in-chief in this battle for "liberty and religion." Upset about the growth of Catholicism and the debauchery of Charles's government, they were determined to establish a "sober and painful" ministry. Those involved took the usual oath of secrecy, and "vast sums" were purportedly collected "over all Ireland" to pay for troops and weapons.[50]

The Irish conspirators reportedly divided up the country, placing an officer, whose duties included recruitment, in charge of each district. Phaire was responsible for county Cork, Walcott for Clare and Limerick. In each Irish garrison a gunsmith was allegedly enlisted in order to purchase and repair used weapons; agents of the earl of Orrery, lord president of Munster, searched the premises of a Limerick gunsmith named Boys, but found only forty-eight weapons. Supposedly funds were liberally used to bribe members of each garrison to join the conspirators. Walcott, for instance, used £300 for this purpose at Limerick, recruiting, among others, a sergeant. The principal conspirators met in Dublin under the guise of pursuing law suits, while a satellite group in Tipperary gathered on the pretext of visiting their sons, who were students of Mr. Wood, "a notorious rogue" whose agents were Captain Lenet and Mr. Rynol. At the appropriate time the schemers expected assistance from the Dutch in the form of money, weapons, and troops. Once the uprising commenced, they allegedly intended to kill those who refused to join them.[51]

Ormond received key information about the conspiracy in February 1666 from Captain Robert Oliver, whose wife Bridget had been approached by Robert Taylor, a former Cromwellian officer living near Charleville, Cork.[52] Taylor seems to have been a friend of the Olivers' who wanted them to salvage what they could before the rebellion erupted. After the Olivers obtained assurances from Ormond that Taylor's life and property would be secure if he revealed what he knew, Taylor confessed. Orrery immediately alerted Sir Ralph Wilson and Colonel Jephson of the plot and instructed them to appoint a trustworthy sergeant or corporal in each company to serve as a spy, particularly to identify the recruiters. Orrery also wanted all the leading "fanatics" in Ireland arrested, but Ormond wisely demurred, not knowing "where to end a list of them" and not wanting to scare them away until some at least had been convicted with "full evidence." Ormond, however, did promise Arlington that he would try to arrest Blood in order to prevent the rebellion from materializing, although as late as 24 February he thought that the plot was still "forming" and not "already formed." But Orrery soon persuaded him otherwise, and by the 27th he was afraid that news of the French declaration of war would encourage the radicals to proceed. The same day Orrery sought permission to organize militia units in his province composed only of men who had taken the oaths of allegiance and supremacy. Otherwise, he wondered, who would maintain order if the garrisons were called out to suppress an insurrection?[53]

In February and March the conspirators made an intensive effort to arm their men. Orrery, who now had spies in every company of foot, reported to Ormond on 2 March: "I find multitudes of arms are fixing amongst the Irish gunsmiths for the Irish, as well as amongst the sectary gunsmiths for the fanaticks." Although 24 March passed without an uprising, dissidents in Ireland still anticipated a "speedy change" as soon as the English lost a major naval battle. Authorities on both sides of the Irish Sea remained vigilant.

When the English dissidents Mr. Ham and Mr. Levington left Berkshire for Ireland in May, Arlington suggested that Ormond interrogate them. The following month Arlington dispatched William Stotesbury, a former quartermaster in Colonel Peter Stubber's regiment of foot, to Ireland to spy on the "disaffected party," while Sir Arthur Forbes investigated reports of an imminent meeting in Ulster concerning a "design." In the meantime Orrery had placed leading dissidents coming to Limerick under close surveillance. Walcott, in fact, was so annoyed that he complained to Sir Ralph Wilson, but Orrery ordered the captain to return to his home in county Clare and prohibited him from entering any garrison without permission.[54]

By August officials in England and Ireland were concentrating on the activities of Blood, Captain Roger Jones, alias "Mene Tekel," and Ralph Alexander, one of the Rathbone conspirators. That month Blood, Jones, Alexander, the Congregationalist minister Thomas or Anthony Palmer, and Lieutenant Timothy (or Simon) Butler left London for Ireland, convinced, according to Arlington's informants, that their chances of instigating a rebellion were better in Ireland than in England. Government informers indicated that Blood would most likely contact such radicals as Captain Thomas Walcott and Colonel Daniel Abbott in Tipperary, or such former Dublin conspirators as Quartermaster Clare, also of Tipperary, Captains Briggs and Grumball of Ormond, Robert Hutcheson of Mountmellick in the Queen's County (Laoighis), and Major John Desborough of the King's County, who had served in Abbott's regiment.[55] To assist in Blood's apprehension, Arlington offered to send two informers to Ireland; one of them, Captain John Gryce (or Grice), was probably a double agent, for Blood knew that he was spying for Arlington but was confident that Gryce would say nothing to hurt the radicals.[56] English dissidents were sufficiently aware of what was happening to send one of their own agents to Ireland to try to stop Arlington's informant, William Ward (or Warde, alias Williams), from helping Ormond capture Blood. Arlington in turn knew of this move and warned Ormond. If Arlington and Orrery were correct, Blood not only eluded Ormond's men but slipped into Scotland in order to assist the Galloway rebels.[57]

By the end of 1666 the serious scheming in Ireland had died down, undoubtedly owing to the government's successful repression of the rebellion in Scotland and the discouraging reports brought by dissidents who had fled to Ireland. Nevertheless the informer William Leeving claimed in December to have learned of yet another conspiracy from a radical who had escaped from prison in York. A number of correspondents noted how quiet the country was in late 1666 and 1667, but in January 1668 there was a complaint that Ralph Alexander and Colonel Robert Shapcote were trying to subvert the Irish settlement involving disputed lands, which undoubtedly remained one of the most potentially explosive issues in the country.[58] Rumors of "a Sudden Change" were rampant in the summer of 1668, some of them involving Scots in the Carrickfergus area, but nothing came of this. There was a baseless report in January 1670 that an attack had been made on Ormond in Dublin and that the city was in an uproar. Rumors of a plot against Dublin Castle were a commonplace each spring but amounted to nothing.[59] Still, some nerves remained on edge. An apprentices' riot in Dublin in July 1671 helped trigger a call for more funds to reward informers, and Orrery was still fretting in August 1672 that there were thousands of discontented persons in Ireland, particularly those who had lost their estates and might rebel.[60] That October Arlington promised the earl of Essex, the new lord lieutenant, that he would be provided with a list of proscribed persons in Scotland to enable him to "shut the doore upon them in Ireland, & soe prevent the Contagion they may bring of their doctrine into Ireland, for which they were banisht from their owne Countrey."[61]

Captain Thomas Walcott, who was troubled about the future of the English in Ireland, continued to conspire. A Baptist, he had served under Ludlow and now had an estate worth £700 or 800 per annum. In October 1672 he tried to recruit Captain Thomas Cullen of Ballynaclohy, a former Cromwellian who had served under Colonel Henry Ingoldsby, for an attempt on Limerick. Although he had no specific plan to seize Dublin Castle or other strongholds, he was convinced that if the rebels could hold Limerick for a month and purchase weapons in the Netherlands with profits from the sale of wool stored in Limerick, they would be successful. Walcott read to Cullen from a declaration that cited offences purportedly committed by the duke of Buckingham, Arlington, Sir George Carteret, and others, and that called for the restoration of the Long Parliament, the abolition of popery and prelacy, the termination of the hearth tax, and the establishment of presbyterianism. The declaration also asserted that the oath of allegiance was not binding because parliamentary privileges and Magna Carta had not been maintained. Walcott subsequently claimed to have copied the declaration from a letter belonging to the countess of Roscommon, though he told Cullen he got it from an unnamed Scotsman. Rejecting the scheme as dangerous, Cullen informed the authorities, who arrested Walcott and sent him to London at the king's behest. There he denied the charges and insisted that he had had no contact with Ludlow since the latter left Ireland.[62]

The evidence against Walcott was shaky. Orrery, who had known him for eighteen years, thought Walcott was "too Judicious a Person, to Engage in it, without haveinge accomplices, & som firmer foundations to carry it on," but Arlington concluded that there was enough substance in the allegations to imagine a link between Walcott and the "designs" of the Dutch. Suspicion was heightened by the fact that shortly before the authorities heard of the purported conspiracy, Baptists and Congregationalists met more frequently than usual. The archbishop of Dublin and lord chancellor of Ireland, Michael Boyle, was probably closest to the mark when he opined that Walcott had "intended mischiefe and as preparatory thereunto he cherished all the discontents he could; but that he was prevented before he could forme it into a designe." If so, the government seems to have had the English dissidents in Ireland well under control. Essex, in fact, while recognizing that Walcott was "a great man with the Anabaptist Partie here," thought the captain could be useful to the government as "an Intelligencer."[63]

Irish Security

The threat to security in Ireland was more complex than that in Scotland and thus offered dissidents greater opportunities to advance their cause, though they failed to capitalize on them. In Scotland surveillance could be concentrated on the Covenanters, whereas in Ireland both Catholic and Protestant dissidents aroused concern. Because the French seem to have hoped for assistance from Scottish dissenters in making a secret landing in Scotland in 1666–67, the prospect of similar plans for Ireland could not be discounted. No one was more troubled than Orrery, who contended that if the French landed in Ireland "there are a crew of desperate English ready to fish in troubled waters." He was worried too that the French would attempt to incite the Ulster Scots. As usual, he pressed the more moderate Ormond to prevent an insurrection by securing the leaders of the Protestant dissidents as well as the Catholics in the western counties, particularly if the French invaded.[64] A French man-of-war entered Kenmare Bay in April 1666, but in the end France showed no serious interest in attacking Ireland. Although Arlington had intelligence in late 1666 that the French intended to intervene in Ireland, Louis XIV's real interests were on the Continent. Early in 1667, therefore, Louis and Charles reached an understanding based on the latter's pledge not to engage in alliances contrary to French interests. Nevertheless as late as June 1667, in the aftermath of the disaster at Chatham, the bishop of Londonderry fretted that France's ally, the Netherlands, might land 20,000 men in his strategic city, while the French invaded southern Ireland to join forces with the Catholics.[65]

During the war years there were other threats to security apart from radical scheming. The most significant of these was the mutiny in May 1666 at Carrickfergus, Antrim, a port described several years earlier as a place with "an Old strong Castle, and . . . fitt to receive his Majesties Stores," though incapable of handling large ships. Much of the population, although prosperous, was "not well affected," being Scottish Presbyterians. Demanding arrears of pay, the troops in the garrison had previously mutinied in April, but none was punished. On 20 May, numbering approximately 117 foot, they rebelled again, seizing both the town and the castle. Formulating a declaration that demanded arrears and calling on other garrisons to join them, they dispatched messengers to Londonderry and Charlemont explaining their actions. The earl of Donegal was inclined to pardon them, but this time Ormond was determined to make an example of the rebels, particularly because of their proximity to the troubled shires of southwestern Scotland and because of the strength of nonconformity in Ulster. Assisted by the earl of Arran, Ormond suppressed them, killing their leader—one Dillon—in the process. A court martial on 30 May sentenced ten ringleaders to death, though one was saved by the countess of Donegal's intervention. Ormond wanted to assign the rest to service abroad, but because of the expense this would entail, Clarendon had him disperse the mutineers throughout Ireland. Their officers, who had remained loyal, were commissioned to recruit new troops in England.[66]

Dissidents in Ireland made no attempt to take advantage of the mutiny, although rumors of insurrections were so rife that Sir Francis Hamilton ordered loyalists in county Cavan to take up arms. There is no evidence to substantiate Orrery's suspicion that Ulster Scots supported the mutineers, but townsfolk in Carrickfergus seem to have been sympathetic. In Scotland Archbishop Burnet thought the mutiny was undertaken with the consent of Scottish dissidents because of correspondence between "fanatics" in the two countries, but again there is no evidence to support his conjecture. By the early autumn of 1667, however, "very many" dissenting ministers were leaving Scotland for Carrickfergus, where their conventicle sermons promised that "times will change shortly," that the bishops would soon be expelled from the English House of Lords, and that the Presbyterian earl of Cassillis had been appointed president of the Scottish Council.[67] Had this activity preceded the mutiny, the latter might well have incited an Irish version of the Galloway uprising.

Ormond and his advisers also had to be concerned about the ever-present possibility of a native Irish revolt. One erupted in county Roscommon in May 1666, led by Cornet Edmund Nangle, brother-in-law of Sir George Lane, the Irish secretary, and Dudley Costellogh (or Costello). With a party of fifty or sixty horse, they mounted an unsuccessful assault on Castle Forbes, burned English homes in Longford in July, and killed various Englishmen. The rebels were finally crushed as Nangle died from a musket-shot wound. Concern had been heightened by fears that his men would be aided by French invaders.[68] The Nangle rebellion sparked a rumor that 10,000 Irishmen were in arms; this and similar false reports upset English settlers throughout this period. In June 1668, for instance, stories circulated of an insurrection in northern Ireland—by one account 1,000 Irish Tories, by another 7,000 Tories or Protestant "fanatics." The problem, as Major Joseph Stroud observed in June 1671 in the context of a suspected Catholic plot, was that "after many false alarms comes a true one at last, and many times when least thought of."[69] Such a possibility made it impossible for officials to concentrate their surveillance on the radicals alone.

The threat to security posed by the Irish Catholics, the radicals, and the Ulster Scots underscored the need to organize the militia, provision the garrisons adequately, and pay arrears to the army. In addition, Orrery wanted to purge suspicious persons from the garrisons, replace all unserviceable weapons, put an artillery train in each province, and order all army officers to return to their garrisons. Orrery, of course, was also the most outspoken advocate of detaining the leading Catholic and Protestant dissidents. As long as the army was unpaid, discipline was lax and mutinies a possibility. In addition to the two Carrickfergus mutinies in 1666, the troops in Connaught committed outrages the same year.[70] An effective militia was clearly required, but efforts to establish one were hampered by inadequate funds and the unwillingness of many Protestants in northern Ireland to take the prescribed oaths of supremacy and allegiance. But Ormond persevered, and by 1667 the militia was an important factor in maintaining security. In October of that year Sir George Rawdon observed in Dublin that "since the militia has been formed we have [had] no alarms of rebellion or Tories, and we hope it will be a security to posterity here." Ormond was not, however, willing to intern Catholic and Protestant dissidents without adequate evidence. Finally, as with fortifications in such English towns as Coventry and Northampton, the Council ordered the citadel of Londonderry pulled down in order to prevent rebels from seizing it.[71]

Nonconformists in Ireland

After the failure of efforts in the early 1660s to produce uniformity among Protestants in Ireland, conventicles increased, particularly in the north. Major Hugh Montgomery, a horse breeder in county Londonderry who raised money for the Presbyterians, provided space on his land for conventicles of as many as 500 to 700 persons. Thomas Boyd of Aghadowey frequently preached to them. Viscount Dungannon ordered the arrest of both men in December 1666, but this did not deter the Presbyterians from holding conventicles. In county Antrim Sir George Rawdon noted in March 1668 that Presbyterian ministers were "taking greater liberty of meeting in every parish almost than formerly." At a conventicle held in a barn at Carnecastle, Antrim, on a September night in 1668, Patrick Adair, Thomas Gowen, Thomas Hall, and William Keyes exhorted their congregants to be faithful to the Covenant rather than yield to the state, assuring them that God would abet them in their struggle. Significantly, those who attended that assembly came from places as scattered as Coleraine, Belfast, Carrickfergus, and Antrim town, and included a number of country gentlemen, among them James McCulloch, whose brother John had been executed as a Galloway insurgent.[72]

Similar meetings, convened throughout Ulster in order to encourage people to remain loyal to the Covenant, helped spread the notion of a "suddaine alteracon" or favorable religious change, one of the favorite themes of Irish dissenters. Some of these assemblies rivaled those in Scotland in terms of size. At Carrickfergus in the spring of 1670, Keyes, the usual preacher, and six Scottish ministers spoke to more than 3,000 persons, many of them from Scotland. In that one service alone there were six sermons and a communion service. Such large conventicles prompted concern that the Presbyterians had "some ill design" in mind.[73] Although there is no proof that this was their intent, such gatherings unquestionably provided the opportunity for militants to discuss their grievances and schemes for their resolution.

A Presbyterian document that the government confiscated by December 1669 did nothing to ease its concerns. The litany of Presbyterian complaints charged that the king had been seduced by evil counselors, that estates were being seized from Protestants and given to Catholics, that money due the army was being channeled to papists, and that Ormond corresponded with Catholic murderers. Likening themselves to the biblical Jonathan, the Presbyterian authors insisted they would stand up for their rights and called on Protestants in all three kingdoms to support them. Their demands included liberty of conscience for Protestants, fidelity to the Solemn League and Covenant, the restoration of Irish lands held in 1659, and the reinstitution of the traditional liberties of the corporations in the three kingdoms.[74] This declaration was significantly less radical than various earlier statements, omitting as it did demands for the abolition of monarchy and episcopacy. Its appeal would have been correspondingly broader, particularly in Ulster, where it reflected the outlook of the more moderate local ministers.

Many Ulster Scots depended on ministers from Scotland for leadership and spiritual sustenance. Recognizing this, the bishop of Londonderry wanted such preachers arrested and forced to provide bonds never to set foot in Londonderry again. Presumably one of those who excited his anger was James Patrick, to whom Major Montgomery played host when Patrick visited Ulster in 1666. Conventicles at such places as Glenarm, Ardclinis, Larne, and probably Coleraine, Ballyrashane, and Dunluce were serviced by itinerant clerics from Scotland. John Shaw left there in the spring of 1668 to return to his former congregation at Ahoghill in Antrim, and shortly thereafter the Galloway rebel John Crookshanks preached at Kilbride in Westmeath and Banagher in Offaly.[75]

The crackdown on conventicles in Scotland in 1668 had the unintended effect of prompting ministers forced out of Ireland by Ormond in 1663 to return. Because of their preaching, Dungannon complained, many parish churches were deserted. As these ministers openly preached the Covenant, he fumed, "all other incitations to rebellion are not wantinge." In some cases the Ulster laity took the initiative and invited preachers to come from Scotland to fill the pulpits of the chapels that they were building. By the summer of 1670 three more Galloway fugitives—Alexander Peden, Gabriel Semple, and Gabriel Maxwell—had come to Ulster and were frequently preaching at Taughboyne and Letterkenny in Donegal. Often, however, such Scottish firebrands did not get along well with Presbyterian clerics in Ulster who preferred to find a *modus vivendi* with the government.[76]

Conventicles continued even in Dublin itself, a city, observed one loyalist, where "all persons except some incorrigible Phanatiques . . . [are] well pleasd with theire present Government." The Congregationalist Samuel Mather, who had gone to England after his ejection from St. Nicholas's in 1660, returned to Ireland after being deprived as curate of Burtonwood, Warrington, Lancashire in 1662. He was briefly incarcerated in 1664 for preaching illegally in Dublin, but he was still holding conventicles in homes in 1668 along with the Congregationalist Timothy Taylor of Carrickfergus. Taylor also spoke frequently at a Thursday morning Presbyterian lecture in Dublin. Conventicles were also held in Dublin in 1668 by (the Presbyterian Samuel?) Cox, the Congregationalist Edward Baines, and the Presbyterian Dr. Gilbert Rule. When efforts were made to curtail these assemblies, the dissenters protested that as long as the Catholics were tolerated, Protestant nonconformists should be left alone.[77]

The uniqueness of Ireland's situation, with its large Catholic population and its mixture of Scottish Presbyterians and English sectaries, made it difficult to conceive and implement an effective religious policy. The sporadic prosecution of conventiclers was ineffective as a deterrent, nor did it make sense to continue chasing Covenanters to Scotland and back again. Voices of moderation were heard: Viscount Conway, for example, tried in 1666 to impress on Rawdon, a hard-liner, the need for liberty of conscience if Ireland hoped to develop its manufacturing and trade while reducing its dependence on cattle export. From a different perspective Major John Ashurst argued the same year that "the removing of soe many godly persons, . . . especially the Ministers," would lead to "an Alteracon" every seven years.[78] Ormond's instructions as lord lieutenant left him room to maneuver: The goal was conformity with the established religion, but not at the cost of endangering the peace of the kingdom. Charles, in fact, clearly expected Ormond to suggest the best course to deal with both Catholic and Protestant nonconformists on the basis of his experience in Ireland, and Ormond—like Lauderdale—favored lenient treatment for moderates. But such a policy had its detractors, among them Rawdon and Sir Nicholas Armorer. "Ah friend," the latter warned Joseph Williamson in August 1669, "if you look not about you, you will all repent indulgence to tender consciences." Even under Ormond severe punishment was meted out: For refusing to take the oath of allegiance, four clergymen—Adam White of Fannet, Thomas Drumond of Ramelton, John Hart of Taughboyne, and William Semple of Letterkenny, the latter two also suspected of complicity in the 1663 Dublin plot—spent seven years in prison.[79]

The problem of dealing with the nonconformists was further complicated by a series of political maneuvers involving the lord deputyship. Undercut politically by Arlington and Buckingham, and with the king intent on tolerating Catholics as part of his shift toward a French alliance, Ormond was replaced as lord lieutenant in March 1669 by John Lord Robartes, a friend of Presbyterians and a supporter of indulgence. Robartes, however, was despised by the Catholics. He resigned in May 1670 after he had angered the king by his seemingly undue sympathy for soldiers at the expense of their officers. His successor, John Lord Berkeley of Stratton, was sympathetic to Catholics and thus was well received by the Irish, but his political ineffectiveness led to his replacement by Arthur Capel, earl of Essex, in February 1672. Like his friend Ormond, Essex favored a policy of limited indulgence. His instructions, issued on 12 July, recognized not only the ideal of religious uniformity but the barriers to its realization: "Wee will that you proceed with Caution therein, and Certify to Us the State of that matter, that Wee may give you thereupon such further Directions as shall be found necessary for the Peace and quiet of that Our Kingdome."[80]

Virtually from the beginning, Essex was confronted with strong remonstrations about nonconformist activity from the bishop of Londonderry. On 27 July 1672 so many Presbyterians assembled in Londonderry town from the surrounding region that the magistrates could not control them. Similar meetings followed. When Essex sought guidance from Westminster about these conventicles, Arlington made it clear that an indulgence of the type recently promulgated in England would be inappropriate. The bishop of Londonderry kept up his demands for a tougher policy, especially after he attempted to prohibit the assembly on 1 September, provoking a riot when soldiers broke up the meeting. Firm action, the bishop insisted, was essential to prevent further "tumultuous practices." Charles ordered the garrison at Londonderry strengthened and instructed Essex to warn the Presbyterians to cease assembling "in Numbers of soe much offence" lest the government be forced to adopt a repressive course. The leaders of the Londonderry Presbyterians—the merchant John Campsie and William Hampton, a Scottish Covenanter—were conciliatory, agreeing not to use their meetinghouse if this offended the king or the lord lieutenant, and generally to meet outside the city walls. "The greater tenderness that is used towards them," said Essex, "the better."[81]

As in Scotland, the government hoped to increase the division between moderate and militant Presbyterians. The latter seem to have been particularly influenced by such fugitives from the Galloway rebellion as John Crookshanks, Gabriel Maxwell, Alexander Peden, and Gabriel Semple. In espousing this policy, the bishop of Down described the militants as "factious, preaching up the peoples libertyes, [and] spreading seditious books printed in Holland since this war." They "excite the people to outrages ag[ain]st their legall incumbents, in which some have been beaten and battered for doing their dutyes, and in Travelling on the high way without any provocation given." Thus the patterns of violence against moderate clergymen spread from Scotland to Ulster. The bishop's plan was to treat moderates kindly, although he urged Essex not to offer them an indulgence, as in England, because this would only encourage the militants. Moderate Presbyterians had an advocate at court in the person of Sir Arthur Forbes, who played a key role in the king's decision to instigate the *regium donum*—small, secret grants to Presbyterian ministers in Ulster. Whether the actual payments began in 1672 or 1676 is not, however, clear. Given the fact that there were, according to Sir William Petty, approximately 100,000 Presbyterians in northern Ireland by 1672, some form of *modus vivendi* was clearly essential.[82]

In both Ireland and Scotland the Quakers contrived to meet throughout this period despite sporadic persecution. The leading Quaker in Ireland, William Edmondson, was imprisoned a number of times. Some twenty Quakers were jailed at Dublin in February

1664 after they refused a magistrate's order to disperse; among them was the bishop of Killaloe's wife. Ralph Sharply, "cheife of the Quakers," was imprisoned at Carrickfergus two years later, as were numerous Friends at Cork between 1667 and 1670, among them William Penn. At the end of the decade, however, less attention was paid to the Quakers. By the time that George Fox, John Stubbs, and three other Quaker missionaries visited Ireland in May 1669, the Friends had approximately thirty settled meetings in Ulster, Leinster, and Munster, including those at Cork, Youghal, and Kinsale. Activities here developed along lines similar to those in England— the organization of provincial and district meetings as well as a national meeting every six months, visits to the conventicles of other sects to win recruits, and an active writing campaign. Philip Ford shipped Quaker books on liberty of conscience and critiques of Catholicism to Francis Rogers in Bristol. At Cork, however, the mayor kept a list of Quakers' names in 1670 "and imprisoned most of the Men Friends in the City." Leniency toward the Quakers did not sit well with the archbishop of Armagh, who complained to Lord Berkeley in August 1670 that they continued to increase in number "and insolence," and generally refused to pay tithes.[83]

Quakers in Scotland did not fare as well. In July 1667 the Council, accusing the Friends of "turbulent and pernitious" behavior, seduction of the king's subjects from their obedience, and contempt for royal authority, ordered the magistrates of Aberdeen, Lanark, and Teviotdale to arrest all male Quakers attending conventicles and send them to the Edinburgh Tolbooth. Heritors, their officers, and parish ministers were made responsible for reporting Quaker meetings to the magistrates. Simultaneously the Councillors summoned George Keith and Alexander Jaffray to answer for holding conventicles.[84] Quaker activities in the shires of Berwick and Roxburgh concerned the Council in 1669, and in June the Councillors again summoned Keith along with Robert Burnett, a tutor at Leys, Kincardine, and ordered the imprisonment of Walter Scott and John Swinton, laird of Swinton. Both men were released in March 1670, but Keith, who had been held a close prisoner in the Edinburgh Tolbooth, was banished. The same month twenty-three Quakers, two of whom were from England, were arrested at the Edinburgh home of the tanner James Brown. The women were not detained, but the men were jailed for a month and then warned that a second offense would result in a sentence twice that long—an onerous penalty for a small artisan or indigent worker. Because Aberdeenshire continued to be one of the most active Quaker regions, in March 1670 the Council ordered the sheriff and his deputies to arrest the offenders and prevent future meetings, in part by punishing those who allowed their houses to be used for conventicles. Those arrested in the ensuing crackdown were incarcerated for the usual term of one month. But Quaker meetings continued, prompting the Council to order a more rigorous enforcement of the laws in 1672 in the shires of Banff, Moray, and Aberdeen.[85]

In neither Scotland nor Ireland was Quaker activity radical in a political sense, for the Friends insisted on nothing more than the right to preach their message and adhere to their own religious and social standards. Although they repudiated royal supremacy, the idea of a state church, and the use of civil authority to enforce religious beliefs, they ceased to pursue their ends by combative means. In contrast, the willingness of militant Covenanters to hold large, armed conventicles, to espouse open defiance of the government, and to embrace violence as a legitimate means of defending their principles marks them as radical. During the late 1660s the Presbyterian ministers in northern Ireland generally showed little inclination for such militancy, though a radical undercurrent was kept alive by itinerant preachers from Scotland. The generally moderate stance of the Ulster clerics is explained by the amount of toleration they enjoyed and probably by the imminent danger posed by the native Irish.

Scottish authorities seem to have regarded the Quakers as a greater threat to their authority than did officials in Ireland, who had apparently come to the realization that the Friends no longer possessed a militant outlook. In Scotland, moreover, officials treated Quakers and Catholics in the same way by the early 1670s, regarding both as threats to royal authority and the maintenance of peace.[86] In Ireland, on the other hand, there could be no question of seriously trying to impose Protestantism on the Catholics, hence a de facto toleration was virtually inevitable. If the Catholics were to be tolerated, it made sense to work out some form of *modus vivendi* with the moderate Presbyterians, isolating the militant Covenanters as well as English radicals who continued to scheme against the Restoration settlement. By the end of our period, then, authorities in both Scotland and England had embarked on a policy of exacerbating the internal tensions that existed within the dissenting community, hoping to weaken its potential to mount further insurrections.

"The Present Distresses"

———————————— ◄ F O U R ► ————————————

The Nonconformist Challenge in England, 1664–1672

In the hands of traditional denominational historians, the story of Protestant dissent in the 1660s and 1670s has focused on the persecution of the godly. The twelve years spent by John Bunyan in the county jail at Bedford for violating the Elizabethan statute against conventicles served as an apt symbol for this historiographical tradition. Such an interpretation, however, makes it difficult to understand why the government of Charles II—the king's own inclination toward toleration notwithstanding—manifested so much concern about illegal services, and why, as late as 1689, one of the conditions for toleration was unlocked doors in dissenting chapels. Were the Stuarts and their supporters alarmist, or was there enough basis for the alleged link between conventicles and seditious activity to justify a suspicion of all illegal religious assemblies?

Assessing Resistance: Passive Disobedience or Sedition?

A large majority of nonconformists posed no violent political threat to the Stuart regime, though the specter of thousands of dissenters willfully disobeying the law on any given Sunday—and often on weekdays, especially in London—was surely regarded as destabilizing. The dominant philosophy in the nonconformist community was passive resistance. Throughout the period Protestant dissenters demonstrated a willingness to defy the law repeatedly, yet they normally stopped short of outright rebellion, partly for fear of renewed civil war, partly because many embraced a theology of suffering on behalf of the Gospel, and partly because they had no one to lead them. Yet the potential for militant action was always present, not least because the nonconformist heritage included the views on tyrannicide espoused a century earlier by John Ponet, Christopher Goodman, and John Knox, and reiterated more recently by John Milton and others.[1]

The laity as well as the clergy amassed multiple convictions, persuaded that it was their spiritual duty to worship in congregations of visible saints, and they were often convinced as well that repressive religious legislation violated "the Lawe of Nature and so [was] voyd in itself." Exhortations to suffer in God's cause were a commonplace of Restoration nonconformity. "The righteous cause of Christ that is now asserted by a remnant of the Lambs faithfull followers is worth suffering for," wrote a Somerset dissenter who faced the threat of imprisonment. As one might expect, Bunyan's writings are filled with comments about suffering, often accompanied by apocalyptic references to divine judgment on persecutors. Magistrates can hardly have welcomed allusions to their eventual punishment in the great

> . . . Prison with its locks and bars,
> Of Gods lasting decree.[2]

Hard evidence linking conventicles to seditious activity was scarce, but the government's supporters were usually reluctant to admit this.[3] A story in the *Intelligencer* on 17 October 1664, for example, alleged that conventicles were rendezvous for plotters. Yet in June of that year one of Viscount Conway's correspondents had observed that despite the use of the trained bands to break up conventicles, the "fanatics" would probably not respond with violence because their preachers advocated patience and nonresistance. Similarly, in September 1667 two magistrates, Sir John Wyrley and John Vernon, reported that their investigation of a conventicle at Oldbury, Worcestershire, uncovered no hint of a disturbance despite the provocative discourse of the preacher. The latter had admonished his hearers "to pray for the Comeing of Christ in Glory to reward all working and suffering saints."[4] That such a theme could still be found potentially inflammatory in 1667 is a reminder that people had not forgotten the use to which such notions had been put by radicals, particularly the Fifth Monarchists.

Christopher Feake, one of the most prominent Fifth Monarchists in the 1650s, was still exciting concern in 1664. He had settled in Dorking, Surrey, under an assumed name the previous autumn, but local magistrates soon discovered that he was receiving allegedly libelous pamphlets as well as suspicious correspondence. One intercepted letter—a call for his spiritual services—emphasized that it was his responsibility to feed the flock, whether in public or in private. When Feake was arrested he volunteered that "hee could not Live in obeaydience to the Governement but would bee willing to suffer" like Shadrach, Meshech, and Abednego. He insisted, however, that none of the literature he had received contained material against the government, nor had he attended unlawful meetings. The past, however, continued to haunt him, for the deputy lieutenants candidly admitted that "people here abouts Are soe Affected to him that wee feare hee will seduce Abundance of his Majesties subjects." The authorities found nothing suspicious in his house but nevertheless regarded him as "A dangerous person and An eminent opposer of Monarchicall Government." Accused of seditious practices, Feake was taken to London in early January and not released until 25 July.[5]

If Feake suffered because of his past, Francis Bampfield, the ejected vicar of Sherborne, Dorset, who had been a royalist during the civil war, was incarcerated for almost nine years for holding conventicles and refusing to take the oath of allegiance. Not even an appeal to Charles from this "Honourer of the King" helped: "As nothing of that turbulent nature can justly be charged upon me with respect to the late war, so I stil abhorre tumultuous insurrections, & have endeavoured to discover & to prevent seditious designes." Imprisoned with four other nonconformist clergymen—Peter Ince, Thomas Hallet, Josiah Banger, and John Sacheverell—Bampfield would have been released had he been willing to post bond for good behavior. Instead he remained in prison, where he gathered his own congregation, preached as often as sixteen times a week, and received other nonconformist ministers as visitors. He was, one magistrate grumbled, "Resolved . . . to remaine in Goale to the Disturbance of his Majesties Government."[6]

This, in essence, was the heart of the charge against conventicles: They disturbed the government. Nonconformists, one of Williamson's correspondents complained, "disquiet church and state." The bishop of Peterborough's description of two unlicensed preachers as "very factious" aptly reflects the general conformist view of dissenters and their illegal meetings. Conformists commonly based their case against conventicles as seditious on several factors, one of which was the content of some of the illegal sermons. The accuracy of the charge is extremely hard to assess because the evidence is from hostile sources; a preacher who engaged in seditious preaching would hardly leave a written account. In May 1664 speakers at London conventicles reputedly expressed their disappointment with the reestablishment of monarchy and indicated no hope for the future; they included such Presbyterians as Henry Stubbes, William Jenkins, and Thomas Watson, a most improbable group of radicals. Another Presbyterian, Thomas Horrockes, was preaching that spring to a Baptist congregation at Hertford that expected a change of government before the end of 1664; by that point the Cavalier Parliament would "lye in the dust." About the same time the Fifth Monarchists Nathaniel Strange and John Vernon, who preached frequently to London conventicles, allegedly indicated their displeasure with Parliament (which had passed the Conventicle Act in May) and expressed their adherence to "the good old cause." At a Warwickshire conventicle in the summer of 1666 Thomas Wincott uttered scandalous words against both the king and the chief magistrate of Warwick. Bedford jurors found that Samuel Fenn, who belonged to the same church Bunyan did, schemed to incite rebellion and to depose the king of his title and authority by denying the royal governorship of the Church of England. The same year Humphrey Merrill, a disgruntled member of the same church, was excommunicated in part for asserting that the congregation "had their hands in the blood of the king: that they were disobedient to government, and that they were not a church." To a degree, then, what conformists saw as sedition, dissenters viewed as their obligation to remain faithful to Scripture. The vast majority of conventicle preachers undoubtedly espoused only passive resistance in their sermons.[7]

If the sermons were less seditious than conformists thought, the conventicles nevertheless were alarming to the extent that their very illegality led the more zealous to defy the magistrates openly. When the mayor of Exeter tried to maintain close surveillance of local conventicles, there was so much popular hostility that he was forced to desist. At an illegal meeting in Evesham, Worcestershire, in December 1664, two or three sectaries urged active resistance when authorities arrested approximately half of the sixty who were present. Lancashire Presbyterians resisted arrest at a Christmas service the following year, and Newcastle upon Tyne Congregationalists, to whom John Davis, the ejected vicar of Bywell St. Peter, was preaching, behaved similarly in November 1666. Dissenters in the southwest, complained one conformist, "openly denounce judgments and pass damning sentences against all that come to the public." Increasingly the dissenters' attitude was one of open defiance, particularly in those areas where they enjoyed the sympathy of some of the local elite. When justices of the peace ordered a conventicle of approximately a thousand at Canterbury to disperse, they refused, insisting that their preacher, the Presbyterian Robert Beake, preach on.[8]

More serious were the occasions on which the conventiclers armed themselves or engaged in violent acts. Recourse to weapons was never as common in England during this period as in Scotland, but the practice nevertheless caused concern. The Baptist congregation at Hertford, some 500 strong, was reportedly armed. There was concern in 1665 when the master of the "Golden Lion," Bread Street, London, and two other disaffected persons bought weapons and horses; they were probably followers of the Fifth Monarchists Thomas Glasse and John Vernon, who periodically preached in Bread Street. Armed Baptists even attended all-night conventicles of forty or fifty in a rented chamber in the White Lion prison, to which they gained access as visitors. Dissenters in the southwest broke open parish church doors in order to have a place to meet.[9]

In April 1664 the Presbyterians of Newbury, Berkshire, engaged in disruptive behavior aimed at the rector, Joseph Sayer, whom they regarded as a turncoat because he had supported Parliament in the civil war and the Protectorate in the 1650s. They were also angered by the repeal of the Triennial Act and by the imprisonment in Windsor Castle of Thomas Voysey (or Voisy), ejected vicar of Thatcham, Berkshire. Voysey, who was charged with complicity in the 1663 northern rebellion, had been living in Newbury and was probably holding conventicles there. When Sayer, the mayor, and other citizens met in the parish vestry to elect churchwardens, more than a hundred dissenters broke into the room, nominated two candidates of their own, and dispersed only when the constables arrived. The ringleaders—William Milton, "A Rigid violent presbyter, [who] has beene A Rebell in the Armies from his cradle," Robert Hyde, and Thomas Stockwell—also tried to prevent parishioners from taking communion at Easter in the belief that "all persons that receave the communion are lost to theire party." Planning was carried out at a coffeehouse owned by Milton, "where all the malecontents of this place frequently meete with great confidence in his secrecy." When Milton was arrested, his accomplices tried unsuccessfully to rescue him. Although peace was restored, conventicles continued to be held in Newbury by the ejected rector, the Presbyterian Benjamin Woodbridge.[10]

The tendency of a small minority of dissenters to commit acts deemed sacrilegious by conformists also contributed to the belief that conventicles were nurseries of sedition. In general such behavior was a continuation of the iconoclastic tradition that grew out of the Reformation, reached its zenith in the 1640s and 1650s, and was renewed in the attacks on the Book of Common Prayer prompted by the passage of the 1662 Act of Uniformity. A dissenter identified only as Harris, who may have had ties to the Congregationalist Thomas Palmer, was banished from Leicester in 1663 for defiling the surplice and chalice; in April 1664 he and other nonconformists were indicted for holding an illegal burial service for the wife of a former Roundhead. At Bolton, Lancashire, the Book of Common Prayer was taken from the parish church, torn in pieces, and thrown into the street in 1666, and a similar incident occurred the same year at St. Anne's, Blackfriars, London.[11]

Suspicion that the conventicles were seditious was heightened by the sizable numbers that many of them drew, although they rarely equaled the largest ones in Scotland until the very late 1660s, and then only in a few places, such as western Wiltshire or Great Yarmouth. "They meete in such numbers," a Great Yarmouth observer wrote in late 1667, "that they put feares into the peoples mindes." He was referring, however, to a conventicle of no more than 300 persons that met at the house of Captain Thomas Ravens (or Raven), a common councillor, but numbers increased sharply in the next few years. English conventicles were seldom larger, although estimates of the 1667 Oldbury meeting referred to earlier placed the number of participants between 300 and 1,000, the latter figure undoubtedly counting the persons unable to squeeze into the building. In the mid-1660s the number of conventicles exceeded 400 at Great Yarmouth, 300 at Dover and Shadwell, Yorkshire, and approximately 200 at Newcastle, Hull, and Covent Garden, London.[12] Chester and Norwich had illegal assemblies exceeding 100, Wrexham and the London parish of St. Mary Abchurch almost that number,[13] but many conventicles drew only 20 to 60 persons.[14] Whatever their size, they siphoned people from the parish churches. There was a complaint in September 1667 that 500 persons attended a conventicle in a barn at Marshfield, Gloucester, while only 2 or 3 went to the parish church. Understandably, the conventiclers assumed that the government would soon have to allow them religious freedom. Such disparities in attendance were probably fairly rare, but the conventicles represented an attack on the established church and the ideal of religious uniformity that to many conservatives was still tantamount to sedition.[15]

Perhaps the strongest reason to suspect conventiclers of seditious behavior was the degree to which well-known radicals of the 1650s preached at them. In London in the years 1664–65 alone, the list of conventicle preachers included the Fifth Monarchists Nathaniel Strange, John Vernon, Thomas Glasse, John Skinner, Henry Danvers, George Cokayne, and Anthony(?) Palmer, as well as the Congregationalists Joseph Caryl, John Rowe, Thomas Brooks, Ralph Venning, and John Knowles. Their services were not isolated incidents but fairly regular events, often involving two or more preachers in the same service and occasionally lasting an entire day. Nonconformists in London could often choose from a variety of illegal services on the same day: at least eight, for instance, on 4 December 1664 or 8 January 1665.[16] Many of these meetings were probably harmless enough, though some were conducted by men implicated in such radical activities of the early 1660s as the Tong plot and the northern rebellion.

There was concern too because the illegal services sometimes attracted persons of note, particularly those with radical backgrounds. In the early 1670s Dr. John Owen's Congregationalist church included such former Cromwellian officers as Charles Fleetwood, John Desborough, James Berry, Jeffrey Ellison, and Griffith Lloyd (a New Model captain), in addition to Mrs. Bridget Bendish, daughter of Henry Ireton and granddaughter of Oliver Cromwell; William Steele, lord chancellor of Ireland in the late 1650s; Fleetwood's son Samuel as well as his son-in-law, Sir John Hartopp, whose aunt was married to Henry Danvers; and Samuel Lee, former dean of Wadham College, Oxford. At East Sheen, Surrey, the conventiclers included John Ireton, the former lord mayor of London and second son of Henry Ireton, at least two former army officers, and one of Cromwell's former justices. Among those present at an illegal London service in August 1664 at which George Cokayne preached were the countesses of Peterborough and Anglesey, four or five knights, and Ladies Mary and Anne Armine.[17] The M.P. Richard Hampden not only had a Presbyterian chaplain and met regularly with Richard Baxter and Thomas Manton, but allowed Baxter to hold conventicles in his London home. The countess of Exeter similarly supported the Presbyterian Thomas Jacomb, who served as her chaplain and preached to various conventicles in the City. The countess herself permitted a congregation to meet each week in her house in Little Britain, and in February 1664 she was present at an illegal meeting in the Whitefriars house of the Presbyterian Arthur Jackson. Manton, William Bates, and Matthew Poole conducted the service, which was also attended by Philip Lord Wharton, Sir William Waller, Richard Hampden, and Lady Mary or Anne Armine.[18]

The participation of such noteworthy persons was valuable to the nonconformists for many reasons, including political and financial support. Their backing also made it possible to have larger conventicles when their homes were used. In February 1665, 80 to 100 dissenters gathered in Wrexham at the home of the gentleman John Manley, a former Roundhead. However, a conventicle at Castle Bytham, Lincolnshire, the following May attracted only 40 people because persons of "qualitie" had been unable to persuade the local minister to let them use the parish church. When 24 worshipers were arrested in June for attending an illegal service of more than 300 at Shadwell chapel, Yorkshire, it was none other than a sympathetic West Riding justice of the peace who suggested that they sue for false imprisonment because the Conventicle Act said nothing about services in parish churches or chapels.[19] For the most part, it was the Presbyterians—and to a lesser degree the Congregationalists—whose conventicles received the support of the influential. The ministers whom they patronized rarely had ties to the radicals. Contemporary assessment of the conventicles was thus rendered difficult by the fact that such meetings ranged from innocuous services conducted in the homes of respectable peers and gentry to surreptitious gatherings addressed by radicals implicated in conspiracies. The government clearly needed a way to discriminate between them, but devotees of the established church opted instead to attempt to crush nonconformity through parliamentary statute, thereby unwittingly prompting "sober" dissenters to close ranks.

Coping with Dissent: The 1664 Conventicle Act

Charles's efforts to procure relief for both Protestant and Catholic nonconformists had foundered in 1663 because of Clarendon's illness and the king's lack of resolve to push his cause in Parliament. For Charles the religious question was not a matter of the greatest import, his anger over Parliament's unwillingness to grant him the dispensing power notwithstanding. The issue of power concerned him more than purely religious questions.

Before the passage of the Conventicle Act in May 1664, magistrates could prosecute dissenters under the old Elizabethan statute against conventicles (35 Eliz. I, c. 1), for refusing the oath of allegiance, or for riotous assembly, but the latter was hard to prove if the meeting was peaceful. The Elizabethan statute, aimed as much at recusancy as at illegal religious assemblies, provided for the arrest and imprisonment of persons over sixteen years of age who refused to attend services of the established church, who persuaded others not to attend, or who were present at conventicles. Detention could continue until a person conformed, with the proviso that someone who refused to conform for three months was subject to exile. Those who harbored or otherwise aided recusants could be fined £10.[20]

Numerous prosecutions were made under the Elizabethan act, the best known being the conviction of John Bunyan, who was imprisoned for twelve years. In late 1663, to cite but one example, the quarter sessions in Suffolk fined some fifty sectaries for nonconformity. The prosecution of dissenters was, however, largely at the discretion of local magistrates. As J.S. Cockburn has demonstrated in his study of assizes, this was true of crimes in general.[21] Although Clarendon himself urged only the arrest of nonconformist leaders, in Berkshire Sir William Armorer imprisoned all the men he found at conventicles; on one Sunday in March 1664, for instance, he jailed forty Quakers and fifteen Baptists for holding unlawful services in Reading. Magistrates in Buckinghamshire were prepared to use the Elizabethan statute to hang twelve General Baptists who refused to conform or leave the country, but the Privy Council wisely prevented this. In contrast, conventiclers in London were mostly ignored. The impact of the northern rebellion encouraged more rigorous attempts to enforce the Elizabethan law throughout much of the country. Roger Lowe of Ashton-in-Makerfield, Lancashire, undoubtedly reflected the worries of many dissenters when he noted in his diary in April 1664 that one could not attend a nonconformist service without some fear of being prosecuted.[22]

Doubt in some minds about the validity of the Elizabethan statute as well as the need for more comprehensive measures to deal with conventicles led the House of Commons to approve a conventicle bill in June 1663 by a vote of 125 to 61. It was not until May 1664, however, that the Lords, having secured some restrictions on the search of their own homes, approved the bill. With the king's efforts on behalf of the dissenters cooled by the northern rebellion, Clarendon and Sheldon both worked for its passage.[23]

Under the terms of the new Conventicle Act (16 Car. II, c. 4), anyone over the age of sixteen who attended an illegal religious service at which more than six persons were present was subject to imprisonment for up to three months or a fine of up to £5 for the first offense—a more realistic penalty for first offenders than that provided in the Elizabethan act, and with ample discretion for magistrates. The punishment doubled for the second offense, but again allowed for considerable flexibility. A third-time offender faced immediate incarceration prior to a trial, and, if convicted, exile to a colony (except New England or Virginia) for a period of seven years. Sheriffs were empowered to distrain the property of the convicted parties to recover transportation costs, but funds for those with insufficient property would be obtained by requiring the deportees to serve as laborers for colonial merchants for five years. Those able to pay a fine of £100 could avoid deportation. Fourth and subsequent offenses were subject to the same penalty as the third. Recognizing the problem of reluctant and negligent magistrates, the act imposed a fine of £5 on an official who failed to punish a first- or second-time offender, and a fine of £40 for a sheriff who was remiss in transporting a third-time offender. Penalties were imposed on the owners of houses in which conventicles met, and on jailers who allowed prisoners to be at large or visitors to attend illegal services in a jail. The act empowered magistrates to use force to enter houses where conventicles were suspected, except in the case of peers. If peers or their spouses were in residence, their homes could be searched only by at least one lord or deputy lieutenant, or two justices of the peace, or a lesser authority with a royal warrant. The act also provided that persons who refused an oath could be transported. Finally, the lords lieutenant and their deputies were instructed to use troops to disperse and prevent illegal meetings.[24]

Enforcement of the new act was irregular. Accurately describing London and the west, the Dutch ambassador informed his government that the sectaries could not be repressed, although a report to Venetian officials optimistically indicated that the campaign "for the destruction of their conventicles is taking a very good turn." By August 1665, fifteen months after the king signed the bill, Henry Muddiman observed that "the Conventicles are now hotly pursued, no meeting but presently snapt and the Brethren prosecuted according to the strictnesse of the Law."[25] In most places the first year of the act brought the greatest efforts to enforce it, but even so, Muddiman's observation was only partially correct. Given the likelihood of lost or incomplete records, drawing firm conclusions based on the

absence of data concerning prosecutions in some counties is hazard-
ous, but it is probable that in such areas the persecution of dissenters
was at least less intensive than in other regions.[26]

During the act's first year, legal proceedings occurred in at least
thirty-one counties and in the cities of London, Bristol, and Chester.
Persecution was most severe in those cities, the counties around
London, and Durham, Somerset, and Staffordshire.[27] To facilitate
the attack on London conventicles, in November 1664 the lord
mayor and two aldermen began searching for illegal meetings each
Sunday. Between 17 July 1664 and 31 December 1665 there were 909
convictions in Middlesex for conventicling, of which 361 involved
females; altogether 782 different persons were convicted, including
one knight (Sir John Vaughan), eight gentlemen, five gentlemen's
wives, nine gentlewomen, two physicians and two physicians' wives,
and six merchants. Several people were fined the maximum £5, but
most paid only 1s. to 5s., and no second offender paid more than £5.[28]

Despite the efforts of magistrates such as Sir John Knight of Bristol and Sir Daniel Fleming in Westmorland, persecution was often
sporadic and penalties relatively light. At Ross-on-Wye, Herefordshire, between 200 and 300 Baptists and Quakers were arrested at
two conventicles in January 1665, but only 12 were jailed. Sir Roger
Bradshaigh, whom Anthony Fletcher has called "a lone campaigner"
to enforce the statute in Lancashire, reported on 29 July 1665 that
only 3 conventiclers had been convicted at the last quarter sessions.
Despite the number of prosecutions in Chester, Sir Geoffrey Shakerley, governor of the castle, complained to Williamson that the
justices "much favoured" the dissenters by imposing light fines.[29]
"This Citty," he grumbled a year later, "doth soe swarme with these
Cardinale Nonconformists who are soe linkt into the Magistracy of
the Citty through Alliance & otherwise, that tis a very difficult matter to bring any of them to punishment." Complaints about magistrates remiss in enforcing the statute became common.[30] By order of
the Privy Council, the deputy lieutenants of Dorset examined the
mayor of Weymouth on charges that he did not punish conventiclers. In Kent, efforts to prosecute the dissenters in the autumn of
1665 were frustrated because so many members of the grand jury
were nonconformists.[31]

Some officials were not only lax in enforcing the act but deliberately supportive of dissenters. Despite the opposition of the governor of York Castle, the lord mayor freed Edward Ord, the ejected curate of Cowesby, after only eighteen days on the grounds that he had been unlawfully committed. When an attempt was made to arrest the Fifth Monarchists John Vernon and Thomas Glasse at a London conventicle in July 1664, a member of the arresting party, the winecooper Captain Cox, not only permitted both men and others to escape, but warned them that some of the conventiclers were informers. At Minehead, Somerset, one sectary defied a magistrate to suppress the Baptist conventicle in late 1667, "presuming upon the favour of the neighbouring justices."[32] Dissenters at Great Yarmouth also benefited from sympathetic magistrates, particularly commencing in 1666 when Presbyterians and other moderates acquired control of the town council.[33] The fact that a sizable body of local officials in England refused to prosecute nonconformists, punished them far less than the law allowed, or even helped them evade magistrates of a different mind underscores the fact that many in the political nation were unwilling to accept indiscriminate attempts to associate conventicles with seditious activity.

Although persecution was only sporadic, the suffering was real enough. Bunyan's dozen years in prison or Francis Bampfield's incarceration of nearly nine years were happily not the norm, but in the Conventicle Act's first year 230 nonconformists, mostly from the London area, were sentenced to transportation. In the end, however, less than 10 percent were actually banished. Maximum penalties were imposed on conventiclers at Wrexham, Denbigh, in February 1665. Seven conventiclers fined 1 mark apiece at the summer assizes in Warwick in 1664 were still in prison in November 1666, as were thirteen others who had refused the oath of allegiance at the lent assizes the same year. There they would remain, said Sir Thomas Tyrell, justice of the Common Pleas, until they paid their fines or received a royal pardon.[34]

The number of dissenters fined or imprisoned would have been considerably higher had many of them not been so adept at eluding the authorities. When Glasse, Vernon, and their friends were tipped off about informers in their midst, they resolved to assemble in the future on only an hour's notice, with no one admitted once the hour had passed. When magistrates did find a conventicle in progress, the nonconformists—with the exception of the Quakers—often tried to escape, helping the minister in particular to get away so that he could continue his surreptitious ministry. Of the nearly one hundred worshipers at a Wrexham conventicle in February 1665, a mere twenty-one were caught by the militia. Because the Fifth Monarchists at Hull the following month used scouts to warn that an arresting party was en route, only twenty of the more than one hundred participants were seized. The use of such sentries became common. Sir Geoffrey Shakerley's men fared better in July 1665 when they arrested sixty of the more than one hundred persons at a conventicle in the house of Dr. Thomas Harrison, a Congregationalist and former chaplain to Henry Cromwell. This was a potentially dangerous group—the "worst stampe of sectaryes," Shakerley called them—that included Major James Jolly, who had served in Ireland, the former aldermen Edward Bradshaw and Peter Lee, and Richard Kirby, who had just arrived from Ireland.[35] Deputy lieutenants in Somerset arrested approximately 120 persons, including eleven ministers, at an illegal assembly in July 1665, but complained that almost as many more dissenting clergymen were still in Taunton and preach "up and downe; and are so close, and secret in their Meetings, as we can never hear thereof till they are gone."[36] Thus nonconformist vigilance, sympathetic or negligent magistrates, and sometimes the support of the powerful mitigated persecution.

Fighting "the Lords Battale": The Quakers and "Antichrists Servants"

The Quakers were the most radical of the major religious groups in their spiritual and social ideas, but the militant behavior they had evinced in the 1650s and early 1660s died out as George Fox's pacifistic principles took hold. The Friends were generally treated differently by the authorities and often responded more disparately to persecution than did other nonconformists. Many dissenters regarded them with deep suspicion, much of it due to their inability to understand Quaker ways, including their mode of speech, their repudiation of such traditional customs as hat doffing, their refusal to pay tithes, and their adamant opposition to oaths. The latter, however, was perhaps less a matter of misunderstanding—the Quaker case was plain enough—than a convenient weapon to use against the Friends. The Quaker combination of plain speech, the language of the Spirit, and the rhetoric of "the Lamb's war" could be easily misunderstood. The title of a 1666 pamphlet by Stephen Crisp aptly illustrates the militant imagery of some Quaker speech: *Epistle to Friends, Concerning the Present and Succeeding Times. Being a Faithful Exhortation and Warning to All Friends, Who Profess the Truth, to Beware of the Manifold Wiles of the Enemy, and to Stand Armed in the Light of the Lord God.* From Carlisle Sir Philip Musgrave, who had had previous experience with militant Quakers, expressed concern to Williamson about the "very suspitious expressions from the Quakers that at this tyme . . . are agitateing some rebellious desine." To Musgrave, as to many traditionalists, they were dangerous people against whom the laws should be vigorously executed.[37]

The Quaker practice of disrupting traditional church services with denunciations of false worship was not only an irritant but a threat to public order. The Quaker message itself was potentially disruptive: When William Penn and William Meade spoke to a crowd of 300 or 400 persons in Gracechurch Street, London, on 14 August 1670, a riot ensued. Suspicion was further aroused when the Friends began holding some of their meetings at night; "from thence wee may receive the suddenest mischeife," cautioned Daniel Fleming.[38]

The Quaker message, particularly to non-Friends, included stern condemnation and the warning of impending judgment. The justices of the peace in Berkshire were described as "Antichrists servants" and threatened with God's "fiery Indignation," while the Church of England was condemned for its pride, cruelty, and use of oaths. Quakers would die, they insisted, before they would make shipwreck of their faith by obeying magistrates in religious matters. In York a Friend gave the lord mayor a paper that proclaimed: "Your day is (even) over, And a darke Gloomie day at hand, in which that which is determined (by the lord) Against you, Will be Accomplished Except that yee doe Repent Spedily." The Quakers also used symbols to convey their message of impending judgment, the most notorious being their "sign" of "going naked." Clad only with a scarf around his "privy parts" and with a pan of coals on his head, one Quaker paraded through Westminster Hall and the palace yard in July 1667.[39]

However much they might jar people's sensibilities or excite concern, by the mid-1660s most Quakers appear to have embraced George Fox's call to pacifism. As he reiterated his principle to the magistrates in January 1664, "wee cannot hurt any man much lesse the king . . . [;] to ayd[,] assist or counsell or countenance or maintaine any that take up armes to disthrone him . . . wee do utterly deny." True Christians, he insisted, use only spiritual weapons to proclaim the gospel of peace. Various Quakers echoed this theme throughout the period. Peter Acklom, imprisoned for fourteen weeks in 1663 on suspicion of plotting, insisted in March 1664 that he would never attempt to remove the king from the throne to which God had restored him. "My Principle," said Henry Jackson from the Warwick jail, "is; To live peaceably with all men & to seek the good peace[,] welfare & prosperity, both of the king, & all his subjects."[40] The peace principle was frequently linked with professions of loyalty to the king, for most Friends probably would have accepted Fox's willingness to embrace any type of government so long as the Quakers enjoyed religious and civil liberty.[41]

As late as December 1663, however, some Quakers were implicated in the northern rebellion, and in later years some still clung to overt forms of resistance. Peter Acklom's own position is unclear. Imprisoned again in 1664, the former major of horse had been holding illegal services at his house in Hornsea in the East Riding, and had allegedly said that "tythes should quickly by putt downe, and if the Lord would putt the sword into their hands, wee should see they would fight the Lords Battale."[42] Another East Riding Friend, John Nicholson, purportedly boasted that "if God putt the sword into his hand he must strike." Whether these statements were intended literally or figuratively is open to question.[43] About 1666 a Quaker named Hutchinson boasted that he had been imprisoned twice, but escaped the last time by killing his jailer. When George Alsop, rector of Chipping Ongar, Essex, tried to preach at the Quaker meetinghouse in Gracechurch Street, London, in July 1670, the Friends physically attacked him, "pulling him by the Neck and otherwise," stripping him of his robe, and bruising his knee and chest, all the while calling him "Popish Priest and Jesuit." Whatever the leaders were saying, at least some of the rank and file had not fully embraced the pacifist gospel.[44]

At first the authorities hoped to control the Quakers by arresting their leaders, the same strategy used for other dissenters. Daniel Fleming thought if Margaret Fell and George Fox were convicted of *praemunire* for refusing the oath of allegiance a second time, it would be a harsh blow to the Quakers, but he was proved wrong. Attempts to stop Quaker meetings by imprisoning leading Friends failed, for members of the rank and file continued to gather until they too were jailed—women and young people as well as men.[45] Unlike other dissenters the Quakers did not flee when magistrates appeared but stood their ground as a witness to their faith. In Wiltshire, however, some attempted to avoid arrest by meeting in groups of three or four, thereby circumventing the provisions of the 1662 Quaker Act. Because they refused to flee, virtually the entire Quaker leadership was in prison in 1664, including Fox, Fell, George White-head, Ambrose Rigge, Francis Howgill, Charles Bayly, and William Dewsbury.[46]

Magistrates had no lack of statutes with which to prosecute the Friends. The 1662 Quaker Act (14 Car. II, c. 1) imposed the same penalties on meetings of five or more that were subsequently adopted in the 1664 Conventicle Act. Two Jacobean statutes (3 Jac. I, c. 4, and 7 Jac. I, c. 6) empowered magistrates to tender the oath of allegiance to any commoner over age eighteen; refusing it twice could bring the penalty of *praemunire*—imprisonment at the royal pleasure and the forfeiture of land and goods to the crown. The various recusancy laws (1 Eliz. I, c. 2; 23 Eliz. I, c. 1; 29 Eliz. I, c. 6; 3 Jac. I, c. 4) authorized magistrates to impose fines ranging from 12*d.* for absence on a Sunday or holy day to £20 per month; those who defaulted could lose two-thirds of their land and all of their goods.[47]

As in the case of other dissenters, the implementation of the laws was far from uniform, although the number of Quakers who were punished was proportionately higher than of other nonconformists. The numbers mounted in 1664: 40 Quaker men jailed at Reading in March; nearly 200 at Bristol in July; some 120 at Newgate prison,

London, in August. By the latter date Newgate held approximately 300 Quakers, though the number had fallen to some 140 by the following May. Twenty-one Quakers were in the Appleby jail in the summer of 1665, 22 in Warwick prison in 1666, and more than 30 in Norwich Castle in September 1669.[48] Even more striking is the fact that of the 804 dissenters imprisoned in London between August 1664 and April 1665, 791 were Quakers. Even allowing for the fact that the term "Quaker" was sometimes used indiscriminately for other sectaries, the extent to which Friends suffered is indisputable. Most of these people were probably imprisoned for relatively short periods, but those unlucky enough to have *praemunire* invoked against them could face long jail terms. Barry Reay has found 80 Quakers so convicted between 1662 and 1664, while by 1672 the number was 125. One of the worst cases involved Ambrose Rigge, imprisoned from May 1662 to February 1672.[49]

The sheer numbers of Quakers who were imprisoned put a severe strain on local resources, leading to cruelly overcrowded prisons and dangerously unsanitary conditions. Simply arresting and prosecuting the Friends must have been onerous for magistrates. Such strains on manpower and resources undoubtedly acted to check the number of Quakers who could be arrested. Given the fact that the Friends were rarely dissuaded from their religious practices by fines and imprisonment, efforts to punish them were inevitably frustrating exercises in futility.

Instances of officials who punished the Friends lightly if at all because of sympathy, inefficiency, laziness, or an unwillingness to regard them as dangerous also occurred. Two judges, Thomas Twysden and Christopher Turner, were so "tyred out" by nine "infinitely impudent & provokeinge" Quakers convicted of *praemunire* that they released them after two and a half years in prison.[50] The Welshpool Quaker Richard Davies traveled rather freely during the seven years he was imprisoned under a penalty of *praemunire*. Complaints of leniency or inactivity were made against justices of the peace in Cheshire, Cumberland, Warwickshire, and the North Riding, against various assize judges, and against such officials as the mayor of Weymouth, Dorset, and the constable of Whitby, Yorkshire.[51]

One measure of the extent of persecution is the degree to which the authorities imposed the high fines that were possible under the recusancy statutes. In some cases the extraordinarily onerous £20 fine was imposed. Quakers in Cambridgeshire had their stocks distrained until such fines were paid, while in Norfolk the Friends were kept in prison until the amount was raised; one Quaker was fined £60 at Norwich in April 1664 for recusancy over a three-month period. When a Norfolk grand jury acquitted Quakers of recusancy, each juror was fined £10; the next jury duly found the Friends guilty. Problems also occurred with juries in Canterbury and London.[52] As Barry Reay has demonstrated, however, the authorities generally preferred to impose the 12*d.* fine, which was easier to collect even though it was roughly the daily wage of a journeyman or laborer. But there was sometimes an ulterior motive for assigning lesser penalties, for if the first and second ones were mild, the third offense—opening the way to banishment—was likely to occur sooner. This, at least, was pointed out by judges at the Norwich assizes to local justices in July 1664. Some Quakers refused to pay the fines and went to prison; Priscilla Moseley of the Isle of Wight died in jail rather than pay a fine of half a crown.[53]

Some magistrates—among them Sir John Lowther of Westmorland, Sir Philip Musgrave of Cumberland, and Sir John Knight of Bristol—were keen on transporting Friends to the colonies. Eight were so sentenced at Hertford in 1664, but only 7 of them were actually put on board the *Ann*. Kept from sailing by contrary winds, the captain finally refused to transport them without their consent; the 7 thereupon remained in prison until 1672. Although Bristol officials had hoped to exile 400 Friends, only 3 were actually sentenced and placed on the *Mary Fortune*. Its crew, however, refused to carry them for fear of divine wrath, and returned them to shore after three weeks. In December 1664 Lowther, hoping to banish 20 or 30 Quakers, asked Bennet to what plantation they should be sent, but the latter's reply has apparently not survived.[54]

Between October 1664 and March 1665, 109 male and 44 female Friends in London and Middlesex were sentenced to banishment, but most of these apparently never left England. W.C. Braithwaite found records of 3 who left in March 1665 (one of them died en route), 7 in April, and 8 in May. However, one of the earl of Huntingdon's correspondents informed him on 27 April that several barges full of Quakers sailed down the Thames each day en route to ships that would transport them to the colonies. The numbers of transported Quakers would have been greater, but the demands of the Dutch War on shipping reduced the number of vessels available to transport them, and many sailors were afraid to risk divine wrath by carrying the Friends. One master deemed it unlawful to transport the Quakers without their consent, while the crew of the *Mary Fortune*, who were of the same mind, were also worried about a Barbados law that prohibited bringing anyone to the island against her or his will. In May 1665 Clarendon backed a proposal to utilize a ship captured from the Dutch to carry "the multitude of Quakers" in prison to the colonies. Finally, in late July and August 55 Quakers—18 of them women—were boarded on the *Black Eagle*. Again the sailors were opposed, and troops from the Tower of London had to be used to get most of the Friends aboard. By the time the ship reached the Downs, half the Quakers had died of the plague. The vessel was eventually captured by the Dutch, and the remaining Friends were liberated in the Netherlands.[55]

There are numerous instances of cruel or illegal treatment of Quakers. In 1664 the mayor of Reading and one of the justices dealt violently with them, pricking women with an instrument akin to a pack needle. Imprisoned in Bridewell for attending a London meeting, Esther Biddle was hit on the mouth and repeatedly pinched, while her son was kicked. For six months the mayor of Colchester had the militia use spiked clubs to beat Quakers who attended illegal services, and their coreligionists in Ireland were periodically assaulted. At Cork Solomon Eccles received at least eighty-seven lashes in 1670 on trumped-up charges of vagrancy, though his going naked as a sign in Galway city the previous year had resulted in no more than a few days in jail. Fifty-six Friends committed at Reading, most of them for fifteen weeks, should have appeared at the sessions under the terms of their mittimuses but were ignored in prison in 1664. That October twenty or thirty Quakers in London were sentenced without receiving the opportunity to plead, although some had wanted to do so. Twenty-two Friends interned in the Warwick jail on life sentences for *praemunire* had not been indicted, convicted, or sentenced in open court. Quaker tradesmen jailed in Cork in 1670 were not allowed to work in prison in order to support their families, and even children were incarcerated in that town the previous year. In 1667 the mayor of Cork had incited gangs of boys to ruin the wares of a Quaker shopkeeper.[56]

Nothing made the Quakers more vulnerable than *praemunire*, for the oath of allegiance could be administered virtually at will. Friends who brought food, drink, and clothing to colleagues in jail—or who simply visited—were sometimes tendered the oath and imprisoned when they refused. Six Quakers dining at a Warwick inn were jailed when they declined to take the oath. Between the fines and the imprisonment, many Quakers were hit hard economically, and only a sustained effort to collect relief funds by Friends at liberty enabled many to weather the persecution. At Reading the magistrates distrained the tools of some Quakers, causing them to lose their trades. Even relatively brief imprisonment during the planting and harvesting seasons was especially hard on farmers. Citing the insensibility of magistrates to law, equity, and mercy, Nottingham Friends accused the king and Parliament of making possible "the desolation of so many honest families" through the loss of grain, cattle, and household goods. Appealing to the government's own economic self-interest, they explained how, because of the persecution, they were no longer able to pay taxes, assist the indigent, or even pay rent.[57] In at least one instance, however, the Privy Council demonstrated some understanding: It transferred John Furly to Newgate prison for business reasons when two ships laden with wine arrived in England.[58]

The Quakers survived the persecution through the strength of their faith, the gradual forsaking of radical political causes in the 1660s, the development of an effective organization and systems of relief, and the espousal of an ethic of suffering. Careful records were kept of those who suffered, a practice in effect creating a Quaker martyrology akin to that of the earliest Christians.[59] Enough persons of substance donated money[60] to enable the Quakers not only to relieve their own needy but to begin constructing meetinghouses, an obvious sign that they had no intention of retreating from their confrontation with the state. By 1670 meetinghouses had been erected in such places as London, Falmouth, Whitby, and Chippenham, Wiltshire.[61]

Apart from their challenge to the ecclesiastical establishment, by the mid-1660s most Quakers were no longer political enemies of the state. As Fox's peace principle spread throughout the Quaker community in the early 1660s, it profoundly altered the movement. Had the Friends, with their radical religious beliefs, continued to embrace their 1650s militancy, the government would undoubtedly have had to repress them vigorously, and their future might have been no brighter than that of the Fifth Monarchists. But the Quakers' increasing willingness to suffer without resorting to seditious or combative behavior allowed the king to experiment with a policy of toleration—a policy also rendered feasible because they generally accepted monarchical government. To the extent that the authorities, particularly at the local level, continued to focus on the Friends rather than the militants scattered among the other nonconformist groups, they missed the mark.

Conflicting Courses: The Toleration Dispute

A combination of factors gave new hope to the nonconformists in 1667. With the end of the Dutch War there was less reason to suspect dissenters of plotting with the enemy, and the fire of London had shifted the animosity of some away from the dissenters to the Catholics, who were widely suspected of arson. Clarendon's dismissal in August breathed new life into the king's 1662–63 scheme for an indulgence. Throughout the last half of 1667 and into early 1668 expectations among nonconformists ran high, though the precise form of relief was a matter of uncertainty. The Presbyterians expected either comprehension or an indulgence, probably restricted to themselves alone, though possibly including Congregationalists as well. Other dissenters anticipated a statute establishing liberty of conscience. "It seems there is a great presumption," Pepys wrote in January 1668, "that there will be a Toleration granted."[62] Conservatives were appalled at the prospect. The specter of comprehension prompted one of Williamson's correspondents to sneer that "all the late fire-brands should be set on horseback, especially those that horsed themselves to join with the Dutch and French."[63] It was yet another manifestation of the old and not unfounded argument linking nonconformity with revolutionary politics.

John Owen, who had been arrested in 1665 for holding a conventicle in his house at Stadhampton, Oxfordshire, responded at length in 1667 to the charges linking nonconformist assemblies with seditious undertakings. Like the Quakers, he was careful to affirm both the king's authority and the willingness of Protestants to defend and assist the government, but he insisted that the kingdom could not be at peace as long as there was an attempt to make religious uniformity its foundation. The nonconformists, Owen insisted, had no intention of imposing a civil or ecclesiastical polity on the nation, nor did they claim the right to exercise power over other persons. "The utmost of our aim is but to pass the residue of our pilgrimage in peace." He repudiated all complicity in seditious conspiracies or ties to states with hostile designs on England; such plans could have no hope of success. Let those, he demanded, who contend that nonconformist assemblies "will be a means to procure and further sedition in the commonwealth, and to advantage men in the pursuit of designs to the disturbance of the kingdom" prove those assertions. The peace of the commonweal could never be endangered, he concluded, by schemes that were "managed by none but such as think to promote and carry them on in assemblies of promiscuous multitudes of men, women, and children; unknown, too, for the most part, unto themselves and to one another."[64]

Owen's plea for toleration was not welcomed by all nonconformists. To a conservative dissenter such as Richard Baxter, the "sin of separating principles" had been responsible for such evils as the corruption of the New Model Army, the upheavals in government between 1649 and 1660, the great ejection in 1662, and now, in 1670, "all this confusion." Throughout the 1660s Baxter and like-minded conservative nonconformists were concerned with finding a *modus vivendi* with conformity rather than with toleration, especially if the latter would benefit the Baptists, Quakers, and Fifth Monarchists.[65]

In *A Proposition for the Safety & Happiness of the King and Kingdom Both in Church and State* (1667), the Presbyterian John Humfrey proposed a moderate course that would include comprehension for "sober" nonconformists and indulgence for the others. For the conformists, Thomas Tompkins was quick to respond in *The Inconveniences of Toleration* (1667), but Humfrey retorted in a second edition of *A Proposition* (1667) and in *A Defense of the Proposition* (1668). The recognition by some Presbyterians of the right of other Protestant dissenters to enjoy religious freedom was welcomed in radical circles: They have "learned . . . by their deare bought Experience," wrote Ludlow, "that Jesus Christ . . . will have his Royal Law of doing unto others, as they would they should doe unto them, to be observed, and that they cannot enjoy their owne Liberty, unless they assist, or at least permit their Brethren & Neighbours to live in the Enjoyment of theirs."[66]

The debate over comprehension and toleration was an accompaniment to efforts in Parliament to procure some form of relief for dissenters. By the fall of 1667 the draft of a comprehension bill that included Presbyterians and possibly some Congregationalists had been completed by Sir Robert Atkins, but in the face of obvious hostility Colonel John Birch did not formally introduce it. In connection with a proposed proclamation to suppress masses and banish native-born priests, consideration was given to a declaration that would "leave some little door of hope to dissenting Protestants" in keeping with the king's wishes. One result of this may have been the Privy Council's directive of 10 December to Westmorland justices of the peace asking them for a list of prisoners, especially Quakers, with the justices' opinion as to which of them deserved the king's mercy and which were "ringleaders of faction." The following month the Quakers were encouraged because some Friends had been released.[67]

During January 1668 a group of moderates, including Sir Orlando Bridgeman, Dr. John Williams, and Sir Matthew Hale, worked with nonconformist leaders such as Richard Baxter, Thomas Manton, and William Bates to draft another comprehension bill. John Wilkins was also interested in toleration, and a bill to that end was prepared by John Owen. When conservatives, led by Archbishop Sheldon and Seth Ward, bishop of Salisbury, learned what was afoot, they launched a successful counterattack. In February the Commons petitioned the king for a proclamation to suppress conventicles, citing information from the counties—especially Staffordshire—

of illegal assemblies and the disruption of services conducted by conformist ministers. Issued on 10 March, the proclamation cited abuses of the recent clemency that had occurred while attempts were under way "for the better union of the Protestant Subjects," and ordered magistrates to be vigilant in executing the statutes against conventicles.[68]

In the Commons, debate raged during the spring over a new conventicle bill. The 1664 act was due to expire at the conclusion of the first parliamentary session subsequent to 17 May 1667 (three years after its passage); the relevant session was prorogued on 1 March 1669, at which point the statute expired. Efforts of dissenters and moderates to temper or delay the "very severe" bill in the Commons were largely unsuccessful despite a warning that nonconformists would be united by it against the government, whereas if left alone they would quarrel with each other. Although "that Act of violence," as one nonconformist called it, was approved by the Commons, the Lords gave it only a first reading.[69]

One of the strongest indictments of the bill came from the Congregationalist and former Cromwellian Nicholas Lockyer, who had been ejected as provost of Eton College, had preached clandestinely in London, and had spent some time as an exile at Rotterdam in the mid-1660s. He judged the proposed act null and void because it contravened Scripture, Magna Carta and other statutes, natural law, and the principle of prudence. On the last point he averred that it was "greatly imprudent to rise up against so considerable a part of the Nation as the Phanatique Interest certainly is," particularly because they played a major role in domestic and foreign trade. Experience has demonstrated, he argued, that persecution, instead of shaking the convictions of nonconformists, only increased their numbers. If the magistrates dispersed a conventicle of a thousand, twenty or thirty smaller but private ones would appear—and in circumstances conducive to plotting. If the state could impose the Book of Common Prayer now, in the future it would have the power to impose the Talmud or the Koran. Lockyer was incensed that the bill virtually ignored Catholics but "enjoyned, hired, and frighted" Protestants "to vex, disturb, prosecute, and ruine one another for worshipping God in their way." He was also angered by the proposed use of informers, which he considered tantamount to the sale of justice.

Legal authorities such as Sir Edward Coke and Sir Henry Finch were cited to buttress his arguments, and he reminded his readers that Edward II and Richard II had been dethroned for perverting the law, and that Richard Empson and Edmund Dudley had been executed for violating Magna Carta.[70] Lockyer thus mixed legal and providential arguments with radical rhetoric and even threats of sedition.

The proclamation of 10 March and the conventicle bill passed by the Commons elicited a response from the nonconformists, published anonymously as *A Few Sober Queries upon the Late Proclamation, for Enforcing Laws Against Conventicles* (1668). The author averred that England's many dissenters were loyal, sober, and industrious, but insisted that only God had the prerogative to rule consciences. If the English government could force Protestants to worship as the state directed, Catholic rulers would be justified in compelling their subjects to embrace popery.[71] With an eye to the state's economic problems, the author contended that liberty of conscience would encourage trade, ease the problem of scarce money, and facilitate London's recovery from the disastrous fire. Acknowledging that some nonconformists engaged in tumultuous gatherings, he nevertheless insisted that it was unjust to penalize all dissenters for the transgressions of some. Whatever the law, the saints, he maintained, would continue to hold their religious services because they had been divinely ordered to do so. Earlier that year, Yarmouth nonconformists had also pushed the economic argument, asserting that "the greatest charge upon the nation is defrayed" by the dissenters, "they being the major part, and the only men of estate, by whom the grand trade of the kingdom is chiefly managed." They also laid claim to be the best tenants of the gentry. The message was clear: Toleration was good business. In the House of Commons, however, the majority did not accept this argument, although in December 1668 the Council of Trade had embraced the principle that religious toleration was a crucial means to increase the nation's trade.[72]

Although the nonconformists had been temporarily embittered by the March proclamation, their spirits soon recovered. The apparent impunity with which dissenters were holding conventicles and constructing meetinghouses "much discourage[d] the Loyall party," though in many places the magistrates themselves contributed to the growth of nonconformist activity by easing enforcement. Various Northamptonshire justices "pretend that they meet with no encouragement above, and therefore resolve to let them [conventicles] & other fanaticks alone." Reports mounted of more frequent meetings of dissenters and a growing reluctance to prosecute them. "It is now become a generall policy," grumbled Daniel Fleming, "to comply with the nonconformists."[73] Margaret Fell's release in June 1668 especially encouraged the Quakers, and in August she began traveling in northern and western England on behalf of the Society. Newcastle dissenters were holding "very great meetings" in December, while at Bicester, Oxfordshire, a conventicle had more worshipers than the parish church. A Dover conformist complained in December of large numbers of seditious and unlawful meetings; "we are overrun with Schisme, and Faction." In April 1669 Sir Brian Broughton estimated that 2,000 people attended illegal services each Sunday in Staffordshire, with one at Wolverhampton drawing 340 and two at Walsall a total of 400. When magistrates arrested some conventiclers at Lichfield, other dissenters rescued them; a preacher at another Staffordshire conventicle similarly escaped, thanks to the women in his group. Coventry nonconformists had two large gatherings every Sunday in Leather Hall, where they "grow very preemptory, to the great discouragement of our Ministers."[74] When Sir Geoffrey Shakerley arrested the Presbyterian John Gartside at a conventicle of more than 200 at Bosley Chapel, Cheshire, some of the congregation resisted, "foule rayling Language" was used, and "som of the Chief of the female Disciples sayd openly that the King tollerated . . . theire meetings." In Hull, where dissidents spoke openly against the government, the number of conventicles—one of which was addressed by an unidentified Scot—was on the rise in the summer of 1669, but the magistrates largely ignored them.[75]

In the London area, where illegal gatherings were virtually irrepressible throughout the 1660s,[76] a government informer reported in March 1668 that some dissenters were almost in a militant mood. At a Southwark conventicle where Nathaniel Strange had been preaching, he found evidence only of "paper" designs by which the dissidents hoped "to gett that small number of old souldiers . . . for the cuting the eares of all government . . . with an endeavour to begett an evill oppinnion of parliaments." At Philip Nye's conventicle in Blue Anchor Alley, Old Street, a preacher from Herefordshire exhorted the people "to be allwayes in a readines to goe when he calles and not before he calls, and when he calls[,] then to seek by prudentiall pollicy to avoyd danger is the only way to be involved in danger." They must, he insisted, be "vallient for the Lord." Vavasor Powell was expected to preach there shortly.[77] Nye provided an important link among nonconformists in the London area, for in addition to his ties to the Fifth Monarchists he participated in the combination lecture at Hackney with his fellow Congregationalists John Owen, Peter Sterry, and Thomas Brooks, and the Presbyterians William Bates and Thomas Watson. Powell was also close to the Baptists Hanserd Knollys and William Kiffin, and the members of the late Henry Jessey's church. A government informer correctly reported that the dissenters were seeking greater unity, undoubtedly as a response to persecution.[78]

In the face of complaints from conservatives, Charles ordered an investigation of the conventicles and the suppression of those which endangered the peace or affronted established worship. Instructions were given to this end in April for Suffolk and Northamptonshire, and on 1 June for Totnes, Devon. He then authorized an inquiry into conventicles in every diocese, with instructions to the bishops to suppress them, if necessary with the assistance of justices of the peace. In response to a directive from the Privy Council, the judges suggested that conventiclers could be prosecuted for disturbing the peace, for recusancy, or for violating the Quaker Act. On 16 July Charles issued a proclamation directing justices of the peace to execute the laws against conventicles because dissenters were meeting "to such a degree as may endanger the publique peace." Arlington ordered the governors of Berwick, Carlisle, Hull, Plymouth, Portsmouth, and other garrisons to prosecute the conventicle ministers and their chief supporters as severely as the law allowed. Similar instructions were given to the lord lieutenant of Devonshire, with special attention to the town of Devon.[79]

The new crackdown gave dissenters pause in such places as Lincoln, Portsmouth, Southampton, and Northamptonshire. Some preachers fled to avoid imprisonment. In Chester only "the bold &

impudent 5th Monarchy people" continued to meet after the proclamation was published, although the strenuous efforts of Sir Geoffrey Shakerley had done much to subdue the dissenters by mid-July.
As recently as 5 July, however, Shakerley himself had complained that
they "assemble[d] in great Numbers, notwithstanding all endevours
used to the Contrary," and another observer reiterated the old charge
that they espoused "dangerous tenents [sic] & doctrine, tending to
sedition if not rebellion." In conjunction with the proclamation, the
arrest of Captain John Travers, a Baptist preacher in Chester, and a
Mr. Boden, "a pittifull broken butter Mercheant" who headed a conventicle at Congleton, temporarily curtailed the dissenters.[80]

In many places, however, the proclamation had little or no effect.
At Coventry dissenters temporarily stopped meeting in Leather Hall
but gathered elsewhere and derided the proclamation. By early August, however, Leather Hall was "as full as has bene knowne." In
Bristol, where a London nonconformist named Percy had arrived in
the spring and was already attracting more than 600 people, the
proclamation was ineffective. One minister was arrested, but he
"preacheth out of the grate to a numerous congregation." George
Fox and Margaret Fell were married in the city in October. The
Presbyterian William Lucke preached to so many people in York that
autumn that a customs collector was reminded of the conventicles
that preceded the 1663 rebellion.[81] Dissenters in Newcastle upon
Tyne were undaunted. On 1 November a group of some 500, calling
themselves "the Congregation of Saints," met in the Barber Sur-
geons' Hall under the leadership of the Congregationalist Richard
Gilpin. There they sang a metrical version of Psalm 149 with obviously militant overtones:

> And in their hands eke let them bear
> a double edged sword,
> To plague the heathen, and correct
> the people with their hands:
> To binde their stately kings in chains,
> their Lords in iron bands;
> To execute on them the doom
> that written is before:
> This honour all his Saints shall have,
> praise ye the Lord therefore.

Three other conventicles met in Newcastle, the leaders of which were the Congregationalist William Durant and the Presbyterians Henry Lever and John Pringle.[82]

Encouraged by supportive magistrates, Great Yarmouth dissenters met "in such numbers that they put feares into the peoples mindes." Those who complained, according to one loyalist, would lose their trades. The Congregationalist William Bridge had been invited to return in 1667 after nonconformists had won control of the town government the previous year, and other dissenting preachers came to minister as well. Feelings against the established church ran so high that people laughed and jeered during burial services using the Book of Common Prayer, and someone tore the prayers and thanksgiving for the king's restoration out of a copy of the Book. In January 1669, after refusing an offer from the deputy lieutenants not to prosecute him if he left Norfolk, Bridge was ordered by the quarter sessions not to come within five miles of Yarmouth. His departure, however, had only minimal impact on the Congregationalists, for in March they were drawing over a thousand persons to their services. When a copy of the king's proclamation against conventicles was posted in the town, it was ripped down the same day, and the dissenters continued to meet "in as great if not greater numbers than formerly." The Congregationalists, moreover, retained their contacts with exiles in the Netherlands. In few English communities were the nonconformists as defiant as in Great Yarmouth.[83]

In early 1670 reports were also received of increased conventicle activity in Cumberland, Westmorland, and Kent. Some Westmorland justices were refusing to prosecute, and there was an illegal assembly involving 200 Congregationalists in Kendal. According to the earl of Winchelsea, some of the illegal meetings in Kent were considerably larger—those of the Presbyterians and Congregationalists in Canterbury numbering more than 600 each, one of similar size at Sandwich, and another nearly that large at Dover; "they meet in those numbers to shew the world how considerable they are."[84] The ineffectiveness of the royal proclamation in many areas prompted hard-liners to renew their efforts to obtain another conventicle act when a new session of Parliament convened in February 1670.

The renewed attempts to suppress conventicles were accompanied by fresh accusations of seditious behavior, though substantive evidence was not provided, presumably because there was none. The charge to a Cheshire grand jury in October 1668 linked dissenters and Catholics as "the moles of our state and Government" because of their secret undertakings to disrupt the peace and unity of church and state. "These violent spirits and secret enemies yet remayninge amonge us . . . wayte onely an opportunity of settinge the whole Kingdome in a new flame." Toleration, in this view, would likely lead to another civil war. The archdeacon of Canterbury, Samuel Parker, gave a much wider voice to such arguments by including them in *A Discourse of Ecclesiastical Politie* (1669), and George Vernon, in an attack on John Owen's principles, argued that the dissenters were "the Incendiaries of humane Societies."[85]

In an interesting riposte to such views, Colonel Matthew Tomlinson, who had supported Ludlow in 1659, allegedly told conformists in Warwickshire that if dissenters did *not* receive religious liberty, "wee shoulde have a warr." But most nonconformists eschewed threats of violence, preferring instead to stress either their loyalty to the king or the economic benefits of liberty to tender consciences. Both arguments were embraced by Lord Wharton, who was convinced that a new conventicle act would force many industrious nonconformists to leave the country, giving foreigners a larger share of the commerce. More than sixty master clothworkers in the west— apparently Presbyterians—petitioned for religious liberty in the summer of 1669, threatening to leave England if it was not granted. Against this background Parliament again took up the nonconformist question in early 1670.[86]

A Nation in Turmoil: From the Second Conventicle Act to the Declaration of Indulgence

Archbishop Sheldon's 1669 survey, although incomplete, revealed the strength of nonconformity. Dissenters were estimated to number between 120,000 and 123,000, with at least 1,138 ministers, 1,234 conventicles, and 907 houses in which services were conducted. The greatest concentration, according to the returns, was in Somerset, Wiltshire, Buckinghamshire, and London. The returns demonstrated that the Presbyterians continued to be the largest group of

Protestant dissenters, roughly three times the size of the Congregationalists, and four times larger than the Baptists. But the usefulness
of the returns is undercut by several factors, not least their incom-
pleteness. There are no returns for four of the twenty-two English
dioceses: Hereford, Gloucester, Rochester, and Bristol. Returns
from dioceses such as Oxford, Peterborough, and Lincoln are partial, with nothing from the counties of Northamptonshire, Lincolnshire, Rutland, Herefordshire, Gloucestershire, Huntingdonshire,
and Cornwall. Moreover, prelates such as John Cosin of Durham
and Richard Sterne of Yorkshire were apparently reluctant to report
Protestant nonconformists in the face of a perceived threat from Catholicism. The accuracy of the reports was also affected by whatever
success the nonconformists had in keeping their meetings secret, and
by the care—or lack of it—that informers used in gathering and
submitting data. In sum, the figures reported in the returns under-
estimate the number of nonconformists and provide an imperfect
picture of their geographic distribution.[87]

   Unless new statistical evidence is discovered, any attempt to map
the geography of dissent must depend primarily on the list of nonconformist congregations compiled by John Evans mostly between
1715 and 1718. This list has been meticulously analyzed by Michael R.
Watts, who checked its figures against other sources and found it
reasonably reliable. By 1715, of course, Protestant dissent was tolerated, hence the overall size of the nonconformist community had
almost certainly increased. Watts estimates the number of nonconformist "hearers" to have been 338,120 in England and perhaps 18,000
in Wales, or approximately 6 percent of the population in each country. In England the Presbyterians were easily the largest group, with
179,350 "hearers," compared to 59,940 Congregationalists, 40,520
Particular Baptists, 18,800 General Baptists, and 39,510 Quakers.[88]

   Numerically the areas with most nonconformists were in the
southeast, notably Middlesex and London (33,220), Essex (18,080),
Surrey and Southwark (12,080), and Kent (11,150), but there were
also sizable numbers in the west, notably Devon (25,610), Somerset
(17,280), and Wiltshire (10,130). The northern counties with the most
nonconformists were Lancashire (20,270) and Yorkshire (18,460). If,
however, one estimates the strength of dissent by percentage of

population, a somewhat different picture emerges. Of the areas mentioned, only in Devon, Essex, and Lancashire were the dissenters more than 10 percent of the population, a figure also applicable to Monmouthshire, Hertfordshire, and especially Bristol, which at 19.60 percent had the highest concentration of nonconformists in the country. Dissenters constituted more than 8 percent of the population in Cheshire, Dorset, Northamptonshire, Somerset, and Wiltshire. Although the largest body of dissenters was in Middlesex and London, they amounted to only 5.72 percent of the population, or less than the national average of 6.22 percent. The shires where dissent was the weakest were in the far north, much of the west, Lincolnshire, and Cornwall. Although these conclusions are based on figures for the early eighteenth century, the pattern of nonconformist distribution they reflect is probably reasonably close to the situation that existed roughly fifty years earlier, though a comparison of the 1668 returns with Evans's figures suggests nonconformists may have doubled in size in this period. If so, one could hazard an estimate that dissenters constituted no more than 4 percent of the English population in 1670.

The majority in both houses of Parliament was sufficiently convinced of the nonconformist threat to push ahead with a conventicle bill notorious for its severity. John Owen again took up his pen in a final attempt to head it off, renewing the old argument that it was bad for the economy and would in any case persuade few to conform. Its real intent, he judged, was to prevent sedition and tumult, but how were such undertakings possible if nonconformist meetings were open to magistrates? Had the dissenters wanted to rebel, he argued, they could have done so during the recent outbreak of the plague or the Dutch War. Speaking to the bill's proviso to use informers to spy on conventicles, he castigated such persons as perjurers and "persons of ill fame and reputation, desperate in their outward fortunes, and profligate in their conversations, whose agency is a scandal unto them by whom they are employed." These views were shared by Lord Wharton, who warned that such an act would make nonconformists not only restless and fearful but useless to the kingdom.[89] He was also troubled by a provision in the bill that would allow a single justice of the peace sweeping powers of enforcement, an authority "greater than [that which] the judges and all the justices of the peace in England together now have or ever had" by virtue of the proposed authority to deprive citizens of their right to trial by a jury of their peers.[90]

As passed, the act (22 Car. II, c. 1), which went into effect on 15 May 1670, prohibited illegal religious meetings of five or more persons (excluding members of a single household gathered in their own residence). A solitary justice of the peace was given the power to convict—without trial—upon either a confession or the testimony of two sworn witnesses, subject to the right to a jury trial if the penalty exceeded 10s. The statute imposed a penalty of 5s. on a conventicler for the first offense, with the fine doubling for a second offense. The minister, however, was liable to a fine of £20 for his first offense and £40 for the second. If he fled or could not pay the fine, his hearers were liable to remit for him, though no conventicler was responsible for more than £10 of that amount. Persons who permitted illegal assemblies to be held in buildings they owned were subject to fines of £20 each. Magistrates were authorized to use force to enter buildings where conventicles were being held, but the homes of peers, if the latter were in residence, could not be searched without a royal warrant unless a lord lieutenant, his deputy, or two justices of the peace were present. For failing to prosecute conventiclers, justices of the peace could be fined £100 and lesser magistrates £5. The most controversial section of the act was undoubtedly the provision that rewarded informants with a third of the fines.[91]

Nonconformists responded to the act with predictable hostility, the Quaker Thomas Ellwood deploring it as "directly contrary to the fundamental laws of England, to common justice, equity, and right reason." Appealing directly to the king, John Lerie pointedly asked if the dissenters were "so Contemptible either for number or quality, as that you should reprove them after this manner, & divest yourselfe of their good will, which . . . you would faine returne afterwards but cannot!" The bishops and their party, he contended, were afraid that conventicles would be nurseries of sedition, when in fact plotting was more likely to occur in taverns, coffeehouses, bowling greens, and race tracks. In his judgment the Turks treated their Christian subjects better than the prelates wanted to deal with Protestant nonconformists. Ministers such as Adam Martindale refused to acknowledge that their services were conventicles, insisting that the latter were by definition meetings to conspire against the king and his government. By year's end a ballad was circulating that lamented freeborn subjects' loss of the birthright to follow their consciences, "and for recovery thereof incited all persons concern'd to take courage and use their swords." Some loyalists, in fact, were afraid that angry dissenters were fomenting another conspiracy.[92]

John Owen kept up a drumbeat of complaint about the restraints on Protestant dissenters, and in particular about the use of informers and the distraint of goods "without notice, warning, or summons, or any intimation of procedure against them." Such a process, he insisted, violated traditional procedures of criminal law, the "light" of nature, the laws of nations, and the citizen's natural right to "common presumptions of right and wrong." Informers were not only persons of obnoxious character but doubly offensive because they could not be cross-examined. As it was implemented in 1670–71, the act, Owen bitterly complained, was often accompanied in the London area with "so much rage and violence, profane swearing, and bloody menaces, as hath occasioned the terror and unspeakable damage of many." In short, the statute was legally, religiously, economically, and morally contemptible.[93]

As the act was implemented, the mood of nonconformists ranged from open belligerence to a quiet resolve to continue meeting, accepting whatever penalties were imposed. Among the latter group were the Presbyterian Thomas Manton (arrested in March for violating the Five-Mile Act), the Congregationalists John Owen and Thomas Goodwin, and the Particular Baptists Edward Harrison and John Tombes. But at a conventicle in Moorfields, London, on 24 April, an unnamed minister prayed, "Convert his [the king's] Evill Counsellours, O Lord, or else Destroy them. . . . Let there be Blood, o Lord; let the Land be coverd with Blood." Reflecting on such sentiments, one of Arlington's correspondents remarked, "Just thus the Trumpet sounded from the Pulpit before the last Rebellion." Again in London, the Baptist Nicholas Cox, a bag-mender from Northamptonshire, allegedly proclaimed that he would be hanged before he would submit to the new act; Charles, he proclaimed, was worse than Nebuchadnezzar because his approval of the act willfully brought violence "upon his owne head." He and his friends, he boasted, would "be true to king Jesus the king of all kinges in this cause of the Lords batell in the gosphell." Guards were posted at nonconformist meetinghouses, services were disrupted, and fines imposed on London conventiclers, prompting the Presbyterian Philip Henry to reflect in his diary on "the noise of war amongst them in time of peace."[94]

Some loyalists were extremely wary of the potentially violent implications that they thought they saw in nonconformist sermons, "pretended Religion being the Refuge under which the worst adversaries of our Roiall kingly goverment doth dayly hide their wicked designs: their very expositions of the Scriptures doth declare their inward intent." Jittery London magistrates briefly imprisoned the Presbyterians Thomas Watson and Thomas Vincent on charges of treason for preaching on Hebrews 12:4—"Ye have not yet resisted unto blood, striving against sin." When the Congregationalist Nathaniel Partridge spoke on Judges 3–7, he compared the children of Israel to the dissenters, and their enemies to the conformists. Such preachers, opined one of Arlington's informers, were not content to attack the king's crown and dignity, but "would gladly smite of[f] his head." At Bell Lane, near Spitalfields, the Seventh-Day-Baptist John Belcher preached on Isaiah 52:2—"Shake thyself from the dust; arise, and sit down, O Jerusalem: loose thyself from the bands of thy neck"—which he interpreted to mean "Arise o Jerusalem, and obey neither prince nor prelate but shake of[f] thy dust till thou sitt downe in peace."[95]

Other areas reported similar unrest. Dissenters in the north, noted Sir Philip Musgrave, were irate at the new act and uttered "bigg words." In Westmorland the Friends were allegedly threatening any who attempted to disrupt their meetings. When the Quaker Thomas Faron was apprehended for illegally preaching at Whitby, Yorkshire, another Friend "laid violent hands" on the arresting magistrate in an unsuccessful attempt to help Faron escape, while others in the group reportedly spoke seditiously. Charges of seditious or treasonable speech were also levied against other nonconformists, including John Bunyan's associate Nehemiah Cox (who was found not guilty but fined for attending a conventicle). At Dover a Baptist preacher exhorted some 200 conventiclers "to stand fast & be not afraid of the wicked," to which one of the sectaries responded that he would "sacrifice his Life for itt [the gospel] & seal itt with his blood." There was an expectation of deliverance in the near future; "this is their tyme now," said a Wiltshire dissenter, "but 'twill not hold soe long."[96]

In the end the nonconformists did not rebel, though many did their best to frustrate the implementation of the statute. Mostly this was done by hindering the distraint of dissenters' goods. When, for example, authorities distrained the possessions of the Quaker Edward Billing, no one would purchase them when they were put up for sale—a pattern repeated in many places. Taking advantage of the act's failure to authorize magistrates to break into locked buildings to distrain goods, Cheshire and Yorkshire nonconformists transferred possession to others before the officials could seize their property. As a result, Shakerley complained, it was impossible to make substantive levies.[97] Nonconformists at Whitby, Yorkshire, constructed a meetinghouse after the act was passed but refused to acknowledge ownership in order to evade the £20 fine on owners of houses in which conventicles were held. When the mayor of Worcester vigorously prosecuted dissenters, he received an anonymous threatening letter, probably from a nonconformist. Dissenters in the parish of All Saints, Sudbury, Suffolk, evaded the statute by holding services in the parish church, which had had no minister for five or six years. The Quakers generally followed their usual course of open defiance of the law by holding meetings at their customary times and places, but they refused to pay fines and jail fees, "the wages of unrighteousness," or to admit who owned the buildings in which they gathered. When magistrates locked the doors of their meetinghouses, they met in the streets.[98]

The heart of the struggle against the new statute was fought in the London area. Nonconformists poured into the capital in the spring of 1670, "knowing that if Conventicles may be prevented in London, they must of necessity lay downe in the Country." According to the lord mayor, on just one Sunday in May 1670 some 12,000 people were at conventicles. One of Arlington's informers cited ten conventicles in one parish alone, including one of more than 200 people where Nathaniel Partridge preached, and two others twice that size where Francis Smith the bookseller and Thomas Doolittle were the "teachers."[99] The lord mayor, Sir Samuel Sterling (or Starling), and the governor of the Tower, Sir John Robinson, took up the challenge. The mayor was authorized to call up the trained bands, which would be used on Sundays and holy days in conjunction with the normal watch "to Rowte all the publique meetings." Two companies were also used to guard the Exchange every night. On 28 May Charles instructed the militia commissioners and field officers of the regiment to search for and arrest dangerous persons and to confiscate their weapons. Even the royal guards were used. In June the king issued a proclamation ordering ex-Cromwellian officers and soldiers out of London for six months, a device previously utilized at peak periods of radical plotting.[100] The government was unmistakably concerned about a recurrence of militant activity.

The effectiveness of these measures was a matter of dispute. According to Sir John Trevor, a principal secretary of state, the situation was very dangerous in late May because the informers and constables were too terrified to act, and the trained bands were reluctant to suppress the dissenters by force. There had been some success, he opined, in breaking up smaller meetings, but three large Presbyterian gatherings involving 3,000 or 4,000 people refused to disperse. Trevor was frankly concerned that if the government directed the royal guards to break up these conventicles by force, "the people universally will bee engaged in the defense," a situation that would lead to bloodshed. But Trevor had been opposed to the act in the first place, and may have been unduly quick to stress the dangers of enforcement.[101]

Robinson, who was intimately involved in the assault on the conventicles, repeatedly expressed his approval of the campaign, though at first he was dissatisfied with the constables and headboroughs. In fact, he complained on 12 June that these officials refused to provide him with information on the conventicles. Both he and the lord mayor, however, had their own informants. Other observers were impressed with the headway made by magistrates in reducing illegal assemblies. As the result of his efforts on 28 and 29 May, Robinson boasted that he had "brooke[n] all the meetings that are considerable in the Citty"; hence peace would soon be restored. "I am confident," he declared, that the dissenters "have a greate Terror upon them, and am confident in a short time [they] will vanish."[102] His satisfaction was premature.

Initially the campaign in the London area made some progress. For preaching at conventicles on 15 and 22 May, fines of £20 each were imposed on eight men, including the Quakers George Fox, William Warwick, and John Burnyeat, and the Congregationalists Anthony Palmer and Seth Wood.[103] The Particular Baptist William Kiffin had been arrested on the 15th; according to Robinson he had been active in the Exchange every day "to promote sedition . . . rebellion and Treason." Although the Presbyterian Samuel Annesley was one of the first to be fined under the new act, his congregation continued to meet. Baptist preachers such as William Reynolds, Thomas Barber, and Henry Russell refused to take the oaths of allegiance and supremacy, and were incarcerated in Newgate or the Tower. Key Particular Baptists such as Edward Harrison and Hanserd Knollys were arrested in the summer. "With a strawe," Robinson exulted, "a man may tumble one of the biggest of them downe." Despite such efforts, one of Williamson's informers reported on 25 July that the dissenters were still meeting in the streets "& doe persist in disobedience with moor Ardent Resolutions then heeretofore." They hoped, he later wrote, "of some strange Catastrophe, or sudden Change."[104]

By 1671 the battle of London was essentially a stalemate, though in the Tower hamlets Robinson was somewhat more successful. The Friends remained irrepressible, even when locked out of their meetinghouses. Quakers whom Robinson caught preaching—among them William Penn—were interned in Newgate for six months. Although he had no success with the Quakers, the lord mayor continued to warn other dissenters, including the Presbyterian Nathaniel Vincent, to cease preaching or face further prosecution. The big coup of 1671 was the arrest of Fifth Monarchists meeting illegally in the parish of St. Sepulchre's during the summer; among them were four leaders of the movement: John Belcher, Arthur Squibb, Richard Goodgroom, and John Jones. Each of the four refused the oath of allegiance and was imprisoned in the Tower.[105]

One of the techniques used against the dissenters, especially in the London area, was the removal of the pulpits and pews from their churches or the confiscation of their meetinghouses as replacements for parish churches destroyed by the great fire. A number of these buildings had been erected after the conflagration by enterprising nonconformists. In June the Privy Council authorized the removal of pulpits and pews from nonconformist meetinghouses in London, Bristol, and other places, and also gave the surveyor-general, Christopher Wren, the right to seize and refit such buildings in London, Westminster, and Southwark for Church of England worship.[106] Eight meetinghouses were confiscated in June, including those used by Seth Wood, Thomas Vincent, Thomas Doolittle, and Thomas Watson. The earliest services in several of these buildings drew sizable crowds, including some who had attended conventicles; this suggests that some of those attracted to nonconformist preachers were simply searching for inspiring sermons.[107] In several instances, as at Mile End and at Horsleydown in Southwark, meetinghouses were dismantled. When the lord mayor discovered that imprisoning Edward Harrison did not discourage his followers from gathering in Petty France, he threatened to pull their chapel down.[108]

Outside the London area the persecution of dissenters, which Sheldon's biographer has called "the most effective . . . in the whole period," was no more productive in most places than in the capital. In Bristol the nonconformists scoffed at the efforts of the mayor, Sir Robert Yeamans, and his fellow magistrates to implement the act. Altogether the dissenters outnumbered the loyalists and "implyed threates" against the magistrates who enforced the law. The tenor of nonconformist speech troubled one loyalist: "They speake strangely but not positively very hard words, which the strictures of lawe calls not Treason yet I thincke it to bee Treason in parables." They also contended that the act violated the ancient laws. New doors were cut in their meetinghouses to facilitate escape, and the Broadmead church protected its minister by having him preach from an adjoining house through a freshly cut window. Officials seized the Quakers' meetinghouse in Bristol, but four times the Friends broke open the doors; sixteen Quakers were imprisoned, but the rest continued to convene in the streets. After threatening the churchwardens, overseers, and constables with charges of negligence, Yeamans and the aldermen finally got their assistance in distraining the goods of dissenters, although no one would purchase them. On 10 September Yeamans reported to Arlington that the nonconformists were being vigorously prosecuted, but another loyalist admitted that the magistrates "cannot suppresse them by reason of theyre many trickes & evasions & meetinge out of the Libertyes of the Citty."[109]

In Devon, magistrates at Exeter had tried in 1669 to suppress conventicles, some of which numbered in excess of 100 or 200 people. After the implementation of the Conventicle Act Bishop Sparrow told Sheldon that they had almost disappeared, although in the November quarter sessions twenty-one dissenters were fined for meeting illegally. Quakers in Cornwall, refusing to submit, met on the beaches, but the Presbyterians tended to gather only in groups of four or five to avoid prosecution.[110]

If Devon and Cornwall were reasonably quiet, untypically large conventicles in Wiltshire began to resemble those in Scotland. In part, the problem was due to the fact that many of the magistrates were sympathetic to the nonconformists or were dissenters themselves. John Eyre, a justice of the peace, fined a number of them in the summer of 1670. Presbyterians attracted as many as 1,000 or 2,000 to some of their services, which were often held in "by Corners . . . in Woods & somtimes on the very Edges of Counties or Hundreds." The largest meetings were at North Bradley near the Somerset border, though the Presbyterians also drew 1,200 to nearby Westbury and 1,000 to Winkfield; this was really the same group, which periodically moved to evade arrest. The Baptists were less numerous, but attracted as many as 400 to North Bradley. Armed conventiclers in both Wiltshire and Somerset used their weapons to prevent arrest. A Presbyterian couple boldly defied the magistrates, asserting that "your lawes are the Devills lawes, and you serve the Devill in doeing this, and the Devill . . . will paie you your wages." A Somerset clothier was even ruder, boasting that "if I had the [Conventicle] Act heere I would wipe my Arse with it," while another man asked a magistrate "what Just Ass of Peace . . . sent you?"[111] Other Presbyterians and Baptists, when told of the statute, retorted that "the King is but the Prince of the Ayre." The Quakers in the region were no less resolute in their determination to meet. To avoid the high fines, some dissenters leased their houses and lands while renting simple cottages, making it difficult for officers to distrain more than £5 worth of goods. Others resorted to the "use," a form of trust, in order to protect their property. When the bishop of Salisbury launched an investigation into the state of affairs in western Wiltshire in September 1670, the local justices protested that the reports of conventicles had been exaggerated, but a mere six days later they had to acknowledge another illegal assembly of some 2,000 persons at which two men spoke treasonably against the king and government.[112] The justices had trouble with constables and churchwardens, who were "more Ready to perjure themselves then to give trew presentments." Because these conventicles drew people from Somerset, they could not be stopped without the support of magistrates in that county, but many of the justices there were unwilling "to disoblige so considerable a partie."[113]

Repeated efforts to disperse Baptists and Presbyterians in Dover had no lasting impact, perhaps because Watson, the mayor in 1670, "weenks att all Conventickles." When other officials implemented the law, the Baptists hindered them by closing their shops and locking their houses, making it difficult to arrest the offenders or distrain their goods. A new mayor in 1671 was more willing to act, in part by removing the pulpit and pews from the Baptist chapel in January, but two days later the Baptists broke into the locked building and held another service. Meanwhile, the Presbyterians were sufficiently numerous to prevent the magistrates from entering their building during a service.[114]

Nonconformists in Great Yarmouth proved especially difficult to control, particularly because they enjoyed the support of such magistrates as Thomas Ravens, an alderman and son-in-law of William Bridge, and Richard Huntington, a justice of the peace and former officer in the parliamentary forces. Meetings were sometimes held on two islands—Lovingland, where they used Ravens's house, and Cobham, the jurisdiction over which was disputed between Yarmouth and Suffolk. In the town itself the dissenters met in a house belonging to Major William Burton, whom the magistrates could not fine because he was an exile in the Netherlands. Among those who preached in Yarmouth were Nathaniel Carter, arrested in June 1670, and Francis English, ejected rector of St. Laurence, Norwich, who attracted between 400 and 500 to a conventicle that summer; sympathetic magistrates declined to prosecute those who attended. Suppressing illegal assemblies was complicated by the fact that "the factious here are so numerous and eminent in trade, that the rest generally depend upon them." Nevertheless, by December 1670 the unrelenting efforts of a churchwarden to prosecute recusants— efforts that included complaints to the Privy Council—temporarily cooled the nonconformists' ardor.[115]

Some success was also enjoyed at Coventry, where on the eve of the act it had been possible to hear as many as six or seven noncon- formist sermons each Sunday. In the aftermath of the act, however, large conventicles were no longer held at Leather Hall, and in gen- eral fewer public ones convened elsewhere. It proved impossible to suppress the private ones.[116] This was also true of the west, though conventicles were prosecuted at Whitchurch, Middlewich, Manches- ter, and especially Chester. In the latter, dissenters were so deter- mined to meet that some were arrested twice in the same day. The moving force in Chester was still Sir Geoffrey Shakerley, but he con- tinued to have difficulty with local officials, some of whom declined to imprison dissenters despite the fact that they refused to take the oath of allegiance.[117] According to one loyalist, the Conventicle Act "so Exasperated" Derbyshire nonconformists "that if anything may be gaithered from the Languadge[,] behavor or the Angrey Looke of them, the[y] threaten nothing but a suddan Insurection" and complain of the great misery that has plagued England at the hands of the Stuarts.[118]

One of the most disaffected places in the north was Hull, where again a sympathetic mayor and his colleagues abetted the noncon- formists. Of greater concern were the "great disturbances" in the garrison occasioned by "seditious meetings in Conventicles" dur- ing the absence of Colonel Anthony Gilby in May 1670. The dissent- ers ceased meeting publicly but continued to gather in private, especially while magistrates watched London to ascertain how vig- orously nonconformists would be punished in the capital. In the meantime, the Presbyterians—estimated by one royalist, with exag- geration, to constitute two-thirds of the city's population—received letters from friends in London that "tell how high their partey are with them, despising the Lawes against them: and speaking openly against [the] government." Nevertheless, by early August the dis- senters' meetings were less frequent, and during the autumn there was speculation that "the Rabble will fall of themselves" when some of the more prominent dissenters drifted away. The city subsequently remained quiet.[119]

Elsewhere in Yorkshire the justices in the Whitby area demonstrated little interest in conventicles, so that during one seven-day period in May 1670 it was possible for the dissenters to hold eight meetings, some with as many as 300 persons, with people traveling as much as forty miles to attend. "The Egg of the Cockatrice must be broken," Sir Thomas Gower insisted. Contempt for the law, even in small matters, could have ill consequences: "If this opposition be not crushed at the very first, it will beget, & nurse up, bold, rather insolent disobedience in others, & at last in all thinges & by degrees shake the foundations of Law, duty & Loyalty." When Sir Philip Musgrave visited Yorkshire in June, he too commented on the "obstinacy" of the nonconformists. Conventicles at Shadwell, north of Leeds, were so numerous that a party of horse had to be dispatched from York to suppress them; it found more than 300 persons in a small chapel.[120] Quakers, of course, were a continuing problem in the north, although some Friends in Westmorland, faced with large fines, began attending their parish churches. Daniel Fleming was imposing fines of 12*d.* for each Sunday they missed in the belief that "a great part of their religion . . . is tyed to their purs-strings." By November 1671 the policy was successful enough to enable him to report that the conventiclers were "pretty quiet," though still meeting. As long as they posed no threat to the public peace, he was willing to impose fines only occasionally—just enough to remind dissenters that the act was still in force.[121]

Despite partial successes, the policy of persecution was bankrupt by 1672. At best, statutes could prevent large public conventicles, but as the nonconformists themselves pointed out, antigovernment plotting was far more likely to occur in small private meetings. Moreover, the 1670 Conventicle Act was so unpopular among some of the country's "natural rulers" that it undermined the very unity it was designed to achieve. The specter of some magistrates winking at or even violating the statute was corrosive to the fundamental notion of a society governed by law. Those officials who embarked on a policy of rigorous enforcement soon had to back off as prisons filled and fines became increasingly difficult to collect. The necessity of using troops to disperse conventicles opened up the possibility not only of soldiers' beating citizens but of dissent within the garrisons, as happened at Hull. Moreover the persecution of nonconformists cannot have been conducive to the maintenance of a strong economy, nor did much of the money raised through fines reach the Exchequer until the 1680s; from 1660 to 1667 total receipts amounted only to £147 15s. 7d.; in contrast, the amount soared to £6,000 in the year 1682–83. Nevertheless the ideal of religious uniformity, so firmly rooted in the medieval past, was far from dead in 1672.[122]

The story behind the declaration of indulgence, to which Charles affixed the royal seal on 15 March 1672, is too well known to need recounting here. The motives stemmed largely from considerations of foreign policy, yet the declaration was also a natural outgrowth of the king's long-standing interest in some form of indulgence.[123] The declaration indicated that seditious conventicles would not be tolerated, but Charles was willing to distinguish between peaceful nonconformist assemblies and meetings devoted to the overthrow of church or state. Licensing was the key: Authorities would know which nonconformists could legally preach and where. In effect the government would establish a master register of all dissenting ministers and their meetinghouses—a bureaucratic coup perfectly conformable with an absolute state, if that was what Charles wished. Religious uniformity was unattainable, but the government could at least know precisely who the nonconformist ministers were and where their congregations met. Surveillance, to whatever degree it was necessary, would be vastly simplified. Those who registered, moreover, could in all likelihood be regarded as tolerably loyal to the state, thus leaving officials free to concentrate on the rest—those, said Dr. Nicholas Butler, "whose wild principles suffer them not to accept this act."[124]

Most nonconformists responded with joy, some even sending addresses of thanks to the king.[125] In Bedfordshire John Bunyan's congregation and four other churches—Keysoe, Cranfield, Stevington, and Newport Pagnell—implemented a carefully conceived plan to provide a network of preachers and teachers throughout northern Bedfordshire and the contiguous areas strong enough to withstand further persecution, should that materialize.[126] Other areas seem to have developed similar organizational schemes. This was not so much a campaign of resistance as an attempt to organize so carefully at the local level that any future attempt to repress dissent would fail. Such organization also made services of worship readily accessible under the direction of "teachers" in numerous villages throughout the land. These local units or cells could in turn monitor the lives of the godly and exhort them to steadfastness in the faith. At root, however, there was nothing surreptitious or seditious about such organizing tactics, particularly since the houses of worship as well as the teachers and preachers were registered with the government and the meetings open to all.

The strength, zeal, and organizational ability so clearly manifested among nonconformists in 1672 was eloquent testimony of how much Sheldon's policy of uniformity had failed. Many conformists were shocked. Sir John Reresby denounced the declaration as "the greatest blowe that ever was given, since the King's restoration, to the Church of England."[127] Daniel Fleming found all of the assize judges at Lancaster displeased; in general that was the reaction of conformists. Altogether licenses were procured by 939 Presbyterians, 458 Congregationalists, and 210 Baptists.[128] In the more tolerant atmosphere of 1672, the hard-core nonconformist community in England and Wales, with Quakers included, must have exceeded 150,000—far too many to coerce into conformity or to risk provoking to militancy, given the limited military force at the king's disposal and the lack of significant public support for such a policy. The actual potential, once the threat of persecution had been lifted, was probably two or three times that number. The trials of nonconformity were far from over, but the battle for survival had been won.

"The True Englishmen's Complaints"

─────────── ▰▰▰ F I V E ▰▰▰ ───────────

The Radical Press, 1664–1672

In January 1664 Sir Henry Bennet predicted that "the *Press* and the *Pen* is beginning as hot a War upon us as if they intended speedily to follow it with the *Sword*." Although the only rebellion to materialize was the 1666 Galloway uprising in Scotland, the radical press in both England and Scotland remained active throughout the period, especially in the London area and among the exiles in the Netherlands. It built not only on the substantial heritage of radical publications from the 1640s and 1650s but on the more than 300 allegedly treasonous and schismatic books that a government spokesman reckoned had been published between 1660 and 1663. In April 1664 the *Intelligencer* reported that the number of publications in the latter category had jumped to 460.[1] Illegal publications continued to inflame discontent with the Stuart regime and, in Scotland in particular, to create a literature of martyrdom honoring Covenanters who suffered in the 1660s, including the executed Galloway insurgents. The government's efforts to crush the radical press were no more effective than its campaign against conventicles; the latter, in fact, were a principal means through which illegal and sometimes seditious literature was disseminated. The state's difficulty in distinguishing between peaceful nonconformists and militant dissidents thus contributed to its inability to suppress the underground press.

The Radical Press in England

Roger L'Estrange's crusade against dissident printers and publishers in the early 1660s had led to the trial in February 1664 of John

Twyn, Simon Dover, Thomas Brewster, and Nathan Brookes. Convicted of high treason for printing *A Treatise of the Execution of Justice*, Twyn was executed the same month, and Dover and Brewster died in prison in April. Two other key figures in the underground press were also in jail in early 1664: Livewell Chapman, who had been arrested on 24 November 1663, was released the following May after posting a bond of £300 and agreeing that neither he nor his wife, Hannah, would print, publish, or disperse illegal books. Twice imprisoned in 1663, Elizabeth Calvert was released from the Gatehouse in April 1664, but only after her son, "the staffe and support of her age," had died.[2] It might have seemed, then, that in early 1664 the government was on the verge of smashing the underground press. Indeed, before the year was out, Livewell Chapman had died. Yet the radical press survived because of the dedication of widows such as Elizabeth Calvert and Joan Simon as well as the care taken to train apprentices who kept the presses operating.

In the aftermath of Twyn's trial, the campaign against allegedly seditious writers, printers, and booksellers resumed in the spring of 1664. L'Estrange obtained a warrant on 17 March to arrest the Congregationalist John Goodwin. The latter had sought anonymity in Bethnal Green, but because he was a celebrated—or notorious—Arminian there had been "a continuall recourse of persons of all sorts" to his house. Secretary Bennet issued a general warrant to L'Estrange on 24 May to arrest authors, printers, binders, publishers, and sellers of unlicensed publications.[3] Specific warrants followed to search the houses and warehouses of thirty-one printers and publishers, some of whom had previously been in trouble. On the list were Colonel John Streater, a suspect in the 1661 Presbyterian plot who had been arrested again in March 1663 in connection with his printing; Peter Lillicrap, apprehended the same year for printing the 1662 farewell sermons; Thomas Leach, arrested as he was about to print accounts of the regicides' trials; Thomas Johnson and Richard Hodgkinson, sought in 1663 in connection with illegal publications; and John Darby (or Derby), arrested for printing *The Poor Whore's Petition*, which satirized the king and Lady Castlemaine. Darby was wanted, with his wife and John Gaines (or Gain, Gayne), in May 1664 for seditious practices. Three of the thirty-one were women: Elizabeth Cotes, Sarah Griffin, and Mary Simmons (or Symons). By 23 July L'Estrange calculated that government agents had seized copies of approximately 130,000 pamphlets and books in the latest crackdown.[4]

The campaign against the radical press inevitably included efforts to identify and suppress printers and publishers of Quaker literature. An undated document from this period in the Public Record Office purportedly identifies forty-three dispensers of Quaker books in England and one in Ireland. Tracking Quaker printers and publishers was rendered more difficult because they generally did not include the printers' names in their works, though one exception was the publication of Richard Hubberthorne's *Works* in 1663 by William Warwick. The latter, identified as a major seller of Quaker publications, was arrested in London in July 1664. Among the London printers who published Quaker material in this period was Simon Dover's widow, Joan, who issued *Englands Warning: or, Englands Sorrow for Londons Misery* (London, 1667) at Benjamin Furly's request. It was a catalogue of sins, such as blasphemy, drunkenness, and whoredom, for which God supposedly punished London with the great fire. Dover also brought out *The Jury-Man Charged; or, a Letter to a Citizen of London* (London, 1664), in which the author, identified only as H.E., argued that Friends and others were not guilty of disobeying the Conventicle Act unless they were demonstrably seditious or wicked. Samuel Simmons published William Bayly's *Pure Encouragements from the Spirit of the Lord* [1664], in which the Quakers were compared to the Hebrews as the latter were driven by the pharaoh into the Red Sea; "the Lord," insisted Bayly, "is on our side." John Redman (or Redmayne) issued Richard Farnworth's *Christian Religious Meetings Allowed by the Liturgie, Are No Seditious Conventicles, Nor Punishable by the Late Act* (1664). In it Farnworth contended that "if the Liturgie do allow of meeting together, according to the Scripture, then they who meet together according to Scripture, are no seditious Sectaries, neither is their religious meetings seditious Conventicles, or punishable by the said Act." This argument was buttressed by the assertion that the Quakers in any case were not the intended target of the Conventicle Act because their meetings were not a cover for seditious conspiracies.

Another widow, Mrs. Jennans, brought out William Smith's *A Book to the Judges and Jury*.[5]

The search for illegal publications extended into the counties. Sixty allegedly seditious books were confiscated at Ipswich, Suffolk, in May, the same month that the rector of Stoke Hammond, Buckinghamshire, alerted authorities to Benjamin Keach's *The Child's Delight: or Instructions for Children and Youth*. Keach, the pastor of a General Baptist church at nearby Winslow, attacked paedobaptism and espoused lay preaching and millenarian tenets in his primer. He was briefly imprisoned, fined £20, and pilloried at Aylesbury and Winslow. Although the common hangman burned the primer, Keach rewrote it, and by 1763 it had gone through thirty editions. Pamphlets and leaflets attacking the Church of England "& otherwise seditious" were seized in June from William Watchers, a tailor at Cranbrook, Kent, who was selling them for a halfpenny a sheet. This did not, however, stem the flow of radical publications in Kent.[6]

In January 1664 the government uncovered links between the underground press in the London area and dissidents in Gloucester. Officials confiscated four boxes of purportedly seditious papers and pamphlets being shipped from William Thompson in London to one Hodgkins in Gloucester. Examining the material, one magistrate recognized the style of Ralph Wallis, formerly of Gloucester but now residing in London. When the correspondence between Wallis and his wife, Elizabeth, who still lived in Gloucester, was tapped, the government learned that he had completed several publications and had others ready for the press. Funds to support his work were being raised by the Scottish Congregationalist James Forbes, who had been ejected as preacher at Gloucester Cathedral; a friend of Anthony Palmer, Forbes now supported himself as a shoemaker in Clapham and Hackney.[7] Warrants for Wallis's arrest were issued on 12 May and 20 June, though he seems not to have been apprehended until September, when Forbes was also arrested. Bennet also dispatched a warrant to Gloucester aldermen authorizing them to search for seditious books and papers in the houses of Elizabeth Wallis, the bookseller Tobias Jordan, the apothecary William Jordan, and Edward Eckly. Copies of the *Sufferers-Catechism* and other allegedly seditious books were discovered in Forbes's study, but he claimed not to have read them or to have any knowledge of how they got there. Wallis admitted having written *Good News from Rome, The Honour of a Hangman*, and *More News from Rome or Magna Charta, Discoursed of Between a Poor Man and His Wife*. In the spring of 1665 Wallis was back in Gloucester, publicly selling his popularly acclaimed works.[8]

More News from Rome, composed in the form of a dialogue between a husband and wife, demanded that "all *Romes* Remnants, Reliques, Rites, &c. now in use in the Church of *England* . . . [be] sent to Hell, from whence they came." Wallis chided "the *Prelatical Cat* and the *Romane Rat*" for sitting as "lovingly close together as might be, without any Schism or Clashing," and satirized "the *Rats* or Cu-Rats" who were ordered by their superiors "to Pottage them well over whatever they do." The Church of England, he claimed, lacked a biblical foundation, whereas Convocation had a Roman constitution. He was especially scathing in his denunciation of those who altered their religious principles so easily in order to retain their ecclesiastical positions: "There is but the breadth of the shears between the *Priest* and the *Taylour*, the one turns a Coat *to get a Living*, the other turns a Coat *to save a Living*." Wallis also made a point of denying the right of magistrates to compel obedience in religious matters.[9]

The anonymous *Sufferers-Catechism* portrayed nonconformists as disciples and servants of Christ who must expect persecution. Although the author did not suggest taking militant action against persecuting rulers, he made it clear that Christians were duty-bound to disobey any commands that contravened God's word. Civil magistrates, he contended, had no right to bind consciences. Although Charles was not explicitly named, it was obvious that the author categorized him with such other persecutors as Nimrod, Nebuchadnezzar, Darius, Nero, and Ahab. As models of suffering Christians he cited the Elizabethans Henry Barrow, John Greenwood, and John Penry.[10]

Contacts also existed between the underground press in London and dissidents in Yorkshire. Early in 1665, copies of Captain Roger Jones's *Mene Tekel* (1663), the printing of which had cost Twyn his life, and George Wither's *New Year's Gift* were circulating in the north, probably owing at least in part to the efforts of John Atkinson. The latter work may have been the broadside *A New-Years-Gift for Papists*, the earliest surviving copy of which was printed in 1667; it was reissued a decade later by Langly Curtis, whose first known publication was an anti-Quaker polemic by Nathaniel Smith entitled *The Quakers Spirituall Cort Proclaim'd* (London, 1669). Atkinson was in any case responsible for sending copies of *Mene Tekel* to the north.[11] When Richard Walker was arrested in Bradford that spring on suspicion of plotting against the state, he had a number of suspicious publications in his possession that he had obtained from Joseph Walley, a London bookseller with strong ties to the nonconformists. They included *Murther Will Out*,[12] copies of which had been found in Simon Dover's shop in October 1663; an attack on clerical turncoats entitled *Covenant-Renouncers Desperate Apostles* (1665); a manuscript containing predictions "tending to sedition" for the year 1665 by Jan Comenius; and assorted letters using aliases that accused the king and Privy Council of fostering popery. One of the magistrates who jailed Walker suspected that he was associated with two 1663 northern rebels, David Lumbey and Simon Butler, both of whom had escaped; Walker, however, refused to confess. For his part, Walley admitted that he had been in Yorkshire in July 1664, that he had sold Bibles to Walker in London, and that the other books had been obtained from the Quaker Martin Grocer in Newgate prison. Walley also confessed that he had written one of the letters Walker was carrying to William Marshall and others in York; in August 1662 Marshall had published the High Commission's examination of Barrow, Greenwood, and Penry.[13]

Still in the north, in August 1665 the authorities arrested Henry Darley and imprisoned him at York when they found "a scheme of a seditious booke" in his possession. Radical works were being published in York by the bookseller Francis Mawborne (or Mawbarne, Mawburne) and the printer Stephen Bulkley (or Bulkeley), including a ballad entitled *The Alewives Outcry Against the Excize*. The two men were released on a £200 bond in November 1666 on condition that they cease printing and selling illegal works as well as English Bibles printed abroad.[14]

Aided by information provided by John Streater, the government arrested Samuel Speed of London in May 1666 for printing *The Power and Practice of Court-leets* (1666), which was objectionable to the state because it reprinted legal material from the interregnum government. Speed had produced other law books in the same vein, thus perpetuating the memory, said the state, of that treasonable era. He was released on a £300 bond on 23 May on condition that he stop printing seditious or unlicensed material and engage in no "designs" against the government.[15]

Given the apocalyptic connotations of the year 1666, the underground press was not unusually prolific. Yet almanac writers such as John Booker, Thomas Nunnes, and John Tanner were telling the people that 1666 would bring the pope's downfall. George Elliott was arrested in March for publishing allegedly seditious material, and two months later the magistrates apprehended Joseph Harrison, who confessed that he had printed *Gods Zeale Thundred Forth Against All Those Magistrates*, the Quaker Edward Burrough's *Antichrist's Government Justly Detected* (1661), and William Bennett's (or Bennit's) *God Only Exalted in His Own Work* (1664), which likened true Christians to the Hebrews saved from the pharaoh's bondage. Warrants were subsequently issued for the arrest of eight persons accused of dispersing *Sigh for the Pitchers: Breathed out in a Personal Contribution to the National Humiliation* (1666), an attack on the Dutch War by George Wither. In it Wither made his views abundantly clear:

> Beyond ret[r]eating we ingaged are
> With *forraign enemies*; and not quite free
> From *Factions*, threatning an *intestine* War,
> If our Presumings unsuccessful be.
>
> . . . .
>
> *Religion* is to *Policy* become
> A servile Handmaid; and few persons are
> Conceivd to be so dangerous as some,
> Who are in *Christian Piety* sincere.

Among those cited with Wither were Sarah Anderton, Elizabeth Goslin, and Margaret Hickes. The Quaker William Dewsbury wrote with apocalyptic fervor in *The Word of the Lord to All the Inhabitants in England* (1666), but seems not to have attracted the government's attention despite the fact that the work was written and published while he was imprisoned at Warwick. His message was abundantly clear: "The pale horse is on his way, passing to and fro in the Nation, and he that rideth thereon is death, smiting and cuting down with the sword of Plague and Pestilence, and if so be you proceed as you have done in executing these cruel Lawes against the innocent, then will the commission of the rider of the pale Horse be enlarged, and what flesh can stand before the pale Horse, seeing the rider thereon is *Death*." [16]

The underground press played an important role in fanning the flames of anti-Catholicism in the aftermath of the London fire. Elizabeth Calvert shipped fifty copies of *A True and Faithful Account of the Several Informations*, which included parliamentary testimony, to Susanna Moone in Bristol, and the bookseller Michael Thomas of the same city sold a copy of the book that he had acquired from the merchant James Light. A similar work, *Londons Flames Discovered by Informations Taken Before the Committee*, also came from the underground press, for copies were found in the London shop of the printer Thomas Leach. It was burned by the hangman at Westminster in September 1667, though copies were dispersed throughout the country. Sir Philip Musgrave confiscated eighteen copies of either this book or *A True and Faithful Account* in Carlisle and discovered that two dozen more had been shipped to Richard Scott, a Presbyterian bookseller. Copies of one of the works also appeared in Westmorland. [17]

At the same time that publications blaming Catholics for the fire of London were circulating around the country, Francis Smith was seeking a printer for the anonymous *Advice to a Painter for Drawing the History of Our Navall Actions*, a satirical account of the fighting in the Dutch War and a hostile treatment in verse of Clarendon, the duke and duchess of York, and other notables of the court. Among those whose aid Smith sought was the printer Thomas Johnson, but the latter had posted a £500 bond in May 1666 not to issue any unlicensed material. The work eventually found its way into print in 1667. In March 1671 Thomas Palmer of Westminster was fined 20 marks and pilloried for two days for selling one of the satirical *Painter* poems, probably Andrew Marvell's *Further Advice to a*

Painter, apparently composed in early 1671. In it Marvell satirized Arlington, Clifford, and others for reveling in "Glorious Bacchanals" while Louis XIV terrorized Christendom.[18]

Despite her earlier legal difficulties, Elizabeth Calvert continued to play a major role in the underground press. In August 1667 the authorities came across an advertisement for *A Trumpet Blown in Sion, Sounding an Alarm in Gods Holy Mountain*, which was being sold at the "Black Spread Eagle" in Barbican—Calvert's shop. After the printer of the advertisement, James Astwood, testified that he had seen a waste sheet of the book in John Darby's shop, Darby and Calvert were arrested.[19] A work with an almost identical title— Benjamin Keach's *A Trumpet Blown in Zion, or an Allarm in Gods Holy Mountain*—was published in 1694, and may have been a later version of the book sold by Calvert; it contained some pointed remarks about the state's persecution of the godly. Darby was in turn involved with Anna (or Anne) Brewster and her son, who sold copies of *The Poor Whore's Petition*, which Darby printed.[20] In the meantime Peter Parker and Samuel Simmons purchased the manuscript of William Dyer's *Christ's Famous Titles, and a Believer's Golden Chain* from Calvert after she assured them it would be licensed. However, they printed it without first obtaining the requisite permission, and were arrested. The contents of this collection of sermons were innocent enough, though Dyer made it clear that as "King of Kings" Christ "breaks mighty kings in pieces for the saints sake." But this was divine work, because no person was allowed to wrong a sovereign. Although the godly were depicted as kings in their own right, the task of punishing errant sovereigns was reserved to Christ, "who will overcome and subdue all our enemies . . . both spiritual and temporal." The arrest of Parker and Simmons was thus the act of a government so frustrated by its inability to crush the underground press that it arrested two booksellers whose only offense was the apparently inadvertent failure to procure a license for a harmless publication acquired from a known radical.[21]

Early in 1668 Wither's *Vox & Lacrimae Anglorum* was posthumously published. In a sweeping indictment of Charles's regime, Wither denounced high taxes, the sale of Dunkirk, forced benevolences, and the poor state of defense. There was criticism too of the decay of trade, the appointment of Catholics to high office, and the extravagance of Henrietta Maria. Wither also denounced the imprisonment of debtors, the corrupt judicial system, and the persecution of nonconformists:

> Thousands there be that could not hurt a worm,
> Imprisoned were, cause they cannot conform.

To compel people to worship against their consciences, he insisted, was contrary to natural law and a violation of Christ's prerogative. He called too for a commission to investigate the fire of London—a Jesuit plot, he suspected, masterminded in France and Spain. "Perfidious *Clarenden*! that potent Thief," came in for some particularly harsh criticism. One of Wither's key recommendations was to place the country firmly in Protestant hands:

> Disarm the Papists, and secure our Ports,
> Place Protestants in Garrisons and Forts.[22]

Wither was perhaps the most eloquent of those who sought to depict Charles's government as a threat to English Protestantism in the 1660s.

In April 1668 L'Estrange wrote to Arlington about seven alleged libels, offering his judgment as to how juries would respond if charges were brought. *Vox & Lacrimae Anglorum* was curiously not one of them. *The Poor Whore's Petition*, he thought, would not interest a jury, nor would the anonymous *Omnia Comesta a Bello* (1667). Bitterly antiprelatical and anticlerical in tone, the latter castigated the "over-grown Cleargy" for impoverishing the nation by their excessive maintenance (which he reckoned at £200,000 per year), their probates and ecclesiastical courts, their religious ceremonies, and their visitations. Thousands of trading people, he blustered, are put to excessive expenses by "the Rigorous and Tyrannical proceedings of the Bishops, in Excommunicating persons." The liturgy, drawn from the mass and breviary, was unfavorably compared to "the Gospel in the Power and Purity of it." Like the old Puritans, the author condemned both the popish vestments and the "swarm" of ecclesiastical offices that had no basis in Scripture or the practices of the Reformed churches.[23]

A similar tone runs through *Felo de Se, or the Bishops Condemned out of Their Own Mouthes* (1668), a work L'Estrange thought might be Wallis's, but was probably by the Presbyterian Thomas Ford, who had been ejected as a preacher at Exeter Cathedral in 1660. This work was an unabashed assault on "Prelatical Tyranny" on behalf of those who "groan to be delivered" from a "yoke of Bondage." Bishops were attacked as cormorants, caterpillars, obstructors of public justice, and evil men without consciences. They appealed to "Romish Records" as the basis of their authority, openly professed their desire to amass power, and appointed "ignorant doltheads, [and] debauched and superstitious Curats" to serve the churches. The bishops "are the most venomous, dangerous, and deadly creatures in the world," Ford declared, and he held them accountable for expelling the Lord's workers from the vineyard, thereby bringing blood and violence to the land.[24] That L'Estrange considered these works, with their blatant disrespect for episcopacy, something that no jury would punish underscores the fact that the pervasive anticlericalism of the 1640s had not substantially diminished.

Of the other four works on L'Estrange's list, one was a Quaker tract, *Several Reasons Rendred by the People of God, (Called Quakers) Why No Outward Force, or Imposition, on the Conscience Ought to Be Used in Matters of Faith and Religion* (1668). Compulsion in religion, the author averred, only creates hypocrisy and enmity. Unless those of differing religious beliefs are tolerated, he insisted, they must according to conventional wisdom be "Destroyed" or exiled. The latter course "makes men more ready to own, then to reject their Faith, and so rather Multiplies, then lessens, the Number of its Professors." Exiling them, however, "renders the Banished as so many Enemies abroad, ready upon all Occasions to Disturb the Peace and Tranquility of their own Native Country," as in fact had been the case in recent years. Imposing one's beliefs on others, he argued, makes the oppressed hate the oppressors. In addition to a few biblical references, the author buttressed his argument by citing none other than James I's 1609 speech to Parliament and "Charles I" in *Eikon Basilike*. Nevertheless, in L'Estrange's judgment this work required refutation rather than punishment, except as an unlicensed pamphlet.[25]

The Saints Freedom from Tyranny Vindicated (1667) he deemed clearly treasonable. Its author contended that no magistrate had the authority "to command any Person to do what God forbids, or to forbid what God commands, in matters Civil, Spiritual, or Ecclesiastical." Subjection to the higher powers was thus limited only to those things specifically ordained by God. L'Estrange thought that Nicholas Lockyer's anonymous *Some Seasonable and Serious Queries upon the Late Act Against Conventicles*, cited in the previous chapter, would be found objectionable by a jury because it reflected adversely on the Cavalier Parliament. The author writes, said one of Musgrave's correspondents, "most subtilly[,] daungerously and Catchingly to such as have the least inclination to . . . [an] alteration of Government."[26]

The final work, Ralph Wallis's *Room for the Cobler of Gloucester and His Wife: With Several Cartloads of Abominable Irregular, Pitiful Stinking Priests* (1668), was "the damnedest thing [that] has come out yet." Taking as his thesis the idea that Church of England clergy were ordained according to Roman rites rather than the Gospel, Wallis satirically compared a bishop and a cobbler, finding the latter more honorable. "The Lord Bishop is much like that Hog, that, when some Children were eating Milk out of a Dish that stood upon a Stool, thrust his Snout into the Dish, and drank up all." The established clergy in general were depicted as ignorant, inebriated, debauched, lazy, and inclined to frequent bawdy houses. After offering a variety of unflattering vignettes about such ministers, he referred "this Cartload of ignorant Sots" and their bishops to an earlier classic of the Separatist tradition, Samuel How's *The Sufficiencie of the Spirits Teaching Without Humane Learning* (1644). L'Estrange, "the Devills bloud-hound," had difficulty tracking Wallis, particularly because he and Forbes moved back and forth between Clapham and Hackney in disguise. *Room for the Cobler* as well as some of the *Painter* satires were printed by Elizabeth Calvert and George Larkin.[27]

The growing use of satire rather than straightforward prose in the late 1660s made it more difficult for the government to prove sedition; hence in the summer of 1668 it accepted L'Estrange's proposal to tighten control over the Stationers' Company. This commenced with a survey of thirty-five printing houses in London and Westminster, excluding the king's printers—the first serious attempt of this kind since the abolition of Star Chamber. In the meantime the search for illegal printers and booksellers continued. A Mr. Willes had been committed to the Gatehouse at Westminster in January for distributing seditious pamphlets, and Elizabeth Poole of Southwark followed in April when an illegal press was found in her home. In July James Cottrell (or Cotterell) went to the Gatehouse when he was arrested for printing seditious books, though he was released after a stay of only a fortnight.[28]

An investigation was launched in October to discover the author and printer of *Nehushtan: or, a Sober and Peaceable Discourse* (1668), a vindication of nonconformists who refused to accept the Book of Common Prayer. All unnecessary things in the church had been grossly abused, the author asserted; superstition and idolatry had thereby been increased. For the safety of people's souls and the peace of the church, the *adiaphora* must be abolished. This, he contended, was the responsibility of the magistrates. Through the testimony of Thomas Leach the government learned that the author was the Presbyterian John Wilson, the ejected vicar of Backford, Cheshire, who had been in trouble in 1665 for illegally preaching in that county. For printing the book Elizabeth Calvert was interned in the King's Bench prison, and Thomas Palmer, a Westminster bookseller, was fined 20 marks and sentenced to two days in the pillory for selling it. The investigation into *Nehushtan* probably led as well to George Larkin, Richard Royston, and John Wright, all of whom were arrested in October. A large number of allegedly seditious but unspecified books were seized from Larkin's press in Southwark.[29]

Attention shifted in December to William Penn's *The Sandy Foundation Shaken* (1668), which caused a considerable stir in both conformist and nonconformist circles by rejecting such Calvinist doctrines as a satisfaction-based atonement and justification by Christ's imputed righteousness. His assertion that the term "Trinity" was unscriptural and his favorable references to Socinians such as John Biddle left him open to a charge of Socinianism, for which he was imprisoned for nine months. For printing the book John Darby also went to prison.[30]

As the campaign against the underground press went forward, there was even a search of the King's Bench prison in late December

1668 for seditious papers and pamphlets. In February 1669 Arlington issued a warrant for the arrest of the Presbyterian Stephen Coven, the suspected author of *The Militant Christian; or, the Good Soldier of Jesus Christ* (London, 1668). Coven specifically repudiated the tenet that Christians had to accept the religion imposed by magistrates or conform to the doctrines and practices of the established church. He mocked the government's efforts to control the press: "This Book may Travel where the Author cannot . . . ; It may have its Liberty, when he is in Bonds; it may speak when his mouth is stopt; it may dwell in *England*, when he is Banished." Coven, the ejected rector of Sampford Peverell, Devon, had reportedly been preaching sedition in 1665, and perhaps had good reason to expect imprisonment or exile. Arlington and Williamson interrogated the bookseller and printer Theodore Sadler in June for possessing copies of *The Brief Method* and *The Passing Bell of Controversies*, and the printer John Winter for a book of unauthorized Catholic meditations. Five years earlier Winter had been suspected of printing unlicensed material.[31]

In July Arlington turned his attention to the Presbyterian Thomas Parkhurst, who was selling an anonymous reply to *A Friendly Debate Between a Conformist and a Nonconformist* (1666), and Thomas Leach, who presumably printed the reply. The author of *A Friendly Debate*, Simon Patrick, bishop of Ely, had attacked several nonconformist works, including Thomas Watson's *The Doctrine of Repentance* (1668), William Bridge's *Christ and the Covenant* (1667), and John Wilson's *Nehushtan* (1668). In Patrick's judgment Wilson's critique of the liturgy amounted to nothing less than an attempt "to throw down the whole Fabrick of the *English* Church." No one, Patrick insisted, had "ever *made an Idol*" of the liturgy or was "guilty of *adoring it*"; such a charge by Wilson entailed "a kind of Conjuring Phrases and Magical words, which make a great Sound, and astonish the silly people, but signifie nothing, save only this, that men care not what they say to serve their cause." He continued his attack in *A Continuation of the Friendly Debate* (1669), adding such new targets as Thomas Case, Jeremiah Burroughs, Thomas Hooker, and Thomas Shepard. Patrick was in turn attacked by the Presbyterian Samuel Rolle (or Rolls), who used the pseudonym "Philagathus," in *A Sober Answer to the Friendly Debate* (1669). Presumably this was the book that Thomas Parkhurst was selling when he got into trouble with Arlington. According to Baxter, other "moderate worthy men" also drafted responses but ultimately declined to print them because of "the danger of the Times." Rolle himself had problems finding a printer: "*I* found it very hard to get any *Midwife*, or else *I* had been sooner *delivered of it*." The delay, however, gave him the opportunity to have "divers persons of great *worth* and judgement" read parts of the work in draft.[32]

Rolle was no radical, having already taken the Oxford oath and demonstrated a willingness, as Baxter put it, to "read some Common prayer." For his moderation he had been allowed to preach at Southwark Hospital and hoped for a better position at Bridewell, where he was elected chaplain in October 1669. The bishop of London, however, refused to license him the following March. Rolle took pains to defend nonconformists from Patrick's charge that they regarded the king as a tyrant; on the contrary, he insisted, dissenters placed their greatest hope for relaxation of the Clarendon Code "in the benignity and good temper of His Majesty." Most of the book, however, was devoted to a defense of moderate nonconformist views on such issues as holy days, the importance of religious experience, the theater, and justification by faith. There is really nothing in the book to set it apart from many other nonconformist works of the period that the government virtually ignored, apart from the fact that Rolle was attacking the writings of a bishop. So far was he from espousing radical tenets that he could "see no reason why *Moderation* should be so odious, which is only a suspension of our zeal as to those things it should not be spent upon; and a *giving unto* C[onformists] the things that *are theirs*, and to N[on] C[onformists] *the things that are theirs*."[33]

Baxter subsequently denounced Patrick for his lack of charity, his methodology in disingenuously abstracting unrepresentative comments from Bridge's work, and his use of "the crude and unmeet Expressions of many well-meaning Women and unlearned private Men, especially that are inclined most to Self-conceitedness, and unwarrantable singularities and separation." In the meantime Patrick wrote a lengthy reply to Rolle, satirizing him as Don Quixote and Antilegon. The nonconformists' plea for religious liberty was deftly turned against them by recalling the practices of the 1640s and 1650s: "That wish would have been better, when you had power to do what you desire. But then you . . . thought it requisite to good Government, that the people should be tyed strictly to the Laws, and punished, according to their fault, if they transgressed."[34]

The passage of the 1670 Conventicle Act led to more illegal publications as nonconformists pushed their case against it. Copies of Nicholas Lockyer's *Some Seasonable and Serious Queries upon the Late Act Against Conventicles*, which had appeared—possibly in an earlier version—in 1668 after the House of Commons approved the bill, were discovered in Chester, Newcastle, and other areas of the north, and plans were afoot to ship copies into Scotland as well. The book was also plentiful at London conventicles. The Friends responded to the act with *A Declaration from the People of God Called Quakers*, denouncing those who used religious assemblies as a cover for treasonous activity. Sir Geoffrey Shakerley found a copy of it when he arrested Quakers in Chester. Allegedly dangerous but unidentified publications were also confiscated in Bristol and Gloucester.[35]

As L'Estrange sought to learn the identity of the author of *Some Seasonable and Serious Queries*, he seized some 300 allegedly seditious books "of old date" from Elizabeth Calvert in May. Two months later a warrant was issued for John Streater's arrest, this time for writing *The Character of a True and False Shepherd* (1670), attacking conformist ministers as hirelings who delivered their parishioners to Satan as reprobates. When government agents went to his shop and tried to arrest his compositor, William Thomas, the entire company of more than twenty persons, vehemently protesting that they were "'free-born subjects, & not be be medled with by such a Warrant,'" helped Thomas escape. Francis Smith, John Darby, and the stationer Francis Siddenham were arrested in September. In Smith's shop were found copies of *That Neither Temporallities Nor Tyths Is Due to the Bishops*, which urged lay peers to expropriate prelatical property for the benefit of the kingdom and the relief of the poor, with supporting justification from the laws and practices of the rulers of England, France, and Judah as well as 120 authors. He was the probable author of *Trap ad Crucem; or, the Papists Watch-word* (1670), another attempt to accuse Catholics of committing arson in London. Yet another anti-Catholic work, a verse burlesque entitled *Come Hither, Topham, Come*, had been found in Chester that June. In November L'Estrange discovered several reputedly seditious pamphlets, including *The Englishman, or a Letter from a Universal Friend* (1670), in the possession of a bookseller named Brooks—possibly the Nathan Brookes who had been tried with John Twyn, Simon Dover, and Thomas Brewster in February 1664. The anonymous author of *The Englishman* provocatively contended that the new Conventicle Act was contrary to the fundamental laws of the realm and called on magistrates not to enforce it.[36]

L'Estrange's efforts to control the press were, to use the king's term, "ineffectual." Although Charles placed the blame on the Stationers' Company for obstructing L'Estrange's efforts, there was no way that the surveyor, with the modest financial resources he had, could curtail the underground press. He had hoped to implement new methods to control the press without additional expense, but by May 1670 he was forced to admit that it was "as foul & Licentious as ever." At that point he proposed recalling the warrants to booksellers and printers that allowed them to hunt for unlicensed publications, thereby leaving his office in charge of all searches. He also requested additional financial support, some of which would be utilized for a deputy and for informers. Tough new rules for the control of printers were approved by the king's counsel, including a requirement that each printer post a £300 bond not to print unlicensed material. In addition, L'Estrange wanted to require all booksellers in London and Westminster to join the Stationers' Company and be subject to its rules, and to prohibit haberdashers from selling books, especially because their stock came from illegal presses. Charles finally approved this reform in August 1671.[37]

The court also gave L'Estrange needed support in September 1670 by using the threat of a *quo warranto* to force the Stationers' Company to cooperate with him in suppressing illegal publications, and by promising essential financial assistance. Even then, however, L'Estrange had to borrow funds to finance his campaign against illegal printers and booksellers. In addition to a constant outlay of £200 per year for a deputy and a coach, there were frequent special costs, as in the case of one prosecution for which he had to examine and maintain twenty-five witnesses in London. In a three-year quest to locate one "most dangerous Private Presse," he had laid out £50 in additional expenses. Despite fiscal problems, in the period from August 1663 to October 1670, he claimed to have suppressed more than 600 seditious publications—an extraordinary average of 7 per month, a testimony not only to his energy but to the vitality of the underground press.[38]

Scotland, the Covenanters, and the Press

Most of the illegal publications in Scotland were religious in nature and reflected the ideals of the militant Covenanters. As early as 1661 the booksellers George Swinton (or Swintoun) and James Glen were in trouble for having works such as Thomas Gataker's *The Covenanter's Plea Against Absolvers* (1661) and speeches of James Guthry and Archibald Campbell printed. Because of the publication of works "prejudiciall to religion," on 19 November 1661 the Scottish Council prohibited the printing of any book or paper that had not been licensed.[39]

Scottish dissidents were provided with publications smuggled into the country from the exile community in the Netherlands. In the spring of 1664 one of Burnet's agents acquired a copy of an unnamed book by Robert MacWard, who had been associated with Archibald Johnston, laird of Wariston, and James Simpson. The book, which was deemed seditious, included letters of encouragement to the "faithful" in Scotland, including Lord Loudon, the laird of Gadgirth, and several ladies. Fresh copies from the Netherlands were apparently smuggled into the country in 1666, for the following January the archbishop of St. Andrews complained that it was "stuffed with more seditious and treasonable assertions then any I have seen . . . against the cause of the king and Church."[40]

On 19 April 1664 the Scottish Council issued a proclamation banning George Buchanan's classic, *De Jure Regni apud Scotos*, reportedly translated by John Crookshanks, who had supported the 1663 Dublin conspiracy. The book, Archbishop Burnet informed Archbishop Sheldon, was supposed to be distributed in Scotland about the time that (unspecified) treasonable pamphlets were to be published in England, "by which your Grace may easily see whether it be crowne or mitre they strike at."[41]

In August 1664 the Council empowered Sir Robert Moray to ascertain who was printing and selling copies of Wariston's speech. The investigation led to the arrest and imprisonment of Archibald Hendry, who was additionally charged with dispersing "other seditious pamphlettis." He was released in November after posting a bond not to sell any more seditious publications on pain of branding on the cheek and exile.[42]

Approximately a year before the Pentland revolt, the exiled minister John Brown of Wamphray wrote *An Apologeticall Relation, of the Particular Sufferings of the Faithfull Ministers & Professours of the Church of Scotland, Since August. 1660* (1665). In it he argued that resistance to those who persecuted the godly is lawful, at least to the extent that Christians are exhorted to fulfill their religious responsibilities even in the face of acts that outlaw them. Moreover the magistrate who commands that which is evil "may be resisted & opposed, without any violence done to the office or ordinance of God." The Christian duty to obey lawful magistrates does not extend, Brown insisted, to tyrants, who are "a terrour to good works" and thus must be resisted. This, of course, was a direct reflection of the continuing influence of John Knox's political thought. Brown praised nonconformist ministers, such as James Guthry, who had suffered at the hands of the state, and defended their freedom to preach in public or private. The right of people to attend conventicles was also asserted. In Brown's judgment Charles II's government "will not have . . . [Christ's] Kingdome a free Kingdome, & consequently they will not have him a free King. They will not allow to him, the liberty of appoynting or instituting his own officers, or to rule his Kingdome by his owne lawes, courts, ordinances, & censures." Prelacy, in short, was depicted as a yoke around the necks of the Scottish people, which in the past had proved to be "so intolerably grievous" that they had thrown it off. Brown urged the nobles to press for an end to episcopacy, but he also insisted that it was the duty of the godly to remember "the good old cause" by fulfilling their spiritual obligations and crying out against oppression. Compromise was out of the question: "Let none say that such precisenesse, & refuseing to cede in a little will prove destructive to the Church, by incenseing the civil Magistrat the more; For God's way is alwayes the best."[43]

On 8 February 1666 the Council condemned Brown's book for its "seditious, treasonable and rebellious principalls," decreeing that it be burned in the High Street of Edinburgh by the hangman. Those who had copies received a brief grace period to surrender them to magistrates or face a fine of £2,000 Scots. Interestingly, a copy of the book was found in the possession of James Guthry's widow; when she and her daughter Sophia refused to identify the supplier, the Council exiled them to Zetland.[44]

One of the most explosive Scottish works of the period was published in 1667 in the Netherlands.[45] Written by the attorney James Stewart of Goodtrees and the minister James Stirling of Paisley, it was entitled *Naphtali, or the Wrestlings of the Church of Scotland for the Kingdom of Christ*. Writing in the conviction that they were living in "the last times, wherein Sin aboundeth, and the love of many is waxed cold," the authors lamented "the Universall decay of Religion." In effect, this was the Scottish version of England's *Speeches and Prayers* of the regicides, for it included the last statements of Argyll, Wariston, and James Guthry, the joint testimony of the Galloway rebels executed in Edinburgh on 7 December 1666, and an account of Hugh McKell's suffering. The insurrection itself was defended as lawful, righteous, and necessary. The authors condemned the use of the military to enforce conformity and castigated the repressive actions of Sir James Turner in the southwest. In the aftermath of the Galloway rebellion, "the whole Kingdom," they reflected, was "so exhausted by exactions and impositions, so vexed by generall oppression and disorder, from which the wickedness of Prelatick Rulers, suffer no place to be exempted, . . . that all are either disabled, disheartened, or disobleiged from the service of King and Countrey."[46]

In addition to being a book of recent martyrs, *Naphtali* brought together the great documents of the Covenanting tradition—the 1560 Confession of Faith, the Solemn League and Covenant, and a Solemn Engagement. Like various contemporary English works, it was also unsparing in its critique of episcopacy. Satirizing prelates as

"Idle drons," Stirling and Stewart damned episcopacy as anti-Christian and condemned "the Tyranny and Illegality of the *High Commission*," the precedent for which, they contended, was the Spanish Inquisition.[47] In its implications this was unmistakably a militant work, as Scottish officials quickly recognized. Sir Robert Moray reported to Lauderdale that it contained "all that a Toung set on fire by hell can say of things & persones hereaway." The Scottish Council issued a proclamation on 11 December 1667 condemning the book, ordering it burned by the common hangman in Edinburgh, and subjecting those who refused to surrender their copies to magistrates to a fine of £2,000 Scots. In the Council's judgment *Naphtali*, if unchecked, would lead to another "unnaturall and bloody warr," or, in the words of the archbishop of St. Andrews, to "a Munster tragedy."[48]

When Dr. Andrew Honeyman, the bishop of Orkney, wrote a response to *Naphtali*, entitled *A Survey of the Insolent and Infamous Libel, Entituled, Naphtali* (1668), Stewart retaliated with *Jus Populi Vindicatum* (1669). The new book, fumed the earl of Kincardine, was "a most wicked piece as ever yet has come out, farre beyond Neptali itself." Stewart defended the Galloway rebellion, praising those who were executed and proclaiming that "the honest cause was never more confirmed then by the death and sufferings of these, whom they cruelly murthered as traitours and rebels." It was, he averred, the right of individual Christians to defend themselves and their Covenanted faith from the tyranny and oppression of all magistrates. Anything done by king or Parliament that contravened the Covenants he deemed "a real and formal subversion of the fundamental constitution of our Christian and reformed Kingdome." Sovereigns, he asserted, were limited not only by the Covenants but by the conditions imposed on them by the people—the so-called "fundamentall lawes"—when they were chosen to govern. In the tradition of John Knox, Stewart defended the right of subjects to resist rulers who issued unjust and iniquitous commands. This "pestiferous" book, complained the archbishop of St. Andrews, casts "a greater reproach upon our religion and nation, than any in print."[49]

On 12 January 1671 the Council ordered an investigation to determine the author, importers, and sellers of *Jus Populi Vindicatum*.

There was some dispute among the Councillors whether to burn this book, for they found "by experience" that burning made "more glorying and more curiosity after the booke," but on 16 February the king's proclamation decreed the same fate for it as had befallen *Naphtali*. To ascertain those responsible for *Jus Populi Vindicatum*, the government offered a reward of £50 sterling to anyone who identified the sellers or dispensers, and £100 sterling to anyone who named the author or importers.[50] In the ensuing crackdown John Ritchie of Borrowstounness, who had been corresponding with John Carstares and other exiles, was arrested for importing allegedly seditious material. Even before the appearance of *Jus Populi Vindicatum* the king had asked the Dutch government in July 1670 to expel Robert Trail, Robert MacWard, and John Nevay, whom he blamed for seditious publications. The three were ordered to leave the Netherlands within fifteen days, though they seem not to have done so, for on 3 February 1671 Kincardine thought it would be strange if the Estates refused to banish them.[51]

By the summer of 1672 the government had learned that Andrew Kennedy (alias Weir) of Closeburn in Dumfries was a key importer of illegal publications. Kennedy, who had been imprisoned in 1663 on a charge of concealing high treason because of his involvement with Wariston, was put to the horn on 20 August when he failed to appear before the Court of Justiciary to answer charges of treason. According to the state, Kennedy "was employed as a fitt and pernicious instrument" with a group of exiles who sent him copies of *Naphtali, Jus Populi Vindicatum*, and other "trumpets and engines of sedition and rebellion." This group included Robert Trail, John Brown, John Livingstone (or Livingston), and Robert MacWard. They were allegedly in touch with former Galloway rebels, and at least some of them reputedly "did traffick and practice in England." Unfortunately the government did not reveal any details about the purported contacts of Scottish exiles with dissidents in England, although the former's use of the press to encourage militant Covenanters in Scotland is clear enough.[52]

Suppressing dissident literature in Scotland was complicated by the fact that most of it was printed in the Netherlands and smuggled into the country, whereas radicals south of the Tweed did most of their printing in London and Bristol. Because virtually all of the illegal Scottish publications were primarily religious in content, an accommodation with the Covenanters, though extremely difficult to achieve, would have resolved the problem of the press. Scottish militants became increasingly adept at using underground publications to justify political rebellion for religious ends, even to the point of turning convicted rebels into martyrs. In contrast, apart from the Quakers the English dissidents generally eschewed this tendency, preferring instead to concentrate their attacks on the evils of the Stuart regime. By opting not to create a literature of martyrdom they lost an opportunity to strengthen the bonds that loosely united them.

The themes most commonly reiterated in the publications of the underground press reinforced the determination of dissenters to resist the government's efforts to make them conform. Whereas Scottish authors expounded the sixteenth-century theory of tyrannicide developed by Knox, Ponet, and Goodman, their English counterparts typically took a less militant tone, urging defiance of unjust laws but stopping short of a call to rebellion. Nonconformists of all stripes in England as well as Scotland repudiated the notion that conventicles were seditious as long as those in attendance worshiped according to Scripture. Magistrates were encouraged not to punish conventiclers, even as the latter were reminded that magistrates had no legitimate authority to compel them to violate their consciences. The 1670 Conventicle Act was even denounced for contravening the fundamental laws of the realm. Thus these publications, which ranged from the advocacy of passive resistance to the fomenting of open rebellion, not only strengthened nonconformist resolve but proposed limits on the power of the state to determine religious issues and compel obedience to the established church.

The ability of the government to rule effectively was further undercut by the barrage of criticism in underground publications. No one was exempt from biting satire or scathing denunciation: Charles II and his bishops were roundly denounced in both English and Scottish publications. Scottish critics also denounced the High Commission, while English authors aimed their barbs at persons as disparate as the duke and duchess of York, Clarendon, and Lady Castlemaine on the one hand and conformist clerics on the other. The repeated and by now familiar attacks on the clergy as mere hirelings, the prelates as corrupt and power-crazed, the liturgy as idolatrous, and the established church as riddled with the dregs of popery can only have reinforced the determination of nonconformists to defy the magistrates and worship in their own manner. Although most of the dissident literature focused on religious themes, there was some attention to more strictly political issues, including hostility to the Second Dutch War, the condition of the economy, the tax burden, and the state of the country's defense.

English critics generally made no effort to exalt new martyrs, but there was an unmistakable insistence in both kingdoms that dissenters were victims of persecution. The Quakers in particular compared themselves to the ancient Hebrews, and wrote of their own ultimate deliverance from the modern pharaoh. Thus there was a tendency for some dissenters, both Quakers and non-Quakers, English and Scots, to see Charles as a persecutor and to look for deliverance, perhaps in an apocalyptic context. Surely stable government would be endangered should the willingness to castigate the king's immorality broaden to include condemnation of him as the very personification of the forces of cosmic evil. The grant of indulgence in 1672 temporarily defused this tendency, thereby calming the underground press for a few years.

"The Militant Christian"

SIX

Kidnappers and Crown Jewels

The failure of the 1663 northern rebellion had encouraged militants to alter their strategy by thinking in terms of an insurrection coordinated with a Dutch invasion, or possibly even reliance on French assistance. The war, however, made it clear to both the Dutch government and the dissidents that such expectations were probably unrealistic. English militants were forced once more to rethink their strategy. Consequently the emphasis in the postwar years was on more limited objectives for which the chances of success were greater. Given the divisions among English dissidents brought on by the war, as well as the inability of English and Scottish militants to forge an effective alliance, an uprising was in any case highly unlikely unless unity could be forged.

The ingredients necessary to rebuild a broad-based dissident movement were, however, present in the late 1660s. The war, with its expense and its conspicuous lack of victories, proved to be highly unpopular by 1667. Discontent over the hearth tax was widespread; there was, for instance, "great murmuring" in Bristol because people believed that tax collectors deliberately called when they were away in order to have an excuse to break into their houses and distrain goods. In the fall of 1666 "mutinies and discontents and uproars" about the taxes erupted in such places as Hereford, Coventry, and Newcastle upon Tyne. Popular hostility against the government continued—so much so that one loyalist compared 1667 to 1641 with respect to the prevalence of "insolent" speech against those who governed.[1] A former republican sailor boasted in July 1667 that within three months a popular army would march on London, replace the Cavalier Parliament with "the old one," and try Charles II as they had tried his father. The country was ruled so badly, another mariner remonstrated, that "the King may come to make the same end his father made."² Rumors and allegations of government misconduct revealed a powerful undercurrent of discontent for the militants to tap.³

The dissidents could also take advantage of the growth of anti-Catholic hostility during the war years. Indeed, the nonconformists in general were instrumental in spreading fears about popery. In Westmorland Daniel Fleming was frankly troubled that "this new zeal enkindled against the Papists" enabled "the Rabble of other Non-conformists [to] escape by the light of it, & grow warm by the heat of that flame to which (some think) they have added no small increase by their declarations & other Acts of insinuation." False rumors concerning the Catholic threat abounded; one, for instance, attributed Buckingham's legal difficulties to his disarming of York-shire Catholics, while another asserted that Albemarle and other peers had been confined to the Tower as part of a papist conspiracy. When suspicion mounted that the king was determined to establish Catholicism, he responded in September 1667 by ordering its suppression. One loyalist compared the "jealousy" of popery that he observed in 1667 to similar feelings in 1642. Occasional reports of armed Catholics in secret meetings fueled the discontent. An anonymous document written in May 1668—almost certainly by a militant—accused the pope of dispatching thousands of missionaries to England to destroy the Protestant faith, and blamed Catholics for burning London in 1666, plotting a massacre of Protestants and a new fire in the City, and enlisting thousands to rendezvous on an hour's notice. The author had hoped to get his manuscript printed, he said, in order to awaken the king and Privy Council, but the government not only intercepted it but branded it a seditious libel. Fears of popish plots were once again a factor to be reckoned with in English politics.⁴

Restless Radicals

Mason's Rescue

The investigation of Buckingham's associations with the militants in the late winter and spring of 1667 uncovered ties to the 1663 north-

ern rebels. His steward, Henry North, had been an agent for Doncaster, Yorkshire, and was at a planning session at the Spa on 9 June
with Dr. Edward Richardson, Jeremiah Marsden, Captain William
Leeving, Lieutenant-Colonel John Beckwith, and others. In February 1667, during the course of the Buckingham investigation, the
state was interested in North's dealings with such northern rebels as
Major Joshua Greathead (who became a government spy), William
Mason of Gainsborough, the Fifth Monarchist James Fisher of Sheffield, and Captain Salmon, Jr. The investigation also turned up the
names of Jeremiah Marsden and Colonel John Mason, a "fat, swar-
thy" man who "habited like a Citisen." A warrant for Mason's arrest
was finally issued on 27 April, with instructions to apprehend those
suspected of corresponding with him. He was incarcerated in the
Tower. On 20 July a new warrant was issued for his transfer—along
with Leeving—to York to stand trial for his part in the northern
rebellion.[5]

Leeving had been briefly imprisoned at York in June on a debt
charge, but was freed after appealing to Arlington with a promise of
bringing the state a new agent—a gentleman who could entice "the
heads of the factions into the King's service." Leeving then visited
friends in Leicestershire, "but liting into ill company & being under
discouragement, was tempted to be an offender of his majestys law."
Once more he went to prison, this time to Newgate, and again he
appealed to Arlington with the prospect of recruiting yet another
agent. It was presumably the latter who had written to Leeving on
29 June suggesting that he be summoned "on pretext of corresponding with Heydon's patron," that is, Buckingham.[6] This web of intrigue provided the background for one of the most famous escapes
engineered by the radicals.

Mason and Leeving left London in the company of Corporal William Darcy and six or seven other troopers. Blood must have been
alerted, perhaps by someone in Buckingham's employ, for he and a
small rescue party, numbering approximately a dozen, surrepti-
tiously left London under cover of darkness. Among them were the
old northern conspirators John Lockyer and Timothy Butler. After
catching up with Darcy's party at a Doncaster inn, they followed
them north, first attacking two straggling troopers and chasing their
horses away. On the evening of 25 July they ambushed the rest in a

narrow lane between Wentbridge and Darrington, southeast of Pon-
tefract. According to one account Blood's well-armed band "fixed
uppon the souldiers backs without saying a word or makeinge any
show of force," but another report had them demanding, "Deliver,
or you are all dead men." A barber traveling with the group was
killed, and Darcy and three of his men were wounded in the fray.
Blood himself was unhorsed three times, cornered in a courtyard,
wounded by a bullet in the shoulder, and struck on the nose with a
pistol before he managed to escape with Mason. Leeving remained
with the troopers and subsequently identified Blood, Lockyer, and
Butler to the authorities. A proclamation issued on 8 August offered
a reward of £100 for the apprehension of Blood, Mason, Lockyer,
Butler, and their confederates.[7]

Leeving was interned in York Castle, where he was poisoned
sometime prior to 31 August, undoubtedly by imprisoned dissidents.
Among the prisoners at this point was another key northern rebel,
John Atkinson, as well as Colonel Aldridge, a Cromwellian who had
once served under Robert Overton in Scotland. Despite Leeving's
fate, another informer, William Fryer (or Freer), was incarcerated in
York Castle in September. Fryer claimed to have information about
Butler as well as those who hid Blood and his associates after Mason's rescue.[8]

All of this had no apparent effect on Buckingham. He continued
his quest for popularity among nonconformists, at least some of
whom revered him as a champion of toleration and "a discoverer off
the papists late designe as they tearme it." When John Wildman was
finally released from prison in October 1667, Buckingham not only
made him his legal adviser and trustee but reportedly praised him as
one of the wisest statesmen in England.[9] The duke's influence was
reputedly such that Viscount Conway complained bitterly that even
the king complied with his wishes out of fear, and that the House of
Commons regarded him as "a premier minister." "He himself,"
grumbled Conway, "thinks to arrive to be another Oliver, and the
fanatics expect a day of redemption under him." Such impressions
were clearly exaggerated, for as Douglas Lacey has shown, the duke's
appeal to nonconformists for political support was not a resounding
success. Despite his attempts to enhance his standing with dissenters

through his patronage of such men as North and Wildman, nonconformists in the country as well as in Parliament were seemingly put
off by his unorthodox religious views, his flagrant liaison with the
countess of Shrewsbury, and his relative lack of concern with issues
of trade and the heavy taxes levied to fight the Dutch. Buckingham's
indiscriminate links to the militants may also have troubled the moderate nonconformists in Parliament.[10]

The duke's quest for the support of dissenters, including those of
a radical bent, may have been related to the hope he shared with
Ashley of making the duke of Monmouth the heir apparent. Efforts
in this direction were under way as early as 1667. But Buckingham
was preeminently concerned with himself, and obviously enjoyed
political maneuvering and intrigue for their own sake. Such traits
prevented him from being a more effective spokesman for religious
toleration and a stable bridge between the court and the dissenting
community.

The London Apprentices' Riot: "Reformation and Reducement"

City radicals received yet another opportunity to strike when
the London area was thrown into disarray by a major apprentices'
riot in March 1668. Unlike early Stuart attacks on brothels by apprentices, which normally took place on Shrove Tuesday, this riot
occurred in Easter week and was greater in size and longer in dura-
tion than its predecessors. As Tim Harris has demonstrated, the 1668
riot was sparked by dissenters who resented the king's proclamation against conventicles (issued on 10 March). They took out their
hostility on bawdy houses, in part because of their association in
people's minds with a promiscuous court, and in part because they,
like conventicles, were illegal but yet were not suppressed. During
the riots, attacks were made on the court, the duke of York, and the
bishops, while demands were made for religious toleration.[11]

The tumult was sparked on Easter Monday, the 23rd, when a buf-
foon in Lincoln's Inn Fields incited apprentices by spoofing "the
gentle Craft of the Taylors in a farce." The satire may well have had
religious connotations, for tailors had been charged for attending
conventicles in the period 1661–66 more frequently than had any
other occupation. At Poplar, near Stepney, some 500 people armed

themselves with iron bars, poleaxes, long staves, and other weapons. On the 24th approximately 300 armed apprentices led by the sawyer Thomas Limerick and the laborers Richard Woodward and John Richardson gathered at St. Andrew's, Holborn. They proceeded to tear down a suspected bordello. A band of 400, led by Edward Cotton and others, attacked brothels at St. Leonard's, Shoreditch. When a troop of the royal guard under the command of Sir Philip Howard ordered them to disperse, they hurled stones at him, some thinking he was the duke of York. Using as their slogans "Liberty of Conscience!" and "Reformation and Reducement!" the rioters warned of a bloody May Day unless they received liberty of conscience. Crying "Hey, now or never," others threatened to storm Whitehall Palace and slaughter the royal guards. Yet another group, this one numbering some 500, gathered at East Smithfield and Moorfields under the leadership of the laborer Richard Beasley (or Bazley), assisted by Peter Messenger (or Messinger), Thomas Appletree, and William Greene. After fashioning a flag by attaching a green apron to a staff, they too attacked brothels; whether they chose that color because of its earlier association with the Levellers is, however, impossible to know.[12]

The apprentices had considerable support from bystanders, but the lord mayor's forces managed to arrest seven of the leaders. Three more were apprehended when the rioters unsuccessfully attempted to rescue their compatriots. When a group of about 300 met at Clerkenwell Green, near the Charterhouse, their leaders, including the tailor Edward Bedell and the laborer Richard Latimer, led them to New Prison. Ordered to depart by a magistrate, they retorted that having been servants for a long time, they would now be masters. When threatened with punishment, they cried, "One dye and all dye." They managed to free two of their colleagues as well as two felons.[13]

Rioting continued on the 25th despite the fact that the militia and the royal guards had been on duty throughout the night. Shouting "Down with the Red-coats," the crowd stoned the troops and, according to Pepys, mocked them. Before the tumult subsided, many purported brothels had been pulled down, two of which belonged to the duke of York. The apprentices, moreover, asserted that they should have dismantled "the great bawdy-house at White hall." A robbery there on the afternoon of the 28th was probably the last gasp of the riot. William Sherwood, Henry Godfrey, and Howard Coney broke into the palace and stole three jewel-studded gold rings along with other jewels and valuables worth in excess of £212. Sherwood and Godfrey were hanged for their crime.[14]

There is some evidence that the militants may have encouraged and participated in the rioting, but no proof that they instigated it. Sir Edward Nicholas's son John learned that former Cromwellian officers were inciting the rioters on the 25th, and that a search was under way for them. Pepys acquired information that some of the demonstrators were ex-Cromwellian troops, and a government spy reported that there was an "abundance of old ollivers officers and souldiers in towne upon the account of work. . . . I heare a whispering as if there were some dableing with the old souldiers." This informer was already on the track of an alleged plot by a group he called "the prudentiall Rant," which met in Whitecross Street on the afternoon of the 25th "to Consult and to informe themselves," presumably about the purported conspiracy rather than the riot. The apprentices, in his view, were the "pander[s]" to the conspirators, that is, their dupes. But he also noted that "the generallyty of the Sectaryes are soe well pleased with those storyes of the prentices that they cannot containe them selves."[15]

Fifteen leaders of the Easter riots were tried for high treason in the Old Bailey. Eight were found guilty, although four of these, including Latimer, received pardons. On 9 May Beasley, Limerick, Cotton, and Messenger were hanged, drawn, and quartered at Tyburn. In the meantime the government investigated the conduct of London officials and Middlesex justices of the peace to ascertain why it had taken so long to suppress the rioters. The militia, they discovered, had not been at full strength; the king thereupon pledged to put an end to the practice of phantom mustering.[16]

A second three-day riot occurred in the spring of 1668 at Taunton in Somerset. Nonconformists were numerous in the town, which, according to one loyalist, "hates the Church & Churchmen." On the 11th, 12th, and 13th they celebrated the lifting of a royal siege in May 1645 with a bonfire and closed shops, "by which they glory in their

rebellion." Although the "meaner sort" engaged in some "great insolencies," the riot had no serious consequences. Among the cele-
brants were many who had been born since 1645; their participation
underscored the fact that a new generation of dissidents was coming
to the fore.[17]

Years of Drifting

From the end of the Dutch War until late 1670 the radicals seem
to have had no clear idea of what they wanted to do, though most
gave up on the idea of a general insurrection. That, perhaps, is why
they were in no position to take advantage of the Easter riots in 1668.
An undated document in the Public Record Office (SP 29/230/108),
filed with the 1667 papers, hints at planning for a general uprising.
Captain Richard Laurence, a prisoner in the Dorchester jail, allegedly told another inmate that all the prisons in England would be
broken into during the early spring and the dissenters liberated. Reportedly this was intended to strengthen a nonconformist army that
would move against the government after first assassinating Albemarle as he walked in St. James's Park. There was probably little
substance to these allegations, although in July 1668 Abraham Goodman, a London gentleman, was convicted of high treason for conspiring to depose the king; he had also spoken traitorously against
Albemarle and the judges.[18]

Serious scheming was hampered by the fact that many prominent
radicals were still in prison. Wildman, however, was now free and in
Buckingham's employ, but he seems to have contented himself with
nothing more than blustery speech: "Neighbour," he reputedly told
a Norwich Quaker in July 1669, "are you whetting your Syth against
harvest—you had more need whett your Sword. . . . Doe you heare
nothing of Warr begun or to be begun?"[19] Samuel Moyer had been
released even earlier, in May 1667. The Fifth Monarchists Richard
Goodgroom, John Portman, and John Rye, imprisoned in 1660
and 1661, were still incarcerated at Hull in September 1667. Vavasor
Powell was finally freed that November after a confinement of six
years, only to be jailed again a year later; he died a prisoner in October 1670. Sir Hardress Waller (d. c. 1666), William Heveningham
(d. 1678), Henry Marten (d. 1680), Robert Tichborne (d. 1682), and

possibly Robert Overton, Thomas Waite, and Henry Smith likewise died in prison. Edward Salmon and Richard Creed were still prisoners in 1670, and Robert Duckenfield, who went to jail only in 1665, apparently was not freed until 1668.[20]

On the Continent there was drift too among the exiles. Ludlow's unwillingness to assume the mantle of leadership during the war sapped most of his prestige among radicals. He continued to correspond with friends in London, especially the Fifth Monarchists Hugh Courtney and Walter Thimbleton, both of whom had reportedly been plotting in Essex in 1666. Apparently he also corresponded, like other exiles, with Philip Alden, who, unknown to Ludlow, was a government agent. Desborough, having obeyed the royal summons to return home, was released from the Tower in February 1667; he attended conventicles but refrained from radical activity until his death in 1680. Dr. Edward Richardson, one of the chief architects of the northern rebellion, shunned radical schemes after fleeing to the Netherlands. Although William Burton of Great Yarmouth had not obeyed the king's proclamation to return in 1666, he sought and was offered a pardon in 1668, but he apparently stayed in the Netherlands and engaged with James Washington and George Gosfright, a former associate of William Kiffin, in shipping "factious" books to England. Washington, a justice of the peace at Leeds in the 1650s, was by March 1668 reputed to be "one of the grand Incendaryes" among the exiles and a key figure in trying to revive the Good Old Cause. Although George Joyce, the abductor of Charles I, showed no signs of wanting to make his peace with the Stuart regime, an unsuccessful attempt to arrest him in Rotterdam forced him into hiding and apparent inactivity. Thus the conspicuous failure of the exiles to restore the fortunes of the Good Old Cause during the war left them impotent.[21]

In the meantime Thomas Tillam, Christopher Pooley, and John Foxey continued their efforts to recruit English citizens for their millenarian community in the Palatinate. Pooley and Foxey returned to England in June 1666 and told potential disciples in the northeast "that they must seperate because the sins of this kingdome are soe great, that the lord will destroy itt; that they hope they must bee the people that must restore & sett up the kingdome of Christ here."

They had no plans to foment rebellion in England, although their covenant unmistakably manifested their religious convictions. Those who joined the Tillam community were required "utterly to re-nounce all powers that ever were, are, or shall bee, opposers and persecutors of the subjects of Christs kingdome." They refused to accept any ruler or judge who was not in communion with them, or to use any coins with images or inscriptions contrary to the word of God. Oaths to unbelievers, bearing arms for unchristian magistrates, and marriage to unbelievers were prohibited. Property could be communal or private, according to the dictates of the individual conscience.[22]

After his tour through the northeast, Pooley went to Notting-hamshire and Suffolk, where he was arrested at Ipswich in the spring of 1667. True to his principles, he refused to take the oath of alle-giance or to acknowledge that he was a subject of the king. In Janu-ary 1668 Pooley and Foxey were at Raby Castle in Durham, where the Baptist Henry Blackett was preaching, and where radical tradi-tions were strong. Lady Vane's steward at Raby Castle, Mr. Cocks, was notorious among conformists for regarding Church of England clerics as "noe better then Roman Catholicks, Teaching for Doctrine the traditions of them." More alarming was the report that there were approximately 140 well-armed men in this area, some of whom were highwaymen or veterans of the 1663 northern rebellion, such as John Ward. According to a government spy, the former Cromwellian soldiers Blackett and Cornet Blenkinsop were convinced that Christ would soon appear on behalf of his followers. In June 1668 Cocks told the same informant that the government intended to butcher imprisoned saints, and hence it was necessary for them to take refuge in the northern castles before they were arrested. Cocks also ex-pected a general uprising in the London area on 4 July of the same year.[23]

Elsewhere in the north dissidents tried to keep their spirits up. Paul Hobson's friend Captain Thomas Gower not only talked of a sudden change in the government but in May 1668 was associating with John or Robert Linton of Shields, Durham, whose guest was the noted Scottish dissident the laird of Swinton. George Bateman, John Atkinson's father-in-law, gave Swinton a prophecy and other (unspecified) papers, which a government spy hoped to see. Sir Philip Musgrave concluded from all this that the dissidents would revolt again as soon as the time was ripe, and that Swinton would be involved. Simultaneously he monitored the activities at Raby Castle, hoping to learn who Cocks's friends were in the north as well as the identity of his London correspondents.[24]

Durham notwithstanding, the north was generally quiet in the postwar era apart from the continuing agitation over conventicles. Daniel Fleming suspected that the dissenters in the northwest "have been, & are now designing some mischeif; for besides the late boldness of the Highway men in divers places, [there are] the many false Rumors & Reports (one of their ancient Policies) which wee have hard of Late in these parts (one which that the Scotts are up in armes, another which, that Bishops & Dean & Chapters Lands will be sold, or annext to the Crowne in the place of the Excise & Hearth-money, & Bishops to be maintained by sallaries out of the Exchequer)." Once again there was the ominous parallel with the early 1640s: "This Party . . . [is] now pursueing . . . the very same practices as the Puritans did in the late Kings time" because they had many of the same grievances. In Yorkshire the sheriff, Sir Philip Monckton, found himself the subject of a complaint to the Privy Council for helping procure the acquittal of John Browne, a former parliamentary soldier charged with denying Charles II's right to the throne and calling him a rogue. Monckton was also accused of inciting sixty suspected plotters "to trouble those that Caused them to be imprison'd, pretendinge they were imprisond without Authority & that he will se[e] them righted." But a report from Chester in August 1670 summarized conditions in most of the north: "The Phanatiques are prettie calme."[25]

Fleming's hint that northern militants may have been involved in robberies is perhaps corroborated by circumstances involving the highwayman Darcy Lascelles.[26] Arrested in the spring of 1669, he gave the authorities information about the 1663 insurrection as well as more recent radical activities. According to him, the Baptist George Marshal, who was at Woodham Moor in Durham with Captain Roger Jones, had carried information about the conspiracy between the north and the conspirators' council in London, to which

Marshal allegedly—but almost certainly did not—belong. Within the past two years Marshal had reportedly taken £20 to dissidents in London who were plotting to assassinate the king and Albemarle, and to seize the Tower of London. The conspiracy also purportedly involved Thomas Stoe of Retford, Nottinghamshire, and Christopher Mansell of London; the latter was supposedly responsible for coining money to pay the plotters. However, Lascelles's garbled account is untrustworthy; among his allegations is the preposterous claim that Ludlow, Doleman, and Whalley had been in London and Yorkshire many times since the 1663 rebellion. Whether Lascelles knew and associated with radicals in the north or simply repeated hearsay to the magistrates is unclear. Various justices of the peace and gentlemen of Cheshire tried to save Lascelles in the belief that he was "fit for his Majesty's service at home or abroad," but he was executed in June 1669.[27]

Most of the concern about radical behavior in the postwar period focused, as usual, on London. In part this was due to fears engendered by the great fire. Letters addressed to a man at the African House in London in the spring of 1669 spoke of persons traveling to the City with fireballs and "grenadoes" to burn Whitehall and the royal stables. The government subsequently intercepted similar letters from the same unknown person. In May 1670 magistrates arrested Mary Worrall, wife of a Stepney yeoman, and Robert Ciprey of St. Leonard's, Shoreditch; the former had fireballs made of gunpowder, sulfur, and other combustible material, and the latter refused to identify persons in Wapping who possessed fireballs. During the same spring magistrates discovered large quantities of gunpowder and balls in London, and arrested those who could not satisfactorily account for them.[28]

The weapons searches in the spring of 1670 were part of the heightened security occasioned by the great influx of nonconformists into the City in the aftermath of the passage of the new Conventicle Act. On 25 May the lord mayor and eleven commissioners expressed concern to Arlington about "the more then ordinary resort of Sectaries & disaffected persons (such especially as were active & engaged in the late Rebellion) from all parts of the kingdome to the City and parts adjacent." To deal with the situation they sought a special commission empowering them to use the militia to maintain order, to execute rebels at their discretion, and to imprison dangerous and suspicious persons as long as they saw fit and to seize their weapons. Charles responded favorably the following day, giving specific instructions to instigate a strict search for dangerous and disaffected persons and to suppress rebels and traitors. The trained bands were called out, and almost immediately moved against the conventicles. They could not find the Presbyterian Thomas Watson but they wrecked his pulpit and seats before nailing shut the doors to his meeting place at Devonshire House, Bishopsgate. Although some officers and soldiers interrupted the Presbyterian Thomas Doolittle in the act of preaching, his congregation helped him escape. A Quaker speaking in Bishopsgate Street similarly got away. Repressive efforts by the trained bands brought "strange looks & hints of dislike amongst spectators," including some who were conformists but "like[d] not this way."[29]

As security was increased in the London area, dissidents who refused to provide bonds for their lawful behavior were interned in Newgate prison. On 10 June the king issued a proclamation ordering all cashiered soldiers and officers of the parliamentary and Cromwellian forces to leave the London area by the 16th, to stay at least twenty miles away, to refrain from using or carrying weapons, and not to return until 10 December. As a further precaution the royal guards were augmented in June. In December the lord mayor instructed the aldermen to make certain that a list was kept with the names of all residents, lodgers, and travelers, and to keep searching for suspicious persons.[30]

One of those arrested in the crackdown was Major or Captain John Hume (or Humes), who had been banished from Scotland in 1660. It seems, however, that instead of leaving the country he went underground, for he corresponded with the northern rebels in 1663. Arrested in Moorfields in 1666 and imprisoned in the Tower, he subsequently escaped. In 1670 he was apprehended at a conventicle in Southwark and returned to the Tower. Among the papers found in his possession was a list of eighteen nonconformist ministers, including the Congregationalist Thomas Brooks and the Presbyterians William Bates, Onesiphorus Rood, Nathaniel Vincent, and Edward

Sheffield. He also had an account of an apparition of a large number of armed riders purportedly seen by a woman and three men at East Brandon, Durham, which one loyalist said was intended to persuade people that a rebellion was imminent. Despite all the security measures in the London area, a small group of radicals mounted a daring though limited attack on Ormond in December 1670.[31]

To Kill a Duke: The Ormond Kidnapping

Following his unsuccessful rescue of Captain John Mason near Darrington, Thomas Blood, the architect of the attack on Ormond, went into hiding at Rumford, Essex, where he practiced medicine. During these years he used a variety of aliases: Dr. Allen, Dr. Clarke, Ayloffe, Aylett or Eylett, and Aleck. A man "of a down look, lean faced, and full of pockholes" who typically wore a short brown periwig, a "Stuff Coat," and a worsted cloak,[32] Blood moved to the Aldgate area, near the Tower, not long before December 1670. He was separated from his wife, Mary, perhaps for reasons of safety; she had operated an apothecary's shop in nearby Shoreditch, but by late 1670 was living with a schoolmaster at Mortlake. Blood's son, commonly known by his alias, Thomas Hunt, was in his early twenties and a Presbyterian like his father. A tall, well-proportioned man with a ruddy complexion, he had a slight limp because of a deformed leg. About 1667 he was apprenticed at Southwark to a Scottish apothecary and former army surgeon, but six months later he moved to Romford and became a grocer, a druggist, or a mercer. By 1670 he was reportedly deeply in debt, and on 4 July he was convicted of robbery, fined 100 marks, and incarcerated in the Marshalsea until August.[33]

The two Bloods were on intimate terms in 1670 with the Fifth Monarchist Richard Halliwell, a tobacco cutter in Petticoat Lane, near Bishopsgate Street. Halliwell had been to Flanders and Virginia, probably prior to 1664, for in that year he was arrested for attending a Baptist conventicle. A former cornet, he was described as a man of demure countenance with a plump, pockmarked face. Halliwell was a deeply religious man whose millenarian convictions persuaded him that the saints should not pray for the "beast," an allusion to the king and the Stuart state. In his judgment the gathered churches should have remained loyal to a republican government. He rebuked the godly for obeying the Conventicle Acts, for their spiritual coldness, and for their transgressions of the Covenant. Like the earlier Seekers, he finally resolved to withdraw from the church until its members repented of their sins. These were the last times, he told his sister, in which Satan lulled the godly to sleep.[34]

The fourth member of this tiny cabal was an old associate of Blood's in Ireland and one of the more elusive conspirators of the 1660s—Colonel William More (or Moore). In 1648 his regiment of foot, which had been in Ulster since 1646, joined Michael Jones, and six years later he was involved in transporting the Irish. When his regiment was sent to the West Indies in the spring of 1657 he was so unhappy that only the threat of a court-martial kept him from returning. In any case he was back in England in November 1658. After the Restoration he joined with Blood in the abortive Dublin plot, and then in 1665, having lost his Irish lands, was allegedly dispatched to Ireland by a meeting of dissidents in Liverpool in order to incite rebellion. By early 1668 he was living in Gray's Inn Lane in London, where he rented lodgings from the Congregationalist Francis Johnson, the ejected master of University College, Oxford, and a former chaplain of Oliver Cromwell. According to Johnson, More was the son of Sir William More of Scotland.[35]

The two Bloods, Halliwell, and More were the core of the group that planned the attack on Ormond. At least two and possibly five others were involved, including the Fifth Monarchist William Smith, who had helped with the preparations for Mason's rescue.[36] Information given to Arlington and presented to a committee of the House of Lords in February 1671 mentions the two Bloods, Halliwell, More, Captain Roger Jones, and one Simons. Jones, of course, was well-known for his involvement in the northern rebellion, and Simons was probably the London goldsmith Symmons who had been associated with a group allegedly planning the king's assassination in 1663. According to this testimony the conventicles with which the six were associated deplored the attempt on Ormond and wanted the culprits punished. Blood subsequently implicated William Smith (alias Mann).[37]

The motives for the assault were straightforward enough. The elder Blood and More had both lost their Irish estates, for which Ormond was held responsible. The younger Blood, now destitute, probably blamed the duke for his misfortune, knowing from his father how the family had lost its Irish lands. Halliwell presumably saw this as an opportunity to avenge the execution of Major-General Thomas Harrison and the persecution of Cornet Wentworth Day, which seemed to trouble him a great deal.[38]

On 6 December Ormond attended a banquet at the Guildhall hosted by the lord mayor to fete William of Orange. While the festivities were under way, Blood and four accomplices, wearing long cloaks and armed with swords, went to the "Bull Head" tavern in Charing Cross, pretending to be graziers. As they waited for Ormond's carriage, each of them downed two pints of wine. It was nearly 7:00 P.M. when a man on foot wearing a cloak came into the tavern and announced, "Make way here for the Duke of Ormond." When the coach passed, Blood's party rode hastily after it, going down Pall Mall and past St. James's Palace toward the duke's residence at Clarendon House. As the duke's six footmen either lagged behind or were dispersed by some of Blood's men, one of the riders prevailed on the coachman to stop in St. James's Street, claiming there was a dead man in the road. While two of the radicals trained their pistols on the coachman, the others forced the duke out of the coach, threatening to pistol-whip him if he resisted. Refusing his offer of 40 guineas and jewels worth £1,000, they tied him to the younger Blood and rode away. As the elder Blood galloped ahead to Tyburn to put a rope on the gallows in order to hang Ormond as a common criminal, the duke threw himself and the younger Blood off their horse into the mud of Piccadilly or the Knightsbridge Road. By this point the page had alerted the duke's porter, who arrived with another member of Ormond's household in time to see the struggle. Although shots were fired at the duke, he escaped with no more than a sword wound and a pistol blow or two on his face. The assailants raced to the Fulham ferry, crossed the Thames, and fled through Lambeth to Southwark, where they disappeared. Sir John Trevor, a secretary of state, immediately ordered the ports watched to prevent their flight from the country.[39]

The next day a proclamation offered a reward of £1,000 to anyone who revealed the identity of any of the six persons thought
to be involved in the attack. A pardon plus the award was offered
to any of the conspirators who freely confessed. The state, however, had little evidence on which to proceed. During the struggle
Ormond had stripped away the younger Blood's pistol, belt, and
sword, with the inscription "T.H." These, as it happened, had been
confiscated from Blood when he was arrested in May, and he had
signed a receipt for them when they were returned on 17 October.
The assailants also left three horses behind, but these proved to be
of little value in the investigation. The tapster and a companion provided an account of the actions of the five men in the tavern but
could name none of them. Michael Beresford, a minister from Hop-
ton, Suffolk, testified that he had seen "Allen"—an alias used by both
of the Bloods—in Covent Garden on the evening of the attack, and
that "Allen" had referred to "great designs" in progress. Beresford
claimed to have known "Allen" when the latter was a footman of the
regicide Sir Michael Livesey; if so, this person could hardly have
been either of the Bloods.[40]

Enough information had been compiled by the 11th to issue warrants for the arrest of Thomas Hunt (Blood junior), Ayliffe (his father), Hollyway (Halliwell), Samuel Holmes, and Mrs. Elizabeth
Price, Holmes's sister. Warrants followed on the 12th for Thomas and
Mary Hurst and Thomas Grantam, and on the 14th for Thomas Sunderland. The *Gazette* for 8–12 December carried descriptions of Halliwell, Hurst, and the two Bloods (under their aliases).[41] Holmes,
the apothecary for whom the younger Blood had worked, could not
be reliably implicated in the scheme. The Hurst in whom authorities
were interested turned out to be a John Hurst, but investigations
turned up three men of this name, none of whom could be indisputably linked to the attack. The most suspicious of these, a Yorkshire
attorney, had recently been in Ireland and Scotland, and was seen
with Halliwell at the Exchange on the 14th or 15th—hardly adequate
evidence that he was one of Ormond's assailants. Sunderland's only
offense was to have spoken favorably of the would-be assassins.[42]

Although a number of arrests were made, the government failed
to apprehend any of the culprits.[43] Three merchants en route to

France, two Gloucestershire butchers, an Irish counterfeiter, and a London cook were among the innocent who were arrested, and suspicion was even temporarily cast on one of the queen's guard. The earl of Ossory accused Buckingham of sponsoring the attempted assassination and threatened to pistol-whip the duke if it happened again, while others suspected the duchess of Cleveland. On 14 January 1671 the House of Lords appointed a committee of sixty-nine peers to investigate the assault; after a month of inquiries it drew up a bill against only three men—the two Bloods (under their aliases) and Halliwell.[44]

While officials were still trying to discover the facts about the Ormond affair, Richard Wilkinson, who had served under Monck in 1659–60 and was more recently the sergeant in a company stationed on the Isle of Wight, related information about an alleged "grand conspiracy" against the king. His source, a former acquaintance in the Cromwellian forces, knew someone who had enlisted fifty men to attack the guards at the gates of Whitehall. The latter person, he subsequently learned, was Captain John Mason. "In steade of armor [they] had designed for themselves close bodied coates Lynd with quiers of paper which would bare carbine bullets." They would act, his source asserted, during an occasion such as "masking & other Jovial sports at courte." This alleged conspiracy would have predated the attack on Ormond, for in late November 1670 Wilkinson was in London with his acquaintance and another man when the latter read part of a declaration that called on the godly to use swords to regain their rights as freeborn citizens. The declaration, they said, had been printed about June 1670. The leader of this alleged conspiracy was none other than Mason (alias Father Thomas), and one of his followers was purportedly a veteran of Venner's 1661 uprising. Wilkinson and other informers also claimed that Blood, Captain John Lockyer, and Timothy Butler were involved. Butler was in the London area in December and at Gravesend the following month, where he was reportedly a steward for Coutnay, whom B.S. Capp has suggested may have been the Fifth Monarchist Hugh Courtney. Another person implicated in the alleged cabal was the Fifth Monarchist Richard Goodgroom. When Wilkinson was examined by Arlington, he could not say if Mason and Butler were involved in the attack on Ormond.

Considering the lengths to which Blood had gone to rescue Mason, it seems likely that if the captain was in the London area he would have been apprised of the Ormond plot; there is, however, no evidence that he participated in it.[45] For his part, Blood soon began planning another exploit.

The Theft of the Crown Jewels

"One of the strangest and [most] infamous actions that any age can paralelle"—so said a newsletter of 9 May 1671 in reference to Blood's attempt to steal the crown jewels from the Tower of London. The robbery itself was the work of at least five men, three of whom were caught in the act: Blood, his son, and the Fifth Monarchist Robert Perrott, a London silk-dyer who had been a lieutenant in Major-General Thomas Harrison's regiment. Perrott had previously associated with Blood, Henry Danvers, John Lockyer, Jeremiah Marsden, and Edward Cary. The fourth man was Halliwell, a veteran of the Ormond assault, and the fifth was either Cary or William More. In addition, William Smith served as a scout for the thieves, and there was suspicion that the brewer Ralph Alexander, a veteran of the Rathbone conspiracy, was also involved.[46]

The groundwork for the robbery began in mid-April when Blood arrived at the Tower dressed in the garb of a minister. With him, he said, was his wife, although the keeper of the crown jewels, Talbot Edwards, subsequently insisted she was an imposter. When "Mrs. Blood" feigned an upset stomach after she had seen the crown, the keeper's wife allowed her to lie down. Three days later Blood returned to the Tower with four pair of new gloves as a token of gratitude for Mrs. Edwards's assistance. Frequent visits ensued, culminating in Blood's suggestion that Edwards's daughter marry his nephew. Agreeing, the keeper arranged for his daughter to meet the young man at 7:00 A.M. on the 9th of May. At the appointed hour Blood appeared with his son, Perrott, and another man, apologizing that Mrs. Blood would be late and asking if his friends could pass the time by viewing the crown. The fifth man remained outside with the horses. Each was armed with a rapier blade hidden in a cane, a dagger, and a pair of pocket-pistols.

When Edwards ushered Blood and his confederates into the room housing the crown, they threw a cloak over his head, gagged him with a plug of wood, and fastened an iron hook to his nose. As he struggled to alert his wife, his daughter, and his daughter-in-law upstairs, the thieves hit him repeatedly with a wooden mallet, then stabbed him in the stomach. Edwards feigned death while Blood stuffed the crown under his cloak, Perrott jammed the orb into his breeches, and Blood junior prepared to file the scepter in two because of its length. At that point Edwards's son arrived unexpectedly and sensed trouble when he was greeted at the door by one of the robbers. While the son went upstairs to check on the women, the conspirators fled, leaving the scepter behind. Edwards struggled to his feet, removed the gag, and cried "Treason, murder!" As his son chased the robbers, his daughter sounded the alarm and others joined the pursuit. At the drawbridge Blood fired his pistol at the warder, who fell to the ground, unhit. The sentinel at the wardhouse gate, a former Cromwellian soldier, made no attempt to stop them, though a servant seized Perrott and an officer captured Blood when the latter again missed his shot and tried to recover the crown he had dropped. The younger Blood made it to his horse, but was nearly thrown off when he struck a pole protruding from a cart; a constable finally arrested him in Gravel Lane. The other two escaped. The orb and the crown were recovered, although a large pearl, a diamond, and some smaller stones had fallen off; these were subsequently recovered and the crown repaired.[47]

The two Bloods and Perrott were returned to the Tower the same day, this time as prisoners of Sir John Robinson. A little book containing sixty "signal deliverances from eminent dangers" was found in the elder Blood's possession, but this seems not to have survived. He refused to cooperate when he was interrogated by the provost marshal, Sir Gilbert Talbot, but on the 12th the king, the duke of York, and others examined him. According to one account this "gallant hardy a villain as ever herded in that sneaking sect of the Anabaptists . . . answered so frankly and undauntedly that every one stood amazed." In Baxter's words, Blood "spake so boldly that all admired him: telling the King, How many of his Subjects were disobliged, and that he was one that took himself to be in a State of

Hostility: and that he took not the Crown as a Thief, but an Enemy, thinking that lawful which was lawful in a War." Blood acknowledged his participation in the attempted assassination of Ormond as well as the theft of the crown jewels. Although a newsletter asserted that the three captured men confessed that "their designe . . . was onely to make their owne advantage by the jewells," Blood insisted that he had acted to avenge Ormond's seizure of his estate and the execution of some of his friends. Many of his associates, he said, had taken an oath to get revenge for their deaths.[48]

Blood also confessed to his involvement in the Battersea plot, an attempt, he alleged, to assassinate the king because of his suppression of the nonconformists. Blood and his confederates were prepared to shoot Charles as he swam in the Thames above Battersea, but, he claimed, when he saw the king from his hiding place in the reeds he was so awed that he called off the attempt. As Baxter recounts the story, Blood reckoned that the king's "Life was better for them than his Death, lest a worse succeed him." If he were executed for his crimes, he told the king, his friends, bound by oaths, would avenge his death with a massacre of the court, but if his life were spared, many would be grateful and the crown would be saved.[49]

Given the number of purported plots to assassinate the king, the Battersea conspiracy is believable enough, but the purpose of relating it was so palpably self-serving that it might seem a contrivance of Blood's imagination. However, on 21 September 1671 Joseph Williamson recorded information given to him by Blood and others to the effect that "Mene Tekel [Captain Roger Jones] put Bl[ood] after L. Ormonds businesse to have killed the K[ing] at the H. of Lords with 300 men." The plans, which Blood claimed he had enough men to implement, also called for the seizure of the earl of Craven and George Morley, bishop of Winchester. The tobacconist John Harrison subsequently testified that Ralph Alexander had told him about "battle-axes or bills with long staves" stored for the conspirators at a house in Thames Street; these were dumped into the river after Blood had revealed the plot. Blood claimed that he forgot to tell the king about this conspiracy; now, however, he clearly had nothing to gain by fabricating a plot. The alleged plan would have been contrived sometime between mid-December 1670, after the attempt on

Ormond failed, and mid-April 1671, when the plot to rob the crown jewels commenced. If true, this lends circumstantial credence to Jones's involvement in the Ormond attack. The Battersea conspiracy had to occur no later than the early fall of 1670, for the king would not have been swimming in the Thames between mid-December 1670 and mid-April 1671, when the Tower scheme got under way. But the attempted theft of the crown jewels only delayed the more ambitious coup, for Blood's associate Ralph Alexander subsequently confessed that indeed "a greate Number of battle-axes or bills with long staves" had been amassed for the plot to overthrow the government. According to Alexander, these weapons, however, were dumped in the Thames when the conspirators learned Blood had confessed.[50]

The state undoubtedly pressed Blood for the names of his accomplices in the Ormond kidnapping and the theft of the crown jewels, but this he seems to have refused until they were offered pardons. However, three days after Blood's examination, John Buxton of Bell Alley, Coleman Street, was committed to the Gatehouse at Westminster "for dangerous practices and combinations with Thomas Blood and his son." Buxton had previously been interrogated in connection with the Ormond assault because of his acquaintance with the Bloods and Halliwell, but so far was he from being a suspect that Arlington had given him a warrant to apprehend Blood junior. Was his arrest in May 1671, then, an act of retribution by the elder Blood, or was he a participant in one of the plots? In any event he was released on 16 May.[51]

Even more puzzling questions are raised by Blood's letter to the king of 19 May, a week after his examination. In this stunning document he asserts that the joint treasurers of the navy, Sir Thomas Osborne and Sir Thomas Littleton, "sett me to steall your Crowne, butt he that feed me with Money was, James Littleton esquire," an employee of the navy treasury office and "a very bold, vilianous fellow, a very rogue." Many times, Blood claimed, James Littleton had given his group payments of £100 to support the planned robbery. On the face of it the letter is preposterous, and its seeming lack of sincerity is buttressed by Blood's flippant pun on his name in signing the letter "youer dutifull subiett, whose name is Blood which I hope is not that your Majestie seeks after." Blood's biographer, W.C. Abbott, interprets the letter as an example of the writer's wit and effrontery, both of which delighted the king and may have been a factor in the bestowal of royal clemency.[52]

The letter hints at something deeper, not least because a man in Blood's position, acting alone, could hardly afford to risk his fate by making unsubstantiated accusations against two powerful men. Osborne's political career had been greatly aided in the late 1660s by his patron, Buckingham, whom he had assisted by attacking Clarendon in the Commons. Sir Thomas Littleton too had been a strong critic of Clarendon, a friend of Buckingham, and though not a nonconformist had opposed the 1670 Conventicle Act.[53] Were Blood's charges therefore an attempt, perhaps instigated by Arlington, to embarrass Buckingham, whose popularity with the nonconformists was well-known, as was his patronage of Osborne? The duke had, after all, only recently recovered from the legal difficulties occasioned by his commission to John Heydon to cast the king's horoscope. Blood, moreover, became Arlington's agent in the immediate post-Tower period, lending credence to the idea that the charge was inspired by Arlington to undermine Buckingham.

Alternatively, was Blood telling the truth—a story so seemingly preposterous that no one believed it? After his imprisonment in 1667 the duke had ample motive for revenge, and he was now the patron of the republican John Wildman, an inveterate plotter. If Ossory was correct in suspecting that Buckingham was behind the attempt on Ormond, it is no more improbable that he worked through Osborne and Littleton to seize the crown. About the time that Blood and his accomplices robbed the Tower, someone broke into the lord keeper's house, apparently in search of the Great Seal.[54] Is it possible, then, that Buckingham engineered a conspiracy to seize power, the prelude to which was the acquisition of the crown, the orb, the scepter, and the Great Seal? Against this view is the apparent fact that neither the Littletons nor Osborne was even interrogated. This possibility thus seems less plausible than the one that attributes Blood's sensational charge to the political machinations of Arlington.

In the aftermath of Blood's arrest royalists anticipated that at last he would "receive the reward of his many wicked attempts" in England and Ireland. But in the inner confines of the court an entirely different fate was being planned for Blood, whether by Buckingham or Arlington is unclear, but certainly with the king's connivance. One of the first steps involved a letter of apology from Blood to his archenemy, the duke of Ormond. Carried personally to the duke by Arlington, Blood's letter was an unqualified—if not necessarily sincere—statement of remorse: "The greatnesse of my Crimes soe farr exceeds expression that weare not my burdened soule incuraged by findin[g] vent to its griefe," he wrote, he could not bear up. Calling himself an "unworthy monster," he expressed regret for his "most hainous Crime" and offered to serve Ormond. Ever the king's loyal servant, the duke accepted the apology.[55]

The Bloods were still closely confined in the Tower at the end of June, but on 14 July Arlington gave Sir John Robinson warrants for the release of the elder Blood and Perrott; Blood junior would stay in prison. On 1 August the elder Blood received a pardon for all treason, murders, and other felonies he had committed since 29 May 1660. The following day he was seen walking in the courtyard at Whitehall, dressed in a new suit and periwig, looking "extraordinary pleasant and jocose." Similar pardons were issued to his son and Perrott on 31 August. As word of Blood's confession spread, radicals were concerned. Ludlow, who had written approvingly of Blood's rescue of Mason but was withholding judgment on the jewel robbery until he heard Blood's explanation, was worried because the latter knew so much about radical activities. At Loughton, Essex, Captain William Poveye (alias Thompson), who had been in London, suggested that Blood and the others should be stabbed.[56]

In addition to his freedom, Blood received a pension of £500 per annum in Irish lands and the return of his English and Irish property. He was expected to keep the government apprised of dissident activity, to improve relations between the Stuart regime and the nonconformists, and to "reduce or disperse" the "absconded persons." His new role was set in the context of the king's plans for an indulgence and a new war with the Dutch. Blood, they hoped, might be the key to preventing renewed attempts to create an alliance between the radicals and the Dutch that would crimp English war efforts. In this area his work probably had minimal impact, but when the indulgence was offered, he acted as an agent to obtain the requisite licenses for Presbyterians, Congregationalists, and Baptists, and in 1672 he worked for the release of imprisoned nonconformists.[57]

The Search for an Accommodation

Considerations of foreign policy dictated alterations in the treatment of the dissenters in 1671. Not only had the crackdown on conventicles in 1670 proved to be a failure, but the government's harsh policy probably contributed to London's refusal to grant the king a loan in September 1670. The obvious solution was to issue an indulgence, which would quiet Protestant dissenters and open the way for more lenient treatment of Catholics. Such a policy would be doubly difficult to implement not only because of legal questions regarding the king's suspensory powers but because of the growth of anti-Catholic feelings, rumblings of discontent about a French alliance, and general hostility toward an indulgence by many conformists and Presbyterians. The more conservative among the latter, including Richard Baxter and Philip Henry, still preferred comprehension within the state church and bridled at a policy that would make them *de facto* separatists.[58] A policy of indulgence, moreover, flew in the face of a House of Commons intent on imposing even tougher restrictions on dissent.

Blood's arrest following his attempted robbery of the crown jewels offered the king a useful instrument with which to pursue his policy. Here was a man with an almost unrivaled knowledge of the radical community in all three kingdoms and the Netherlands, and with a reputation as a fearless opponent of the regime. His arrest and subsequent pardon offered him the opportunity to serve as an intermediary between the state and his former associates—exactly the role Charles and Arlington envisioned for him. While the pardon destroyed Blood's credibility as a militant, leaving no opportunity for him to return to the radical community as a spy, it had obviously not been granted in return for a damaging disclosure that incriminated others in seditious acts. No series of arrests ensued. Blood was thus in a unique position to deal with his former comrades, with whom he had been linked in underground activity for nearly a dozen years.

His own pardon was clear proof that others could be treated similarly. John Bunyan liked to preach that Christ offered forgiveness to the greatest sinners first; thanks to the capture of Blood, Charles could act similarly in pardoning this impudent rebel.

To be sure, the government continued to utilize spies and agents, but in the immediate postwar period the espionage corps had undergone some crucial alterations. Chief among them were the mysterious deaths or murders of the three principal witnesses against Buckingham in 1667—George Middleton (alias Fawcet), John Gryce, and William Leeving. Gryce's testimony had been instrumental in convicting eight of the Rathbone conspirators in 1666, and Leeving had been spying on Blood and Jones for Arlington. After their deaths the government used informants such as William Fryer, who was ineffective, and William Haggett, a veteran who had served under Major-General Thomas Kelsey in Kent during the 1650s. Unlike Blood, neither had extensive contacts in the radical community.[59]

The useful life of a spy was typically rather brief. Leeving's periodic efforts to recruit more agents suggest a government in need of a regular supply of fresh spies. Indeed, the 1670 Conventicle Act virtually included an open invitation to would-be informants to spy on conventicles, with a third of the fines as their reward rather than the usual remuneration from a financially strapped government—an inexpensive means of gathering intelligence. Some spies managed to continue for rather lengthy periods, as in the case of the shoemaker Joseph Bincks (or Binckes), who had informed on Venner and was still spying a decade later, and Joseph Strangways.[60] In 1671 Blood, though no spy, opened up a new channel for intelligence on behalf of Arlington and Williamson. He was not, however, so much an informant as an intermediary—to nonconformist ministers as well as to militants willing to explore the offer of a royal pardon. In the beginning he worked with Dr. Nicholas Butler and Mr. Church, the clerk of the Fleet prison, both of whom developed their own ties to the nonconformists.

The principal body of evidence for the activities of Blood, Butler, and Church between Blood's pardon and the Declaration of Indulgence consists of Williamson's highly cryptic notes, written in a cramped, sometimes virtually undecipherable script. Interpreting his notes is rendered more difficult by the fact that they indiscriminately lump tales of court machinations, spy reports, records of conventicles, and references to divisions among Presbyterians over royal policy.

Arrangements with Blood were worked out in September 1671 in negotiations conducted successively with two peers known for their support of nonconformists, Lords Holles and Ashley.[61] Blood wanted the governorship of a plantation but had to settle for the financial benefits previously noted. His dealings with Ashley occurred at a time not only when the latter's position at court was on the rise but when his relations with Arlington improved considerably. Blood was thus asked to persuade nonconformists to accept the government's pro-French, anti-Dutch foreign policy, and to decipher and identify the authors of letters intercepted from radicals in the Netherlands. His efforts put him at odds with pro-Dutch dissidents such as Captain Roger Jones. The earl of Anglesey, himself a Presbyterian, seems to have known enough of what was happening to "blast" Blood among London nonconformists.[62]

By October Blood was meeting regularly with Butler and Church, and he was also working with James Innes (or Ennys, Ennis), a Scottish nonconformist with whom Ashley was intimate. Innes, who had been a preacher at Durham in the late 1640s and subsequently rector of St. Breock, Cornwall, had worked with Thomas Manton, William Bates, and Thomas Jacomb in an effort to persuade the king to grant religious freedom to nonconformists; he was introduced to court circles by Sir Robert Moray. Presumably with Blood's assistance, Church was attempting to establish contacts with sources in Ireland who could provide intelligence. Blood maintained contact with Williamson (and thus Arlington) through Sir John Robinson, while Williamson also conferred directly with Church and Butler.[63] Williamson was worried that the prospects of a new Dutch war had emboldened the nonconformists, and that if the Dutch fared well in the fighting England might face a "desperate danger" from an alliance of the Dutch and the militants. In part this reflected what he had learned from Church, who insisted that it would be madness not to reach some form of settlement with the dissenters before the outbreak of war. If Parliament imposed more penalties on nonconformists, he concluded, dissidents would be driven to extreme actions.

As conventicle activity picked up in the fall of 1671, Williamson wondered if it might not be due to the encouragement of Dutch agents and their partisans, although there is no evidence to support the notion that the former were involved. Charles's advisers were split as to the appropriate response to the conventicles. Some felt he should essentially ignore them, but others, including Williamson, urged that public assemblies should be repressed as long as meetings in homes were tolerated. This course, Williamson thought, would restore ministerial leadership, which had been eroding in the face of congregational militancy. Ministers who were reluctant to preach in the aftermath of the 1670 Conventicle Act were being told by their congregations that others would be found if they refused. The Presbyterian clergy divided, the old guard—who came to be known as "Dons"—opting to obey the law, while the more defiant ones—the "Ducklings"—took the plunge and held conventicles. Williamson compiled a list of those who openly held illegal services: they included the Vincent brothers, Thomas and Nathaniel; Samuel Annesley; Edward West; Thomas Doolittle; and James Janeway. Thomas Manton, Thomas Jacomb, and William Bates were among the Dons. Each group duly censured the other. The dissenters with whom Blood was most intimate were not holding conventicles in early November, whereas Innes's contacts were. To protect his sources Williamson wanted to summon Watson, creating the false impression that he was an informant.[64]

As all parties jockeyed for position, the intrigue deepened. Innes, acting as a spokesman for the Ducklings, urged Blood to ask the king to give liberty of conscience to the great meetinghouses, but Blood refused. On the night of 8 November Innes took his case directly to Charles, who professed sympathy but nevertheless demurred. Instead he told Innes "that they must order their meetings discreetly that you may strengthen my hands & not weaken them." The king was clearly not prepared to act, though he had Butler canvas "the Meeting-house men" and knew they were "stout sturdy dissatisfied people." What he did not realize, however, was that Innes and Blood were secretly meeting, whether to concoct a common strategy or simply to exchange information is unclear. Blood, Williamson noted, "sees privately & cunningly Innes & his friends[,] but of that not a word[,] not to the K[ing]." Williamson, in turn, wanted to ensure that the Presbyterian clergy did not know that he corresponded with Innes through Blood.[65]

From his survey of the Ducklings, Butler concluded that their indignation toward the government was probably more intense than officials had been led to believe. The king, Butler surmised, should therefore appease the dissenters now inasmuch as future demands under conditions of stress would undoubtedly be greater, as Charles I's experience had demonstrated. Williamson concluded that care should be taken to satisfy the nonconforming gentry because there would be no great disturbance without their participation. This was doubly significant for Williamson inasmuch as he recognized that there was no popular enthusiasm for another Dutch war, which people correctly connected to the Anglo-French alliance. It was thus too risky not to reach a settlement with the Protestant dissenters, particularly because they could join forces with an invading Dutch army.[66]

In the meantime Charles attempted to keep the situation under control by having the lord mayor and Innes warn the Ducklings to cease holding public meetings or risk losing the king's willingness to tolerate private services. But the meetings continued—and with substantial popular support, because, as Williamson admitted, "our men do not preach judiciously [and] effectionately."[67]

Between 16 November and 4 December Blood switched his primary allegiance from Arlington to Lauderdale, despite the fact that the latter was, according to Butler and Church, roundly disliked by English dissenters, certainly more so than Arlington. Blood's new relationship with Lauderdale was either the cause or the consequence of his break with Butler and Church, who no longer trusted him. Henceforth Butler made his own arrangements for intelligence from Scotland, and Church finally succeeded in gathering information from Ireland without consulting Blood. The latter continued to maintain close contact with Innes, although Innes informed Butler that two or three of Blood's old acquaintances still supported him. Moreover, if Butler and Church were telling the truth, the money Blood was given to conduct his intelligence work was instead spent on personal items. Nevertheless Williamson, who still retained hopes that Blood could gain information about radical schemes, made no immediate attempt to dismiss him, though he wanted the latter to preserve whatever credibility he still retained with the "phanaticks" by seeing the king secretly rather than publicly. In his role as an intermediary, however, Blood made little effort to conceal his actions, even revealing to dissidents that he was on intimate terms with Butler, a quasi-official government agent. Williamson was clearly concerned by the way Blood handled himself in these dealings: He "leaps over all heads, & his company may ruine them [Church and Butler] to the Phanaticks." Butler and Church were convinced in early December that Blood was "quite lost amongst the phanaticks."[68]

The assessment of Blood's status by Butler and Church was biased, for Blood continued to serve as a link between the crown and London nonconformists. Yet he was always less important in this respect than Butler and Innes. The latter helped arrange a conference between the two Presbyterian factions in December. In recording the meeting, Williamson observed that the Dons drew most of their support from the gentry, whereas the Ducklings appealed primarily to the middling sort. But Williamson, remembering the failure of the Savoy Conference, was chary of any public meetings and preferred that his agents foster private discussions. This, of course, severely complicates the task of ascertaining the role of Blood and Innes. The latter solidified his contacts in the dissenting community in 1671 by marrying the sister of Nathaniel Vincent, one of the preachers who most concerned Williamson because of his insistence on holding public conventicles; he was, said Williamson, the "most violent" of the Presbyterians. Blood knew Vincent through the ties each man had with Innes, though Vincent seems to have had little regard for Blood.[69]

Through his fidelity to Lauderdale, Blood became further enmeshed in the political infighting that plagued the later years of the Cabal. In late 1671 two Scotsmen with information about the Scottish nonconformists offered their services to Sir Robert Moray, a leading advocate of a moderate position toward dissenters. Moray's relations with Lauderdale were now strained, perhaps, as Julia Buck-royd suggests, because the countess of Dysart, who was jealous of Moray, had promoted distrust between the two men. In any event, Moray sent the the two Scotsmen to Sir John Baber, who, with his Puritan background and links to Thomas Manton, was used by Charles as an agent to English dissenters. Baber in turn directed them to Arlington. Questioned by Butler, they painted a grim pic-ture of Lauderdale's difficulties in Scotland and of growing noncon-formist strength: "The dissenters are 100 to one & on this will de-pend much as to all present affaires." Blood, however, was convinced that Baber and Dr. Benjamin Worsley were attempting to discredit him with Arlington, and he was therefore probably responsible for inciting Lauderdale's ire against the two Scottish informants. By the end of 1671 Arlington was reportedly disgusted not only with Blood but with Innes, who established close ties to Lauderdale and main-tained his association with Ashley. Innes, Williamson observed, "is all one with Blood."[70]

At the same time that the government was seeking an accommo-dation with the nonconformists preparatory to war with the Dutch, it made a sustained effort to offer pardons to leading radicals in re-turn for oaths of loyalty tendered in the king's presence. In this en-deavor Blood played a key role, not least because his own example was proof that the king was indeed willing to forgive. Some dis-sidents, including Captain Roger Jones, were willing to accept a pardon, but not on the condition of appearing before Charles and taking the oath of allegiance. They were probably hoping, as Wil-liamson surmised, that they could still advance their cause by work-ing with the Dutch. Major John Gladman, who was "hearty to Bloods way," sought private audiences with the king and William-son, but there is no hint of the outcome in the records. Captain John Lockyer, a northern plotter and one of the party that rescued Mason, and Nicholas Lockyer, the minister who wrote *Some Seasonable and Serious Queries upon the Late Act Against Conventicles*, both accepted pardons, at least one of them through Blood's intervention. Mason, however, did not, but there is a curious note in Williamson's records to the effect that "Mason was of Jo. Goodwins there to tea[c]he." Goodwin, of course, had died in 1665, but his old Coleman Street congregation seems to have divided in the 1660s; in December 1671 part of them were apparently following the Congregationalist Nathaniel Holmes, and the rest Mason, a General Baptist.[71]

Most of those who accepted the pardon were inconsequential radicals, although some prominent men made their peace with the regime. Chief among them was Major-General Thomas Kelsey, who returned to England from the Netherlands in November 1671. Pardons were bestowed on Cornet Daniel Carey, a northern conspirator; Ralph Alexander, a Rathbone plotter; and Major William Burton, who had allegedly aided the Dutch in the last war and had been offered a pardon in May 1668. Contact was made, presumably through Blood, with Major Thomas White in the Netherlands, but he declined to cooperate. So too did the Fifth Monarchist William Smith. Blood was instrumental in procuring a pardon in 1672 for Major William Lowe of Dublin, "a man of parts and esteeme in that [militant] party in Ireland," and another in 1675 for Captain Humphrey Spurway, formerly of Tiverton, Devon, a veteran of the Tong conspiracy. Spurway settled on an overseas plantation financed by London merchants, including one Nelthorpe, probably James Nelthorpe, whose son Richard was a prominent conspirator in the 1680s. An unnamed person offered to "pay" for the release of the regicide Robert Tichborne, but he remained in prison until his death in 1682. Warrants of 6 December 1672 for the transfer of Colonel Robert Overton from Jersey to London and his appearance before Arlington coincide with and may have been part of the amnesty program, but Overton's health was bad and he may not have survived the trip.[72]

The offer of amnesty, the granting of the indulgence, and the failed attempts on Ormond and the crown jewels contributed to a relative calm. As usual, hostile remarks about the king and his court could be heard, as could threats such as the one to "take of[f] the branches first & then have at the roote."[73] Charles's policy toward the nonconformists was bearing fruit, although a storm clearly awaited him when the Parliament returned. One of the informers in the 1663 northern rebellion, Joseph Strangways, discovered in January 1672 that dissidents at Hull were agitating for change, were angry over the excise and the customs, and had as their agent a former associate of Dr. Edward Richardson. The potential trouble in Hull, Strangways judged, was worse than that in the northern rebellion, "for the Streme runs not as it did at the Spaw, it is among the Sea men & marchants."[74] In February 1672 two counterfeiters tried to ingratiate themselves with the magistrates by alleging a conspiracy involving Colonel Richard Buffett, Edmund Ludlow, and 10,000 men from Ireland. The accusations were baseless, but any report of correspondence between militants and the Dutch had to be investigated. The story also mentioned commissions from Richard Cromwell, who had been the object of an intensive government search the previous June, instigated, said some, by Blood's confession.[75]

Of the limited efforts of the radicals in the postwar period, only the rescue of Mason was successful. Ormond, however, escaped with his life solely because Blood's party missed when they tried to shoot him. The attempted theft of the crown jewels enabled the state, at last, to capture Blood and to use him to further the king's ends. When coupled with the amnesty program, the policy of indulgence—the most effective means to deal with the conventicles—finally provided a creative way to reduce the radical threat, particularly the appeal of militants to the broader nonconformist community. But the solution was formulated as part of an inherently unpopular war policy, and was never given a chance of success by building support for it in Parliament. As such, the means to achieve an accommodation rested on an unsatisfactory foundation consisting of the king's suspensory powers and his ability to obtain sufficient funds from France to rule without Parliament. When Parliament met in 1673, the accommodation was destroyed at least in part because of the broader policy of which it was an element, and the radical cause acquired new life.

Conclusion

Radicalism and the Policy of Indulgence

At no time in the reign of Charles II was the government closer to negating the radical threat than in 1672. The provision of *de facto* liberty of conscience effectively resolved the single grievance that offered radical recruiters the most hope. In the aftermath of the tumultuous 1650s the appeal of republicanism was too weak to attract sufficient support for an uprising in the three kingdoms. By 1670 the republican cause in Ireland and Scotland was virtually nonexistent, though it remained strong in militant circles in England and among the exiles. Moreover the arrest of Thomas Blood and his associates, followed by the offer of amnesty, further weakened the rebel cause. Charles was in a position to embark on his third war against the Netherlands relatively free of concern about Dutch support for a radical insurrection.

The Impact of the Indulgence in England

The solution to the radical threat was put forth partly for the wrong reasons. A policy of toleration and amnesty, linked to a pro-Dutch, essentially Protestant foreign policy, might have resolved the radical challenge permanently,[1] but this solution would have been possible only if the king could have garnered adequate parliamentary support for toleration grounded in statute. Given Charles's quest to tolerate Catholics as part of his French-oriented foreign policy, the parliamentary reaction to the Declaration of Indulgence in 1673 was probably a foregone conclusion. That reaction, however, inadvertently breathed new life into the radical movement by once again raising the potent issue of religious freedom. Before the 1670s were over, the king himself further enhanced the radical appeal through his pro-French, pro-Catholic policies.

The 1672 Declaration was significant in another respect. As a means of implementing the promise of liberty to tender consciences in the Declaration of Breda, the indulgence would have made religious dissent legitimate for the first time in the context of traditional monarchical government. As important as the experiments of the 1650s had been, they were only a precursor of the permanent system of legal dissent finally—but imperfectly—achieved in 1689. The issue was extremely complex, involving far more than the question of spiritual freedom. To legalize dissent raised the thorny issue of property, including the fate of mandatory tithing and the rights of lay proprietors. Related to this was the threat to gentry preeminence if nonconformity were allowed. The universities, moreover, would lose their monopoly over the training of the clergy, just as the bishops—and indirectly the monarchy—would no longer monopolize the supervision of the clergy. Legalizing dissent could only be accomplished at the expense of the gentry, the bishops, and the universities; this fact was now more significant than the challenge to the old argument that religious diversity was inimical to a strong, unified state.

Whether Charles could have won approval for a toleration bill in the Convention of 1660, with its rather strong nonconformist representation and its absence of bishops, is a moot point. But the Cavalier House of Commons was indisputably more hostile to such notions, and the recurring radical conspiracies only hardened the Commons' resolve to repress dissent. Charles was therefore driven to the constitutionally dubious course of implementing toleration by using the suspensory power. The stakes were high, and the religious issue per se was not the crux of the matter. Had the king succeeded in legitimating dissent, he would have substantially altered the political framework of his and subsequent reigns by integrating dissent into the political order. Nonconformists could have become a truly viable political bloc, enabling the king to play them off against other factions. Indeed, by the late 1660s he was already treating the dissenters as if they were an identifiable constituency in the political system, but they had no opportunity to benefit from the indulgence politically before Parliament reconvened in 1673. The financial necessities of war thus defeated Charles's scheme. The Test Act was a response to the king's challenge to the political order as well as a defense of the privileged position of the gentry, the bishops, and the universities.

It is in a sense ironic that Charles's efforts to incorporate nonconformists more effectively into the political system included overtures to the very radicals who had been plotting against his regime since 1660. The program of amnesty that commenced with Blood, coupled with the offer of toleration to nonconformists, was thus a bold stroke. That such an attempt was linked to a foreign policy intolerable to most of the king's English, Scottish, and northern Irish subjects doomed it to failure, although in the short term it calmed the radicals throughout most of the 1670s.

Although the Declaration of Indulgence was officially canceled in March 1673, the resumption of persecution was sporadic and seems to have had relatively little impact on dissenting meetings. Some dissenters continued to regard their licenses to meet and preach as valid, thereby confusing various magistrates. There was also a manifest reluctance to relinquish the new liberty, and on occasion this led to acts of violence against magistrates. At Norwich in late 1674 an informer was beaten and chased by hundreds of Presbyterians, who cried "Fall on & Kill the Rogue." About the same time Great Yarmouth nonconformists dragged two informers through a hog sty and a pond; one of them subsequently died from the physical abuse. Nonconformists at Norwich, Great Yarmouth, and elsewhere subsequently claimed to have letters from the king prohibiting the justices from issuing warrants against them.[2] At last, Charles was persuaded to announce a proclamation on 3 February 1675 ordering the suppression of conventicles and reiterating that the licenses to preach were invalid. Letters were later sent by the Council to justices of the peace directing them to suppress illegal meetings. Even so, there were those, such as Coventry, who wanted "modest and quiet" dissenters left alone and only the "Insolent and presumptuous" severely prosecuted.[3]

Instead of quashing nonconformity, the revival of a more vigorous

policy of repression inflamed feelings. At Margate, dissenters ignored the proclamation and pushed ahead with the construction of
a meetinghouse, while at Great Yarmouth they continued to hold
services, often aided by the constables' reluctance to prosecute. By
August 1675 the number of dissenters at Great Yarmouth exceeded
that during the period of indulgence, and in the coming year their
supporters even gained control of the militia.[4] Only briefly did sporadic enforcement of the Conventicle Act discourage illegal meetings. In the fiery words of one Congregationalist layman, "where
they mett ten let them meete twenty & where twenty a hundred &
a hundred a thousand, & so make theire numbers as considerable as
they can, and then if any came to disturbe them let them beate them,
this would put all in a flame."[5]

The clearest indication of the unmistakable link between radicalism and religious toleration is the relative absence of militant activity
in England in the period immediately after the promulgation of the
1672 Indulgence. Even the expressions of popular hostility toward
the Stuarts and the established church seem to have tapered off,
though there were occasional reports of malcontents hoping for the
king's violent death or longing for the heady days of Oliver Cromwell, "a great zealot for the law of God." Charles was still accused of
being a "whoremaster" who "minded his whores, and neglected the
concernes of the Kingdome." At York hundreds of young people
disrupted services in the cathedral, and on Shrove Tuesday in 1673
broke open the church doors and later assaulted Dr. John Lake, the
canon residentiary, and vandalized his house.[6] But such instances
were now few.

In the aftermath of the Indulgence the themes in the publications
of the radical press shifted. The great motifs of the pre-1672 period—the emphasis on persecution and the right of the saints to
disobey the Conventicle Acts—temporarily receded, and the government was increasingly faced with controversial works dealing with
constitutional issues. The mere issuance of the Indulgence sparked a
freer exchange of views, both orally and in print, prompting the government to issue a proclamation on 14 June 1672 ordering citizens
not to write or speak about affairs of state. The state's efforts to
curtail radical publications never abated, as repeated general war-

rants to search for and seize seditious literature make manifest. Moreover, growing attention was given to stopping the importation of dissident literature, both radical and Catholic, from the Netherlands and Flanders. As part of that campaign the English ambassador, Sir William Temple, protested to the Dutch States General in the summer of 1674 about the publication of dissident literature for the English market. A number of persons were arrested in connection with the radical press in the mid-1670s: Samuel Medley for corresponding with smugglers of illegal books, Henry Stubbes for printing and publishing unlicensed papers, and the printers and booksellers Elizabeth Calvert, Peter Lillicrap, Robert Crouch, Thomas Philpott, and Joshua Waterhouse.[7]

In late 1675, with the outbreak of inflammatory political issues, reports of popular hostility again began to increase, including allegedly treasonable words against the king and the duke of York. Some of this was fanned by the underground press in verse that harshly satirized Charles. *The Busse or the Royal Kiss or Prorogation, 22 November 1675* referred to the moment when,

> . . . red-hot with wine and whore,
> He turned the Parliament out of door.

The equally satirical lines of *The Chronicle* not only criticized the king's incontinence, his corruption of Parliament, and his stop of the Exchequer, but the Indulgence itself, thus reflecting concern about the questionable way in which toleration had been bestowed. The anonymous author may have been an exile, for he or she referred to the restoration as the "curse and banishment" of "Israel's nation." The writer also bitingly referred to Thomas Blood,

> . . . that wears treason in his face,
> Villain complete in parson's gown,
> How much is he at Court in grace
> For stealing Ormonde and the crown!
> Since loyalty does no man good,
> Let's seize the King and outdo Blood.[8]

Such radical activity as did occur in the period 1672 to 1674 was associated with the Third Dutch War, and was largely confined to espionage. These efforts have already been thoroughly investigated by K.H.D. Haley and need only brief recapitulation here. The key figure was Peter Du Moulin, a member of the Council of Trade who had contacts with dissenting congregations in London. Suspected of passing information to the Dutch, he fled to the Netherlands in the summer of 1672 and there entered William of Orange's employ. The following fall and winter he established contacts with friends in London with a view to obtaining further intelligence. Chief among them were William Medley, Venner's son-in-law and a key figure in the Fifth Monarchist movement in the 1660s, and John Trenchard, who would sit for Taunton in the Exclusion Parliaments. Among the other members of this "fifth column" were John Ayloffe, William (later Lord) Howard, Andrew Marvell, Richard Goodenough, and the Scot William Carstares, several of whom would later engage in the Rye House conspiracy.[9]

Unlike the plotting that had occurred during the Second Dutch War, the intent here was to force England out of the fighting—an objective accomplished in the 1674 Treaty of Westminster—but not to overthrow the Stuart regime. Some members of this group, such as Trenchard and Medley, did, however, hope to move from the cessation of fighting to the prohibition of a Catholic succession. As early as January and February 1674, various antipopish proposals were discussed in Parliament, including an abortive one that would have banned anyone who married a Catholic from the succession. While such a proposal was of obvious interest to William and thus Du Moulin, the espionage network collapsed when several of its members, including William Carr and the printer Robert Crouch (alias Cross) began passing information to Williamson. Goodenough went to the Tower; Howard apparently told the king little but nevertheless escaped punishment; and the government was unable to get its hands on the other principal conspirators.[10]

Against this background, the first significant radical work to concern the government in the aftermath of the Indulgence, the anonymous *Letter from a Person of Quality, to His Friend in the Country*, possibly by Shaftesbury, appeared in the fall of 1675. Efforts to pass the Test Bill, the author argued, would not only make a distinct party of "High Episcopal" men but, if successful, would make the polity of the established church unalterable. The intent of the Test's supporters, according to the *Letter*, was to make the government both absolute and arbitrary. The Test's "*design*" was purportedly "*to declare us first into another Government more Absolute, and Arbitrary, then the Oath of Allegiance, or old Law knew*, and then make us *swear unto it*, as it is so established." The Corporation, Militia, Uniformity, and Five-Mile Acts were supposedly part of the plan to establish *jure divino* monarchy and episcopacy. Copies of the *Letter* were found in the St. Giles home of the widow Catherine Knight, who professed ignorance of its contents.[11]

As both sides enlisted supporters, Shaftesbury's ally, Buckingham, spoke in the Lords on 16 November 1675 in favor of relief for Protestant dissenters. That speech, together with Shaftesbury's of the 20th attacking *jure divino* monarchy, were published, ostensibly in Amsterdam. Shaftesbury insisted that *jure divino* monarchy was a serious threat to the Magna Carta: "All our Claims of right by the Law, or Constitution of the Government, All the Jurisdiction and Priviledge of this House, All the Rights and Priviledges of the House of Commons, All the Properties and Liberties of the People, are to give way . . . to . . . the will and pleasure of the Crown" if this doctrine is embraced.[12]

Anonymously, Shaftesbury also published *Two Seasonable Discourses Concerning This Present Parliament* (Oxford, 1675), recounting his arguments in favor of dissolving Parliament and electing new ones frequently. Taunting the bishops for their opposition to new elections and their fears that dissolution might prove fatal to the episcopalian establishment, he argued that a church that could not command the support of Parliament could only be maintained by military force. No friend of the church could possibly accept this, he insisted, for "a *standing Parliament* and a *standing Army* are like those *Twins* that have their lower parts united . . . and cannot long outlive each other." He also alluded to the exploratory talks then under way to forge a loose alliance between Catholics and Protestant dissenters, holding out hope that a new Parliament would provide liberty to the latter and relief to the former, though excluding papists from access to court and the right to hold office and bear arms.[13]

Shaftesbury's use of the underground press helped transform it from a tool of religious radicals and militants into a more broad-

based political weapon. The government struck back with a proclamation on 7 January 1676 denouncing the publication of seditious
libels that sought "to stirre up and dispose the minde of his Majesties
Subjects to Sedition & Rebellion." As the controversy between the
court and Shaftesbury's faction intensified, the dispute became a
popular subject of conversation in coffee shops, prompting the
Council to decree that no unlicensed books be allowed in them and
that no coffeehouses be permitted to operate without a license. Warrants were issued for the arrest of dissidents who wrote or dispersed
libels against church or state.[14]

On 29 March L'Estrange obtained a warrant to search for and
seize *A Letter from a Person of Quality* and *Two Seasonable Discourses*
as well as the *Two Speeches* and Herbert Croft's *The Naked Truth*
(1675), and to arrest their authors, printers, and publishers. Croft's
Naked Truth, published anonymously and without license, was,
however, an important but not a truly radical work; it called for
reforms within the established church to permit nonconformists lati-
tude with respect to such issues as kneeling to receive communion
and the use of the sign of the cross in baptism. Croft's offense was
not radicalism but publishing without a license, a charge to which
others were also subjected. An increasingly jittery government was
determined to enforce licensing as the best means to stem the revival
of radical publications, especially those that attacked the government
as arbitrary and tyrannical.[15]

The political assault on the regime intensified when Francis Jenks,
a Cornhill linen draper, made a speech in the Guildhall on 24 June
urging the lord mayor to summon the Common Council so that it
could petition Charles to call a new Parliament. The old one, he
averred, was dissolved because it had been prorogued for more than
a year. Jenks raised the specter of a popish plot to place James on the
throne, insisting that this threatened property, liberties, lives, and
true religion. He was interrogated by the Council, which hoped to
discover who put him up to this, and then jailed, but his speech was
rushed into print and attracted immediate attention.[16]

Impassioned rhetoric reflected mounting concern about the country's future. On 2 July a member of the Temple defended Jenks's
views: "What signifies the Parliament when the People of England

shall appear on Black heath," he warned, for the people will "crush them to noothing." Sir Philip Monckton expressed fears for religion and property if the king should die without first consulting Parliament about "some fitting Redress"; without this, he opined, the French would invade and popery triumph. As inflammatory rhetoric spread, Williamson complained of "so exorbitant a licenciousness of writing & speaking of the Government, & all that relates to it." As early as 9 July he had ordered L'Estrange to confiscate *Jenkes His Case* and any other printed material concerning Jenks's speech, his examination before the Council, or his incarceration. John Marlow went to prison for printing the speech. A search was also instigated for *An Account of the Proceedings at Guild-Hall, London, . . . Held 24th. of June 1676.*[17]

For publishing the second part of Andrew Marvell's *The Rehearsal Transpros'd* Nathaniel Ponder was also imprisoned in 1676. Originally issued under license in May 1673, the second edition of this work appeared the following year without authorization. But this seems to have sparked concern only in May 1676, when Williamson found it objectionable not only because it was unlicensed but also because it was purportedly seditious in content. The second edition did step up the attack on Samuel Parker, the apologist for those who opposed religious toleration; he was now accused of suffering from venereal disease. The appearance of the second part in 1673, so close on the heels of the Indulgence, had been safe enough for Marvell; the king himself had intervened to ensure that the first part could be sold. But by 1676 toleration for Protestants had become a prominent part of the ideology of the government's political critics, and in this context Marvell's biting satire was therefore deemed seditious. In less than four years the cause of toleration had gone from royal policy to its earlier linkage with radical political ideology.[18]

As fears of popery mounted, contacts between radicals and the most stringent of the king's parliamentary critics became closer. The key figure was Buckingham, who not only continued his close association with John Wildman but had ties to London radicals such as Jenks as well as the Quakers William Penn, Thomas Rudyard, and Edward Billing. The duke's circle also included Sir Robert Peyton, who in the fall of 1676 was under investigation for seditious speech.[19]

A year later Blood provided Williamson with information that Peyton and his "gang" were conspiring "to sett up Richard [Cromwell] at first as a stiripp to what else afterwards they shall sett up," especially to issue commissions, apparently for military units to be used in a coup against the government. According to Blood, this group intended to denounce the French alliance, popery, and the government's "invasion of liberty." Reportedly they had already made attempts to recruit supporters in Buckinghamshire, Berkshire, and Bedfordshire. Peyton was associated with Shaftesbury as well as Buckingham, and Blood's report may therefore have reflected discussions among the more militant members of the incipient Green Ribbon Club.[20]

The partial confession in March 1677 of Henry North, a former servant of Buckingham's, may relate in part to this alleged conspiracy, for he claimed at that time that the duke "is now led by a faction." North also referred to a plot in which Buckingham "would not have . . . engaged but by the frequent importunity of an Eminent man . . . [;] there was a party who were very much dissatisfied with the Government & were resolved with lives & fortunes to remove divers persons from [their] place[s], & that there was a party of the Parliament that . . . will engage at the begining of theire sitting." Unfortunately North was executed after the government refused a reprieve in return for a full confession. But whether the caballing to which North alluded was virtually contemporaneous or from an earlier period (or both), it corroborates other evidence linking Buckingham to radical scheming.[21]

For their efforts to procure the dissolution of the Cavalier Parliament on the grounds that it had been prorogued for more than a year, Buckingham, Shaftesbury, Wharton, and Salisbury were sent to the Tower in February 1677; all were released in July except for Shaftesbury, who remained in prison until the following February. One of Shaftesbury's attorneys, the future Rye House conspirator Aaron Smith, was forced to flee when the House of Lords ordered his arrest for impugning the legitimacy of the new session of Parliament. Such actions further inflamed radical opinion. Harrington, who had bailed Monckton after his arrest for speaking about the succession, not only defended Jenks but advocated the legitimacy of rebellion against the government and accused Danby of holding his place with the help of a French whore. England, he charged, had been sold to the French by the corruption of two or three ministers, and "this King did bugger this parliament much like the buggering of an old woman."[22]

Dr. Nicholas Cary also went to the Tower in February 1677, but his offense was commissioning the printing of Denzil Holles's anonymous tract, *Some Considerations upon the Question, Whether the Parliament Is Dissolved*, which answered that question affirmatively, adding that Parliament must meet each year. In the ensuing months warrants were issued for the arrest of others accused of publishing seditious material, including Joseph Browne, clerk of the Coopers' Company, John Goznold and his associate John Clarke, Nathaniel Thomson, and Anthony Lawrence. At least five London coffeehouse keepers, including the widow Rebecca Weeden, were arrested in September 1677 for dispersing papers containing false and scandalous news, a telltale sign of a nervous government.[23] Not surprisingly then, the Privy Council was defensive about the republication of Nathaniel Bacon's *Continuation of an Historical Discourse, of the Government of England*, an interregnum work, and its predecessor, *An Historical Discourse of the Uniformity of the Government of England*, which discussed the origins of royal authority. John Starkey was responsible for their reappearance. Reminders of the revolutionary era were also evident when some 1,900 copies of the Westminster Confession and the Larger and Shorter Catechisms of the Westminster Assembly were found at the printing house of Evan Tiler and Ralph Holt; they had been commissioned by Dorman Newman, who in 1682 would publish John Bunyan's *Holy War*, an allegory highly critical of the Stuart government.[24]

By 1677 Charles had impaled himself on the horns of a dilemma. The policy of indulgence had not only raised serious constitutional issues but provoked the ire of staunchly conservative defenders of the established church, thus intensifying the divisions within the realm. Yet to repress conventicles with any consistency, especially after an interlude of toleration, risked inciting rebellion. When, therefore, nonconformists were zealously prosecuted by Bristol magistrates, Charles directed his lord keeper to halt or mitigate the proceedings. However, this had to be done in a fashion that would not encourage dissenters; do not give them, Coventry told the bishop of Bristol, "any Occasion to believe we either credited or feared their railings."[25] Given the events of the 1640s and 1650s, the greater danger was probably in the excessive prosecution of nonconformists, among whom former military officers such as James Berry, Thomas Kelsey, John Desborough, and Henry Danvers continued to be active.[26] Had it not been for the hysteria triggered by the alleged Popish Plot, the king's loosely defined policy of informally tolerating moderates while repressing militants might have been sufficient to allow time for the formation of a consensus in favor of modest Protestant toleration. But fears of popery were sufficiently pronounced by 1675 to raise the issue of the succession in political circles. The prospect of James as king exacerbated fears that Protestant dissent was endangered, especially as efforts to suppress conventicles intensified in 1675–76.[27] The return to serious repression set the stage for the tales of Titus Oates, the abortive efforts to exclude James from the throne, and the revival of intensive radical plotting.

Scotland: The Flawed Compromise

Militant dissidents in Scotland, unlike those in England, were little pacified by the policy of indulgence, primarily because the Scottish version was a compromise settlement that many Covenanters found obnoxious. Instead of decreasing illegal religious activity, the Scottish indulgence caused it to mushroom. As early as October 1672, the "meaner sort" in Edinburgh demonstrated against the election of a new provost expected to be less lenient toward nonconformists. But the provost, influenced by the burghers' wives, most of whom were dissenters, in fact chose to ignore the conventicles, prompting a complaint from the Scottish Privy Council. Part of the problem was that deprived ministers assigned to churches outside the capital under the terms of the indulgence refused to leave the city. In March 1673 they were expelled from Edinburgh. By May the king was resigned to the fact that these men could not be forced to serve parishes, though he insisted they provide assurances that they would not hold illegal services. Adamant that those who expected a broadening of the indulgence were mistaken, Charles authorized Lauderdale to restrict it.[28]

Conventicle activity began increasing in 1673. "Private conventivcles abound," complained the earl of Kincardine, "where very disaffected persons preach dangerous doctrins." Once the archbishop of Glasgow had returned to London, illegal meetings sprouted in the southwest, a development that especially troubled the king because of fresh reports that the Dutch hoped to instigate trouble in Scotland. From Dublin Sir Arthur Forbes reported to Essex that his agents had learned that dissidents in Scotland were engaged in "dangerous desines." Essex was concerned because "a Cloud from that Quarter has bin more fatall to England, then any other"—yet another reminder that militant activity in one kingdom was rightly recognized as having an impact on the other two.[29]

As conventicles spread throughout the west, south, and east, the threat to security increased proportionally. Nonconformists posted armed sentries to guard their meetings, and armed men escorted the preachers. When Blackader preached near St. Andrews in January 1674, students drew swords to protect worshipers from the militia. In the west militant women stoned a conforming preacher in April, and two months later "phanatik women" in Edinburgh demonstrated on behalf of the Covenanters' cause. In addition to convening conventicles in the fields, deprived clergy sometimes appropriated vacant pulpits, infuriating conservatives. Charles responded to the disorder with a proclamation in June in which he offered substantial rewards for the apprehension of conventicle preachers, clergy who invaded pulpits, and those who summoned worshipers to illegal meetings. He also offered 2,000 merks for the arrest of John Welsh, Gabriel Semple, and Samuel Arnot. A companion proclamation required masters of families to prevent their charges from attending conventicles, and heritors and landlords to require their tenants to subscribe bonds not to attend such services.[30]

The proclamations were ineffectual. In cities such as Glasgow and Stirling, the troopers who posted the proclamations were stoned by women; one soldier, in fact, was killed at Stirling, and in Fife armed Covenanters confronted the Horse Guards. Although Kincardine detected a decline in the number of field conventicles in Fife and the

Lothians in the immediate aftermath of the proclamations, "it is not to be imagined to what a height of malice & discontent peoples spirits are raised not only amongst the foolish phanatick partie but even amongst all sorts of people."[31] The Council's attempt to enforce the proclamations seems to have produced a temporary decline in illegal religious activity throughout the summer, though Welsh, Robert Lockhart, Blackader, and others refused to be silenced. Welsh preached to assemblies that may have exceeded 8,000 in Fife, and Blackader had an audience of 3,000 near Dunfermline. When the Council summoned more than forty deprived ministers for holding field conventicles, they refused to appear. Conventiclers in West Lothian fired on government troops. Arresting the offending ministers was complicated by the ease with which they moved between Scotland and northern Ireland. In an attempt to maintain order, Charles and Lauderdale approved Major-General George Monro's plan to march the army through the country in a show of force.[32]

Officials were concerned that armed conventiclers were potential revolutionaries. The arrest of several leading Covenanters, including Major Montgomery in King's County, Ireland, William Carstares, and James Stewart the younger, son of the former provost of Edinburgh, was small comfort. In March 1675 Coventry intercepted a letter to a fugitive in the Netherlands that he interpreted as evidence of a planned insurrection, probably to take place in Scotland, but with links to England and Ireland; one of the alleged conspirators was the former Tong plotter Captain Spurway. Three months later, Coventry learned that dissidents in Scotland and northern England intended to meet at Berwick on 16 July "to consult of carrying on the Comon Concerne," and that six Scottish Presbyterian clerics had gone to London to confer with their brethren "concerning the ordering of their Church." While the core of these discussions was undoubtedly religious, at this point such considerations had undeniable political overtones and were a legitimate government concern. Indeed, during the same spring both deprived and indulged ministers meeting in Ayr issued instructions "for keeping fasts and other illegal injunctions, as if they had been a judicature."[33]

The state's inability to prohibit the gathering of armed conventiclers, sometimes by the thousands, was eloquent testimony to the failure of the indulgence policy in Scotland. Efforts to suppress them were likely to end in the kind of violence that could incite the very rebellion officials were desperate to prevent. In the parish of Bathgate, West Lothian, conventiclers exchanged gunfire with soldiers in March 1675, and two months later conventiclers forcibly rescued a servant of Lord Cardross who had been arrested for attending an illegal service. The minister James Kirkton was freed by a sword-wielding Covenanter, and a party of cavalry dispatched to break up a large conventicle in southern Scotland ran into stiff opposition in February 1677. Such militancy perhaps inevitably carried over into armed attacks on conforming ministers.[34]

The sermons preached at the conventicles ranged from the innocuous to the seditious. At the former extreme there were, for instance, the 1671–72 sermons of John Campbell on various aspects of the spiritual life, such as sobriety, the importance of justification by faith for Christian living, the covenant of grace, and the differences between fallen man and true believers. At most, these sermons would have intensified the Covenanters' sense of identity and reinforced their notion of Covenant obligations. But there was nothing seditious here, and echoes can be found in many nonconformist works of this period. The 1674 sermons of James Wodrow were largely cut of similar cloth; hearers were urged to cast off the works of darkness and don the wedding garment of Christ. Emphasis was placed on performing Gospel duties, upholding one's bargain with God, and cleansing one's life to prepare to meet God. But in one sermon Wodrow reminded his audience that Christ had not come to bring peace but the sword, and there was talk of obedience to Gospel commands even to the point of death. There was sustenance here for those inclined to militancy.[35]

That tone was even more pronounced in some of the sermons of Donald Cargill. While he regularly discussed such traditional themes as backsliding and repentance, he often preached an unmistakably apocalyptic message. God, he thundered, "is saying to Brittan, who rules here? ere it be long he will make them know who rules in Brittan." Evil magistrates will "fall from the throne to eternall fire." Kings and priests will be overturned, and "as the Lord lives you shall be a part of this overturning." Monarchs, nobles, and generals are all worm-eaten, so "doun it must be." The king who is an enemy of God can only be branded as a wicked prince. "Thus sayes the Lord, take away the croune, remove the diadem, this is the Lord disrobing sin." And who will the new rulers be, Cargill asked? "They ar sitting low indeed whom he will set up." Preached to defiant worshipers protected by armed sentries, the effect must have been electrifying.[36]

John Welsh could be just as fiery, as when he preached in Ayr and Renfrew in the fall of 1677. Upon accusing the king, the nobles, and the prelates of being "the Murtherers of Christ," he went on to ask: "O people . . . tell mee what good the King hath done since his coming, yea hath he not done all the mischiefe that a Tyrant could doe both by his Life & Laws?" There was pressure on ministers to preach in this fashion, for in a presbytery of which Welsh was moderator, Gilbert Kennedy was formally censured for not being sufficiently outspoken in his condemnation of the wicked ways of the nobles, the bishops, and their supporters. The same presbytery took up the question of rebellion, but decided for the moment that "the people should not rise in Arms till they should be someway oppressed & provoked, and that then the Signes should be given them to make ready; That all the World might see they would not invade the right of the worst pretenders without just cause." Thus the government was unquestionably correct in perceiving the activities of militant Covenanters as a threat to the stability of the kingdom.[37]

The Scottish policy of a severely limited indulgence was manifestly bankrupt. As early as June 1674, Lauderdale, the principal proponent of moderation, had embraced Archbishop Sharp's insistence on treating dissenters harshly. The result had been the proclamation of 16 June 1674, noted earlier, but the revival of repression was no more successful in curbing dissent. Any realistic hope for continuation of a moderate policy had probably been dashed in the fall of 1674 when Alexander Burnet replaced Robert Leighton as archbishop of Glasgow. At the heart of the policy of severity was a decision to garrison the countryside with a standing army, though practical problems delayed its implementation. A proclamation of March 1676 sought to tighten measures to curb conventicles, but by this point the Covenanters were too well organized to curtail so easily.[38]

Early in 1676, therefore, the duke of Hamilton apparently sponsored efforts to issue a new indulgence, but this the bishops stridently opposed. By the summer of 1677, Lauderdale again changed course, despairing that repression would succeed. He was now prepared to revive the old plan to divide nonconformists by indulging moderates while crushing militants. A proclamation of 2 August again called on masters of families to ensure that their charges attended legal church services, and on landlords to require their tenants to subscribe bonds not to attend conventicles. Renewed efforts were made to imprison conventiclers, but to little avail.[39]

By October Lauderdale had decided to pacify the western shires with an occupying army of Highlanders. To garner support for this scheme he warned that the militants were in reality Fifth Monarchists, of whom "no measures off reason can be expected." "Nothing can Fright them more From Rebellion then the knowledge [that] so many thousand highlanders will be poured upon them." Hamilton was properly dubious, but Lauderdale's scheme was intended in part to demonstrate to the nonconformists that Hamilton could no longer protect them. If, moreover, westerners rebelled against the Highlanders, Lauderdale would have a convenient excuse to crush the west militarily, destroying Hamilton in the process. Apprised of the danger of a Covenanter uprising, Charles further strengthened Lauderdale's hand by ordering the duke of Newcastle to have a thousand militiamen ready in Northumberland to go to Lauderdale's assistance, and by placing troops in Ireland at his disposal. In Scotland the bishops generally endorsed the new policy, so long as the troops were quartered only on nonconformists. Once the west was pacified, they wanted the army to enforce conformity in Teviotdale, Stirling, and Fife.[40]

In the short term, the threat of military force seems to have had the desired effect, for Sir Christopher Musgrave reported to Williamson that "the West was very apprehensive the Lords of the Councell would call in the English Forces upon them, & Fearful that the Highlanders would be drawne downe." The undisciplined behavior of the Highlanders, who descended on the southwest "lyke a Torrent," proved to be severe punishment, forcing the Council to replace them with the militia. Over the long run, however, the use of the military was not only an ineffective solution but opened Lauderdale to renewed criticism that he was seeking to provide the king with a standing army.[41] That criticism was extended to the duke of York in 1678 by Sir John Dalrymple, though almost certainly without justification, for at that point James was principally interested in organizing an expeditionary force to help the Dutch against France. More importantly, Lauderdale's plans for an occupying force in Scotland coincided with fears in England that Charles hoped to raise troops allegedly to fight the French but in fact to rule without Parliament. Thus Lauderdale's recourse to military force not only intensified the hostility of nonconformists toward the government but unwittingly contributed to the growth of anti-army ideology.[42]

De Facto Toleration in Ireland

In Ireland the mid-1670s were largely peaceful. Insubstantial rumors of plotting continued, but Essex rightly attributed them to disgruntled Catholics and nonconformists, each of whom accused the other of seditious activity. "Should I have troubled your Lordship," he told Arlington, "with a narration of every litle Plott, which I have bin informed of, it would have bin endless." By early 1674 both court and Parliament were convinced that the only real threat to Irish security was posed by native Catholics, not former Cromwellians so long as their property was secure.[43] Yet neither Essex nor Charles was willing to entrust security to the militia because that would have entailed arming large numbers of Scottish Presbyterians and ex-Cromwellians. Only an army could be trusted, especially in view of lingering doubts of nonconformist loyalty should England again go to war against the Netherlands.[44]

Toward the dissenters Essex preferred a policy of de facto toleration. He insisted, however, on keeping a watchful eye on the activities of banned Scottish Covenanters who sought refuge in Ulster. These men, he observed, were followed by the multitude, especially in coastal counties of the north. Yet he never thought the Covenanters were as dangerous as the bishops of Londonderry and Down made them out to be, for "they have no man of eminent popularitie to head them." Nevertheless, given the frequent contact between Ulster and Scotland, there was a constant possibility that Covenanter unrest could disrupt northern Ireland. The situation was further complicated by links between nonconformists in Ireland and the exile community in the Netherlands. Arlington and Essex were both worried when, in December 1673, Robert Trail, who had been exiled from Scotland, left the Netherlands for England en route to Ireland. Ulster was, of course, a convenient place to embark for Scotland as well as a place of refuge for Covenanters such as Robert Rule, who had been exiled from Scotland, Gilbert Kennedy, Archibald Hamilton, and Michael Bruce, "a fierce & pernicious Zealott." Travel and communications between southwestern Scotland and Ulster were so simple that the Covenanters enjoyed virtually limitless sanctuary in northern Ireland.[45]

As conditions in Scotland worsened in 1674, Essex dispatched additional troops to Belfast, Carrickfergus, Londonderry, and Charlemont. He also wanted a frigate stationed at Carrickfergus, and urged Westminster to establish a regular post between that port and Edinburgh to ensure that Sir Arthur Forbes was kept apprised of Scottish developments. Essex, in fact, saw his army as an essential key to the security of all three kingdoms, especially considering that "the Kingdome of England is not in the most composd condition that could bee wisht, [and] That of Scotland very uneasy." In June 1676 Coventry received intelligence from Scotland that the Covenanters intended to dispatch a party to Ulster, and wanted to know what additional supplies Essex needed to repulse them.[46]

The security of Ireland was intimately linked with Scotland. When, therefore, Presbyterians in Londonderry renewed the Covenant, the Committee on Foreign Affairs resolved to proceed against them "as high as by Law can be, to the utmost extremity, Ecclesiastically and Civilly." Two preachers who proved to be especially troublesome were William Hendry and Samuel Halliday, both of county Donegal. According to an incensed bishop of Killala, they rode "up and downe the Country like Martiall Evangelists with Sword and Pistolls, as if they came not to prate downe, but storme our Religion." When the bishop arrested Hendry, he found a copy of a paper containing ten reasons why the godly could resist the authority of evil magistrates. The last of these was an unequivocal statement of contract theory: "That Band between a Prince & People is reciprocall and alsoe Princes are not only bound to keep promises to their Subjects, but also in case they faile they may be bridled." The essence of this bridling was set forth in the sixth point, with reference to Jehu in 2 Kings 9:7—"Subjects are commanded to execute Gods Judgments against their King, as upon him." Not surprisingly, Orrery, musing on Hendry's tenets, likened the Covenanters in general to a black cloud hanging over Scotland and Ireland.[47]

Because of the impact of Scottish militants, Ormond concluded in September 1677 that the nonconformists had become the greatest threat to royal authority in Ireland. "Thay are much increased, spread, & imboldned beyond what thay were about 8 or 9 yeares since," not least because immigrants from Scotland had joined them, attracted by the informal toleration. To enforce Catholic-oriented recusancy laws on Protestant nonconformists rather than papists would, Ormond believed, incite substantial clamor. Yet to implement the laws against both groups would inundate the prisons, drive dissenters from homes and jobs, and undermine the economy. Not to punish nonconformists, however, would encourage them to think the government was afraid, thereby increasing their numbers and insolency. For the present, he opted to continue unofficial toleration so long as efforts were not made to renew the Covenant or establish "illegal jurisdiction." The wisdom of this policy enabled Ireland to continue enjoying the absence of serious disruption by nonconformists.[48]

A Retrospect

Although conspiratorial activity continued throughout the Second Dutch War, in neither England nor Ireland did the dissidents mount an insurrection. The single uprising of the war years—the 1666 Galloway rebellion in Scotland—was not instigated as part of a radical scheme, although Scottish dissidents had been planning some form of action against the government. Once the revolt was under way, many of the leading Scottish dissidents supported it. The insurrection failed, particularly when neither the English radicals nor the Dutch government provided crucial backing. Such assistance as the Ulster Scots furnished was woefully inadequate. Thus for the second time in the 1660s coordinated uprisings in the three kingdoms failed to materialize. In the postwar years the dissidents were again forced to rethink their strategy. For most, this was a period of relative inactivity, whereas others, such as Thomas Blood and James Mitchell, contrived less ambitious schemes, the most important of which entailed the assassination of key figures such as the king, the duke of Ormond, and the archbishop of St. Andrews.

Government efforts to monitor the activities of the radical community were severely complicated by the fact that virtually all dissidents were Protestant nonconformists. But the majority of the latter had no real ties to the radicals, despite sharing a desire for religious toleration, a dislike of prelacy, anger over taxes, and a pronounced fear of popery. Of course, some of these attitudes extended beyond the world of nonconformity, thereby providing the radicals with a large potential audience. If the radicals' problem was enlisting this larger community in an insurrection, the government's difficulty was distinguishing between militants intent on overthrowing the regime and nonconformists determined to gather in conventicles but otherwise in no sense revolutionary. Given the presence of strong political support in Parliament and the ecclesiastical hierarchy for an exclusive church and penal legislation to repress nonconformity, the simplest solution to the government's problem—a policy of toleration for Protestants—remained beyond reach. The government was indeed fortunate that throughout the country many magistrates demonstrated little or no inclination to enforce the penal laws dealing with nonconformity on a regular basis. Had they done so, radical ranks might have been swelled to the point where a successful insurrection would have been feasible.

The historian is confronted, as was the Stuart government, with the fact that there was actually a spectrum of disaffection, ranging from those who might be accommodated within the system to those who rejected the system itself. The former included moderate nonconformists such as Richard Baxter and Edmund Calamy, who would have preferred an accommodation that brought Presbyterians into the state church. At the other extreme were militant republicans and dissenters who espoused nothing less than the abolition of monarchy and episcopacy. In general, the gradations on this spectrum do not correlate with religious groupings. Among the most active militants in the 1660s were Thomas Blood, Gilby Carr, James Wallace, and James Mitchell, all committed Presbyterians; yet most people of this persuasion, especially in England, shunned radical activity, seeking only the freedom to conduct their own worship services and, especially beginning in 1675, political reforms designed to prevent a Catholic succession. Congregationalists such as Edward Richardson, architect of the 1663 northern rebellion, and Robert Ferguson were militants, though the former became quiescent as an exile. Other Congregationalists, such as Dr. John Owen and George Griffith, posed no real political threat to the Stuart regime until the early 1680s. The Baptists too were divided on the question of militant action, with men such as Henry Danvers, John Mason, and Nathaniel Strange active in conspiracies against the government. After 1663 most Quakers repudiated their earlier militancy as George Fox's "peace principle" won acceptance. The Quaker challenge—though radical in its own way—was to social customs and traditional religious practices, not monarchical government. Quaker rejection of such basic tokens of authority as oaths and hat doffing, as well as their willingness to court martyrdom, made them seem more threatening than they really were. Charles was relatively quick to recognize this. Persecuted, the Quakers were dangerous as models of resistance to established authority; left alone, they were essentially harmless. Yet the extremity of their convictions complicated efforts to implement religious toleration, thereby making it more difficult to reduce the radical threat.

Although the percentage of militants was probably higher among Congregationalists and Baptists than other nonconformists, the majority of these groups were not committed to violent action against the regime. The government's problem was to identify and isolate the militants, a task compounded by their intimate association with pacific nonconformists willing to do little more than convene illegally for worship. But the conventicles, harmless though most undoubtedly were, always had the potential for danger, not least as a recruiting ground for militants.

The range of attitudes toward the regime meant, of course, a lack of unanimity among dissidents concerning goals. It was easy enough to formulate negative positions on which most disaffected persons could agree: hostility to prelates, the Clarendon Code, the lasciviousness of the court, the level of taxes, the popish threat, the possibility of a Catholic succession, and, beginning in 1675, the king's refusal to hold new parliamentary elections. It was considerably more difficult to agree upon a plan of reform. The 1663 Dublin plotters had called for, among other things, "libertie of conscience," but according to them this meant "establischeing the Protestant religion in puretie, according to the tenor of the Solemne League and Covenant."[49] Such an aim was shared by the Covenanters in Scotland and would probably have been acceptable to most English Presbyterians (setting aside the question of Erastian, or lay, control), but not to Congregationalists, Baptists, and Quakers. In addition to disagreements over the meaning of liberty of conscience, there was considerable divergence with respect to the nature of government. In general, Presbyterians, no matter how militant, were not antimonarchical; they sought a godly, Covenanted sovereign, not a republic or a protectorate. Had the radicals succeeded in toppling the Stuart regime, they would have been confronted with the same problems and divisiveness that had baffled them in 1659. There is no reason to suppose they solved the problem of legitimacy in the post-Restoration decades, or that they commanded a base of support adequate to establish a nonmonarchical government in the three kingdoms. It would have taken a gross miscalculation by the government—the stringent, consistent enforcement of penal legislation against the nonconformists, or a blatant attempt to impose Catholicism as the state religion, or excessive subordination to France in foreign policy in such a way as seriously to hurt English economic interests—to create a climate of discontent so pervasive that militants could have enlisted sufficient support to reimpose an alternative to monarchy.

The effect of divisions within the dissident community was reflected in their inability to cooperate effectively against the regime. The experience of the 1640s had demonstrated to English radicals how incompatible the ideals of Scottish Covenanters were with their own. Thus when the Covenanters rebelled in 1666, English militants refused to come to their aid. Even within the exile community there were divisions. Ludlow, for instance, would support an invasion of England only if it were restricted to troops of the Reformed faith, but Sidney and others were willing to discuss French involvement. Plots to assassinate the king or duke of York were abhorrent to most nonconformists, no matter how much they disapproved of court life or the repression of Protestant dissent.

There were, moreover, interests unique to each of the three kingdoms. Dissidents in Ireland were markedly concerned with the restoration of their lands, whereas the aims of the Scottish Covenanters were almost exclusively religious and framed so as to make them unappealing to English sectaries. The freedom of religion sought by the latter was not the goal of Presbyterians in Ireland or Scotland, though their English colleagues began to embrace it in the 1670s and 1680s as they put greater emphasis on the common heritage of nonconformity and shared the experience of persecution.

Religious differences did not always divide militants. In the late 1660s, the Presbyterian Thomas Blood, for example, worked closely with the Fifth Monarchists and Baptists Richard Halliwell and Robert Perrott. Militant Congregationalists, Baptists, and Quakers had cooperated in the 1663 northern rebellion. But such coalitions were of necessity temporary, based largely on common grievances rather than a constructive program of reform. In retrospect such opposition may not seem to have been all that threatening to the government, but the latter could not afford to assume that future coalitions would always be impotent.

That the government survived the radical challenge in the period 1664–77 was not due to the effectiveness of its own action. The press was nearly as ill-controlled in 1677 as it had been in the mid-1660s. Although the government still relied on a network of informers that extended from Ireland to the Netherlands, the quality of information it provided was never high, given the tendency of some informers to see conspiracy in most conventicles, particularly when preachers used militant religious imagery. Nor was the English militia in a sufficient state of readiness to deal with an insurrection, as James II discovered as late as 1685. In coping with the radical threat the two most effective government policies were its reliance on regional authorities, notably the Scottish Council during the Galloway rebellion, and its relative leniency in punishing conspirators and rebels. The number of executions could have been much higher, and the handling of crises in Scotland and Ireland could have been severely complicated if the king had insisted on taking active control of decision making. Perhaps Charles also deserves some credit for not pushing magistrates to implement the penal legislation against nonconformists more strenuously. Had religious persecution been more intense, the radical ranks undoubtedly would have been expanded.

The dissidents themselves were responsible for the fact that most of their plans came to naught. Had Ludlow forthrightly joined Sidney and Say in the early stages of the Second Dutch War, Dutch assistance to radicals in England would almost certainly have materialized. Had dissidents in England, Scotland, and northern Ireland forged a common alliance, the Galloway rebellion might have mushroomed into another civil war, possibly complicated by Dutch involvement. But as in the early 1660s, the dissidents suffered greatly from inadequate leadership. The causes were there, and the money and supplies could probably have been raised, but strong, experienced leaders were lacking. With Lambert in prison and Ludlow in Vevey, only the Thomas Bloods and John Masons were active. From such men effective leadership in a general insurrection was impossible.

Even if the radicals had been blessed with strong leaders, a return to civil war was highly improbable for a variety of reasons. Unlike the militant reformers of the 1640s, the most strident critics of the regime in the 1660s and early 1670s had no institutional base in Parliament. Nor, in the absence of stringent, consistent religious persecution did they have a cause that could rally large numbers of recruits. The substantial differences of opinion among dissidents on religious and political issues made a working alliance extremely difficult, and the conflicting aims of Scottish Covenanters and most English militants further complicated matters. In the absence of unity there was no hope of procuring Dutch assistance. The radicals therefore were forced to resort to conspiracies with highly restricted aims. Indeed, the duke of Ormond and the archbishop of St. Andrews narrowly escaped assassination, and Blood—if he was telling the truth—could have killed the king at Battersea. Yet even these plots went awry, and instead of sparking insurrections they probably only discredited the radical cause in many circles.

Thus the rumblings of discontent, so unmistakable in the early 1660s, continued throughout that decade and into the 1670s. Government informers had a difficult time distinguishing between genuinely conspiratorial meetings and illegal conventicles that sometimes used militant religious imagery but were politically harmless. Nor was Roger L'Estrange effective in his campaign against the underground press, again largely because the government failed to discriminate adequately between truly subversive publications and unlicensed but otherwise innocuous works.[50] Despite all the difficulties inherent in assessing the radical threat, the government could not ignore it, nor should the historian. The radical tradition that flowered in the revolutionary 1640s and 1650s continued throughout the 1660s, 1670s, and 1680s, keeping alive the ideals of responsible republican government, and of religious liberty and freedom of the press for Protestants.

The existence of militant nonconformity had a significant impact on the history of England, Scotland, and Ireland in the 1660s and 1670s, as this study has shown, as well as in the 1680s. Clearly, the traditional picture of quiescent Restoration dissent is no longer tenable. The Good Old Cause was kept alive by militants, most of whom were nonconformists, willing to embrace violent measures to achieve their ends. Ultimately the Monmouth rebellion of 1685 was but the most famous of their failed efforts.

Charles II's government was constantly faced with the necessity of monitoring radical activity and employing repressive measures to reduce or eliminate the threat it posed to the regime. Historians are cognizant that the militants were unsuccessful in their efforts to establish a godly state, or even to win toleration for all Protestants. Yet for the most part, historians have been unaware of much of what the militants were attempting to do, perhaps because evidence of genuine radical activity is so easily overlooked amid the flood of spurious accusations from malicious informers, agents provocateurs, and enemies of nonconformity. The king and his officers, however, had no choice but to evaluate the reports, and that task affected how they governed.

The actions of the militants, the government's uncertainty as to their numerical strength, the possibility of their obtaining powerful support from the Dutch or the French, and concern about what they might attempt in the future had a direct impact on events. The government expended appreciable effort to control the press, suppress conventicles, monitor passage between Ireland and Scotland, employ informers to gather information about dissidents at home and abroad, and confiscate illegal caches of weapons.

When conventiclers in Scotland, the borders, and southwestern England not only armed themselves but threatened magistrates who had been ordered to disperse them, the government's very ability to rule within its own borders was threatened. No one can read the records of the Scottish Privy Council without being impressed by the amount of time it spent seeking to curb conventicles. The controversy over illegal assemblies in the three kingdoms was not merely, or even primarily, a dispute over liturgy and polity but an issue of law and authority. Although some conventicles were peaceful and apparently harmless, they nevertheless contributed to an atmosphere of defiance against the regime.

In nonconformist circles, the crucial question was not whether unjust laws could be broken, but what form disobedience could take. Violence, as magistrates knew too well, was always a possibility. Such considerations, including concern about how far militant dissidents would go, were factors in the passage of the 1670 Conventicle Act and the political maneuvering surrounding the 1672 Declaration of Indulgence. The government could not even engage the Netherlands in war without contemplating the possibility of radical involvement, including militant support for a Dutch invasion of England and Scotland, or a French incursion into Ireland. Ultimately, radicals endorsed and participated in William of Orange's invasion in 1688.

To ignore the role of militant dissidents in the period from the Restoration to the Glorious Revolution is to create a world that neither Charles and his supporters nor the nonconformists would have recognized. Although the radicals never succeeded in toppling Charles's government or compelling it to establish lasting freedom of religion for Protestants, they made their presence felt.

NOTES

Notes

Abbreviations

Abbott, *Blood* Wilbur Cortez Abbott, *Colonel Thomas Blood, Crown-Stealer* (1911), reprinted in *Conflicts with Oblivion*, 2nd ed. (Cambridge, Mass.: Harvard University Press, 1935)

Abbott, "Conspiracy" Wilbur Cortez Abbott, "English Conspiracy and Dissent, 1660–1674" *American Historical Review* 14 (1908–1909): 503–28, 696–722

Add. MSS Additional Manuscripts, British Library

APS *The Acts of the Parliaments of Scotland*, vols. 7 and 8 (1820)

Ashcraft Richard Ashcraft, *Revolutionary Politics & Locke's Two Treatises of Government* (Princeton, N.J.: Princeton University Press, 1986)

Ashley, *Wildman* Maurice Ashley, *John Wildman: Plotter and Postmaster: A Study of the English Republican Movement in the Seventeenth Century* (New Haven, Conn.: Yale University Press, 1947)

BDBR *Biographical Dictionary of British Radicals in the Seventeenth Century*, ed. Richard L. Greaves and Robert Zaller, 3 vols. (Brighton: Harvester Press, 1982–84)

BL British Library

Blackader Mem. Andrew Crichton, *Memoirs of Rev. John Blackader* (Edinburgh: Archibald Constable & Company, 1823)

Bodl. Bodleian Library, Oxford

Buckroyd, *CS* Julia Buckroyd, *Church and State in Scotland 1660–1681* (Edinburgh: John Donald Publishers, 1980)

Burnet Gilbert Burnet, *History of His Own Time*, new ed. (London: William Smith, 1838)

Capp, *FMM* B.S. Capp, *The Fifth Monarchy Men: A Study in Seven-*

	teenth-Century English Millenarianism (London: Faber and Faber, 1972)
Carte	Thomas Carte, *An History of the Life of James Duke of Ormonde*, 2 vols. (London: J. Bettenham, 1736)
CCSP	*Calendar of the Clarendon State Papers Preserved in the Bodleian Library*, vol. 5, *1660–1726*, ed. F.J. Routledge (Oxford: Clarendon Press, 1970)
CH	Huntington Library, San Marino, Calif.
CJ	*Journals of the House of Commons 1547–1714*, 17 vols. (1742ff.)
CMHS	*Collections of the Massachusetts Historical Society*
Cobbett	William Cobbett, *Cobbett's Parliamentary History of England*, vol. 4 (London: R. Bagshaw, 1808)
Cosin	John Cosin, *The Correspondence of John Cosin, D.D., Lord Bishop of Durham*, Surtees Society, vol. 55 (1872)
Cowan	Ian B. Cowan, *The Scottish Covenanters 1660–1688* (London: Victor Gollancz, 1976)
CR	A.G. Matthews, *Calamy Revised* (Oxford: Clarendon Press, 1934)
Crosby	Thomas Crosby, *The History of the English Baptists*, 4 vols. (London: For the Author, 1738–40)
CSPD	*Calendar of State Papers, Domestic Series, 1603–1714*
CSPI	*Calendar of State Papers Relating to Ireland*
CSPV	*Calendar of State Papers . . . Venice*
DCY	*Depositions from the Castle of York, Relating to Offences Committed in the Northern Counties in the Seventeenth Century*, ed. J. Raine, Surtees Society, vol. 40 (1861)
DNB	*Dictionary of National Biography*
DWL	Dr. Williams's Library, London
EUL	Edinburgh University Library
Evelyn	*The Diary of John Evelyn*, ed. E.S. de Beer, 6 vols. (Oxford: Clarendon Press, 1955)
Firth and Davies	Charles Firth and Godfrey Davies, *The Regimental History of Cromwell's Army*, 2 vols. (Oxford: Clarendon Press, 1940)
Greaves, *DUFE*	Richard L. Greaves, *Deliver Us from Evil: The Radical Underground in Britain, 1660–1663* (New York and Oxford: Oxford University Press, 1986)
Greaves, *Saints and Rebels*	Richard L. Greaves, *Saints and Rebels: Seven Nonconformists in Stuart England* (Macon, Ga.: Mercer University Press, 1985)

Grey, *Debates*	*Debates of the House of Commons from the Year 1667 to the Year 1694*, ed. Anchitel Grey. 10 vols. London, 1763.
Harl. MSS	Harleian Manuscripts, British Library
Henry	Philip Henry, *Diaries and Letters of Philip Henry*, ed. Matthew Henry Lee (London: Kegan Paul, Trench & Co., 1882)
HMC	*Historical Manuscripts Commission, Reports*
Hodgson	John Hodgson, *Original Memoirs* (Edinburgh: Arch. Constable; London: John Murray, 1806)
Hutton	Ronald Hutton, *The Restoration: A Political and Religious History of England and Wales 1658–1667* (Oxford: Clarendon Press, 1985)
Int.	*Intelligencer*
JEH	*Journal of Ecclesiastical History*
JR	*The Records of the Proceedings of the Justiciary Court Edinburgh 1661–1678*, ed. W.G. Scott-Moncrieff, 2 vols., Publications of the Scottish History Society, vols. 48 and 49 (Edinburgh: T. and A. Constable, 1905)
KI	*Kingdomes Intelligencer*
Lacey	Douglas R. Lacey, *Dissent and Parliamentary Politics in England, 1661–1689* (New Brunswick, N.J.: Rutgers University Press, 1969)
Latimer, *Annals*	John Latimer, *The Annals of Bristol in the Seventeenth Century* (Bristol: William George's Sons, 1900)
Lister	T.H. Lister, *Life and Administration of Edward, First Earl of Clarendon*, 3 vols. (London: Longman, 1837)
LJ	*Journals of the House of Lords* (1767ff.)
LP	*The Lauderdale Papers*, ed. Osmund Airy, 2 vols., Camden Society, n.s., nos. 34 and 36 (1884–85)
Ludlow, *Memoirs*	*The Memoirs of Edmund Ludlow*, ed. C.H. Firth (Oxford: Clarendon Press, 1894)
Ludlow, "Voyce"	Edmund Ludlow, "A Voyce from the Watch Tower," Bodleian Eng. Hist. MS c. 487
Ludlow, *Voyce*	Edmund Ludlow, *A Voyce from the Watch Tower Part Five: 1660–1662*, ed. A.B. Worden, Camden Society, 4th ser., vol. 21 (London, 1978)
MCR	*Middlesex County Records*, ed. John Cordy Jeaffreson, 4 vols. (London: Middlesex County Records Society, 1886–92)
Misc. Aul.	Thomas Brown, *Miscellanea Aulica* (London: J. Hartley, Rob. Gibson, & Tho. Hodgson, 1702)

MP | *Mercurius Publicus*
MVB | *Memoirs of Mr. William Veitch, and George Brysson, Written by Themselves*, ed. Thomas McCrie (Edinburgh: William Blackwood, 1825)
NLS | National Library of Scotland, Edinburgh
Nicoll | John Nicoll, *A Diary of Public Transactions and Other Occurrences, Chiefly in Scotland*, Bannatyne Club, vol. 52 (Edinburgh, 1836)
NRR | *Quarter Sessions Records*, ed. J.C. Atkinson, North Riding Record Society, vol. 6 (London: Printed for the Society, 1888)
Orrery Coll. | *A Collection of the State Letters of . . . Roger Boyle, the First Earl of Orrery*, ed. Thomas Morrice, 2 vols. (Dublin: George Faulkner, 1743)
Parker, *History* | Samuel Parker, *History of His Own Time*, trans. Thomas Newlin (London: Charles Rivington, 1727)
Pepys | Samuel Pepys, *The Diary of Samuel Pepys*, ed. Robert Latham and William Matthews, 9 vols. (Berkeley and Los Angeles: University of California Press, 1970–75)
Plomer, *DBP* | Henry R. Plomer, *A Dictionary of the Booksellers and Printers Who Were at Work in England, Scotland and Ireland from 1641 to 1667* (London: Blades, East and Blades for the Bibliographical Society, 1907)
Plomer, *DPB* | Henry R. Plomer, *A Dictionary of the Printers and Booksellers Who Were at Work in England, Scotland and Ireland from 1668 to 1725* (Oxford: Oxford University Press for the Bibliographical Society, 1922)
PRO SP | Public Record Office (London), State Papers
Rel. Bax. | Richard Baxter, *Reliquiae Baxterianae: or, Mr. Richard Baxter's Narrative of the Most Memorable Passages of His Life and Times*, ed. Matthew Sylvester (London, 1696)
Reresby | *Memoirs of Sir John Reresby*, ed. Andrew Browning (Glasgow: Jackson, Son, & Co., 1936)
RPCS | *The Register of the Privy Council of Scotland*, ed. P. Hume Brown, 3rd ser., vols. 1–3 (Edinburgh: H.M. General Register House, 1908–10)
Schwoerer | Lois G. Schwoerer, *"No Standing Armies!": The Antiarmy Ideology in Seventeenth-Century England* (Baltimore and London: The Johns Hopkins University Press, 1974)
Som. Tr. | W. Scott, ed., *Collection of Scarce and Valuable Tracts . . . of the Late Lord Somers*, 13 vols. (1809–15)

Sprunger	Keith L. Sprunger, *Dutch Puritanism* (Leiden: E.J. Brill, 1982)
SR	*Statutes of the Realm*
ST	W. Cobbett, T.B. Howell, et al., eds., *Cobbett's Complete Collection of State Trials and Proceedings*, 34 vols. (London: R. Bagshaw, 1809–28)
Strype	John Strype, *A Survey of the Cities of London and Westminster* (London: A. Churchill, et al., 1720)
TRHS	*Transactions of the Royal Historical Society*
Turner	*Original Records of Early Nonconformity*, ed. G. Lyon Turner, 3 vols. (London: T. Fisher Unwin, 1911–14)
Var. Coll.	*Various Collections*
Walker, "Secret Service"	James Walker, "The Secret Service Under Charles II and James II," *TRHS*, 4th ser., 15 (1932): 211–35
Watts	Michael R. Watts, *The Dissenters: From the Reformation to the French Revolution* (Oxford: Clarendon Press, 1978)
Whiting	C.E. Whiting, *Studies in English Puritanism from the Restoration to the Revolution, 1660–1688* (London: Society for Promoting Christian Knowledge, 1931)
Wodrow	Robert Wodrow, *The History of the Sufferings of the Church of Scotland from the Restoration to the Revolution*, ed. Robert Burns, 4 vols. (Glasgow: Blackie, Fullarton, & Co., 1829)

Preface

1. G.E. Aylmer, "Collective Mentalities in Mid-Seventeenth-Century England: III. Varieties of Radicalism," in *TRHS*, 5th ser., 38 (1988): 1–25.

2. J.C.D. Clark, *English Society 1688–1832* (Cambridge: Cambridge University Press, 1985), p. 278.

3. J.C.D. Clark, *Revolution and Rebellion: State and Society in England in the Seventeenth and Eighteenth Centuries* (Cambridge: Cambridge University Press, 1986), pp. 110–11.

4. Clark, *English Society*, p. 348.

5. Ibid., p. 279.

6. BL Add. MSS 32,520, fol. 181r-v.

Chapter 1

1. Cf., e.g., *DCY*, p. 134; PRO SP 29/178/88; 29/180/88; 29/181/15, 50; *MCR*, 3:338–39.

2. PRO SP 29/200/54.1.

3. PRO SP 29/102/6; 29/103/148; 29/143/139; *DCY*, pp. 141, 147. Cf. PRO SP 29/96/3.

4. PRO SP 29/81/103, 104; *MCR*, 3:335, 339; *DCY*, pp. 83, 124. Cf. PRO SP 29/128/51; *DCY*, pp. 115–16.

5. Pepys, 6:267; PRO SP 29/101/23, 40; 29/159/7.1. Cf. PRO SP 29/187/169.

6. PRO SP 29/86/22; 29/90/88.1; 29/154/38.1; 29/179/176; *DCY*, pp. 146–47.

7. PRO SP 29/97/91; 29/159/7.1; 29/178/92; *DCY*, pp. 93–94.

8. PRO SP 29/95/67; 29/125/51.1; 29/131/53; *DCY*, p. 83. Cf. PRO SP 29/94/114; 29/97/53; 29/106/9; *DCY*, pp. 116, 141; *MCR*, 3:371, 389; *Warwick County Records: Quarter Sessions Order Book Easter, 1657, to Epiphany, 1665*, ed. S.C. Ratcliff and H.C. Johnson (Warwick: L. Edgar Stephens, 1938), p. 305.

9. Pepys, 4:372; *MCR*, 3:368; PRO SP 29/148/56; 29/180/6. Cf. *DCY*, p. 145.

10. Capp, *FMM*, pp. 213–14.

11. *Newes* 16 (17 December 1663), pp. 121–22; 70 (1 September 1664), p. 568; *Int.* 31 (18 April 1664), p. 251; 57 (18 July 1664), p. 464; PRO SP 29/97/32.1. Cf. PRO SP 29/81/85.

12. PRO SP 29/94/1, 20; 29/172/13; 29/197/118; *DCY*, p. 100. Cf. PRO SP 29/100/108.1–2.

13. PRO SP 29/94/9; 29/98/63; 29/449/26. A dissident in Durham told Christopher Sanderson, one of Sir Philip Musgrave's correspondents, that his study of Esther had convinced him that "the people of God had noe peace untill Hamans tenn sonnes were destroyed; the application," Sanderson concluded, "is obvious." PRO SP 29/105/81.

14. PRO SP 29/91/90; 29/96/84, 97; 29/187/169.

15. The three, who were associated with Major Colbourne, were Roger Card, the cutler John Campe of Wellington, and a Mr. Priest. In June 1664 there were reports that militants would again seek funds by a robbery at Taunton, Bristol, or Tavistock. *Newes* 60 (28 July 1664), p. 481; 66 (18 August 1664), p. 5634; PRO SP 29/99/128; 29/101/45, 45.1, 45.4, 45.7–11; 29/103/73; *Int.* 73 (12 September 1664), pp. 585–86.

16. *CSPD 1663–64*, pp. 464, 494, 524; PRO SP 29/92/96; 29/93/91.

17. PRO SP 29/92/20, 95; 29/97/67 (cf. 29/94/75).

18. PRO SP 29/94/34; 29/95/17; 29/109/93; Bodl. Carte MSS 81, fol. 262r. Cf. *HMC* 25, *Le Fleming*, pp. 32–33.

19. PRO SP 29/97/19, 34; 29/98/63. Cf. PRO SP 29/109/29.

20. *CSPD 1663–64*, p. 430; PRO SP 29/91/91 (which has Elton at Plymouth); 29/95/104–109; 29/96/26, 54; *Int.* 31 (18 April 1664), p. 251.

21. PRO SP 29/90/51; 29/91/73; 29/92/99.

22. PRO SP 29/91/42; 29/93/12; 29/94/13.1; *CSPD 1664–65*, p. 348.

23. *CSPD 1663–64*, p. 446; PRO SP 29/91/100; 29/97/31; 29/99/21.3; 29/100/47.

24. Bodl. Clarendon MSS 81, fols. 32r, 172r; PRO SP 29/91/69; 29/95/63; 29/96/37, 81; 29/97/47; 29/98/64, 79; *CSPD 1663–64*, p. 457; *CCSP*, 5:361.

25. PRO SP 29/98/63; 29/99/119.

26. PRO SP 29/98/59; 29/99/143, 144; 29/100/17, 26, 45.

27. PRO SP 29/100/26, 85, 86; 29/116/12.1; *CSPD 1663–64*, p. 654.

28. PRO SP 29/100/34, 46, 107; Pepys, 3:186.

29. PRO SP 29/96/13, 14; 29/97/33.2; 29/101/16. The latter document, dated 5 August, must be misdated, for the warrant to take Holmes to Windsor Castle was issued on 1 April 1664. See also PRO SP 29/217/47.1.

30. PRO SP 29/102/36, 97.

31. PRO SP 29/102/48. Also in the group were Captain John Lockyer, George Rumford, Robert Joplin, and Captain Samuel Wise.

32. PRO SP 29/102/97, 129; 29/103/74. One of those involved in the shipment of arms was the tailor Ralph Alexander of Moorfields. PRO SP 29/109/58. This may have been the Ralph Alexander who was allegedly involved in the 1663 northern rebellion. Greaves, *DUFE*, p. 195.

33. PRO SP 29/103/110. Joplin wrote on his cell wall that he "would be for King Jesus." PRO SP 29/180/68. The malcontents in the bishopric of Durham at this time included Captains George Gray, Robert Hutton, Edward Shepperdson (or Shiperson), Sharpe, and Hunter. The last five lived in the Sunderland area. PRO SP 29/109/50.

34. PRO SP 29/102/136; 29/104/17, 43; *CSPD 1664–65*, pp. 79, 451.

35. PRO SP 29/107/28.1; 29/110/9; 29/111/6; *CCSP*, 5:463, 465.

36. PRO SP 29/110/77. A warrant was issued on 17 January 1665 to search all the warehouses and goods connected with Robert Hawsey, a carrier between London and Bristol. *CSPD 1664–65*, p. 172.

37. PRO SP 29/112/89; 29/113/19. Cf. PRO SP 29/107/68 (for Durham dissidents); 29/109/48.

38. PRO SP 29/113/19. At Ely, Cornet Graves, who had served under Colonel Francis Hacker, mustered a group of ex-Cromwellian soldiers in February, but then dismissed them, "having notice to meet noe more[,] but we shall have a day of it for all this." PRO SP 29/113/40.

39. *CSPD 1663–64*, p. 515. Hill formally became minister of the English Reformed church in Middelburg only in 1667. Sprunger, p. 188.

40. Bodl. Clarendon MSS 81, fols. 203r-204r; *CCSP*, 5:390; PRO SP 29/90/1; 29/98/56.

41. PRO SP 29/98/56. Richardson was preaching at Amsterdam in February 1664. *CCSP*, 5:373. He received the M.D. degree at Leiden University the same year. Sprunger, p. 415.

42. PRO SP 29/103/59; BL Add. MSS 41,818, fol. 35r; Greaves, *DUFE*, p. 119. Cf. BL Add. MSS 41,818, fol. 35r.

43. PRO SP 29/100/64; 29/101/66.

44. PRO SP 29/110/77. Cf. PRO SP 29/109/20. The Dutch encouraged nonconformists to come to the Netherlands by offering liberty of conscience. *HMC* 78, *Hastings*, 2:145. In May 1664 the Dutch published the Conventicle Act with the comment that it was designed to suppress the Gospel. *HMC* 53, *Montagu*, p. 166.

45. Pepys, 5:264; PRO SP 29/99/109, 117; 29/103/62; 29/105/81 (which also refers to the militants' hopes that the government would have trouble with the Scottish Presbyterians). There was apparently some feeling among the malcontents that the English navy would have difficulties with the Dutch because so many qualified officers had been dismissed for having served the interregnum governments. PRO SP 29/101/74, 74.1. In the spring of 1664, however, a number of these officers received new commands. *CSPD 1663–64*, p. 597.

46. Pepys, 5:296; George Wilson Meadley, *Memoirs of Algernon Sydney* (London: Cradock and Joy, 1813), pp. 136–37, 141; Ludlow, *Memoirs*, 2:346; Alexander Charles Ewald, *The Life and Times of the Hon. Algernon Sydney 1622–1683*, 2 vols. (London: Tinsley Brothers, 1873), 1:383–88, 392.

47. PRO SP 29/86/109; 29/101/29.1; *CSPD 1663–64*, p. 380. There is a proposal in the Public Record Office from an unidentified source urging the dispatch of a spy in the guise of an escaped prisoner to learn more about the exiles in the Lausanne area. PRO SP 29/86/17.

48. PRO SP 29/86/110; 29/101/22; Ludlow, *Memoirs*, 2: 359–62. In 1666 an unnamed woman who claimed to be familiar with Ludlow's haunts offered to capture him in return for a reward. PRO SP 29/168/156.

49. Ludlow, "Voyce," pp. 1026–28, 1038–39; Ludlow, *Memoirs*, 2:373–74, 427, 488–89.

50. Ludlow, "Voyce," p. 1056.

51. *CCSP*, 5:487, 493; PRO SP 29/110/77; 29/112/89.

52. PRO SP 29/109/20; 29/113/19; 29/142/72. In Yorkshire the dissidents understood that there were two regiments of English exiles in Holland. PRO SP 29/113/55.

53. PRO SP 29/112/23. The merchant was Mr. Lane.

54. *CCSP*, 5:473; PRO SP 29/127/61.

55. See J.L. Price, "Restoration England and Europe," in *The Restored Monarchy 1660–1688*, ed. J.R. Jones (Totowa, N.J.: Rowman and Littlefield, 1979), pp. 121, 124–25.

56. PRO SP 29/112/122; 29/114/89; 29/116/96. Atkinson was now a poor man, having lost his estate. He had to support a wife and four children. PRO SP 29/115/36.

57. PRO SP 29/115/38; 29/116/96. I have been unable to trace this book.

58. PRO SP 29/117/38; BL Egerton MSS 3349, fol. 260r. The name John Atkinson appears twice, raising the possibility that there were two dissidents

of this name. PRO SP 29/117/37. A warrant for the arrest of Atkinson the hosier was issued on 18 March 1665. *HMC 22, Eleventh Report*, Appendix, Part VII, p. 7.

59. PRO SP 29/117/37.

60. PRO SP 29/117/67; 29/125/15. One of Atkinson's friends, John Taylor, was certain Atkinson would not betray the militants because he was "a very stubborne fellow." PRO SP 29/121/93.3

61. PRO SP 29/113/56; 29/114/22, 89; 29/116/12.

62. PRO SP 29/114/89; 29/187/57, 159.

63. PRO SP 29/114/11. A warrant for Strange's arrest was issued on 2 March 1665, but he eluded the magistrates. He was now using the alias Captain L'Estrange. *CSPD 1664–65*, p. 234.

64. PRO SP 29/114/11. Cf. PRO SP 29/116/127; *BDBR*, s.v. "Cox, Owen." There were rumors during the war that Lambert was planning an escape. Cf. PRO SP 29/112/135.

65. PRO SP 29/104/13; 29/113/61, 66, 66.1; 29/117/2; 29/120/24; 29/121/93.4; 29/122/50; 29/124/24; *CCSP*, 5:474.

66. PRO SP 29/116/11; *HMC 25, Le Fleming*, p. 35; *HMC 35, Fourteenth Report*, Appendix, Part IV, pp. 75–76; *HMC 55, Var. Coll.*, 2:379–80; *HMC 31, Thirteenth Report*, Appendix, Part IV, pp. 464–65.

67. *Newes* 48 (22 June 1665), pp. 484–85; PRO SP 29/124/42, 49, 134; Bodl. Carte MSS 79, fol. 13r.

68. PRO SP 29/129/98; 29/131/52; BL Harl. MSS 7010, fol. 396v. Colonel Thomas Doleman fought with De Witt. BL Add. MSS 22,920, fol. 162r. One of Lauderdale's agents in the Netherlands noted in July 1665 that some 300 Scots as well as an undetermined number of Englishmen served in the Dutch fleet. He attributed the large number to sermons by preachers such as James Simpson and John Livingston that called for Charles II and his advisers to repent and condemned the nation's profanity. NLS MS 597, fol. 130r.

69. PRO SP 29/159/4, 108.1; *CSPD 1665–66*, p. 567; BL Harl. MSS 7010, fols. 566r-567r.

70. PRO SP 29/160/103; 29/161/24.

71. *CSPD 1665–66*, p. 519; *HMC 25, Le Fleming*, p. 40; *HMC 31, Thirteenth Report*, Appendix, Part IV, p. 467; Arthur John Hawkes, *Sir Roger Bradshaigh of Haigh, Knight and Baronet 1628–1684 with Notes of His Immediate Forbears* (Manchester: Lancashire and Cheshire Antiquarian Society, 1945), p. 32; BL Add. MSS 41,254, fol. 3r-v.

72. *Misc. Aul.*, pp. 406–407; PRO SP 29/161/17.

73. PRO SP 29/160/65; 29/163/11, 30, 64; 29/164/24.

74. PRO SP 29/160/19, 104. Cf. *DCY*, p. 144; *CSPD 1665–66*, p. 522.

75. PRO SP 29/159/9, 10, 71; *CSPD 1665–66*, p. 526 (which appears to be an

encoded statement about radical plans, including contacts with the exiles). Cf. *CSPD 1665–66*, p. 568.

76. Herbert H. Rowen, *John de Witt, Grand Pensionary of Holland, 1625–1672* (Princeton: Princeton University Press, 1978), pp. 591–93.

77. *CSPV 1666–68*, p. 114; PRO SP 29/188/27; Pepys, 8:155 n. 1.

78. Bodl. Carte MSS 47, fols. 158r, 486r-v; Rowen, *John de Witt*, pp. 595–96; PRO SP 29/209/86.1; 29/223/189; Abbott, "Conspiracy," p. 709. English citizens captured in the service of France or the Netherlands could be hanged. PRO SP 29/165/103. Among the agents in England who were allegedly coordinating radical activity with the Dutch assault were a Mr. Mead and Captain Pierce. Mead met with Dutch agents. Pierce left for New England in June 1667, and was reportedly responsible for having helped William Goffe and Edward Whalley escape there in 1660. *CCSP*, 5:618. Robert Hammond of Reading was thought to have carried information on the damage at Chatham to the Dutch following their raid. PRO SP 29/206/151, 152; 29/207/14.

79. PRO SP 29/205/63, 128; 29/206/47, 48, 63, 64, 116.1; 29/207/107; 29/209/150.1; *MCR*, 4:2–3; Pepys, 8:332.

80. PRO SP 29/205/117; 29/207/12; 29/209/101.

81. PRO SP 29/205/64; 29/207/2; Abbott, "Conspiracy," p. 709; Pepys, 8:332. Among the other security measures were the use of two troops of horse and two companies of foot to secure the Isle of Ely against both the militants and the Dutch; the arrest of Major Edmund Rolfe; the inspection of letters to dissidents in Bristol; and Sir Philip Musgrave's stepped-up intelligence activities in the north, including the dispatch of an agent to Scotland. PRO SP 29/206/1, 1.1, 1.2, 7; 29/207/2, 141.

82. Schwoerer, pp. 90–91; PRO SP 29/210/121.

83. *CCSP*, 5:376; Burnet, p. 153; Ewald, *Sydney*, 1:396, 400–401; Ludlow, "Voyce," pp. 1056–57. One of Williamson's correspondents asserted that as early as June 1664 various English militants made an offer to the States General to raise 20,000 supporters in England. *CSPD 1663–64*, p. 610. Sidney's political views have been thoroughly analyzed by Jonathan Scott, *Algernon Sidney and the English Republic 1623–1677* (Cambridge: Cambridge University Press, 1988).

84. Ludlow, "Voyce," p. 1057; Ludlow, *Memoirs*, 2:378–80.

85. Ludlow, "Voyce," pp. 1057, 1059–60.

86. Ibid., pp. 1064–65.

87. Ibid., pp. 1065–67, 1079–81, 1101. The subsequent assertion, made in 1683, that Ludlow had joined Sidney at Nieupoort's house and had there demanded £200,000 and forty ships, is erroneous. PRO SP 29/433/39.

88. PRO SP 29/124/72; Lister, 3:388–89; *CCSP*, 5:495.

89. PRO SP 29/150/5; 29/151/7; 29/153/46, 57; BL Egerton MSS 2618, fol. 123v; James Waylen, *The House of Cromwell and the Story of Dunkirk* (London: Elliot Stock, 1891), pp. 16–18; M.A. Everett Green, "Richard Cromwell," *The Athenaeum* 1798 (12 April 1862): 498. During the preceding month the States of Holland, to the dismay of some other provinces, had imposed a loyalty oath on those exiles who accepted commissions in their forces. BL Harl. MSS 7010, fols. 489r-v, 491r.

90. The others were John White, William Burton, John Nicholas, Robert Honeywood, Jr., John Grove, John Phelps, and William Scott. Nicholas's name appeared for the first time in the printed proclamation (21 April).

91. PRO SP 29/153/57, 58; [London] *Gazette* 47 (23–26 April 1666); Green, "Richard Cromwell," p. 498.

92. Sir William Temple, *Memoirs of the Life, Works, and Correspondence of Sir William Temple, Bart.*, ed. Thomas Peregrine Courtenay, 2 vols. (London: Longman, 1836), 1:234–35, 237–39; PRO SP 29/128/15; 29/135/25; Walker, "Secret Service," pp. 225–26. Captain James Hely, former governor of Salisbury, also carried intelligence reports to and from the Netherlands. PRO SP 29/133/97.

93. PRO SP 29/187/148; *The Tanner Letters*, ed. Charles McNeill (Dublin: Stationery Office, 1943), p. 405.

94. PRO SP 29/162/105; 29/165/12; *CSPD 1665–66*, p. 544; K.H.D. Haley, *An English Diplomat in the Low Countries: Sir William Temple and John De Witt, 1665–1672* (Oxford: Clarendon Press, 1986), p. 90. His return made possible the release of Nathaniel Desborough from the Tower in August. PRO SP 29/167/52; 29/168/76; 29/176/109.

95. Ludlow, *Memoirs*, 2:389–91.

96. Ludlow, "Voyce," pp. 1111–13.

97. Ibid., p. 1114.

98. Ibid., pp. 1115–16, 1122–25; Meadley, *Memoirs*, pp. 144–46; Ewald, *Sydney*, 1:402–405.

99. Ludlow, "Voyce," pp. 1127–28; *CSPD 1665–66*, p. 522; Bodl. Carte MSS 46, fol. 329v.

100. Bodl. Carte MSS 35, fols. 5v, 285r, 313v; Carte MSS 46, fols. 329r, 432r-v; Carte MSS 47, fol. 470r; BL Add. MSS 23,125, fol. 267r.

101. Angeline Goreau, *Reconstructing Aphra: A Social Biography of Aphra Behn* (New York: Dial Press, 1980), pp. 95, 100; PRO SP 29/167/159, 160; 29/172/81.2.

102. Rowen, *John de Witt*, p. 231; PRO SP 29/171/20, 65, 81.2; 29/172/14.1. Cf. PRO SP 29/143/135.

103. PRO SP 29/167/159; 29/172/14.

104. Ludlow, "Voyce," pp. 1144–46, 1154. Cf. *CSPD 1667–68*, p. 56.

105. Ludlow, "Voyce," p. 1093; Pepys, 6:184; PRO SP 29/127/81, 136; 29/128/53; 29/129/29, 63; 29/132/51; *CSPD 1664–65*, p. 542; *Int.* 74 (11 September 1665), pp. 850–51.

106. PRO SP 29/129/11; Hawkes, *Bradshaigh*, p. 30.

107. PRO SP 29/131/88. Among the others allegedly involved were Captain Lyons of Lundy Island, Devon, and a Bristol minister, William Troughton (or Throton), formerly chaplain to Robert Hammond, governor of the Isle of Wight in 1647. PRO SP 29/131/88. John Read (or Rede), former governor of Poole, was interrogated but denied knowing Dale or Buffett. He subsequently insisted to Arlington that he abhorred plots and submitted to the government, but urged modest freedom for nonconformists to worship in peace. PRO SP 29/132/2, 30. Dale does not appear in the lists of Tower prisoners. Cf. PRO SP 29/74/58; 29/75/161; 29/81/32; 29/90/112; 29/95/68.

108. *CSPD 1664–65*, p. 518.

109. PRO SP 29/449/90.

110. PRO SP 29/129/11, 40, 45, 60; *HMC* 55, *Var. Coll.*, 7:428; *HMC* 25, *Le Fleming*, p. 38. Cf. Hawkes, *Bradshaigh*, p. 30; PRO SP 29/128/89; 29/129/59. Sir William Coventry complained to Arlington on 8 August that the militia in the West Riding was still unsettled and short of officers. PRO SP 29/128/62.

111. *HMC* 55, *Var. Coll.*, 2:120; PRO SP 29/129/18, 31, 77; 29/131/46, 52.

112. Abbott misdates the plot in the early summer, thus erroneously attributing earlier crackdowns to it. Abbott, "Conspiracy," pp. 699–700.

113. The other seven were William Saunderson (alias Saunders), yeoman; Henry Tucker, tailor; Thomas Flint, gentleman; Thomas Evans, millener; John Miles, carpenter; William Wescott, yeoman; and John Cole, tailor. The latter may have been the Captain John Cole who served in Richard Coote's regiment in Ireland. *MCR*, 3:376; *CMHS*, 8:215; *Gazette* 48 (26–30 April 1666); Pepys, 6:209; Parker, *History*, pp. 94–96; PRO SP 29/154/74; Firth and Davies, p. 620; Thomas Long, *A Compendious History of All the Popish & Fanatical Plots and Conspiracies* (London, 1684), p. 131. Cf. PRO SP 29/156/101.

114. PRO SP 29/135/37.

115. The other two were Captains (Clement?) Nedham (or Needham) and Sherwood.

116. Croxton, Duckenfield, and Hope denied any involvement in a conspiracy. PRO SP 29/134/29, 50; 29/136/70. Cf. PRO SP 29/134/51. Duckenfield had been imprisoned in the Tower in August. For Duckenfield see *BDBR*, s.v.

117. PRO SP 29/133/102; Bodl. Carte MSS 34, fol. 446r; Carte MSS 46, fol. 207r-v.

118. Bodl. Carte MSS 34, fol. 446r; PRO SP 29/132/28; 29/133/4; 29/134/13.

For lists of other arrested dissidents see PRO SP 29/133/103 (Newcastle); 29/132/39 (Staffordshire); *CSPD 1664–65*, p. 567, and PRO SP 29/137/120 (Berkshire); 29/132/24 (Cheshire); 29/143/138 (Herefordshire). Cf. *HMC 55, Var. Coll.*, 2:120–21; PRO SP 29/143/137.

119. PRO SP 29/133/11; 29/143/136; Henry, pp. 175–76.

120. *CCSP*, 5:514–15, 519; *CSPD 1665–66*, p. 97; PRO SP 29/139/23; *LJ*, 11:688. On 1 September Albemarle committed the following dissidents to the Tower: William Pride, Robert Kingsford, Captain John Gryce (who was subsequently discharged and became an informer), Owen Baxter, Richard Sandford, Henry Tucker, and Thomas Flint (or Flynt). Tucker and Flint were among the eight executed for the Rathbone plot. PRO SP 29/149/87. Gryce formerly served in Ireland. Ludlow, "Voyce," pp. 942, 1117.

121. PRO SP 29/134/57, 81.

122. PRO SP 29/135/42, 43; *CSPD 1665–66*, pp. 24–25; *HMC 35, Fourteenth Report*, Appendix, Part IV, p. 76; Bodl. Carte MSS 46, fol. 231r.

123. PRO SP 29/127/44. Cf. *DCY*, p. 134.

124. *CCSP*, 5:514; PRO SP 29/139/64; 29/149/87.

125. Hodgson, pp. 194–95; PRO SP 29/140/4. In August there were more than eighty prisoners in York Castle. Captain Lascelles died in prison. Hodgson, pp. 195–96.

126. PRO SP 29/140/4.

127. PRO SP 29/139/60, 60.1, 64, 102; 29/145/7, 36; *HMC 55, Var. Coll.*, 2:121; *Orrery Coll.*, 1:215.

128. PRO SP 29/149/42. Cf. PRO SP 29/146/66.

129. PRO SP 29/120/25; 29/129/11; *CSPD 1664–65*, p. 512; BL Harl. MSS 4631, vol. 1, fol. 130r. Among the others arrested were Sir Hugh Campbell, Sir James Stewart, and Sir William Muir. Abbott erroneously makes the arrest of the Scottish generals a consequence of the Rathbone plot. "Conspiracy," p. 700.

130. PRO SP 29/112/61; 29/120/25; *CCSP*, 5:473; Burnet, p. 153.

131. *JR*, 1:135–39; Nicoll, pp. 442–43. A proclamation ordering the return of all military personnel in the service of the States General who were Charles II's subjects had been issued on 14 October 1665. *Int.* 86 (23 October 1665), pp. 1019–20. The twelve officers were Colonels John Kirkpatrick, Walter Scott, and Louis Erskine, Lieutenant-Colonels Thomas Livingston, George Lauder, and Coutts, Majors John Kirkpatrick and Henry Graham, and Captains George Coutts, Evertson Kirkpatrick, Colzier, and Sir William Sandilands.

132. PRO SP 29/144/26, 71.1.

133. PRO SP 29/149/66, 66.2, 66.3.

134. *CSPI 1663–65*, pp. 662, 679; *Misc. Aul.*, pp. 369–70; *Tanner Letters*, pp. 405–406.

135. *CSPI 1666–69*, pp. 8, 25–26, 33–35; *Orrery Coll.*, 1:229–30; PRO SP 29/147/111; 29/168/152.

136. PRO SP 29/147/86.1. Collins was the pastor of a nonconformist church in Dover. PRO SP 29/147/86.1. Cf. PRO SP 29/147/86.

137. PRO SP 29/156/107.1.

138. PRO SP 29/154/10; 29/155/15; *Gazette* 48 (26–30 April 1666). Cf. PRO SP 29/149/43.

139. PRO SP 29/155/17, 53; *CSPD 1665–66*, p. 416. Cf. PRO SP 29/157/21.

140. PRO SP 29/165/15, 54, 93; 29/166/14, 15, 54; 29/168/55. For another alleged plot, this one involving the London silk-weaver Henry Bellard, see PRO SP 29/230/112.

141. PRO SP 29/166/39; 29/167/68; 29/168/43, 147; *HMC* 25, *Le Fleming*, p. 41. Cf. PRO SP 29/187/159.

142. PRO SP 29/169/51; 29/173/3, 4; BL Add. MSS 41,818, fol. 35r; Goreau, *Aphra*, p. 304.

143. PRO SP 29/174/58; 29/176/127; 29/190/30.

144. PRO SP 29/178/133–35, 174.1–2; 29/179/118; 29/180/32, 42, 89; 29/189/29; Latimer, *Annals*, p. 342. Troops were sent to secure Leeds in late November or early December. PRO SP 29/180/120.

145. PRO SP 29/173/83; 29/178/130, 135; 29/180/5; *CSPD 1666–67*, pp. 197, 242–43, 245, 252.

146. PRO SP 29/178/103, 125, 166; *CSPD 1666–67*, pp. 231–32, 236. Cf. PRO SP 29/181/46.

147. *CSPD 1666–67*, pp. 231–32, 250, 287; PRO SP 29/179/94; 29/180/25; 29/182/37, 60, 70; 29/206/16; *Gazette* 112 (10–13 December 1666); 115 (20–24 December 1666).

148. PRO SP 29/187/173. One proposal to improve security centered around the recruitment of "ould rebellious Fannatikes [and] Fift Monarkye men" for an army that would serve the Venetians. PRO SP 29/143/85.

149. PRO SP 29/170/44; 29/173/35; 29/174/13, 13.1, 80, 81; 29/175/142.

150. PRO SP 29/175/87; 29/176/108; 29/180/68; 29/189/20; *CSPD 1667*, pp. 1–2.

151. PRO SP 29/188/26.

152. *CCSP*, 5:580, 582, 605; *CSPD 1667*, p. 3; PRO SP 29/188/168; 29/200/4, 55; 29/201/92. There were also reports—probably spurious—in February 1667 that Colonel Richard Ingoldsby, the earl of Derby, Christopher Eyon, and a Captain Rowld were heading a conspiracy to return Richard Cromwell to power. Derby was associated with Buckingham, though there is no reliable evidence to tie them to this alleged plot. One of the sources for this information was a scrivener and tutor named Rawlinson. PRO SP 29/190/104.1; 29/197/21, 21.1; *CSPD 1666–67*, pp. 495–96.

153. *CSPD 1666–67*, pp. 512, 533, 552–53, 555, 560; *HMC* 25, *Le Fleming*,

p. 45; PRO SP 29/197/161; BL Althorp MSS H2, fol. 1r. The informer William Leeving claimed that in 1665 North told him Buckingham had asked North to "assure the trusty fanatics that he would appear for them on opportunity." Leeving blamed North for revealing his status as an informer to the dissidents. *CSPD 1666–67*, p. 511.

154. *CSPD 1667–68*, p. 259; Bodl. Carte MSS 35, fol. 304r; Carte MSS 47, fol. 174r; Abbott, "Conspiracy," pp. 708–10; *CSPD 1667*, p. 360; Ludlow, "Voyce," p. 1160; R.W. Harris, *Clarendon and the English Revolution* (London: Chatto and Windus, 1983), p. 373. Cf. *CSPD 1667*, pp. 114, 170, 265, 511. Richard Baxter, however, sneered that Buckingham "was of no Religion, but notoriously and professedly lustful; And yet of greater wit and parts, and sounder Principles as to the interest of Humanity, and the Common good, than most Lords in the Court." *Rel. Bax.*, pt. 3, par. 49 (p. 21); cf. pt. 3, par. 54, 56 (p. 22).

155. PRO SP 29/170/102, 114, 152; 29/172/106; *HMC* 13, *Tenth Report*, Appendix, Part IV, p. 115; BL Add. MSS 41,254, fol. 7r. Cf. PRO SP 29/171/24. Ludlow referred to 3 September as "a day as observed fatall to Monarchy." "Voyce," p. 1131.

156. *DCY*, pp. 145–46; *MCR*, 3:387. For others see *MCR*, 3:384–86.

157. *MCR*, 3:385; PRO SP 29/178/154; 29/204/30; 29/207/75, 78; 29/211/65, 111; *HMC* 31, *Thirteenth Report*, Appendix, Part IV, p. 348; William Lilly, *Mr. William Lilly's History of His Life and Times* (London, 1715), pp. 95–98.

158. PRO SP 29/171/34, 52, 111, 128; Ludlow, "Voyce," p. 1132; *Rel. Bax.*, pt. 3, par. 38 (p. 18). According to Ludlow some of the Scots blamed the king and Henrietta Maria. "Voyce," p. 1136.

159. *Londons Flames Discovered by Informations Taken Before the Committee* (1667); Pepys, 8:439.

160. *A True and Faithful Account of the Several Informations* (1667), p. 32.

161. [Francis Smith?], *Trap ad Crucem; or, the Papists Watch-word* (1670).

162. *HMC* 78, *Hastings*, 2:371–72; PRO SP 29/173/132; 29/450/36; *HMC* 55, *Var. Coll.*, 2:123–24.

163. *CSPD 1666–67*, p. 99; PRO SP 29/170/152, 157; 29/171/12, 56, 73, 111, 112, 129; 29/181/29.

164. Cf., e.g., PRO SP 29/172/6; 29/173/39.

165. *Gazette* 85 (3–10 September 1666); PRO SP 29/170/50; 29/171/141. Radicals were found especially in such London parishes as Allhallows the Great, Allhallows Lombard Street, St. Thomas the Apostle, St. Mary Abchurch, and St. Magnus Martyr. See Tai Liu, *Puritan London: A Study of Religion and Society in the City Parishes* (Newark: University of Delaware Press; London and Toronto: Associated University Presses, 1986), pp. 110–18.

Chapter 2

1. *KI* 23 (3–10 June 1661), pp. 359–60; Nicoll, p. 335; F.N. McCoy, *Robert Baillie and the Second Scots Reformation* (Berkeley and Los Angeles: University of California Press, 1974), pp. 211–14.

2. *ST*, 5:1369-1541; *KI* 23 (3–10 June 1661), pp. 359–60; "The Old Tolbooth: With Extracts from the Original Records," ed. John A. Fairley, in *The Book of the Old Edinburgh Club*, vol. 4 (Edinburgh: T. and A. Constable, 1911), p. 140.

3. *KI* (18–25 February 1661), p. 128; Nicoll, pp. 333–34; *KI* 21 (20–27 May 1661), p. 327; 22 (27 May-3 June 1661), p. 339; *APS*, 7:26.

4. *RPCS 1661–64*, pp. 28–29; Bodl. Clarendon MSS 75, fol. 427r.

5. F.D. Dow, *Cromwellian Scotland 1651–1660* (Edinburgh: John Donald Publishers, 1979), p. 273; *RPCS 1661–64*, pp. 28–32.

6. *RPCS 1661–64*, pp. 130–31, 260–61, 269–70.

7. *KI* (25 February–4 March 1661), p. 144; William Steven, *The History of the Scottish Church, Rotterdam* (Edinburgh: Waugh & Innes; Rotterdam: Vander Meer & Verbruggen, 1832), p. 28. MacWard subsequently went to the Netherlands, where he wrote books defending his views and corresponded with supporters in Scotland. Ibid., p. 29; Burnet, p. 79; *Extracts from the Records of the Burgh of Glasgow, A.D. 1663–1690*, ed. J.D. Marwick (Glasgow: Scottish Burgh Records Society, 1905), p. 2 n. 1; *KI* 29 (15–22 July 1661), p. 463.

8. *KI* (10–17 November 1662), p. 742; *RPCS 1661–64*, pp. 278, 305–306, 312; "The Old Tolbooth: With Extracts from the Original Records," ed. John A. Fairley, in *The Book of the Old Edinburgh Club*, vol. 5 (Edinburgh: T. and A. Constable, 1912), p. 104.

9. *MP* 44 (24–31 October 1661), p. 680; *KI* 43 (21–28 October 1661), p. 688.

10. Gordon Donaldson, *Scotland: James V to James VII* (New York and Washington: Frederick A. Praeger, 1966), pp. 365–66; Dow, *Cromwellian Scotland*, pp. 273–74; Cowan, pp. 52–54; Andrew McKerral, *Kintyre in the Seventeenth Century* (Edinburgh and London: Oliver and Boyd, 1948), p. 112. See Cowan's words of caution on these statistics (pp. 52–54).

11. *Extracts from Glasgow, 1663–1690*, p. 2 n. 1. According to the Council, Cargill's "cariadge hes bein most seditious." *RPCS 1661–64*, p. 270.

12. Robert Herbert Story, *William Carstares: A Character and Career of the Revolutionary Epoch (1649–1715)* (London: Macmillan, 1874), p. 18; A. Ian Dunlop, *William Carstares and the Kirk by Law Established* (Edinburgh: Saint Andrew Press, 1967), p. 25; *RPCS 1661–64*, pp. 312–15.

13. *HMC* 78, *Hastings*, 4:367.

14. *RPCS 1661–64*, pp. 264, 302–303, 311–12, 319; *KI* 23 (2–9 June 1662), p. 366; 25 (16–23 June 1662), p. 389; 27 (30 June-7 July 1662), p. 432; 51 (15–22 December 1662), p. 822; *MP* 24 (12–19 June 1662), p. 384. James Simpson of Airth had been exiled in 1661. Wodrow, 1:197.

15. *APS*, 7:377–79; Wodrow, 1:197–99; *RPCS 1661–64*, pp. 264, 397.

16. *RPCS 1661–64*, p. 350; *HMC 72, Laing*, 1:335; Buckroyd, *CS*, p. 54.

17. *RPCS 1661–64*, pp. 403–404; PRO SP 29/78/82.

18. *LP*, 1:157; *RPCS 1661–64*, pp. 408–409, 455–56, 462; Wodrow, 1: 384–86.

19. "Old Tolbooth," 5:114; *HMC 50, Heathcote*, p. 151. Cf. "Old Tolbooth," 5:122–23; *LP*, 2:iii; *HMC 72, Laing*, 1:340; EUL MS La.III.350, fol. 3r.

20. *LP*, 2:i-ii; *RPCS 1661–64*, pp. 511, 624–25; PRO SP 29/105/8, 23.

21. *RPCS 1661–64*, p. 520; *LP*, 1:204–205. Cf. NLS MS 2512, fol. 64r.

22. *RPCS 1665–69*, pp. 107–109; PRO SP 29/138/59.

23. *KI* 24 (10–17 June 1661), p. 365; 25 (17–24 June 1661), p. 392; *MP* 1 (2–9 January 1662), p. 8; *KI* 25 (16–23 June 1662), p. 400; *Int.* 43 (30 May 1664), p. 352; *Newes* 62 (10 August 1665), p. 707; 85 (19 October 1665), p. 1003.

24. Pepys, 4:138; PRO SP 29/28/93, 93.1; 29/43/91.

25. *HMC 51, Popham*, pp. 189–90.

26. PRO SP 29/73/35; BL Add. MSS 23,135, fol. 170r-v.

27. PRO SP 29/75/71; 29/103/95.

28. *CSPV 1661–64*, p. 200 (cf. p. 188); *HMC 21, Hamilton*, Supplementary Report, p. 81; PRO SP 29/143/28; *Oxford Gazette* 12 (21–25 December 1665); Nicoll, pp. 433–34.

29. *CSPI 1661–64*, p. 277; *RPCS 1661–64*, pp. 282, 290–91, 355; *JR*, 1: 54–55.

30. *RPCS 1661–64*, pp. 263, 397, 491; *KI* 47 (17–24 November 1662), p. 752; Ambrose Barnes, *Memoirs of the Life of Mr. Ambrose Barnes, Late Merchant and Sometime Alderman of Newcastle upon Tyne*, Surtees Society, vol. 50 (Durham, 1867), p. 392; Greaves, *DUFE*, pp. 125–27. Cf. *The Rawdon Papers*, ed. Edward Berwick (London: John Nichols and Son, 1819), p. 166.

31. *CCSP*, 5:290; *LP*, 1:209, 215.

32. *KI* (4–11 March 1661), pp. 156–58; Nicoll, p. 323; *RPCS 1661–64*, pp. 42, 371–72; Pepys, 4:168–69.

33. NLS MS 2512, fol. 82r; *RPCS 1661–64*, pp. 439–42, 466, 551, 587–88; Wodrow, 2:5; Buckroyd, *CS*, p. 64.

34. *RPCS 1661–64*, pp. 339, 368–70, 666; *KI* 11 (9–16 March 1663), p. 171; 23 (1–8 June 1663), p. 368; "Old Tolbooth," 5:105.

35. *RPCS 1661–64*, pp. 596, 616, 626; "Old Tolbooth," 5:121, 125; *RPCS 1665–69*, p. 36; PRO SP 29/134/14; 29/135/39.

36. NLS MS 2512, fol. 82r; PRO SP 29/136/69; *RPCS 1665–69*, pp. 135–36.

37. Burnet, p. 145; *LP*, 1:236–37; 2:xxii; *HMC 21, Hamilton*, Supplementary Report, pp. 82–83.

38. Nicoll, p. 436; *LP*, 1:223.

39. *MVB*, pp. 385–86; PRO SP 29/124/98; Wodrow, 1:425; PRO SP 29/131/31; *Letters from Archibald, Earl of Argyll, to John, Duke of Lauderdale* (Edinburgh: Bannatyne Club, 1829), pp. 28–29; Bodl. Carte MSS 45, fol. 189r. The "refractory" Wallace and Hugh Peebles had been suspended by the church in the spring of 1664. NLS MS 2512, fol. 38r.

40. *MVB*, pp. 36, 377–79; Thomas Stephen, *The History of the Church of Scotland from the Reformation to the Present Time*, 4 vols. (London: John Lendrum, 1843–45), 2:557.

41. PRO SP 29/148/102; 29/149/42; 29/168/72; *CSPV 1666–68*, p. 19.

42. Burnet, p. 143; Willie Thompson, "The Kirk and the Cameronians," in *Rebels and Their Causes: Essays in Honour of A.L. Morton*, ed. Maurice Cornforth (Atlantic Highlands, N.J.: Humanities Press, 1979), pp. 95, 98; *Extracts from the Records of the Burgh of Glasgow, A.D. 1630–1662*, ed. J.D. Marwick (Glasgow: Scottish Burgh Records Society, 1881), p. 495; *HMC 78, Hastings*, 4:367.

43. Dow, *Cromwellian Scotland*, p. 275; Cowan, p. 55; *CCSP*, 5:272.

44. *RPCS 1661–64*, pp. 338–39, 349–50; *KI* 14 (30 March–6 April 1663), pp. 209–10.

45. *RPCS 1661–64*, pp. 350–51; *CMHS*, 8:209.

46. *RPCS 1661–64*, pp. 357–59, 372–77, 384, 390, 401–403, 408, 419–21; "Old Tolbooth," 5:108–10; PRO SP 29/73/18; Pepys, 4:130; *HMC 36, Ormonde*, n.s., 3:52.

47. *KI* 23 (1–8 June 1663), p. 367; *LP*, 1:154–55, 169.

48. *RPCS 1661–64*, pp. 389, 396–97; Sir James Turner, *Memoirs of His Own Life and Times*, ed. Thomas Thomson (Edinburgh: Bannatyne Club, 1829), pp. 139–40; *Newes* 9 (29 October 1663), p. 72; BL Add. MSS 23,119, fol. 126r.

49. Thompson, "Kirk," p. 97; *LP*, 1:194n; 2:iv, ix.

50. *LP*, 1:222; 2:xviii, xxx–xxxi; PRO SP 29/115/43; BL Harl. MSS 7010, fol. 231v; Burnet, p. 143; *HMC 21, Hamilton*, Supplementary Report, p. 83; BL Add. MSS 35,125, fol. 115r.

51. *LP*, 1:235; 2:xix; *HMC 21, Hamilton*, Supplementary Report, p. 82; *HMC 50, Heathcote*, p. 191; PRO SP 29/147/82.

52. NLS MS 2512, fol. 84r; PRO SP 29/135/39; 29/147/82; *LP*, 1:234–35.

53. Wodrow, 2:4–5; *LP*, 1:235n; 2:xxviii–xxix; PRO SP 29/138/16; Andrew Crichton, *The Life and Diary of Lieut. Col. J. Blackader, of the Cameronian Regiment* (Edinburgh: H.S. Baynes, 1824), p. 18; John C. Johnston, *Treasury of the Scottish Covenant* (Edinburgh: Andrew Elliot, 1887), p. 352.

54. *LP*, 1:236; Bodl. Carte MSS 45, fol. 189r; *HMC 39, Fifteenth Report*,

Appendix, Part II, p. 53; Bodl. Carte MSS 77, fol. 575r-v; BL Add. MSS 4631, vol. 1, fol. 132r. Cf. PRO SP 29/175/178.1.

55. NLS MS 597, fol. 129r-v; Burnet, p. 144; *RPCS 1665–69*, pp. 407–409; [James Stewart and James Stirling], *Naphtali, or the Wrestlings of the Church of Scotland for the Kingdom of Christ* (n.p., 1667), pp. 287–98.

56. Turner, *Memoirs*, pp. 140–45; *LP*, 1:234, 242; 2:xxxiv. John Black-ader's house was one of those pillaged by Turner's men. Crichton, *Life and Diary*, p. 20. Turner's original manuscript is BL Add. MSS 23,125, fols. 218r-241v.

57. Cowan, p. 63; Charles Sanford Terry, *The Pentland Rising and Rullion Green* (Glasgow: James MacLehose and Sons, 1905), p. 3; Andrew Lang, *A History of Scotland from the Roman Occupation*, 4 vols. (Edinburgh and London: William Blackwood and Sons, 1900–1907), 3:309; Donaldson, *Scotland*, p. 368; Wodrow, 2:33, 60.

58. *LP*, 2:15; *Letters from Argyll*, p. 41; *HMC* 25, *Le Fleming*, p. 43; Tweeddale, in *LP*, 2:35; Wodrow, 2:31; Turner, *Memoirs*, p. 144; PRO SP 29/179/107. Cf. Burnet, p. 158.

59. *LP*, 1:245n, 262–63; BL Add. MSS 23,125, fol. 246r; Bodl. Carte MSS 45, fol. 201r. For Kennedy see Hew Scott, *Fasti Ecclesiae Scotticanae: The Succession of Ministers in the Church of Scotland from the Reformation*, new ed., 7 vols. (Edinburgh: Oliver and Boyd, 1915–28), 7:531.

60. Buckroyd, *CS*, pp. 66–67. Cf. William Ferguson, *Scotland's Relations with England: A Survey to 1707* (Edinburgh: John Donald Publishers, 1977), p. 153, who also cites the plotting between the Dutch and dissident Scottish Presbyterians, but concludes that the uprising was probably spontaneous. Foreign conspiracy of a different sort is cited—on the flimsiest evidence—by Leopold von Ranke, who contends that the rebellion was caused "by means of secret and ambiguous influences from abroad," influences possibly due to the activities of a Jesuit in disguise. According to a French emissary, a Jesuit from Douai had assumed the identity of a "Puritan," using the alias Semple—perhaps, mused von Ranke, the Gabriel Semple whose preaching enflamed the rebels! Leopold von Ranke, *A History of England Principally in the Seventeenth Century*, 6 vols. (Oxford: Clarendon Press, 1875), 3:507–508.

61. Turner, *Memoirs*, p. 148; *MVB*, p. 381; NLS MS 3473, fol. 39.

62. NLS MS 597, fols. 136r, 138r-v; BL Add. MSS 23,125, fol. 250r. Welsh of Cornley was a petty vassal of the archbishop of Glasgow. NLS MS 2512, fol. 91r.

63. BL Harl. MSS 4631, vol. 1, fol. 137v; Stewart and Stirling, *Naphtali*, p. 137; *Blackader Mem.*, pp. 136–37; NLS MS 3473, fol. 40; Turner, *Memoirs*, pp. 148–49.

64. PRO SP 29/178/67; *HMC* 25, *Le Fleming*, pp. 42–43; *Gazette* 106

(19–22 November 1666); Turner, *Memoirs*, pp. 149–50; *RPCS, 1665–69*, p. 409; *Blackader Mem.*, pp. 137–39; Cowan, p. 65; *MVB*, pp. 49, 391; NLS MS 597, fol. 136v. One of Welsh's recruits was the minister William Veitch. *MVB*, p. 23.

65. PRO SP 29/178/102; Turner, *Memoirs*, p. 151; *Gazette* 107 (22–26 November 1666); *Extracts from the Records of the Burgh of Edinburgh 1665 to 1680*, ed. Marguerite Wood (Edinburgh: Oliver and Boyd, 1950), pp. 23–24; PRO SP 29/179/57; Cowan, p. 65; Robert Law, *Memorialls: or, the Memorable Things That Fell out Within This Island of Brittain from 1638 to 1684*, ed. Charles Kirkpatrick Sharpe (Edinburgh: A. Constable and Co., 1818), p. 16.

66. NLS MS 3473, fol. 41; *MVB*, pp. 381–83, 388–89.

67. Turner, *Memoirs*, pp. 151–54; Wodrow, 2:18; Parker, *History*, pp. 108–109; Bodl. Carte MSS 46, fol. 400r; *HMC* 25, *Le Fleming*, pp. 42–43; PRO SP 29/178/67.

68. Wodrow, 2:18; *RPCS 1665–69*, pp. 211–12; *HMC* 25, *Le Fleming*, p. 43; *MVB*, p. 391. Cf. PRO SP 29/179/41; 29/180/41. Captain Grey was almost certainly the Andrew Grey who was riding with a band of fugitive Scottish rebels in Northumberland in 1678. *Gazette* 1341 (23–26 September 1678).

69. *RPCS 1665–69*, pp. 210–14; BL Add. MSS 23,125, fol. 149r; Nicoll, p. 452; *Extracts from Glasgow, 1663–1690*, p. 89.

70. *HMC* 78, *Hastings*, 2:374; *The Right Honourable the Earl of Arlington's Letters to Sir W. Temple, Bar.*, ed. Thomas Bebington, 2 vols. (London: Thomas Bennet, 1701), 2:208; PRO SP 29/179/3; Bodl. Carte MSS 46, fol. 402v. Cf. NLS MS 2512, fol. 93r.

71. Turner, *Memoirs*, pp. 155–56; BL Stowe MSS 199, fols. 3r-4r.

72. Some of Dalziel's officers were convinced that the insurgents could have been routed had they been attacked at this stage of the insurrection. *LP*, 2:67–68.

73. Turner, *Memoirs*, pp. 158–60; *Gazette* 110 (3–6 December 1666); *RPCS 1665–69*, pp. 217–18; *JR*, 1:159–60; *MVB*, p. 26.

74. *RPCS 1665–69*, pp. 214–18; PRO SP 29/179/9.

75. Turner, *Memoirs*, pp. 162–63, 166; Cowan, p. 68; PRO SP 29/179/9; *RPCS 1673–76*, p. 152; Wodrow, 2:23; *MVB*, pp. 388–90, 394–97.

76. BL Harl. MSS 4631, vol. 1, fols. 141v-142r, 146r-v; Wodrow, 2:23–24; Turner, *Memoirs*, pp. 164–66; *MVB*, pp. 399–401.

77. *Gazette* 108 (26–29 November 1666); Turner, *Memoirs*, pp. 166–68; *HMC* 25, *Le Fleming*, p. 43; *MVB*, pp. 404–405; Wodrow, 2:26; *JR*, 1:159–60; BL Add. MSS 23,125, fol. 153r.

78. *HMC* 25, *Le Fleming*, p. 43; PRO SP 29/178/155, 156; Bodl. Carte MSS 46, fol. 406r; *Misc. Aul.*, p. 429; *CSPD 1660–85, Addenda*, p. 165. The sources disagree on the number of troops raised by the rebels; some put the number of horse at 1,500 or 2,000, but another writer gives a figure of only 400.

79. *RPCS 1665–69*, pp. 222–25; *Extracts from Edinburgh*, pp. 23–24. On 27 November Lord Bellenden informed Rothes that officials in Edinburgh had expressed "great readyenes" to defend the city. BL Add. MSS 23,125, fol. 155r.

80. PRO SP 29/179/24, 26. The Westmorland and Cumberland militias were dismissed as soon as Annandale's forces positioned themselves between the rebels and the English border. PRO SP 299/179/69.

81. Bodl. Carte MSS 46, fol. 404r; Carte MSS 47, fol. 466r; PRO SP 29/179/35, 41. Cf. *HMC 25, Le Fleming*, p. 43.

82. PRO SP 29/179/57, 58; Charles Dalton, *The Scots Army 1661–1668* (London: Eyre and Spottiswoode; Edinburgh: William Brown, 1909), p. 24; *MVB*, pp. 28, 405; Wodrow, 2:25; Terry, *Rising*, p. 37; *JR*, 1:164; Turner, *Memoirs*, p. 169; *LP*, 2:xl–xli; Lang, *History*, 3:308–309. Other estimates put the size of the rebel force at no more than 1,100 to 1,500. According to Turner the rebels never had more than 1,100 horse and foot, but he was not in a position to assess the number accurately. Turner, *Memoirs*, p. 170; PRO SP 29/179/69, 70; *Gazette* 109 (29 November–3 December 1666).

83. Burnet, p. 159; BL Add. MSS 23,125, fol. 198r. Cf. BL Add. MSS 23,125, fols. 175r, 255r; PRO SP 29/178/102; 29/180/110; 29/441/16; *LP*, 1:252.

84. *MVB*, pp. 406, 415; PRO SP 29/179/57, 70; Turner, *Memoirs*, p. 170; *Gazette* 109 (29 November–3 December 1666); Wodrow, 2:26. Archbishop Burnet estimated the number of clergymen with the insurgents at twenty. *LP*, 2:xl–xli.

85. *MVB*, p. 29; Turner, *Memoirs*, pp. 174–75; *LP*, 1:246, 267; *RPCS 1665–69*, p. 226; PRO SP 29/179/105; 29/180/110; BL Add. MSS 23,125, fol. 269r. Cf. Cosin, 2:158–60.

86. Turner, *Memoirs*, pp. 176–77; *LP*, 1:246; PRO SP 29/179/105; *Blackader Mem.*, p. 141; *MVB*, pp. 30–31, 40, 408; BL Add. MSS 23,125, fol. 155r.

87. *LP*, 1:246; *RPCS 1665–69*, pp. 210, 226–27; PRO SP 29/179/104, 105, 107; 29/183/18; Turner, *Memoirs*, pp. 178–80.

88. *RPCS 1665–69*, p. 227.

89. John Willcock, *A Scots Earl in Covenanting Times: Being [the] Life and Times of Archibald 9th Earl of Argyll (1629–1685)* (Edinburgh: Andrew Elliot, 1907), p. 144; Bodl. Carte MSS 72, fol. 3r; *HMC 52, Astley*, p. 29; Burnet, pp. 158–59; *MVB*, p. 413; Turner, *Memoirs*, pp. 181–87.

90. PRO SP 29/179/106, 107, 148; *MVB*, pp. 415–19; *RPCS 1665–69*, p. 228; Bodl. Carte MSS 46, fol. 410r; *Gazette* 110 (3–6 December 1666); BL Add. MSS 23,125, fols. 161r, 173r, 185r; 35,125, fols. 143r-144v; Dalton, *Scots Army*, p. 24; M. Sidgwick, "The Pentland Rising and the Battle of Rullion Green," *Scottish Historical Review* 3 (July 1906): 450. Cf. PRO SP 29/180/10. Dalziel had 600 horse and 2,000 infantry. Willcock, *A Scots Earl*, p. 144. Drummond reckoned the number of prisoners at not more than 140, but Cowan thinks

the number was approximately 80. Dalton, *Scots Army*, p. 25; Cowan, p. 69. Wallace claimed the total number of his men who had been killed or captured had not exceeded 100. *MVB*, p. 419.

91. *Arlington's Letters*, 1:108; Story, *Carstares*, p. 20; Wodrow, 2:28; PRO SP 29/180/76; *Gazette* 112 (10–13 December 1666); *MVB*, pp. 420–22; BL Add. MSS 23,125, fol. 175v.

92. PRO SP 29/181/39; *MVB*, p. 384.

93. Wodrow, 2:22; PRO SP 29/179/135.

94. PRO SP 29/180/76, 110; 29/441/16; *CSPD 1666–67*, p. 293.

95. NLS MS 7033, fol. 68v; *RPCS 1665–69*, p. 239; BL Harl. MSS 4631, fols. 149v-150r; *Gazette* 117 (27–31 December 1666); *JR*, 1:187–88; Wodrow, 2:52–53; PRO SP 29/181/14.

96. *HMC* 78, *Hastings*, 2:374; *Orrery Coll.*, 2:95; Bodl. Carte MSS 35, fol. 128r; PRO SP 29/196/6. Cf. *Som. Tr.*, 8:444n. Abbott believes that Blood was involved. Abbott, *Blood*, pp. 122–23.

97. *CSPD 1666–67*, pp. 285–86; PRO SP 29/180/41; *LP*, 1:265. The entry on Carr in *BDBR* should read: "He reportedly had command of some 4,000 men in the Pentland Rising." The actual number, of course, was probably half that. There had been a report in July 1666 that Carr was in Scotland. BL Add. MSS 23,125, fol. 32r.

98. *MVB*, p. 416; BL Add. MSS 23,125, fol. 185v; *RPCS 1665–69*, p. 595; *CSPD 1666–67*, p. 293. Cf. PRO SP 29/179/111.

99. *RPCS 1665–69*, pp. 228–29; PRO SP 29/179/117, 136.

100. NLS MS 7033, fol. 67r; *LP*, 1:253; *RPCS 1665–69*, pp. 229–31; Bodl. Carte MSS 35, fol. 146r; PRO SP 29/180/77, 95; *CSPD 1666–67*, p. 320.

101. Bodl. Carte MSS 45, fol. 202r; Carte MSS 46, fol. 410r; *CSPI 1666–69*, p. 251. Ormond also sought information about the activities of a preacher named Kennedy. Bodl. Carte MSS 45, fol. 202r.

102. *LP*, 1:261–62; *Letters from Argyll*, pp. 42–43; *CSPI 1666–69*, p. 278; BL Add. MSS 23,125, fol. 199r-v.

103. *LP*, 1:256–57, 267; 2:xliii–xliv; BL Add. MSS 23,125, fol. 269r; PRO SP 29/181/39.

104. BL Add. MSS 23,125, fols. 259r, 267r; *LP*, 1:256, 262–63; *Arlington's Letters*, 2:210.

105. PRO SP 29/182/114; 29/202/91; *RPCS 1665–69*, pp. 285–86; *RPCS 1669–72*, p. 666.

106. PRO SP 29/180/110, 124; 29/181/12, 97; 29/441/16; *JR*, 1:182–83; *RPCS 1665–69*, p. 231.

107. *RPCS 1665–69*, pp. 235–36; *LP*, 2:xlii; PRO SP 29/181/13, 55; *Arlington's Letters*, 1:112.

108. BL Add. MSS 23,125, fol. 185r. Cf. PRO SP 29/180/125; NLS MS 597, fol. 143r-v. Rothes thought only of making examples of ten or twelve of

those with the "most dangerous principals." BL Add. MSS 23,125, fol. 244v.

109. *JR*, 1:186–87; NLS MS 597, fols. 140r-141v; PRO SP 29/181/13, 55, 131, 145; *Gazette* 114 (17–20 December 1666); 115 (20–24 December 1666); *RPCS 1665–69*, pp. 236–38; BL Add. MSS 23,125, fol. 250r; 35,125, fol. 145r; Lang, *History*, 3:312.

110. *JR*, 1:188–89; PRO SP 29/182/75, 78; Nicoll, p. 453.

111. *JR*, 1:187–88; PRO SP 29/180/76; 29/181/55; 29/182/10, 98; Nicoll, p. 452; *Gazette* 116 (24–27 December 1666); 117 (27–31 December 1666).

112. *JR*, 1:189; Wodrow, 2:53–54; *Gazette* 121 (10–14 January 1667).

113. *Gazette* 121 (10–14 January 1667); 122 (14–17 January 1667); PRO SP 29/180/76; 29/188/126; Burnet, p. 161; Lang, *History*, 3:313; HMC 21, *Hamilton*, Supplementary Report, p. 83; P. Hume Brown, *History of Scotland*, 3 vols. (Cambridge: At the University Press, 1909–12), 2:399.

114. *Letters from Argyll*, p. 59; *RPCS 1665–69*, pp. 267–68, 272–76, 284–86, 290–92, 352–53; *CSPD 1666–67*, p. 585. The provost of Glasgow went to Edinburgh to petition the Council to allow "honest" persons to bear arms for their protection. *Extracts from Glasgow, 1663–1690*, p. 92.

115. *MVB*, pp. 361–62; Willcock, *A Scots Earl*, p. 149; Burnet, p. 160; *JR*, 1:232; Dalton, *Scots Army*, p. 25 n. 5.

116. NLS MS 7024, fol. 53r; *RPCS 1665–69*, pp. 307–308, 318–19, 339. Forty-four of the rebels escaped from the tolbooth in Edinburgh in the spring of 1667 but were recaptured. PRO SP 29/207/143.

117. NLS MS 7033, fol. 95r; *JR*, 1:241–42; 2:64–66.

118. NLS MS 7033, fol. 96r; *RPCS 1665–69*, pp. 340–41, 343–45, 347–49; "Thirty-four Letters Written to James Sharp, Archbishop of St. Andrews, by the Duke and Duchess of Lauderdale . . . 1660–1677," ed. John Dowden, in *Miscellany of the Scottish Historical Society*, vol. 1, Publications of the Scottish Historical Society, vol. 15 (Edinburgh, 1893), p. 263. For the value of estates forfeited by the rebels, see NLS MS 7033, fol. 168r. The largest of these belonged to William Muir of Caldwell (9,000 merks), Robert Ker of Kersland (5,000), John Cuningham of Bedland (2,000), William Maxwell of Monreith (2,000), and John Nelson of Corsock (1,500).

119. NLS MS 7033, fol. 139r; BL Add. MSS 23,130, fol. 5r; 35,125, fol. 197r; *RPCS 1665–69*, pp. 350–51, 412–14, 451–54, 470, 474, 501–503, 507, 534, 556, 572–73; *RPCS 1669–72*, pp. 22–23; *LP*, 2:74–75, 96.

120. PRO SP 29/182/141, 142.

Chapter 3

1. NLS MS 573, fol. 66r; PRO SP 29/181/11; *LP*, 2:xxxix, 65–66.

2. Buckroyd, *CS*, pp. 71–72; *LP*, 1:279, 281; 2:13–15, 34, 37, 83; HMC 29, *Portland*, 3:305.

3. Buckroyd, *CS*, p. 73; PRO SP 29/241/227; 29/244/207; 29/245/12, 73, 180. Because much of the southwest had been disarmed, it was generally incapable of providing a militia for several years. *RPCS 1665–69*, p. 275; PRO SP 29/241/227.

4. *HMC 72, Laing*, 1:357; *LP*, 2:lviii, 26; PRO SP 29/180/126; 29/209/19; *Letters from Archibald, Earl of Argyll, to John, Duke of Lauderdale* (Edinburgh: Bannatyne Club, 1829), p. 61; *RPCS 1665–69*, pp. 234, 285–86.

5. PRO SP 29/222/130; *RPCS 1665–69*, pp. 398–99; *LP*, 2:98.

6. NLS MS 2512, fols. 100r, 116r; PRO SP 29/239/211; *RPCS 1665–69*, pp. 444–45, 466–67, 480, 491, 501, 557, 572–73, 615; *LP*, 2:102; *CSPD 1667–68*, pp. 516–17.

7. BL Harl. MSS 4631, vol. 1, fol. 163v; *RPCS 1665–69*, pp. 459–60, 504; "The Old Tolbooth: With Extracts from the Original Records," ed. John A. Fairley, in *The Book of the Old Edinburgh Club*, vol. 5 (Edinburgh: T. and A. Constable, 1912), p. 140; *LP*, 2:106–107; Wodrow, 2:111–12; James Seaton Reid, *History of the Presbyterian Church in Ireland*, new ed., 3 vols. (Belfast: William Mullan, 1867), 2:318.

8. *RPCS 1665–69*, p. 504; *RPCS 1669–72*, p. 23; "Old Tolbooth," 5:141. The authorities also captured William Ferguson of Lanark, who had been encouraging dissidents not to provide bonds of security; he was banished to Virginia. *LP*, 2:104. John McKilligen was also illegally preaching in Moray.

9. BL Add. MSS 23,130, fol. 108v; Cowan, p. 82; *LP*, 2:122–23; *Blackader Mem.*, p. 147.

10. BL Add. MSS 23,130, fol. 42r-v; *LP*, 2:103–104; *HMC 72, Laing*, 1:370–71.

11. NLS MS 7024, fols. 113r, 150r, 161r; BL Add. MSS 23,130, fol. 42r; 23,131, fols. 103r-v, 111v; *LP*, 2:121, 125–26, 129; *RPCS 1665–69*, pp. 614–16, 621, 626; *RPCS 1669–72*, p. 2; *Extracts from the Records of the Burgh of Edinburgh 1665 to 1680*, ed. Marguerite Wood (Edinburgh: Oliver and Boyd, 1950), p. 56.

12. BL Add. MSS 23,131, fol. 192v; *RPCS 1665–69*, pp. 620–21, 625–26; *RPCS 1669–72*, pp. 1, 3, 13, 24–26; *LP*, 2:136. Cf. NLS MS 7033, fol. 146r.

13. BL Add. MSS 23,131, fols. 181r, 186r; *LP*, 2:131. But the provost of Ayrshire reported conventicles in his area. BL Add. MSS 23,131, fol. 188v.

14. The others were John Spalding of Dreghorn, James Alexander of Kilmacolm, Andrew Dalrymple of Auchinleck, John Hutcheson of Maybole, Hugh Campbell of Riccarton, John Gemill of Symington, John Wallace of Largs, William Fullerton of St. Quivox, and Hugh Archbald of Avondale. *RPCS 1669–72*, p. 3. Cf. BL Add. MSS 23,131, fol. 123r.

15. *RPCS 1669–72*, pp. 20, 30, 625–27. Blantyre was taken to the Edinburgh Tolbooth on 15 June. "Old Tolbooth," 5:146–47.

16. CH Ellesmere MSS 8544; *RPCS 1669–72*, pp. 38–40, 47. Cf. PRO SP

29/266/140. Archbishops Sharp and Burnet opposed the indulgence. NLS MS 2512, fols. 126r, 130r; PRO SP 29/266/119.

17. NLS MS 597, fols. 201r, 202r; BL Add. MSS 23,132, fols. 46r, 47v, 49r, 50r; *RPCS 1669–72*, pp. 47, 62, 70, 77, 103–104, 149, 586–88; CH Ellesmere MSS 8545. The sources differ as to the precise number of ministers who accepted the indulgence. Cf. Bodl. Carte MSS 81, fol. 292r; *HMC 72, Laing*, 1:375–76; Cowan, pp. 77–78.

18. NLS MS 7024, fol. 166r; MS 7025, fols. 4r, 9r-v; MS 7033, fol. 70r (which should be dated 1669); BL Add. MSS 23,131, fol. 190r; 23,132, fol. 52r; 23,133, fol. 4v; *RPCS 1669–72*, p. 123; Buckroyd, *CS*, pp. 85–86, 88; *LP*, 2:133; Bodl. Carte MSS 81, fol. 292r. Because the indulgence benefited the more turbulent districts, nonconformists in the calmer areas felt they were being penalized for their quiescence. BL Add. MSS 23,132, fol. 65r.

19. NLS MS 7025, fols. 4r, 9r, 10r, 11r, 37r; BL Add. MSS 35,125, fol. 205r; *RPCS 1669–72*, pp. 61–62, 104, 124, 130–32, 157–58, 161, 168–69, 178, 180; *LP*, 2:177–78; *Blackader Mem.*, pp. 148–51. One of the offending preachers in Edinburgh was George Johnston, the deprived minister of Newbattle, Midlothian. *RPCS 1669–72*, p. 161.

20. NLS MS 7034, fol. 3r; *RPCS 1669–72*, pp. 157–59, 161.

21. *RPCS 1669–72*, pp. 180–81, 185–86, 190–91, 197–99, 204, 206–208, 217, 229–30, 320, 660–61, 665–66, 670; NLS MS 7025, fol. 19r; BL Add. MSS 23,134, fol. 42r-v; *LP*, 2:183; Sir George Mackenzie, *Memoirs of the Affairs of Scotland from the Restoration of King Charles II. A.D. M.D.C.L.X.* (Edinburgh: no pub., 1821), pp. 188–89; Burnet, p. 196; Andrew Lang, *A History of Scotland from the Roman Occupation*, 4 vols. (Edinburgh and London: William Blackwood and Sons, 1900–1907), 3:322; *Blackader Mem.*, pp. 153–57; Buckroyd, *CS*, p. 92.

22. PRO SP 29/277/7; NLS MS 2512, fol. 134r; BL Add. MSS 23,134, fol. 26r; *RPCS 1669–72*, pp. 184–85, 188, 199, 662–63.

23. BL Add. MSS 23,134, fol. 138r; *LP*, 2:184 (cf. pp. 185–87); PRO SP 29/277/117; *APS*, 8:9–10. Julia Buckroyd has plausibly pointed to two other motives that would explain the shift to a stringent policy of dealing with dissent: (1) to undermine the duke of Hamilton's argument that a standing army, which would enhance his own power, should be raised to suppress conventicles; and (2) to placate hard-line English bishops inclined to support Alexander Burnet, recently dismissed as archbishop of Glasgow. Buckroyd, *CS*, pp. 92–93. Lauderdale gave the Clanking Act its name, presumably in the expectation that it would have a striking impact on conventicles, like a clanking chain.

24. *RPCS 1669–72*, pp. 204–205, 208; BL Add. MSS 23,134, fol. 57r. In June, Hamilton and Sharp had called for a proclamation to apprehend Gabriel Maxwell and Gabriel Semple. *RPCS 1669–72*, p. 665.

25. Buckroyd, *CS*, p. 102; BL Add. MSS 23,135, fol. 19r; *RPCS 1669–72*, pp. 277, 308, 312, 347, 393, 463–64; PRO SP 29/303/159. Cf. BL Add. MSS 23,135, fol. 28r; *HMC 25, Le Fleming*, p. 89. When officials seized the papers of William Carstares upon his return to Scotland from Amsterdam, they discovered that the Dutch were interested in inciting a Covenanter insurrection, but Lauderdale was prepared to crush it. Lang, *History*, 3:325. Carmichael was subsequently deported to London, where he established a Scottish Presbyterian congregation in Founders' Hall; he served as its minister until his death in July 1677. Hew Scott, *Fasti Ecclesiae Scotticanae: The Succession of Ministers in the Church of Scotland from the Reformation*, new ed., 7 vols. (Edinburgh: Oliver and Boyd, 1915–28), 7:489.

26. *APS*, 8:71–73, 89; *RPCS 1669–72*, pp. 545–47, 549–51, 558–61, 583–85; BL Add. MSS 23,135, fol. 182r; *CSPD 1672*, pp. 384–85; "The Old Tolbooth: With Extracts from the Original Records," ed. John A. Fairley, in *The Book of the Old Edinburgh Club*, vol. 6 (Edinburgh: T. and A. Constable, 1913), p. 114.

27. Buckroyd, *CS*, pp. 100–101, 106; *RPCS 1669–72*, pp. 588–90; *HMC 21, Hamilton*, p. 142; Wodrow, 2:206–10; Cowan, pp. 79–80.

28. *RPCS 1669–72*, pp. 590–91; Burnet, p. 197; *HMC 21, Hamilton*, pp. 142–43; *Blackader Mem.*, pp. 166–72.

29. NLS MS 7033, fols. 81v-82r; Burnet, p. 160; *LP*, 2:1; Cowan, p. 71.

30. PRO SP 29/207/94; *LP*, 2:xlvi-xlvii, 18–19, 23–24, 26; *RPCS 1665–69*, p. 292; *CSPD 1667*, pp. 523, 536–37, 555; NLS MS 2512, fol. 102r.

31. Margaret Carse of West Calder, who was allegedly involved in the attack on James Brown, had reputedly participated in the Galloway rebellion. *RPCS 1665–69*, p. 503.

32. NLS MS 7033, fols. 110r, 111r; "Old Tolbooth," 5:138–39; *RPCS 1665–69*, pp. 503, 549; *JR*, 1:313.

33. *RPCS 1673–76*, p. 152; Wodrow, 2:115; PRO SP 29/243/154; EUL MS La.II.27, vol. 4, fol. 19r.

34. PRO SP 29/243/33, 34; Wodrow, 2:115–16; BL Harl. MSS 4631, vol. 1, fol. 165r; Burnet, p. 187; "Thirty-four Letters Written to James Sharp, Archbishop of St. Andrews, by the Duke and Duchess of Lauderdale . . . 1660–1677," ed. John Dowden, in *Miscellany of the Scottish History Society*, vol. 1, Publications of the Scottish History Society, vol. 15 (Edinburgh, 1893), p. 263 n. 2; *LP*, 2:109–10; *Gazette* 280 (20–23 July 1668); BL Add. MSS 23,129, fols. 215r-v, 223r. For a general overview of anticlericalism, primarily at the highest levels of Scottish society, see Julia Buckroyd, "Anti-Clericalism in Scotland During the Restoration," in *Church, Politics and Society: Scotland 1408–1929*, ed. Norman Macdougall (Edinburgh: John Donald Publishers, 1983), pp. 167–85. Buckroyd's biography of Sharp devotes little attention to the attempted assassination: *The Life of James Sharp, Archbishop of St. Andrews 1618–1679: A Political Biography* (Edinburgh: John Donald, 1987), pp. 90–91.

35. PRO SP 29/243/34A, 154; 29/244/165; 29/245/158; *RPCS 1665–69*, pp. 488, 503; *HMC 72, Laing*, 1:369–70; NLS MS 7033, fol. 119r; BL Add. MSS 23,129, fols. 221v-222r, 245r, 251r, 276r, 288r; *LP*, 2:111, 116.

36. *HMC 72, Laing*, 1:369–70; PRO SP 29/243/99, 154; *RPCS 1665–69*, pp. 494–95, 500–503; BL Add. MSS 23,129, fols. 245r, 249r, 251r.

37. NLS MS 2512, fol. 118r; MS 7024, fol. 109r; Buckroyd, *CS*, p. 79; BL Add. MSS 23,129, fol. 288r; *LP*, 2:114; *RPCS 1665–69*, p. 500. Cf. PRO SP 29/244/165.

38. PRO SP 29/244/108, 109; *Gazette* 288 (10–13 August 1668); *RPCS 1665–69*, pp. 344–45, 518–19, 522–23, 540–41; *CSPD 1667–68*, p. 548; Lang, *History*, 3:317, 330–32; *RPCS 1673–76*, pp. 135, 152–53, 172, 494, 500–501, 509; Thomas Long, *A Compendious History Of All the Popish & Fanatical Plots and Conspiracies* (London, 1684), p. 130; NLS MS 7024, fol. 117v; BL Add. MSS 23,130, fols. 5r, 22r-v, 62v-63r, 64r, 95r; EUL MS La.II.27, vol. 4, fols. 19r, 20r; MS La.II.89, fol. 130r; *A True Account of the Horrid Murther* (London, 1679), p. 4. Mitchell's execution inspired some verse; EUL MS La.II.89, fols. 241r-246v.

39. *RPCS 1665–69*, p. 541; *LP*, 2:lxiii; Buckroyd, *CS*, p. 89; "Old Tolbooth," 5:151–52; *RPCS 1669–72*, pp. 86, 99–102, 116, 127–29, 156, 159, 162, 170–71, 208–10, 368–69, 402, 441–45, 702; PRO SP 29/277/117; 29/315/43; *HMC 21, Hamilton*, Supplementary Report, pp. 84–85; NLS MS 2512, fol. 134r; MS 7033, fol. 70r (which should be dated 1669). Cf. BL Add. MSS 23,132, fol. 135v.

40. Greaves, *DUFE*, pp. 85, 110, 150, 171.

41. Ibid., pp. 124–25, 175, 182, 184, 186, 191, 256 n. 69.

42. *Warwick County Records: Orders Made at the Quarter Sessions: Easter, 1665, to Epiphany, 1674*, ed. S.C. Ratcliff and H.C. Johnson (Warwick: L. Edgar Stephens, 1939), p. 57; *RPCS 1665–69*, pp. 451–54; PRO SP 29/187/39.

43. BL Add. MSS 35,125, fol. 201r; PRO SP 29/277/22.

44. Greaves, *DUFE*, pp. 54, 187; PRO SP 29/243/100; 29/261/131, 133; *LP*, 2:104–105; *RPCS 1665–69*, pp. 4551–54.

45. *RPCS 1669–72*, pp. 299, 538–39.

46. PRO SP 29/223/134; 29/224/76; *RPCS 1669–72*, p. 296; BL Add. MSS 23,134, fol. 218r. Cf. BL Add. MSS 23,129, fol. 264r. On 28 November 1671 the Council summoned him to appear before them because he had not provided security. *RPCS 1669–72*, p. 412.

47. Bodl. Carte MSS 34, fol. 181r. See chapter 1.

48. Bodl. Carte MSS 34, fols. 181r, 494r; Carte MSS 45, fol. 173r-v.

49. See chapter 1.

50. *Orrery Coll.*, 1:225–26, 239–40; Carte, 2:324–25.

51. *Orrery Coll.*, 1:225, 240–41, 243, 248–49, 252–53, 255; Carte, 2:324–25. Limerick as well as Kinsale had been the object of a contemplated conspiracy in 1664, which allegedly involved such ex-Cromwellians as Lieutenant-

Colonel William Allen, Sir Henry Ingoldsby, and Lieutenant-Colonel John Nelson. PRO SP 29/109/93.

52. *Orrery Coll.*, 1:225–26, 228–29, 231–33, 236–41. A Captain Taylor had been arrested in the crackdown on suspicious persons that followed Thomas Venner's uprising. Greaves, *DUFE*, p. 242 n. 19.

53. *Orrery Coll.*, 1:232–33, 241, 244–45, 247; *CSPI 1666–69*, p. 33.

54. *Orrery Coll.*, 1:250–51, 255, 267; 2:21; Bodl. Carte MSS 34, fol. 763r; Carte MSS 46, fol. 321v; *Misc. Aul.*, p. 401; *HMC* 36, *Ormonde*, n.s., 3:226.

55. Bodl. Carte MSS 35, fols. 50r-v, 52r-v, 54r; PRO SP 29/168/148, 149, 150. Cf. *CSPI 1666–69*, p. 214. In connection with the search for Blood and his accomplices, Williamson ordered the interception of all letters between John Knipe of London and Daniel Edgerton of Dublin. PRO SP 29/168/151.

56. Bodl. Carte MSS 46, fol. 357v. Gryce made a copy of a letter from a dissident identified only as E.D. that promised that "deliverance" was imminent. PRO SP 29/169/14.

57. Bodl. Carte MSS 46, fols. 383r, 392v; *Orrery Coll.*, 2:95.

58. Bodl. Carte MSS 35, fol. 181r; Carte MSS 36, fol. 117r; PRO SP 29/166/71; 29/167/58; *CSPD 1666–67*, p. 560; *CSPD 1667*, p. 152; *CSPI 1666–69*, p. 439.

59. Bodl. Carte MSS 35, fol. 181r; Carte MSS 36, fols. 446r, 486r; PRO SP 29/272/15; *CSPD 1671*, p. 259.

60. Bodl. Carte MSS 37, fols. 578r, 586r-v; BL Stowe MSS 200, fol. 127r. Cf. Arlington's similar concern, voiced in July 1666. Bodl. Carte MSS 46, fol. 331v.

61. BL Stowe MSS 200, fol. 326v.

62. *HMC* 36, *Ormonde*, n.s., 3:321–22; BL Stowe MSS 200, fols. 346r, 348r, 349r, 361r, 363r-v, 396r-v, 406r-v, 419r; Stowe MSS 201, fols. 5r, 28r-29r, 115v, 117r, 147v, 154r, 377r; PRO SP 63/332/39, 39.1, 43.1, 47, 49, 52, 53.1, 59, 60, 68, 70, 70.1, 70.3, 96; 63/333/5, 39; 63/335/7; *CSPD 1673*, pp. 116–17; BL Egerton MSS 3327, fols. 22r-23v. Walcott described himself at one point as "being for the Congregational way." PRO SP 63/332/53.1.

63. PRO SP 63/332/104, 120; 63/333/21; BL Stowe MSS 200, fols. 396r-v, 437v-438r; Stowe MSS 201, fols. 5r, 28v-29r; Stowe MSS 213, fols. 98r, 196r.

64. Bodl. Carte MSS 34, fol. 628r; *Orrery Coll.*, 1:271, 283–84; 2:47, 51; *CCSP*, 5:545.

65. *Misc. Aul.*, pp. 433–34 (cf. *HMC* 78, *Hastings*, 2:375); Bodl. Carte MSS 35, fol. 506r.

66. Bodl. Carte MSS 34, fols. 698r-v, 700r, 708r-v, 714r-v, 724r-v, 726r-v; Carte MSS 37, fols. 93r-94r; Carte MSS 46, fols. 319r, 321r; Carte MSS 68, fol. 118v; *CSPI 1666–69*, pp. 110–11, 115–17; Carte, 2:326–27; CH MS HA 1950; *Gazette* 61 (11–14 June 1666); 67 (2–5 July 1666); Lister, 3:435.

67. Carte, 2:327; *Orrery Coll.*, 2:4; *CSPI 1666–69*, pp. 115, 117, 484; *LP*, 2:xxxvi. Lay persons also came from Scotland in substantial numbers. Bodl. Carte MSS 36, fol. 209r.

68. Bodl. Carte MSS 34, fols. 385r-v, 654r-v, 736r-v, 747r-748r, 764r; Carte MSS 35, fol. 17r-v; *Orrery Coll.*, 1:265–66; Carte, 2:328; PRO SP 29/165/11; *CSPI 1666–69*, pp. 62–63, 137, 139, 155–61; *CSPD 1665–66*, p. 581; *The Rawdon Papers*, ed. Edward Berwick (London: John Nichols and Son, 1819), p. 223; *Calendar of the Orrery Papers*, ed. Edward MacLysaght (Dublin: Stationery Office, 1941), p. 57; *HMC* 36, *Ormonde*, n.s., 3:227.

69. PRO SP 29/165/17; 29/241/132, 155; *CSPI 1666–69*, pp. 252, 612; *CSPD 1671*, pp. 339–40. Cf. *CCSP*, 5:545; *CSPD 1666–67*, p. 491, for more rumors.

70. Bodl. Carte MSS 34, fol. 24r; *Orrery Coll.*, 2:97–99, 101, 103; *CCSP*, 5:545; PRO SP 29/182/144.

71. Bodl. Carte MSS 35, fols. 113r, 617r-v (cf. fol. 636r); *CSPI 1666–69*, pp. 104–105, 138, 397, 474; *Orrery Coll.*, 2:132–33.

72. *Rawdon Papers*, p. 222; Bodl. Carte MSS 35, fols. 136r-v, 140r-v; Carte MSS 36, fol. 488r; *CSPI 1666–69*, p. 585.

73. Bodl. Carte MSS 36, fols. 488r, 490r; *CSPI 1669–70*, pp. 147–48.

74. Bodl. Carte MSS 37, fol. 99r-v.

75. Bodl. Carte MSS 35, fols. 136r-v, 138r; Carte MSS 36, fol. 511r-v.

76. Bodl. Carte MSS 36, fol. 607r-v; *CSPI 1666–69*, pp. 226–27, 237–38, 703; *CSPD 1671*, p. 575; J.C. Beckett, *Confrontations: Studies in Irish History* (Totowa, N.J.: Rowman and Littlefield, 1972), pp. 36–37; Reid, *History*, 2:313 n. 21.

77. PRO SP 29/276/74; *CR*, s.v. "Mather, Samuel"; Bodl. Carte MSS 36, fols. 468r, 513r-514v. Baines went to England in September 1668. Bodl. Carte MSS 36, fol. 493v.

78. CH HA 6786; *HMC* 78, *Hastings*, 2:375; PRO SP 29/147/83.

79. *CSPI 1666–69*, pp. 741, 771; *CSPI 1669–70*, pp. 22, 194, 226–27, 649; William Thomas Latimer, *A History of the Irish Presbyterians*, 2nd ed. (Belfast: James Cleeland and William Mullan, 1902), p. 142. The four were released in October 1670. For the first set of Ormond's instructions see *CSPI 1660–62*, p. 556.

80. Bodl. Carte MSS 37, fol. 707v; James I. McGuire, "Why Was Ormond Dismissed in 1669?" *Irish Historical Studies* 18 (March 1973): 295–312. For the instructions of Robartes and Berkeley see *CSPI 1666–69*, p. 761; *CSPI 1669–70*, pp. 78–79.

81. Clement E. Pike, "The Origin of the *Regium Donum*," *TRHS*, 3rd ser., 3 (1909): 265–67; BL Stowe MSS 200, fols. 184v-185r, 195r-v, 235r, 287r, 301r (cf. fol. 326v); Stowe 213, fols. 11v-12r, 57v; PRO SP 63/331/130, 130.1, 168, 175, 175.1. Essex was less charitable in the case of the former Dublin plotter Robert Chambers, Blood's brother-in-law, whom he regarded as "a very desperate bold fellow" unfit to minister to a dissenting congregation in Dublin. BL Stowe MSS 213, fol. 180r; Stowe 214, fol. 293v.

82. BL Stowe MSS 200, fol. 334r-v; Beckett, *Confrontations*, p. 36; Pike, "The Origin of the *Regium Donum*," pp. 265, 268–69; Reid, *History*, 2:317;

David W. Miller, *Queen's Rebels: Ulster Loyalism in Historical Perspective* (Dublin: Gill and Macmillan, 1978), p. 22; *DNB*, s.v. "Forbes, Sir Arthur"; J.C. Beckett, *The Making of Modern Ireland 1603–1923* (London: Faber and Faber, 1966), p. 132; BL Add. MSS 23,135, fol. 213r.

83. *BDBR* and *DNB*, s.v. "Edmondson, William"; *HMC* 63, *Egmont*, 2:8; Bodl. Carte MSS 45, fol. 187r; William C. Braithwaite, *The Second Period of Quakerism* (London: Macmillan and Co., 1919), pp. 260–62; *CSPI 1669–70*, pp. 151–52, 226–27; Thomas Holme, *A Brief Relation of Some Part of the Sufferings of the True Christians . . . in Ireland . . . from 1660. until 1671* (1672), pp. 13, 16–17, 19–23, 25–40, 42–49. The three Quaker missionaries who visited Ireland with Fox and Stubbs in 1669 were John Lancaster, Thomas Briggs, and Robert Lodge.

84. *RPCS 1665–69*, pp. 312–13; *RPCS 1669–72*, p. 640. The Council ordered the arrest of David Falconer in December 1667 for illegally marrying Quakers. *RPCS 1665–69*, p. 376.

85. BL Add. MSS 23,133, fols. 31r-v, 34r-v, 42r-v; *RPCS 1669–72*, pp. 17, 22, 30–31, 52, 148–49, 153, 155–56, 162, 480–81 (cf. pp. 441–42); "Old Tolbooth," 5:148–49; *LP*, 2:179–81.

86. Cf., e.g., *RPCS 1669–72*, pp. 480–81.

Chapter 4

1. For examples of multiple offenders see *MCR*, 3:350–53; PRO SP 29/94/65; 29/112/25.

2. PRO SP 29/97/47.1; 29/137/97; *The Miscellaneous Works of John Bunyan*, vol. 6, *The Poems*, ed. Graham Midgley (Oxford: Clarendon Press, 1980), p. 93.

3. *Int.* 81 (17 October 1664), p. 666. Cf. the commission to a captain in the earl of Oxford's regiment in August 1665, which ordered him to take command of two troops of horse and several companies of foot "for the better secureing of those parts [the Salisbury area, which the court was visiting] against the daingerous attempts of Seditious Conventicles and meetings." PRO SP 29/129/81.

4. PRO SP 29/99/9; 29/217/15, 60, 60.1. Witnesses identified the preacher as Mr. Frazer or (Thomas?) Worden. For Thomas Worden, a Congregationalist minister, see Greaves, *DUFE*, p. 54. The Quakers subsequently denied the involvement of any Friends in the northern rebellion. Anon., *The Innocency and Conscientiousness of the Quakers Asserted and Cleared* (London, 1664), p. 13.

5. PRO SP 29/90/11, 11.1, 12, 27, 27.1, 29; 29/100/111; *CSPD 1663–64*, pp. 430, 432, 650. For Feake's career see *BDBR*, s.v.

6. PRO SP 29/93/8; 29/98/152, 153; 29/99/48–52; Greaves, *Saints and Rebels*, pp. 187–88.

7. PRO SP 29/99/7; 29/136/72; 29/178/57; *HMC* 53, *Montagu*, p. 168; W.M. Wigfield, "Recusancy and Nonconformity in Bedfordshire Illustrated by Select Documents Between 1622 and 1842," in *Publications of the Bedfordshire Historical Record Society*, vol. 20 (1938), p. 179; *The Minutes of the First Independent Church (Now Bunyan Meeting) at Bedford 1656–1766*, ed. H.G. Tibbutt, vol. 55 of *Publications of the Bedfordshire Historical Record Society* (1976), p. 42. For Stubbes, Jenkins, Watson, and Horrockes see *CR*, s.vv.

8. Allan Brockett, *Nonconformity in Exeter 1650–1875* (Manchester: Manchester University Press of the University of Exeter, 1962), p. 22; *Newes* 96 (8 December 1664), p. 784; PRO SP 29/146/68; 29/179/95; *CSPD 1667*, p. 455; *CSPD 1667–68*, p. 69; Frank Bate, *The Declaration of Indulgence 1672: A Study in the Rise of Organised Dissent* (London: University Press of Liverpool by Archibald Constable and Co., 1908), p. 57.

9. PRO SP 29/99/7; 29/110/108; 29/111/67; 29/115/44; *CSPD 1667*, p. 455.

10. PRO SP 29/96/97, 110, 110.1, 114, 114.1, 129; *Int.* 31 (18 April 1664), pp. 251–52; 33 (25 April 1664), p. 266; *Newes* 14 (16 February 1665), pp. 110–11; 17 (27 February 1665), p. 134. For Voysey see *CR*, s.v.

11. *Int.* 33 (25 April 1664), pp. 267–68; PRO SP 29/146/68; *CSPD 1665–66*, p. 300.

12. PRO SP 29/101/102; 29/115/40; 29/126/1.1; 29/129/14; 29/217/60.1; 29/220/32; 29/225/9, 39. Cf. *CSPV 1664–66*, p. 73. The tendency of nonconformist ministers to gather in the towns was another matter of concern. London, of course, attracted many, sometimes only for brief visits. In Exeter there were twenty-two dissenting clergy in January 1664, and nearly forty in April 1665, though Bishop Ward listed only sixteen later that year. Brockett, *Nonconformity in Exeter*, pp. 23–24, 26; PRO SP 29/119/19. Cf. PRO SP 29/107/100, 101 (Dorchester); Thomas Richards, *Wales Under the Penal Code (1662–1687)* (London: National Eisteddfod Association, 1925), pp. 37–38 (Swansea).

13. PRO SP 29/112/125; 29/126/13; 29/174/35; DWL Turner MSS 89.32.

14. E.g., *Newes* 96 (8 December 1664), p. 784 (Evesham); 98 (15 December 1664), p. 806 (Exeter); PRO SP 29/179/95 (Newcastle upon Tyne); *MCR*, 3:343–45, 350–53 (Stepney and east London); *CSPD 1665–66*, p. 566 (Lyme); *Surrey Quarter Sessions Records: The Order Book and the Sessions Rolls. Easter, 1663-Epiphany, 1666*, ed. Dorothy L. Powell and Hilary Jenkinson, Surrey Record Society, no. 39, vol. 16 (1938), p. 190 (Reigate).

15. *CSPD 1667*, p. 455. At Huntingdon, where "the Spiritt [of] Oliver . . . [hovers] yet among them," there were only some twenty communicants at Christmas 1663, although approximately 400 families lived in the town. PRO SP 29/93/22.

16. PRO SP 29/99/3, 7; 29/100/7; 29/101/102; 29/103/136; 29/105/37; 29/110/108; 29/449/33.

17. Peter Toon, *God's Statesman: The Life and Work of John Owen, Pastor,*

Educator, Theologian (Exeter: Paternoster Press, 1971), pp. 151–52; Greaves, *Saints and Rebels*, p. 177; PRO SP 29/101/102; 29/109/64. The countess of Anglesey was a member of John Owen's church. Lacey, p. 307 n. 21.

18. PRO SP 29/93/3; 29/109/56; 29/110/108.

19. PRO SP 29/112/125, 125.1; 29/121/71; 29/126/1, 1.1–2. The preacher at Shadwell may have been the Presbyterian Thomas Hardcastle, arrested for speaking there in August 1665. *CR*, s.v.

20. *SR*, 4, pt. 2, pp. 841–43.

21. PRO SP 29/91/41; J.S. Cockburn, *A History of English Assizes, 1558–1774* (Cambridge: Cambridge University Press, 1972). For Bristol see Latimer, *Annals*, p. 326; PRO SP 29/90/10.1; *Int.* 7 (25 January 1664), p. 57.

22. Bodl. Tanner MSS 81, fol. 199r; *CCSP*, 5:386; Crosby, 2:180–85; Greaves, *DUFE*, pp. 205–206; *The Diary of Roger Lowe of Ashton-in-Maker-field, Lancashire 1663–74*, ed. William L. Sachse (New Haven: Yale University Press, 1938), pp. 58–59. A story in the *Newes* about a Baptist conventicle in Nottingham on 20 March 1664 alluded to the revolutionary London council when it noted that the preacher, who had come from the capital, "doubtless had his *Mission* from the *Metropolitan Committee.*" *Newes* 24 (24 March 1664), p. 199.

23. Lacey, p. 53.

24. *SR*, 5:516–20.

25. *CSPD 1663–64*, pp. 670–71; *CSPV 1664–66*, p. 45; PRO SP 29/129/99. Cf. Henry, p. 175.

26. Hutton's assertion (p. 210) that nonconformists were not persecuted in Norwich is erroneous; Presbyterians and Congregationalists were arrested in the fall of 1666. PRO SP 29/174/35. Other dissenters apparently were arrested in 1665. PRO SP 29/136/17. Norwich nonconformists were undoubtedly helped by the fact that Bishop Reynolds was not inclined to persecute them. John T. Evans, *Seventeenth-Century Norwich: Politics, Religion, and Government, 1620–1690* (Oxford: Clarendon Press, 1979), p. 245; cf. BL Add. MSS 41,656, fol. 75r. Anthony Fletcher found no reference to the enforcement of the act in the Sussex order books for the period 1664–70, but dissenters were cited in ecclesiastical courts for refusing to have their children legally baptized. *Churchwardens' Presentments (17th Century) Part 1. Archdeaconry of Chichester*, ed. Hilda Johnstone, Sussex Record Society, vol. 49 (1947–48), p. 129; Anthony Fletcher, "The Enforcement of the Conventicle Acts 1664–1679," in *Persecution and Toleration*, ed. W.J. Sheils, Studies in Church History, vol. 21 (1984), p. 244.

27. Hutton, p. 209. Cf., e.g., Latimer, *Annals*, p. 326; Wigfield, "Recusancy," pp. 166, 172–76; Whiting, p. 368; *Newes* 2 (5 January 1665), p. 9.

28. PRO SP 29/104/146; *MCR*, 3:341–45, 349. Cf. *Newes* 66 (18 August 1664), p. 536; DWL Turner MSS 89.32; Pepys, 6:199.

29. *Newes* 4 (12 January 1665), pp. 25–26; Fletcher, "Enforcement," p. 239; PRO SP 29/127/7, 47. Cf. PRO SP 29/113/107; *Int.* 71 (5 September 1664), p. 575; 75 (26 September 1664), p. 623.

30. Cf., e.g., PRO SP 29/125/50 (Isle of Wight); *CSPD 1667*, p. 169 (northern Oxfordshire); *CCSP*, 5:589 (Wiltshire); PRO SP 29/225/132 (Great Yarmouth).

31. PRO SP 29/134/102; 29/136/34; 29/161/39. Bishop Seth Ward complained in December 1663 that at least fourteen justices of the peace in Devon were "arrant" Presbyterians. Brockett, *Nonconformity in Exeter*, pp. 21–22.

32. PRO SP 29/143/141; 29/449/33; *CSPD 1667–68*, p. 69. In April 1664 two unnamed deputy lieutenants personally bailed Captain John Williams, Owen Morgan, and three other conventiclers from prison. PRO SP 29/97/76.

33. PRO SP 29/166/96; 29/225/132; Watts, p. 245.

34. Hutton, pp. 209–10; Henry, p. 168; PRO SP 29/178/57.

35. PRO SP 29/112/125; 29/115/40; 29/126/13; 29/129/14; 29/449/33; Firth and Davies, p. 489.

36. PRO SP 29/126/109. See also PRO SP 29/99/7; 29/165/51; *CSPD 1667*, p. 527.

37. PRO SP 29/90/86; 29/168/70. Cf. *HMC 25, Le Fleming*, p. 33; *HMC 33, Lonsdale*, p. 93; PRO SP 29/128/90. Cf. anon., *The Innocency and Conscientiousness of the Quakers Asserted and Cleared*, in which the Friends defend themselves from some of the more common accusations as voiced by Judge Keeling.

38. *HMC 55, Var. Coll.*, 1:19; *HMC 25, Le Fleming*, p. 44; Henry, p. 233; PRO SP 29/441/1.

39. PRO SP 29/100/106; 29/441/74; *HMC 78, Hastings*, 2:154. See Richard Bauman, *Let Your Words Be Few: Symbolism of Speaking and Silence Among Seventeenth-Century Quakers* (Cambridge: Cambridge University Press, 1983).

40. PRO SP 29/91/7.1; 29/95/66; 29/178/115. Cf. Greaves, *DUFE*, p. 58.

41. PRO SP 29/102/59; 29/235/26; 29/292/113; George Fox, *A Collection of the Several Books and Writings* (London, 1665), p. 118.

42. Greaves, *DUFE*, pp. 200–201; PRO SP 29/113/63, 63.1–2; *Int.* 11 (8 February 1664), p. 96.

43. PRO SP 29/113/63.1. A "well Mounted" Durham Quaker told one loyalist that "it was time then or never to Looke about them or they would be all run downe"; the implication was clearly that some kind of militant action was required. PRO SP 29/260/136.

44. PRO SP 29/187/160; 29/277/14; DWL Turner MSS 89.32. An interesting example of Quaker passive resistance—a prototype of the kind widely used in modern times, e.g., in the English women's suffrage movement, the American civil rights movement, and the American protests against the Vietnam War—occurred at Pakefield, Suffolk, in the summer of 1671. When

eleven Quakers refused to give their names to the chief constable, he procured a warrant to bring them before the justice of the peace, but they refused to go. He got a cart, and when they declined to get into it, he and his assistants lifted them aboard. Because the first Quakers into the cart would not stand or sit, the entire group had to be laid on top of each other. When they arrived at the justice's house, they refused to climb out of the cart, forcing the driver to dump them unceremoniously on the ground. By that point they were willing to give the justice their names. PRO SP 29/292/27.

45. PRO SP 29/90/38; 29/93/23; 29/95/2; 29/103/2; 29/117/110; 29/275/168.2; 29/441/1; *Int.* 65 (15 August 1664), pp. 527–28.

46. *Newes* 68 (25 August 1664), p. 552; PRO SP 29/100/8; 29/292/113; BL Egerton MSS 3349, fols. 232r, 262r; *BDBR*, s.vv. "Fox," "Fell," "Whitehead," "Rigge," "Howgill," "Bayly," and "Dewsbury."

47. They could also be excommunicated by the church courts. Barry Reay, "The Authorities and Early Restoration Quakerism," *JEH* 34 (January 1983): 77–79.

48. "Letters of Early Friends," in *The Friends' Library*, ed. William Evans and Thomas Evans, vol. 11 (Philadelphia: Joseph Rakestraw, 1847), pp. 362, 365, 367, 370; Bodl. Clarendon MSS 81, fols. 182v–183r; Joseph Besse, *A Collection of the Sufferings of the People Called Quakers*, 2 vols. (London, 1753), 1:394; *HMC* 33, *Lonsdale*, p. 92 (cf. p. 90); PRO SP 29/265/21; Reay, "The Authorities," p. 81 n. 73.

49. Hutton, p. 210; Reay, "The Authorities," p. 76; PRO SP 29/292/113; *BDBR*, s.v. "Rigge." Cf. PRO SP 29/178/115.1; 29/303/4 (Francis Hart). See Craig W. Horle, *The Quakers and the English Legal System 1660–1688* (Philadelphia: University of Pennsylvania Press, 1988).

50. PRO SP 29/112/134, 134.1; *CSPD 1664–65*, p. 218. Among the nine was Thomas Taylor; but see *BDBR*, s.v. "Taylor, Christopher and Thomas."

51. Reay, "The Authorities," pp. 80–81; PRO SP 29/161/39; 29/275/168.2.

52. PRO SP 29/97/5; 29/103/75, 105; 29/134/102. Cf. *Rel. Bax.*, pt. 3, par. 190 (p. 87). In Lancashire in January 1664 some Quakers were fined and had their goods distrained at treble the value of the fines. PRO SP 29/91/7. Sixty were fined at the Lancaster assizes in January 1664. PRO SP 29/90/100.

53. Reay, "The Authorities," p. 77; *Newes* 98 (15 December 1664), pp. 799–800; PRO SP 29/100/110; *CSPD 1664–65*, pp. 108–109.

54. *HMC* 33, *Lonsdale*, p. 93; PRO SP 29/105/20; 29/107/25, 25.1; 29/110/42; 29/128/90; *Int.* 71 (5 September 1664), p. 569; *Newes* 6 (19 January 1665), p. 41; anon., *Another Cry of the Innocent and Oppressed for Justice* (1665), which records the names of twenty-four Quakers sentenced to banishment, of whom five were women; William C. Braithwaite, *The Second Period of Quakerism* (London: Macmillan and Co., 1919), pp. 43–44.

55. PRO SP 29/121/95, 95.1; Braithwaite, *Second Period*, pp. 45–48; *HMC*

78, *Hastings*, 2:151; *CSPD 1664–65*, p. 373. See also Bodl. Carte MSS, fols. 255r, 256r-v. The Friends responded to the threat of banishment with a sense of resignation and resolution to suffer for their faith. See, e.g., R[ichard] F[arnworth] and Thomas Salthouse, *A Loving Salutation with Several Seasonable Exhortations* (1665); George Whitehead, *This Is an Epistle for the Remnant of Friends, and Chosen of God* (1665), which reflects especially on Quaker losses sustained from the plague while in prison; M[organ] W[atkins], *A Lamentation over England* (1664), especially pp. 46–47; G[eorge] W[hitehead], *The Conscientious Cause of the Sufferers, Called Quakers* (London, 1664).

56. PRO SP 29/100/36, 37; 29/103/75, 105; 29/178/115.1; Besse, *Collection*, 1:199–202. Thomas Holme, *A Brief Relation of Some Part of the Sufferings of the True Christians . . . in Ireland . . . from 1660. until 1671* (1672), pp. 20, 22, 32, 41, 43–45, 48. Cf. PRO SP 29/225/265.

57. PRO SP 29/100/37, 77 (cf. 29/276/201); 29/178/55, 115, 115.1; 29/287/69A; 29/441/70. Some officials refused to allow Quaker merchants to keep their shops open on holy days. PRO SP 29/140/9; 29/294/224.

58. PRO SP 29/96/93–95; 29/105/115.

59. PRO SP 29/113/63.1; 29/277/174.1; 29/280/124.

60. Legacies could be a problem; see PRO SP 29/292/26; *CSPD 1671*, p. 325.

61. *CSPD 1667*, p. 9; PRO SP 29/275/168.1; 29/278/113.1; *HMC* 55, *Var. Coll.*, 1:150. Other nonconformists were building meetinghouses too. PRO SP 29/241/3.

62. PRO SP 29/211/55; 29/217/174; 29/232/187; *CSPD 1667*, pp. 437, 457; *CSPD 1667–68*, pp. 203, 209, 242; BL Egerton MSS 2539, fol. 119r; Pepys, 9:31. In 1667 the London astrologer Peter Heyden predicted "full freedom" of conscience in time. PRO SP 29/192/164. For a general overview see Roger Thomas, "Comprehension and Indulgence," in *From Uniformity to Unity 1662–1962*, ed. Geoffrey F. Nuttall and Owen Chadwick (London: S.P.C.K., 1962), pp. 195–207.

63. *CSPD 1667*, p. 550.

64. PRO SP 29/113/84; John Owen, *The Grounds and Reasons on Which Protestant Dissenters Desire Their Liberty*, in *The Works of John Owen*, ed. William H. Goold, 16 vols. (London: Johnstone and Hunter, 1850–53), 13:578; *Indulgence and Toleration Considered*, in *Works*, 13:531; *A Peace-Offering*, in *Works*, 13:548–49, 570–71. For subsequent statements by Owen on this theme, see Ashcraft, pp. 42–44, 46–47, 49, 52–53, 65–67, 70–71, 73–74.

65. DWL Baxter MSS 59.1.9; cf. 59.1–6 passim.

66. Ludlow, "Voyce," p. 1282. For more on Humfrey's subsequent arguments, see Ashcraft, pp. 43, 47–49, 52.

67. Lacey, p. 56; Walter G. Simon, "Comprehension in the Age of Charles

II," *Church History* 31 (December 1962): 440–41; *CSPD 1667*, p. 447; *CSPD 1667–68*, p. 203; *HMC* 25, *Le Fleming*, p. 54.

68. Lacey, pp. 57–58; Cobbett, 4:413; *CJ*, 9:60; Pepys, 9:96; BL Egerton MSS 2539, fol. 162v; PRO SP 29/236/64; *Rel. Bax.*, pt. 3, pars. 62–63 (pp. 23–24), 81 (p. 36).

69. PRO SP 29/239/141.1; 29/258/43; Pepys, 9:177 (cf. pp. 180–81); Cobbett, 4:421; BL Egerton MSS 2539, fol. 170r; Lacey, p. 59.

70. *BDBR*, s.v. "Lockyer, Nicholas"; *DNB*, s.v. "Lockyer, Nicholas"; [Nicholas Lockyer], *Some Seasonable and Serious Queries upon the Late Act Against Conventicles* ([London, 1670]), pp. 5–13; this work was written in 1668.

71. In January 1667 Thomas Curtis, a Quaker in the Reading jail, suggested that the use of force in religious matters, whether by Protestants or Catholics, smacked of Antichrist. *CCSP*, 5:578. The conformist Richard Bower, however, sneered at nonconformist appeals to conscience as "a Cloake for all things unwarranted," including "errors in opinion & practice." PRO SP 29/232/70.

72. Anon., *A Few Sober Queries upon the Late Proclamation, for Enforcing Laws Against Conventicles* (London, 1668), pp. 3–8, 14; *CSPD 1667–68*, p. 250; BL Egerton MSS 2539, fol. 305v.

73. PRO SP 29/225/111; 29/232/104, 187; 29/236/74; 29/241/3; *CSPD 1667–68*, pp. 255–56; *CSPD 1668–69*, p. 96; Pepys, 8:584; 9:385; *HMC* 25, *Le Fleming*, p. 58.

74. *CSPD 1667–68*, p. 546; *BDBR*, s.v. "Fell, Margaret"; BL Egerton MSS 2539, fol. 294v; *CSPD 1668–69*, pp. 151, 236; Bodl. Carte MSS 37, fol. 39r (cf. fols. 34r, 37r); Carte MSS 39, fols. 68r-69r; PRO SP 29/250/65; 29/258/92. Cf. *CSPD 1667*, p. 377. An undated document in the Public Record Office from about this period records four services each Sunday at the Leather Hall, attended by approximately 700 persons. Three of the preachers were ejected clergymen: Samuel Bryan, George Martyn, and Thomas Evans, all Presbyterians. PRO SP 29/270/141.1. The bishop of Coventry wanted to station a troop of horse in Coventry to stop the conventicles. PRO SP 29/270/141.

75. PRO SP 29/261/22; 29/262/105; *CSPD 1667–68*, p. 481; *CSPD 1668–69*, pp. 394, 623.

76. For earlier conventicles in the London area see, e.g., PRO SP 29/93/3; 29/99/7; 29/100/7; 29/103/136; 29/105/37; 29/109/56; 29/110/108; 29/111/67; 29/116/13; 29/121/38; 29/157/10; *Surrey Quarter Sessions 1663–1666*, pp. 188–90; *MCR*, 3:340, 350–51.

77. PRO SP 29/237/140. For Powell's activities see R. Tudur Jones, "The Sufferings of Vavasor," in *Welsh Baptist Studies*, ed. Mansel John (n.p.: South Wales Baptist College, 1976), pp. 82–87. A Fifth Monarchist conventicle was

reported at the house of Ursula Adman in Hillingdon, Middlesex, on 6 June 1669. Only two of the thirteen who were arrested were found guilty. *MCR*, 4:14–15; *BDBR*, s.v.

78. Greaves, *Saints and Rebels*, p. 91; Jones, "The Sufferings of Vavasor," pp. 87–88; PRO SP 29/237/140.

79. *CSPD 1668–69*, p. 294; *HMC 43, Fifteenth Report*, Appendix, Part VII, p. 103; *HMC 25, Le Fleming*, pp. 64–65; PRO SP 29/262/15, 175; 29/263/2; 29/270/137. The perennially suspicious Sir Philip Musgrave, who had been utilizing informers to spy on nonconformists, told Williamson that he was "much joyed to fynde the Nonconformist[s] are discovered to be as You know I ever accounted them." PRO SP 29/263/54.

80. PRO SP 29/261/135, 145; 29/262/107, 154, 154.1, 170; 29/264/43, 56, 127; 29/265/14, 159; 29/276/143. For the suppression of conventicles by the vice-chancellor of Oxford see CH HA 9602; *HMC 78, Hastings*, 2:315–16.

81. PRO SP 29/261/137; 29/263/97, 158 (cf. 29/265/50); 29/265/15; Latimer, *Annals*, p. 351; *CSPD 1668–69*, p. 516.

82. *CSPD 1667–68*, p. 551; PRO SP 29/249/146, 146.1, 171, 172; 29/258/132; *CSPD 1668–69*, p. 91; BL Egerton MSS 2539, fol. 294v. The dean of Carlisle put the number at 3,000. Ambrose Barnes, *Memoirs of the Life of Mr. Ambrose Barnes, Late Merchant and Sometime Alderman of Newcastle upon Tyne*, Surtees Society, vol. 50 (Durham, 1867), Appendix, pp. 407–409; *DCY*, pp. 173–74; Whiting, pp. 400–401. The text of the hymn comes from a hostile source, the Newcastle minister Thomas Naylor.

83. PRO SP 29/225/9, 39, 132; 29/230/83; 29/236/76; 29/241/111, 188; 29/250/70, 96, 126, 157; 29/262/17; 29/264/99, 140; 29/265/16, 75; 29/287/117; *CSPD 1667–68*, pp. 67–68, 186, 232–33; *CSPD 1668–69*, pp. 10–11, 160, 221, 297; DWL Harmer MSS 76.2; Whiting, pp. 381–83.

84. PRO SP 29/272/28, 76; *HMC 25, Le Fleming*, pp. 68–69; (but also see PRO SP 29/264/141 for Cumberland).

85. Sir Peter Leicester, *Charges to the Grand Jury at Quarter Sessions 1660–1677*, ed. Elizabeth M. Halcrow, Chetham Society, 3rd ser., vol. 5 (1953), pp. 44, 46–48; [George Vernon], *A Letter to a Friend Concerning Some of Dr. Owens Principles and Practices* (London, 1670), p. 51. Cf. *CSPV 1669–70*, p. 167; *Rel. Bax.*, pt. 3, par. 93 (pp. 41–42).

86. PRO SP 29/264/139; Bodl. Carte MSS 81, fol. 305r-v; *CSPV 1669–70*, p. 84.

87. Turner, 3:69–70, 105–39. Some of the bishops were ineffective in procuring the information. BL Harl. MSS 7377, fol. 6r. The bishop of Bangor dubiously claimed that there were no conventicles in his diocese. Richards, *Wales Under the Penal Code*, pp. 125–26.

88. Watts, pp. 491–510.

89. Owen, *The State of the Kingdom with Respect to the Present Bill Against Conventicles*, in *Works*, 13:583–86; Bodl. Carte MSS 81, fol. 331r-v (cf. fol. 311r).

90. Quoted in Lacey, p. 61.

91. *SR*, 5:648–51. The bill was approved in the Lords by a division of 140 to 80. *CSPI 1669–70*, p. 85. See also Cobbett, 4:443–47; *HMC* 35, *Fourteenth Report*, Appendix, Part IV, pp. 84–85; Grey, *Debates*, 1:146–47, 174–76, 220–23, 245–50, 254, 263–65; Ashcraft, pp. 26–27.

92. Thomas Ellwood, *The History of the Life of Thomas Ellwood*, ed. C.G. Crump (London: Methuen and Co., 1900), p. 169; PRO SP 29/274/126, 154; 29/281/91; Adam Martindale, *The Life of Adam Martindale, Written by Himself*, ed. Richard Parkinson, Chetham Society, vol. 4 (1845), pp. 194–95; *Rel. Bax.*, pt. 3, par. 163 (p. 74); BL Add. MSS 56,240 (unbound; 7 June 1670, John Cooke [to Monsr. Blathwayt]).

93. Owen, *The Present Distresses on Nonconformists Examined*, in *Works*, 13:579–82; *A Word of Advice to the Citizens of London*, in *Works*, 13:590–91.

94. PRO SP 29/275/14, 134.1–2; 29/276/14; *HMC* 29, *Portland*, 3:313; *CSPV 1669–70*, p. 174; *Rel. Bax.*, pt. 3, par. 167 (p. 74); Henry, p. 228. For Tombes see also PRO SP 29/239/173. Capp identifies Cox as a Fifth Monarchist. Capp, *FMM*, p. 247.

95. Henry, p. 228; PRO SP 29/278/153; 29/291/112.1. Partridge had been an army chaplain in Ireland in the 1650s. *CR*, s.v.

96. PRO SP 29/276/82, 127; 29/278/116.1; 29/281/97; Wigfield, "Recusancy," pp. 181–83. Cf. *MCR*, 4:19; PRO SP 29/278/148; 29/279/8.

97. PRO SP 29/276/14, 101, 128; 29/278/19.

98. PRO SP 29/276/95, 171; 29/278/119; *CSPD 1670*, p. 303; Burnet, p. 184.

99. PRO SP 29/275/104, 152, 173; 29/276/63; *The Parliamentary Diary of Sir Edward Dering 1670–1673*, ed. Basil Duke Henning (New Haven: Yale University Press, 1940), pp. 4–6. Doolittle was a Presbyterian, Smith a Baptist.

100. PRO SP 29/275/158; 29/276/63, 72; Cosin, 2:243 (cf. Schwoerer, p. 76); *HMC* 25, *Le Fleming*, p. 71. Among those arrested in the spring 1670 sweep were the alderman James Hayes, John Jekyll (or Jekell), Gerrard Roberts, Thomas Rudyard, and Captain William Mead. PRO SP 29/276/72, 114. Hayes and Jekyll were "eminent Sticklers among the Conventiclers." PRO SP 29/276/105; *HMC* 25, *Le Fleming*, p. 71. Major-General William Boteler had been arrested several days earlier. PRO SP 29/275/174.

101. PRO SP 29/275/174.

102. PRO SP 29/275/140, 173; 29/276/1, 15, 118, 206; DWL Turner MSS 89.32; CH HA 9607; *HMC* 78, *Hastings*, 2:319–20; Cosin, 2:243.

103. PRO SP 29/275/135. See also *MCR*, 4:18; PRO SP 29/277/93.

104. PRO SP 29/275/152, 173; 29/276/118; 29/277/3, 95; 29/278/89A; DWL Turner MSS 89.32.

105. PRO SP 29/291/112, 112.2; 29/294/216; *MCR*, 4:29–31; *HMC* 25, *Le Fleming*, p. 80. Two others from the parish of St. Sepulchre's, possibly Fifth Monarchists, had been arrested in May. *MCR*, 4:28. On 18 July twenty-seven Fifth Monarchists were found guilty in London and subjected to the penalty of *praemunire*. PRO SP 29/291/207. Richard Wilkinson and his friends, who also informed on Blood, Mason, John Lockyer, and Timothy Butler, alerted authorities to this group. PRO SP 29/294/68.

106. Burnet, p. 183; PRO SP 29/276/114, 130A; 29/277/69; 29/302/118; *HMC* 25, *Le Fleming*, p. 71; *CSPV 1669–70*, pp. 215–16. Cf. *CMHS*, 8:220.

107. *Gazette* 478 (13–16 June 1670); DWL Turner MSS 89.32; PRO 29/276/154, 206. Sheldon directed John Brackshaw to leave Bedfordshire in order to minister in the parish of St. Michael, Crooked Lane, where in the absence of a preacher the people attended the conventicle of the Congregationalist Thomas Brooks. BL Harl. MSS 7377, fol. 15v.

108. PRO SP 29/278/5; DWL Turner MSS 89.32.

109. Victor S. Sutch, *Gilbert Sheldon: Architect of Anglican Survival, 1640–1675* (The Hague: Martinus Nijhoff, 1973), p. 115; PRO SP 29/275/162, 163 (cf. 29/92/91); 29/276/75; 29/278/149, 158, 163; *The Records of a Church of Christ in Bristol, 1640–1687*, ed. Roger Hayden, Bristol Record Society, vol. 27 (1974), p. 128. On the first Sunday the act was in force, the constables left Bristol rather than enforce the law. PRO SP 29/276/14.

110. Brockett, *Nonconformity in Exeter*, pp. 30–32; PRO SP 29/277/29; [John Hicks], *A True and Faithful Narrative* (n.p., 1671). Cf. *Som. Tr.*, 7:586–615.

111. PRO SP 29/276/76; 29/277/11, 204, 204.1; *HMC* 55, *Var. Coll.*, 1:151.

112. PRO SP 29/277/204; 29/278/22, 137, 206; 29/279/8; *Rel. Bax.*, pt. 3, par. 185 (p. 86). The two men—Nathaniel Barnard and John Love—were convicted.

113. PRO SP 29/276/14; 29/277/11; 29/278/37, 116. Cf. *Quarter Sessions Records for the County of Somerset*, vol. 4, *Charles II. 1666–1677*, ed. E.H. Bates-Harbin and M.C.B. Dawes, Somerset Record Society, vol. 34 (1919), pp. 101–102.

114. CH HA 9606; PRO SP 29/276/172; 29/277/24, 112; 29/287/57, 71; *HMC* 25, *Le Fleming*, p. 75. For Deal, where nonconformists were encouraged by London dissenters, see also PRO SP 29/277/123.

115. Whiting, pp. 383–85; PRO SP 29/276/77; 29/277/28, 126, 165, 166, 206; 29/278/171; 29/279/69 [newly renumbered 167 and 171]; 29/279/111 [newly renumbered 218]; 29/280/72, 82; 29/281/54, 73; CH HA 9609.

116. *CSPD 1670*, pp. 90–91; PRO SP 29/275/154; 29/278/61. Cf. Wigfield, "Recusancy," pp. 179–81 (Bedford); *CSPD 1670*, pp. 352, 407; PRO SP 29/276/130A (Hertfordshire).

117. PRO SP 29/275/138; 29/276/66, 81, 144; 29/277/10; 29/294/69; *HMC* 35,

Fourteenth Report, Appendix, Part IV, pp. 90–91. Cf. Leicester, *Charges*, p. 69. Baptists and Quakers in Gloucestershire and other western shires received effective legal assistance from Walter Clemens, which helped some of them escape punishment. For his efforts he was jailed at Gloucester. PRO SP 29/289/71, 71.1.

118. PRO SP 29/275/172.

119. PRO SP 29/275/172; 29/276/4, 65, 113, 176; 29/277/2, 192 (cf. 29/279/4); 29/279/74 [newly renumbered 172]; 29/281/8; 29/289/113.

120. PRO SP 29/275/168; 29/276/178; 29/277/12; 29/278/76, 76.1. For other conventicles see *NRR*, pp. 151, 158.

121. PRO SP 29/278/76.1; *HMC* 25, *Le Fleming*, pp. 71, 86. Cf. PRO SP 29/274/163.

122. *Correspondence of the Family of Hatton: Being Chiefly Letters Addressed to Christopher First Viscount Hatton A.D. 1601–1704*, ed. Edward Maunde Thompson, 2 vols., Camden Society, n.s., vols. 22–23 (1878), 1:58; Reay, "The Authorities," p. 81 n. 75. Cf. *CSPV 1671–72*, p. 29.

123. Cf. Baxter's observation that Manton, Watson, Whitaker, Annesley, and Vincent had reported that Charles told them "he was against Persecution, and hoped ere long to stand on his own Legs, and then they should see how much he was against it." Baxter's own view is unclear. *Rel. Bax.*, pt. 3, pars. 191–92 (pp. 87–88).

124. White Kennet, *The History of England from the Commencement of the Reign of Charles I. to the End of the Reign of William III.* (London, 1706), p. 287; *CSPD 1671–72*, pp. 217–18. Williamson annotated Butler's phrase thus: "Quakers, Fifth Monarchy."

125. *CSPD 1671–72*, p. 226. Cf. Burnet, p. 206; Lacey, pp. 64–66.

126. Richard L. Greaves, "The Organizational Response of Nonconformity to Repression and Indulgence: The Case of Bedfordshire," *Church History* 44 (December 1975): 472–84.

127. Reresby, p. 84.

128. *HMC* 25, *Le Fleming*, p. 90 (cf. Henry, p. 250); Turner, 3:726–36. These numbers should be used with care because denominational labels were sometimes used incautiously.

Chapter 5

1. *Misc. Aul.*, p. 335; anon., *An Exact Narrative of the Tryal and Condemnation of John Twyn* (London, 1664), sig. A3v; *Int.* 31 (18 April 1664), p. 250.

2. PRO SP 29/90/16; 29/95/98; 29/96/64; 29/98/25, 37; *CSPD 1663–64*, pp. 465, 536, 549, 581. George Piggott was also in prison in the Gatehouse for printing a seditious ballad he claimed he had found in the street. PRO SP 29/96/55, 56.

3. *CSPD 1663–64*, pp. 519, 594; PRO SP 29/90/61.

4. Greaves, *DUFE*, pp. 70–72, 219–20, 266 n. 42; *CSPD 1663–64*, p. 577; PRO SP 29/99/162–65; George Kitchin, *Sir Roger L'Estrange: A Contribution to the History of the Press in the Seventeenth Century* (London: Kegan Paul, Trench, Trubner & Co., 1913), pp. 124, 168; *Int.* 59 (25 July 1664), p. 480. For Cotes, Griffin, and Simmons see Plomer, *DBP*, pp. 52, 87, 164; the first two and possibly Simmons were widows. Gaines is probably the John Gain who was sued by the Stationers' Company in 1681 for illegally printing primers. Elizabeth Cotes may have been Ellen Cotes, widow of Richard Cotes. Plomer, *DBP*, p. 52. Warrants were issued in November 1664 for the arrest of Elizabeth Ward, Sarah Kent (or Keat), and John Westcombe and his wife. *CSPD 1664–65*, p. 89.

5. PRO SP 29/109/44, 92; *Int.* 55 (11 July 1664), pp. 441–42; William Bayly, *Pure Encouragements from the Spirit of the Lord* [1664], pp. 2–3; R[ichard] F[arnworth], *Christian Religious Meetings Allowed by the Liturgie* (1664), pp. 2–6. *Englands Warning* was sold by Thomas Passenger and William Whitwood. Plomer, *DBP*, pp. 145, 193. Plomer (*DBP*, p. 189) suggests that Warwick may have been a bookseller at Colchester in 1663; he was in London the following year. Plomer (ibid., p. 165) also suggests that Samuel Simmons was the son or nephew of Matthew Simmons, who printed Milton's *Paradise Lost* in 1667.

6. PRO SP 29/98/116, 138; 29/99/117; *BDBR*, s.v. "Keach, Benjamin"; *Int.* 69 (29 August 1664), p. 560.

7. PRO SP 29/90/78, 78.1, 111, 111.1; 29/103/1; *CSPD 1663–64*, p. 434; *CSPD 1664–65*, p. 8. Another Scottish dissident, James Nesbitt, also lived in Clapham at this time and was purportedly "the manager of the disaffected Scots in England." Quoted in Kitchin, *L'Estrange*, p. 171.

8. *CSPD 1664–65*, pp. 8, 309; PRO SP 29/102/124. Baxter disapproved of Wallis's efforts to ridicule the "notoriously scandalous" behavior of some conformists because of "the great temptation of many of the Nonconformists, to be glad of other Mens sin, as that which by accident might diminish the interest of the Prelatists." *Rel. Bax.*, pt. 3, par. 59 (p. 23). Tobias Jordan had been sheriff of Gloucester in 1644 and mayor in 1659. Plomer, *DBP*, p. 108.

9. [Ralph Wallis], *More News from Rome or Magna Charta, Discoursed of Between a Poor Man and His Wife* (London, 1666), sig. A2v, pp. 2, 7, 10, 30, 32, 36.

10. Anon., *The Sufferers-Catechism, Wherein Are Many Necessary and Seasonable Questions and Cases of Conscience Resolved* (n.p., 1664), pp. 1, 3–4, 7–8, 23.

11. PRO SP 29/116/12, 96. For Curtis see Plomer, *DPB*, p. 96. A list of Wither's "authentic published works" by Charles S. Hensley does not in-

clude the *New Year's Gift. The Later Career of George Wither* (The Hague and Paris: Mouton, 1969), pp. 144–53. For Wither's radicalism see Christopher Hill, *The Collected Essays of Christopher Hill*, 2 vols. (Amherst: University of Massachusetts Press, 1985–86), 1:133–50.

12. On 29 January 1665 handbills inscribed "Murder Will Out" were posted on twenty doors in Paternoster Row and Ludgate Hill in London. PRO SP 29/111/67.

13. PRO SP 29/121/93, 93.1–2; 29/123/1; 29/125/109; Greaves, *DUFE*, pp. 195, 218. For Walley see Plomer, *DBP*, p. 188.

14. PRO SP 29/131/30, 73; 29/179/47–49; 29/187/166; *CSPD 1666–67*, p. 287. For Mawborne and Bulkley see Plomer, *DBP*, pp. 38–39, 124.

15. PRO SP 29/156/105, 106; *CSPD 1665–66*, p. 386; Plomer, *DBP*, pp. 169–70. The author of *The Power and Practice of Court-leets* identified himself only as Ph. Ag.

16. Bernard Capp, *English Almanacs 1500–1800: Astrology and the Popular Press* (Ithaca, N.Y.: Cornell University Press, 1979), pp. 172–75; BL Add. MSS 41,656, fol. 52r; *CSPD 1665–66*, pp. 325, 569; William Dewsbury, *The Word of the Lord to All the Inhabitants in England* (1666), p. 5. Burrough's *Antichrist's Government Justly Detected* had originally been published in 1661 by Robert Wilson; it argued, among other things, that any attempt to impose religion by law was contrary to true Christian teaching.

17. PRO SP 29/187/172; 29/209/75, 75.1–2; 29/441/24; Pepys, 8:439; *CSPD 1667*, pp. 393, 401; Plomer, *DBP*, pp. 114, 162.

18. PRO SP 29/155/70 (cf. 29/450/100); 29/187/172; 29/211/13; *MCR*, 4:25–26; Mary Tom Osborne, *Advice-to-a-Painter Poems and Letters of Andrew Marvell*, 3rd ed., ed. H.M. Margoliouth and rev. by Pierre Legouis and E.E. Duncan-Jones, 2 vols. (Oxford: Clarendon Press, 1971), 1:176–77.

19. *CSPD 1667*, pp. 353, 355, 395; *CSPD 1667–68*, p. 178; Plomer, *DBP*, p. 42. Astwood was imprisoned, and a warrant was issued for the arrest of his printer, Robert White. Calvert was kept in the Gatehouse as a close prisoner. *CSPD 1667–68*, p. 363; PRO SP 29/239/156. For White see Plomer, *DBP*, p. 193.

20. PRO SP 29/239/5, 6; *CSPD 1667–68*, p. 378. PRO SP 29/88/68 should probably be dated 1668, not 1663. If so, warrants were again issued for Roger Norton and Thomas Newcomb. Newcomb had once been in trouble for printing one of John Lilburne's works. Plomer, *DBP*, p. 136.

21. *CSPD 1668–69*, p. 130; William Dyer, *Christ's Famous Titles, and a Believer's Golden Chain* (Philadelphia: Stewart and Cochran, 1743), pp. 18, 20, 41. In August 1667 another widow, Ann Maxwell, entered a bond of £200 not to print any unlicensed material. *CSPD 1667*, p. 390; cf. Plomer, *DBP*, p. 125. For Parker see Plomer, *DBP*, p. 144; Plomer, *DPB*, p. 230.

22. [George Wither], *Vox & Lacrimae Anglorum: or, the True English-mens Complaints, to 1668* ([London, 1668]), pp. 3–10, 13, 15.

23. Anon., *Omnia Comesta a Bello* (n.p., 1667), pp. 5–8, 10, 12.

24. [Thomas Ford], *Felo de Se, or the Bishops Condemned out of Their Own Mouthes* ([London], 1668), pp. 8–10, 20.

25. Anon., *Several Reasons Rendred by the People of God, (Called Quakers) Why No Outward Force, or Imposition, on the Conscience Ought to Be Used in Matters of Faith and Religion* (n.p., 1668), pp. 3–8.

26. *CSPD 1667–68*, p. 358; A.B., *The Saints Freedom from Tyranny Vindicated* (London, 1667), pp. 19, 36, 40; PRO SP 29/276/178.1.

27. *CSPD 1667–68*, p. 358; [Ralph Wallis], *Room for the Cobler of Gloucester and His Wife: With Several Cartloads of Abominable Irregular, Pitiful Stinking Priests* ([London], 1668), pp. 14, 34, 39–40; PRO SP 29/99/73; Kitchin, *L'Estrange*, p. 174. Larkin was also the publisher of John Bunyan's spiritual autobiography, *Grace Abounding to the Chief of Sinners* (1666). The Presbyterian Samuel Rolle referred to *Room for the Cobler* in refuting Simon Patrick, bishop of Ely: "You have been pleased to come forth, like the *Cobler of Glocester*, with your two *Dust-Carts*, or *Dung-Carts*, fetching away one Load from T[homas] W[atson] and another from W[illiam] B[ridge]." *A Sober Answer to the Friendly Debate* (London, 1669), p. 52; cf. pp. 133–34. This literary skirmish is discussed later in this chapter.

28. Kitchin, *L'Estrange*, p. 177; *CSPD 1667–68*, pp. 178, 350, 363, 369, 409, 495; PRO SP 29/239/93. Cottrell had been arrested in 1664 for illegally printing law books. Plomer, *DBP*, p. 54.

29. [John Wilson], *Nehushtan: or, a Sober and Peaceable Discourse, Concerning the Abolishing of Things Abused to Superstition and Idolatry* (London, 1668), sigs. A3r-v, A5r-v, pp. 87–93; *CSPD 1668–69*, pp. 30, 32, 37, 133–34; *CR*, s.v. "Wilson, John"; PRO SP 29/113/128; 29/248/88; *MCR*, 4:26–27; *Gazette* 560 (27–30 March 1671); Kitchin, *L'Estrange*, p. 183. Royston had been in trouble during the interregnum for publishing royalist works. Plomer, *DBP*, pp. 158–59. For Wright see Plomer, *DBP*, p. 198; Plomer, *DPB*, p. 321. In the *DNB* entry, Gordon Goodwin attributes *Nehushtan* to James Forbes. *DNB*, s.v.

30. *CSPD 1668–69*, pp. 92, 98; *HMC* 25, *Le Fleming*, pp. 60, 61, 65.

31. *CSPD 1668–69*, pp. 121, 201, 216, 409; PRO SP 29/99/163; 29/261/37; [Stephen Coven], *The Militant Christian; or,the Good Soldier of Jesus Christ* (London, 1668), sig. ₂A2v, pp. 249–50; Plomer, *DBP*, pp. 144, 160; Plomer, *DPB*, pp. 230–31, 260, 319. In December 1668 Leach had assisted John Redman in printing a "somewhat dangerous" sheet dealing with Ireland. PRO SP 29/250/132.

32. [Simon Patrick], *A Friendly Debate Between a Conformist and a Non-Conformist*, 2nd ed. (London, 1669), pp. 20–39, 123–43, 188–91 (pp. 125, 142

quoted); *Rel. Bax.*, pt. 3, par. 92 (p. 41); [Samuel Rolle], *A Sober Answer*, sigs. C3v-C4r.

33. *Rel. Bax.*, pt. 3, par. 92 (p. 41); [Rolle], *A Sober Answer*, passim (pp. 8, 219 quoted).

34. *Rel. Bax.*, pt. 3, par. 88 (pp. 39–40); [Simon Patrick], *A Further Continuation and Defence, or, a Third Part of the Friendly Debate* (London, 1670), pp. 27–29, 75, 239–40. Antilegon was the name of a character in Arthur Dent's *Plaine Mans Path-way to Heaven* (1601).

35. PRO SP 29/275/131, 139, 152, 163, 164.

36. PRO SP 29/275/155; 29/276/64; 29/277/35; 29/280/138; *CSPD 1670*, pp. 322, 437; DWL Turner MSS 89.32; Kitchin, *L'Estrange*, p. 188; *HMC 71, Finch*, 2:1; Plomer, *DBP*, pp. 34–35. Illegal Quaker publications continued to create concern in 1671. PRO SP 29/289/72; *CSPD 1671*, pp. 128–29. In March the bookseller (George or Thomas?) Palmer was fined 40 marks and pilloried for distributing seditious material. *CSPD 1671*, p. 157; Plomer, *DBP*, p. 143; Plomer, *DPB*, pp. 227–28. See also PRO SP 29/294/172.

37. *CSPD 1668–69*, p. 446; PRO SP 29/262/85; 29/275/155, 155.1; 29/278/167; *CSPD 1671*, p. 447; N.H. Keeble, *The Literary Culture of Nonconformity in Later Seventeenth-Century England* (Athens: University of Georgia Press, 1987), p. 127. Cf. *CSPD 1670*, pp. 642–43. Illegal books were also distributed by peddlers and petty chapmen. *CSPD 1664–65*, p. 400.

38. *HMC 71, Finch*, 2:1–2 (cf. PRO SP 29/279/51 [newly renumbered 147]); PRO SP 29/280/15.

39. *RPCS 1661–64*, pp. 73, 90 (cf. p. 119); Plomer, *DBP*, pp. 83, 174.

40. BL Add. MSS 35,125, fol. 130r; Greaves, *DUFE*, p. 127; PRO SP 29/96/9. No copy of this book seems to have survived.

41. *Int.* 39 (16 May 1664), pp. 313–14; *LP*, 2:iv; *RPCS 1661–64*, p. 527. The translator of Buchanan's *De Jure Regni apud Scotos* used the pseudonym Philalethes.

42. *RPCS 1661–64*, pp. 584, 623, 696; *Newes* 66 (18 August 1664), p. 529; "The Old Tolbooth: With Extracts from the Original Records," ed. John A. Fairley, in *The Book of the Old Edinburgh Club*, vol. 5 (Edinburgh: T. and A. Constable, 1912), p. 121.

43. [John Brown], *An Apologeticall Relation, of the Particular Sufferings of the Faithfull Ministers & Professours of the Church of Scotland, Since August. 1660* (1665), sigs. **1r, **5v, **6v, pp. 69–90, 153–56, 305–15, 422. Argyll was also praised.

44. Cowan, p. 61; *RPCS 1665–69*, pp. 138–39.

45. BL Add. MSS 23,128, fol. 217r; *LP*, 2:88. I erroneously listed the place of publication as Edinburgh in *DUFE*, p. 236 n. 27.

46. [James Stewart and James Stirling], *Naphtali, or the Wrestlings of the Church of Scotland for the Kingdom of Christ* (n.p., 1667), sig. B1r, pp. 130–37, 155, 175, 193–286.

47. Ibid., sig. B4r, p. 123.

48. *LP*, 2:88; *RPCS 1665–69*, pp. 375–76; BL Add. MSS 23,128, fol. 217r; Wodrow, 2:100; NLS MS 2512, fol. 110r.

49. *HMC 72, Laing*, 1:380; "Thirty-four Letters Written to James Sharp, Archbishop of St. Andrews, by the Duke and Duchess of Lauderdale . . . 1660–1677," ed. John Dowden, in *Miscellany of the Scottish Historical Society*, vol. 1, Publications of the Scottish Historical Society, vol. 15 (Edinburgh, 1893), p. 265 n. 1; [James Stewart], *Jus Populi Vindicatum* (n.p., 1669), fol. *5v, pp. 5, 95–96, 266–67; NLS MS 2512, fol. 136r; BL Add. MSS 23,134, fols. 187r, 204r, 211r. Some thought the author was John Brown, who had written *An Apologeticall Relation. LP*, 2:213.

50. *RPCS 1669–72*, pp. 265, 296–97; *HMC 72, Laing*, 1:381–82.

51. *RPCS 1669–72*, p. 582; *HMC 72, Laing*, 1:380–81; William Steven, *The History of the Scottish Church, Rotterdam* (Edinburgh: Waugh & Innes; Rotterdam: Vander Meer & Verbruggen, 1832), p. 36.

52. Greaves, *DUFE*, p. 127; *JR*, 2:110–12. Wodrow (2:225–26) erroneously dates Kennedy's being put to the horn in 1673.

Chapter 6

1. *CSPD 1667*, pp. 360–61, 498; *HMC 78, Hastings*, 2:374; Bodl. Carte MSS 35, fol. 148v; PRO SP 29/180/41, 85.

2. PRO SP 29/209/150, 150.1–4; *DCY*, p. 124. The sailor, John Groscomb of Limehouse, Middlesex, was imprisoned. PRO SP 29/230/106; *CSPD 1667*, p. 353. Cf. *DCY*, p. 176; PRO SP 29/275/134, 178; 29/276/116; 29/279/73 [renumbered 171].

3. PRO SP 29/206/148; 29/211/28; 29/212/32, 88; 29/215/34; *MCR*, 4:4, 6–7; *DCY*, p. 158. The Dutch were quick to report such discontent. PRO SP 29/209/101.

4. PRO SP 29/165/23, 23.1; 29/189/2 (cf. 29/217/75); 29/207/10; *CSPD 1666–67*, pp. 568, 575; *CSPD 1667*, pp. 409–10, 428, 457 (cf. PRO SP 29/217/127); *HMC 25, Le Fleming*, p. 53; *CSPD 1667–68*, pp. 413–15. Cf. Wharton's concern with the growth of Catholicism in England. Bodl. Carte MSS 81, fols. 318r, 324r-v.

5. Greaves, *DUFE*, p. 179; PRO SP 29/192/112; *CSPD 1667*, pp. 57, 245, 310. Two yeomen, John Browne of Syke House and Richard Wilson of Barforth, were accused of high treason along with Mason. *DCY*, pp. 98–99.

6. *CSPD 1667*, pp. 170, 265; PRO SP 29/209/44.

7. PRO SP 29/210/151; 29/211/17, 60; *Som. Tr.*, 8:442–44; *CSPD 1667*, pp. 352, 369; *HMC 25, Le Fleming*, pp. 51–52; *Gazette* 181 (8–12 August 1667). Reresby, pp. 69–70, is inaccurate. Gower regarded the rescue as proof that the rebels did not want "the bottom of the design"—the 1663 rebellion—discovered. *CSPD 1667*, p. 388.

8. *CSPD 1667*, pp. 427, 488. The government also had at least four other informers imprisoned in York Castle to spy on the dissidents: Joshua Westerman, Luke Lone, Jacob Ellis, and William Dickinson. PRO SP 29/277/8.

9. Ashley, *Wildman*, p. 205; PRO SP 29/225/40; Bodl. Carte MSS 47, fol. 174r. Ludlow wrote favorably of Buckingham for "having lately asserted the peoples Interest against Tiranny, & Popery." "Voyce," p. 1160. The duke was married to a Presbyterian, the daughter of General Fairfax.

10. *CSPD 1667–68*, p. 259 (cf. p. 238); Lacey, pp. 43–44; Hutton, p. 286.

11. Tim Harris, "The Bawdy House Riots of 1668," *Historical Journal* 29 (September 1986): 537–56. For the broader context, see Tim Harris, *London Crowds in the Reign of Charles II: Propaganda and Politics from the Restoration Until the Exclusion Crisis* (Cambridge: Cambridge University Press, 1987).

12. BL Egerton MSS 2539, fol. 180r; *MCR*, 4:8–12; *Gazette* 246 (23–26 March 1668); Pepys, 9:129; *ST*, 6:887–89; Harris, "The Bawdy House Riots," pp. 550–51. Whether the adoption of the color green was accidental or a deliberate evocation of the traditional Leveller hue can only be a matter of speculation. See Harris, "The Bawdy House Riots," p. 553.

13. Pepys, 9:129–30; BL Egerton MSS 2539, fol. 180r; PRO SP 29/237/59; *ST*, 6:886; *MCR*, 4:9. A broadside entitled *The Whores Petition to the London Prentices* (London, 1668) chides the rioters because they attempted "By crooked ways to seek to make things *streight*."

14. *ST*, 6:880; Pepys, 9:132; *MCR*, 4:9–10, 12. Coney escaped. *CSPD 1667–68*, pp. 328, 330, 339, 425; *CSPD 1668–69*, p. 172.

15. BL Egerton MSS 2539, fol. 182v; Pepys, 9:132; PRO SP 29/237/59, 82.

16. *ST*, 6:879–914; BL Egerton MSS 2539, fols. 185r, 194r; *Gazette* 259 (7–11 May 1668); PRO SP 29/237/191. Cf. PRO SP 29/237/133.

17. *HMC* 25, *Le Fleming*, p. 56; PRO SP 29/290/179.

18. PRO SP 29/230/108; *MCR*, 4:12.

19. PRO SP 29/263/70. Wildman was allowed to go abroad for health reasons in July 1670. *CSPD 1670*, p. 322.

20. PRO SP 29/202/130; 29/217/122; 29/250/37–43, 78; *CSPD 1667*, p. 498; *CSPD 1667–68*, p. 229; *CSPD 1668–69*, pp. 92, 128, 389; *CSPD 1670*, p. 624; *CSPD 1682*, p. 285; *HMC* 25, *Le Fleming*, p. 61; *BDBR*, s.v. "Powell, Vavasor."

21. Ludlow, *Voyce*, p. 13; *CSPD 1667*, pp. 553–55; *BDBR*, s.v. "Courtney," "Thimbleton," "Desborough"; PRO SP 29/236/18, 88, 107; Ludlow, *Memoirs*, 2:424–25; *The Tanner Letters*, ed. Charles McNeill (Dublin: Stationery Office, 1943), p. 406. While Doleman and his men assisted the Dutch in their 1667 attack on England, Washington, Burton, and Kelsey held services in their houses to pray for Dutch success. PRO SP 29/205/73.

22. PRO SP 29/181/116, 116.1.

23. PRO SP 29/182/11; 29/190/104; 29/207/1; 29/232/10; 29/239/200; 29/241/129.1. Cf. SP 29/263/54.1.

24. PRO SP 29/239/94, 158; 29/241/129.

25. PRO SP 29/260/23; 29/275/118; 29/277/179. Cf. *CSPD 1667*, p. 511; *CSPD 1668–69*, p. 232.

26. PRO SP 29/258/155. Cf. *HMC* 35, *Fourteenth Report*, Appendix, Part IV, p. 82; *CSPD 1668–69*, pp. 145, 208–209.

27. Greaves, *DUFE*, p. 191; PRO SP 29/258/155.1; 29/261/164; *CSPD 1668–69*, pp. 333, 351. The self-styled Kempsey Levellers of Worcestershire appear to have had no connection with the radicals, but were traditional rural demonstrators or outlaws. PRO SP 29/281/63; *CSPD 1670*, p. 597; *HMC* 25, *Le Fleming*, p. 74.

28. *CSPD 1668–69*, p. 316; *MCR*, 4:19–20; PRO SP 29/274/200; *CSPD 1670*, p. 253. Cf. PRO SP 29/441/53. For dissent in Oxford see PRO SP 29/275/177.

29. PRO SP 29/275/184, 184.1; 29/276/2; *CSPD 1670*, p. 237; *HMC* 15, *Tenth Report*, Appendix, Part IV, p. 180. At the end of 1669 there were reportedly almost 20,000 ex-Cromwellian soldiers in London. Ashcraft, p. 30.

30. PRO SP 29/276/2, 96, 111, 135; 29/281/109; *Gazette* 477 (9–13 June 1670). Several men got licenses permitting them to remain in the London area. *CSPD 1670*, pp. 278, 281; PRO SP 29/276/138.

31. Greaves, *DUFE*, pp. 47, 259 n. 69; PRO SP 29/276/250; 29/277/20, 21, 27, 27.1; *CSPD 1670*, p. 317. Vincent was arrested in August 1670 for violating the Five-Mile Act and imprisoned for six months. *CSPD 1670*, p. 388; PRO SP 29/280/130.

32. *Gazette* 529 (8–12 December 1670); *Rel. Bax.*, pt. 3, par. 194 (p. 88). The story erroneously gave his age as approximately 36; he was probably closer to 50. On 28 May 1670 Sir John Trevor had issued a warrant for the arrest of Henry Danvers and William Allen (alias Blood)—probably Thomas Blood. *CSPD 1670*, p. 239.

33. *HMC* 7, *Eighth Report*, Appendix, Part I, pp. 155, 157; *Gazette* 529 (8–12 December 1670).

34. *Gazette* 529 (8–12 December 1670); *HMC* 7, *Eighth Report*, Appendix, Part I, pp. 155, 158.

35. Arthur John Hawkes, *Sir Roger Bradshaigh of Haigh, Knight and Baronet 1628–1684 with Notes of His Immediate Forbears* (Manchester: Lancashire and Cheshire Antiquarian Society, 1945), p. 43; Firth and Davies, pp. 598, 705, 726–27; Greaves, *DUFE*, p. 147; *CSPI 1663–65*, p. 662; *CR*, s.v. "Johnson, Francis"; *HMC* 7, *Eighth Report*, Appendix, Part I, p. 159.

36. One eyewitness put the number at five; the proclamation for their arrest cited six persons; and Blood allegedly claimed that nine men had been involved. *HMC* 7, *Eighth Report*, Appendix, Part I, pp. 156–57; *CSPD 1670*, p. 567; *HMC* 25, *Le Fleming*, p. 78; *CSPD 1678*, pp. 290, 302–303.

37. Greaves, *DUFE*, pp. 160–61; *HMC* 7, *Eighth Report*, Appendix, Part

I, p. 159; PRO SP 29/405/91, 106, 107, 108. The Presbyterian Philip Henry called Ormond's attackers "Ruffians." Henry, p. 235.

38. *HMC* 7, *Eighth Report*, Appendix, Part I, p. 158. Ludlow attributed the attack to "some personall animossity." "Voyce," p. 1259.

39. *Gazette* 528 (5–8 December 1670); 529 (8–12 December 1670); *HMC* 7, *Eighth Report*, Appendix, Part I, pp. 154–57; *Som. Tr.*, 8:444; *CSPV 1669–70*, p. 314; Carte, 2:421–22; *HMC* 63, *Egmont*, 2:24; *The Rawdon Papers*, ed. Edward Berwick (London: John Nichols and Son, 1819), pp. 246–47; Margaret M. Verney, *Memoirs of the Verney Family from the Restoration to the Revolution 1660 to 1696*, vol. 4 (London: Longmans, Green, 1892), p. 228; *CSPD 1670*, p. 565. According to Baxter, Blood and his associates intended to take Ormond to the Netherlands, where he reputedly had funds and could be forced to pay "his Arrears," but they supposedly intended him no harm. *Rel. Bax.*, pt. 3, par. 194 (pp. 88–89).

40. *CSPD 1670*, p. 567; PRO SP 29/281/15; 29/292/219; *HMC* 7, *Eighth Report*, Appendix, Part I, pp. 155, 158; *LJ*, 12:447.

41. *CSPD 1670*, pp. 573, 576; *Gazette* 529 (8–12 December 1670). Cf. *Gazette* 531 (15–19 December 1670).

42. *HMC* 7, *Eighth Report*, Appendix, Part I, pp. 156–57; *CSPD 1670*, p. 576.

43. In February 1671 a special search was made for Thomas and "Mark" Blood and William More in Lancashire, "for there is new mischiefe Brewing" in that county and Cheshire. Hawkes, *Bradshaigh*, p. 43.

44. PRO SP 29/281/24, 28, 28.1, 42, 99; 29/287/40, 41, 41.1–2, 54, 60, 102, 102.1, 110; *CSPD 1671*, p. 23; *HMC* 25, *Le Fleming*, p. 75; *HMC* 7, *Eighth Report*, Appendix, Part I, pp. 156, 159 (cf. PRO SP 29/281/75, 77); *Som. Tr.*, 8:448n; Carte, 2:424–25; *LJ*, 12:404; Abbott, *Blood*, pp. 102–103.

45. PRO SP 29/281/57.1, 74, 91, 91.1; 29/287/131, 173; 29/294/124; 29/333/82; Capp, *FMM*, p. 247. After Mason's escape he was recaptured and incarcerated at Windsor Castle, where he was a prisoner in September 1667. *CSPD 1667*, p. 465. Wilkinson's brother had been accused of complicity in the 1663 northern rebellion and had narrowly escaped execution.

46. *HMC* 25, *Le Fleming*, p. 78; BL Lansdowne MSS 1152, fol. 238r; PRO SP 29/405/91, 106, 107, 108; 29/427/75; Strype, 1:94; *BDBR*, s.v. "Perrott, Robert"; Hawkes, *Bradshaigh*, p. 44; *CSPD 1678*, p. 290; *CSPD 1683*, 2:30. Halliwell (or Holloway) is identified as a "crownstealer" in 1683. *CSPD 1683*, 1:105. According to Capp, *FMM*, p. 244, Edward Cary was one of the thieves, but I have found no evidence to support this claim. William More and Ralph Alexander may also have been involved.

47. *Som. Tr.*, 8:447–48; Strype, 1:92–93; PRO SP 29/289/187; *CSPV 1671–72*, p. 49; *Gazette* 572 (8–11 May 1671); *HMC* 25, *Le Fleming*, p. 78; Evelyn, 3:576; *Rel. Bax.*, pt. 3, par. 194 (pp. 88–89).

48. *CSPD 1671*, p. 225; *HMC 5, Sixth Report*, Appendix, Part I, p. 370; Abbott, *Blood*, pp. 134–35; Abbott, "Conspiracy," p. 715; PRO SP 29/289/214; 29/290/5; Carte, 2:422; *Som. Tr.*, 8:448; *Rel. Bax.*, pt. 3, par. 194 (p. 88).

49. Carte, 2:423; *Rel. Bax.*, pt. 3, par. 194 (pp. 88–89).

50. PRO SP 29/293/28; 29/422/152; *CSPD 1683*, 1:103.

51. *CSPD 1671*, pp. 242, 244; *HMC 7, Eighth Report*, Appendix, Part I, p. 157.

52. PRO SP 29/290/11; Abbott, *Blood*, pp. 137–38.

53. Lacey, pp. 280, 287; Maurice Lee, Jr., *The Cabal* (Urbana: University of Illinois Press, 1965), p. 178; R.W. Harris, *Clarendon and the English Revolution* (London: Chatto and Windus, 1983), pp. 383–87.

54. Abbott, *Blood*, p. 134.

55. *CSPD 1671*, p. 244 (cf. *CSPV 1671–72*, p. 74); Carte, 2:423; Bodl. Carte MSS 69, fol. 164r; *Rel. Bax.*, pt. 3, par. 194 (p. 89). According to Baxter two views of Blood's pardon were current: Some attributed it to "his Gallantry [which] took much with the King, having been a Soldier of his Father's: Most say, that he put the King in fear of his Life, and came off upon Condition that he would endeavour to keep the discontented Party quiet." *Rel. Bax.*, pt. 3, par. 194 (p. 89). Blood's subsequent career suggests that the latter view is correct.

56. PRO SP 29/291/82–84, 207; 29/292/10.1; *CSPD 1671*, pp. 409, 460; *HMC 5, Sixth Report*, Appendix, Part I, p. 370; Ludlow, "Voyce," p. 1265.

57. *Rel. Bax.*, pt. 3, par. 96 (pp. 42–43), par. 215 (pp. 100–101); Turner, 3:231–45; PRO SP 29/369/165; *CSPD 1672*, p. 45. This may be the second occasion when Blood acted as a government agent, for in 1666 a Mr. Blood pressed Arlington not to allow certain unnamed spies to be arrested. In 1665–66 the same man was concerned with the fate of several imprisoned nonconformists. PRO SP 29/140/93; 29/173/131.

58. Carte, 2:423 (cf. PRO SP 29/441/119); Abbott, *Blood*, p. 142; *BDBR*, s.v. "Blood, Thomas"; Watts, p. 248.

59. PRO SP 29/152/60; 29/162/87.1–2; 29/181/136; 29/239/200; *CSPD 1665–66*, pp. 26–27; *CSPD 1666–67*, p. 580; *HMC 13, Tenth Report*, Appendix, Part IV, pp. 112–13.

60. PRO SP 29/204/31; 29/275/79; 29/278/142; 29/292/24; 29/302/136.

61. When a stranger told Blood that if his attempts on Ormond and the crown jewels had been successful, "it might have bene a happy day," Blood suspected a trap and reported the incident to Williamson. PRO SP 29/293/12.

62. PRO SP 29/293/28; *Rel. Bax.*, pt. 3, par. 85 (p. 36), par. 191 (p. 87); *CR*, s.v. "Innes, James."

63. PRO SP 29/293/28, 135.

64. PRO SP 29/293/22, 28, 222, 233; 29/294/235.

65. PRO SP 29/294/14, 15.

66. PRO SP 29/294/15.

67. PRO SP 29/294/36, 64.

68. PRO SP 29/294/139, 157, 178.

69. PRO SP 29/294/178, 235.

70. Lacey, p. 303; PRO SP 29/294/235; 29/441/87; Buckroyd, *CS*, p. 103.

71. PRO SP 29/293/28, 222; 29/294/28, 36, 139, 178.

72. *CSPD 1671–72*, pp. 13, 65, 116; PRO SP 29/293/164; 29/294/15, 139; 29/317/94; 29/369/165; *BDBR*, s.v. "Overton, Robert"; *CSPD 1675–76*, pp. 56, 60; *CSPD 1678*, p. 290; *CSPD 1682*, pp. 357–58. In November 1671 pardons were also issued to Robert Boulter, John Knight, Thomas Gealing, Thomas Frenchfield, and Thomas Jones. Pardons were granted to John Barnes and John Hickes in January, and to Thomas Swetnam (or Swetman, Sweetham), Captain John Nicholas, and Jonathan Jennings in February. *CSPD 1671*, p. 565; *CSPD 1671–72*, pp. 46–47, 65, 116, 170. Jennings, who was brought to the government by Blood, may have been the Captain Jennings who was allegedly scheming in the summer of 1661. Greaves, *DUFE*, p. 69.

73. PRO SP 29/289/31, 60, 60.1; 29/291/143; 29/293/164; *CSPD 1671*, p. 245; *MCR*, 4:26, 29.

74. PRO SP 29/302/136.

75. PRO SP 29/303/15, 28, 95. For the Cromwell search see *CSPD 1671*, p. 335; PRO SP 29/291/39, 48, 48.1; *HMC 24, Rutland*, 2:19. Among the houses searched were those of the Congregationalist ministers George Griffith, Anthony Palmer, and George Cokayne.

Conclusion

1. Cf. Thomas Walcott: "I know Acts of Indulgence and Mercy in the King would make him sit much easier in his Government, and cause his Subject[s] to sit much easier under it." *A True Copy of a Paper Written by Capt. Tho. Walcott* (London, 1683), p. 2.

2. PRO SP 29/335/13, 302; 29/362/67, 169; 29/363/25, 53, 71; *CSPD Add. 1660–85*, pp. 402–403; *CSPD 1672–73*, pp. 332–33 (misdated); Bodl. MS Rawl. Letters 104, fol. 92r-v; DWL Turner MSS 89.32. Cf. PRO SP 29/362/135, 261; 29/363/93.

3. BL Stowe MSS 207, fols. 114r-v, 120v-121r, 184r; BL Add. MSS 25,124, fols. 14r, 16r (cf. 15r, 22r); *London Gazette* 962 (4–8 February 1675). Cf. *London Gazette* 965 (15–18 February 1675). The bishop of London was troubled by the activities of "dangerous" Fifth Monarchist preachers in 1677. BL Add. MSS 28,093, fols. 212r, 213v.

4. PRO SP 29/368/54, 72, 90, 107, 128, 232; 29/369/158; 29/374/238; 29/379/46; 29/382/42; *CSPD 1675–76*, pp. 234, 275.

5. PRO SP 29/382/87, 121; 29/383/41, 54, 74, 74.1, 115; 29/386/16; *CSPD 1676–77*, pp. 266–67, 311–12. Cf. PRO SP 29/392/3.

6. PRO SP 29/309/160, 160.1; 29/332/140; 29/333/89; 29/369/270; 29/370/10; 29/375/43 (but cf. 29/375/44).

7. *London Gazette* 686 (13–17 June 1672); *CSPD 1672*, pp. 30, 673; *CSPD 1673*, pp. 93, 599; *CSPD 1673–75*, pp. 122–23, 132, 567; *CSPD 1676–77*, p. 274; PRO SP 29/333/181; 29/334/198, 212, 213, 214; 29/336/15.1; 44/28, fols. 94v, 102r, 116v; 44/40, pp. 1, 2, 21; BL Stowe MSS 215, fol. 217v.

8. PRO SP 29/378/36; 44/43, p. 169; *CSPD 1675–76*, p. 510; *CSPD 1676–77*, pp. 97–98, 369; *CSPD 1677–78*, pp. 407–408. For publishing *The Chronicle Freake* (the Fifth Monarchist Christopher Feake?) and Ratford were sent to the Tower in May 1676. BL Stowe MSS 209, fols. 261r, 309r; Stowe 210, fol. 1r.

9. K.H.D. Haley, *William of Orange and the English Opposition 1672–4* (Oxford: Clarendon Press, 1953), chap. 4. One of Blood's friends, a Mr. Newman, was dispatched to the Netherlands as a government spy in the spring of 1672. *CSPD 1672*, p. 683.

10. BL Stowe MSS 204, fol. 42r; Haley, *William of Orange*, chap. 10.

11. [Anthony Ashley Cooper, earl of Shaftesbury?], *A Letter from a Person of Quality, to His Friend in the Country* (n.p., 1675), pp. 1–3, 32; *CSPD 1675–76*, pp. 393, 395; PRO SP 29/374/261, 281.

12. *Two Speeches. I. The Earl of Shaftesbury's Speech in the House of Lords the 20th. of October, 1675. II. The D. of Buckinghams Speech in the House of Lords the 16th. of November 1675.* (Amsterdam, 1675), p. 11.

13. [Anthony Ashley Cooper, earl of Shaftesbury], *Two Seasonable Discourses Concerning This Present Parliament* (Oxford, 1675), pp. 9–10; Lacey, pp. 79–80, 82.

14. Lacey, pp. 76–79; PRO SP 29/378/35.1, 40, 48, 76, 77, 79; 29/379/151; *CSPD 1675–76*, p. 511 (cf. p. 503).

15. *CSPD 1676–77*, p. 51; [Herbert Croft], *The Naked Truth* (n.p., 1675), sig. A3r-v, pp. 18–19, 66. Among those cited for unlicensed printing was Thomas Parkhurst for issuing Thomas Danson's *A Friendly-Debate Between Satan and Sherlock* (1676); *CSPD 1676–77*, pp. 429–30, 479. Note the regular linkage between searches for unlicensed and seditious material. *CSPD 1677–78*, pp. 2, 4, 152; PRO SP 44/28, fol. 173v; 44/334, p. 373. Cf. PRO SP 44/43, p. 118.

16. PRO SP 29/382/142; *CSPD 1676–77*, pp. 193–94. Some attention was also given to illegal Catholic publications. Cf., e.g., PRO SP 29/366, p. 263; BL Stowe MSS 216, fol. 101r-v; *CSPD 1676–77*, p. 328.

17. BL Stowe MSS 210, fols. 1r, 6r, 12r-13v, 14r-v, 89r-v; *CSPD 1676–77*, pp. 215, 251–52, 285; PRO SP 44/43, p. 117.

18. PRO SP 29/366, p. 161; Andrew Marvell, *The Rehearsal Transpros'd and the Rehearsal Transpros'd, the Second Part*, ed. D.I.B. Smith (Oxford: Clarendon Press, 1971), pp. 147–327.

19. PRO SP 29/385/246; 29/391/23; 44/28, fol. 166r.

20. PRO SP 29/397/7.

21. PRO SP 29/392/98, 112; cf. 29/392/46.1, 46.2. In July 1677 the secretaries of state also obtained information about a group of some twenty conspirators who were allegedly planning to kidnap the lord treasurer. Cf. PRO SP 29/395/49.

22. *London Gazette* 1205 (4–7 June 1677); PRO SP 29/392/14.

23. *CSPD 1676–77*, pp. 525, 534–35, 543–44, 563; PRO SP 29/391/110; 44/28, fols. 173r, 174r; 44/344, pp. 363–64, 367, 373, 409–12; *CSPD 1677–78*, p. 152. The government also ordered the arrest of John Mackerness and Mrs. Nathaniel Thompson for publishing William Penn's anonymous *Commentary upon the Present Condition of the Kingdom and Its Melioration* (1677)—a sweeping indictment of royal policy and in particular the established church, not least because "all External Worship is in some degree or other Antichristian" (p. 28). PRO SP 29/393/162; 44/334, pp. 364–65.

24. PRO SP 29/397/51, 55, 56, 76; 44/334, p. 432. The printer of Bacon's works was William Rawlins, and the binder John Barksdale.

25. PRO SP 29/368/210; 29/380/76; 29/385/296.1; BL Add. MSS 25,124, fols. 22r, 33r, 38r, 129r, 130r.

26. PRO SP 29/375/104; 29/379/50; 29/385/112; cf. 29/398/131.

27. Cf. BL Add. MSS 25,124, fols. 33r, 38r; Stowe MSS 209, fol. 237v; PRO SP 29/369/182; 29/383/54; *CSPD 1675–76*, pp. 9–10, 61; *CSPD 1676–77*, pp. 46, 132, 308, 407, 454, 547.

28. *CSPD 1672–73*, p. 129; *CSPD 1673*, pp. 321–22, 516; BL Add. MSS 23,135, fol. 254r; 23,136, fol. 3r; PRO SP 29/333/62; *HMC* 21, *Hamilton*, pp. 86–87; NLS MS 597, fol. 255v.

29. BL Add. MSS 23,135, fol. 284r-v; NLS MS 7006, fol. 16r-v; MS 7034, fols. 29r-30r (contradicted by *Blackader Mem.*, pp. 195–96); *CSPD 1673*, p. 189; BL Stowe MSS 208, fol. 398r; Stowe 213, fol. 354v.

30. BL Add. MSS 23,135, fol. 284r-v; 23,136, fol. 136r; *Blackader Mem.*, pp. 174–77, 195–96; NLS MS 7034, fol. 252r; PRO SP 29/337/185; 29/361/97, 98; *CSPD 1673–75*, p. 253.

31. BL Stowe MSS 214, fol. 232v; *CSPD 1673–75*, pp. 288–89; BL Add. MSS 23,136, fol. 165v-166r.

32. BL Add. MSS 23,136, fols. 167r, 169r-v, 186r-v; 35,125, fol. 260r; *CSPD 1673–75*, pp. 302–303, 364, 381; PRO SP 29/361/135, 135.1; *Blackader Mem.*, pp. 179–84; BL Stowe MSS 214, fols. 223r, 239v, 289v; Stowe 205, fol. 346r. On 2 July 1674 the Council prematurely boasted that "the insolence of that party is at a stand, and their Seditious practises in a greate measure abated." BL Egerton MSS 3340, fol. 14r.

33. BL Stowe MSS 207, fol. 251r-v; Stowe 215, fols. 11r, 192r; *CSPD 1673–75*, pp. 608–609; *CSPD 1675–76*, pp. 161–62; BL Add. MSS 28,747, fol. 17r-v.

34. *CSPD 1675–76*, pp. 161–62; *CSPD 1676–77*, pp. 548–49; *CSPD 1677–78*,

p. 323; PRO SP 63/338/85; BL Add. MSS 23,137, fols. 54r-v, 68r; 23,138, fols. 13r, 67r.

35. NLS MS 2123; MS 2762.

36. EUL MS La.III.684, especially pp. 80–83.

37. PRO SP 29/397/146.

38. Buckroyd, *CS*, pp. 113–19.

39. BL Add. MSS 23,137, fol. 110r; 23,138, fol. 17r (cf. 21r); 32,094, fol. 396r; NLS MS 2512, fol. 203r; PRO SP 29/395/127; 63/338/99.

40. NLS MS 597, fols. 270v-271r; BL Add. MSS 12,068, fol. 12r; 23,138, fols. 71r-v, 81r-v; PRO SP 29/398/124. See also PRO SP 29/397/210 and 29/398/51 for Westmorland. The military unwittingly drove some of the dissidents into Northumberland, reinforcing what Dr. George Hickes called "a correspondence betwixt the two factions in both nations." *HMC 29, Portland*, 2:40.

41. PRO SP 29/398/133 (cf. 29/408/118); 63/338/135. Cf. PRO SP 63/338/140; BL Add. MSS 23,138, fols. 93r-94r, 97r. The charge against Lauderdale was made in 1674 in connection with his support for the 1669 Scottish Militia Act. Schwoerer, p. 105.

42. Wodrow, 2:372; Buckroyd, *CS*, p. 127; Maurice Ashley, *James II* (Minneapolis: University of Minnesota Press, 1977), pp. 117–18; Schwoerer, pp. 118–19.

43. PRO SP 63/333/202; BL Stowe MSS 204, fol. 209r; Stowe 213, fols. 233v-234r. Cf. Stowe MSS 201, fol. 349r. For reports of quiet conditions see *CSPD 1673–75*, pp. 22–23; BL Stowe MSS 208, fols. 239r, 324r, 382v; Stowe 213, fols. 355v, 356v, 357r, 361r, 365r; Stowe 214, fol. 289v.

44. BL Stowe MSS 204, fol. 304r; Stowe 213, fol. 358r. In October 1674 Essex arrested a number of officers who were enlisting men for military service with the Dutch. BL Egerton MSS 3327, fol. 80r-v.

45. BL Stowe MSS 203, fol. 305r; Stowe 205, fol. 346r; Stowe 213, fols. 34v-35r, 56r-v, 179v-180r, 295r-296v, 338v; Stowe 214, fols. 8r, 223r, 232r, 235r, 301r. Cf. Stowe MSS 200, fols. 326v, 334r-v; Stowe 216, fols. 148r-v, 163r.

46. BL Stowe MSS 214, fols. 239v, 289v, 303r; Stowe 216, fols. 63r-v, 93r-v. Cf. Stowe MSS 204, fols. 209r, 283r-v, 313v, 347r.

47. BL Stowe MSS 210, fols. 194r, 197r-v; Stowe 211, fols. 45r, 110v-111r, 114r, 120r, 155v, 238v; Stowe 216, fol. 143r; Stowe 217, fols. 31v-32r, 33r-34r, 39v, 75v, 76v, 78r.

48. BL Add. MSS 32,095, fols. 32r-33v.

49. *MVB*, p. 509.

50. Before the French Revolution, the Old Regime government was also inept in imposing censorship, not least by categorizing "its most advanced philosophy with its most debased pornography." Robert Darnton, *The Literary Underground of the Old Regime* (Cambridge, Mass.: Harvard University Press, 1982), p. 207.

Index

In this index an "f" after a number indicates a separate reference on the next page, and an "ff" indicates separate references on the next two pages. A continuous discussion over two or more pages is indicated by a span of page numbers, e.g., "pp. 57–58." *Passim* is used for a cluster of references in close but not consecutive sequence.

Abbott, Col. Daniel, 107
Abbott, W.C., 213
Aberdeen: Aberdeen (town), 57; Towie, 100; other refs., 99, 118f
Acklom, Peter, 136
Act against Separation and Disobedience, 52–53
Act of Indemnity (1662), 60
Active resistance, views on, 122, 125, 185, 189, 233–34, 242–43
Adair, Patrick, 113
Adman, Ursula, 289
Albemarle, duke of, 21, 32–39 *passim*, 43f, 198, 265. *See also* Monck, George
Alden, Philip, 27, 39, 104, 199
Aldridge, Col., 194
Alexander, Lt.-Col. Ralph, 34, 107f, 209, 211f, 222, 259, 300
Allen, Lt.-Col. William, 8, 280
Anderson, Cornelius, 80
Anderton, Sarah, 173
Andrew, Robert, 50
Anglesey: Holyhead, 44
Anglesey, countess of, 128, 284
Anglesey, earl of, 217
Angus, countess of, 91

Annandale, earl of, 70–76 *passim*
Annesley, Samuel, 159, 218, 292
Anticlericalism, 5, 176–77, 178, 186–90 *passim*, 278
Antrim: Ahoghill, 114; Antrim (town), 113; Ardclinis, 114; Ballyrashane, 114; Carnecastle, 113; Dunluce, 114; Carrickfergus, 108–18 *passim*, 242; Glenarm, 114; Larne, 114; other refs., 104, 113
Apocalyptic themes, 5, 104, 122, 173–74, 190, 200, 238
Apprentices' riots: Dublin (1671), 108; London (1668), 195–97, 298
Archibald, Robert, 63
Argyll: Kintyre, 52
Argyll, eighth earl and marquis of, 50, 186, 296
Argyll, ninth earl of, 73
Arlington, Lord: investigates radical activity, 18, 37, 75, 212, 216, 222; and the Second Dutch War, 22, 27, 30, 62; political rivalries of, 44, 116, 213; attitude toward nonconformists of, 57, 148, 221; and security of Ireland, 71, 77, 107f, 110, 242, 280; and the radical press, 180; and Thomas Blood, Sr.,

214–19 *passim*, 301; other refs., 47, 109. *See also* Bennet, Henry

Armagh: Charlemont, 110, 242; other refs., 104

Armine, Lady Anne, 128

Armine, Lady Mary, 128

Armorer, Sir Nicholas, 115

Arnot, Capt. Andrew, 70, 72, 78

Arnot, Samuel, 63, 81, 236

Arran, earl of, 111

Ashurst, Maj. John, 115

Ashley, Anthony Ashley Cooper, Lord, 195, 217, 221

Assassination schemes, 14, 41, 97–99, 101, 202, 205, 211

Assaults on English clergy, 136–37, 227

Assaults on Scottish clergy, 96–100, 117, 236, 238, 278

Atkins, Sir Robert, 144

Atkinson, John, 7, 11, 17, 45, 172, 194, 260–61

Aylmer, G.E., vii

Ayloffe, John, 229

Ayres, George, 39, 105

Ayrshire: Auchinleck, 100; Ayr, 64f, 68f, 79, 237; Dalmellington, 68; Irvine, 64, 80; Kilmarnock, 63f, 100; Stewarton, 100; other refs., 55, 63, 69, 80, 88ff, 92ff, 99, 239, 276

Baber, Sir John, 221

Bacon, Nathaniel, 234, 304

Baines, Edward, 115, 281

Ballantyne, Sir William, 80

Bampfield, Col. Joseph, 13, 17, 30f

Bampfield, Francis, 123, 133

Banff, 99, 119

Banger, Francis, 123

Bangor, Diocese of, 289

Baptists: and Second Dutch War, 21, 40, 42, 44; in Ireland, 103–9 *passim*; conventicles of in England, 124f, 130, 132f, 155–62 *passim*, 200, 284, 290; adherents of, 152; and licenses, 166, 215; and radical press, 170; radical activities of after Second Dutch War, 201,

204–10 *passim*, 214, 247; other refs., 1, 7, 143, 148f, 201, 222, 245f, 292. *See also individual Baptists by name*

Barber, Thomas, 159

Barclay, Col. David, 50

Barker, Capt. John, 33

Barkstead, Sir John, 24, 29

Barrow, Henry, 171f

Barton, Maj. Nathaniel, 34

Bateman, George, 18, 200

Bates, William, 128, 144, 148, 203, 217f

Battersea plot, 211–12

Baxter, Richard, 128, 143f, 181, 210–11, 215, 244, 267, 292f, 300f

Bayly, William, 169

Beake, Robert, 125

Beckwith, Capt. Matthew, 33

Beckwith, Lt.-Col. John, 193

Bedfordshire: Bedford, 124; Cranfield, 165; Keysoe, 165; Newport Pagnell, 165; Stevington, 165; other refs., 233

Behn, Aphra, 30f

Belcher, John, 156, 159

Belfast, 113, 242

Bellard, Henry, 266

Bendish, Bridget, 128

Bennet, Henry, 13, 19, 21, 167f, 170. *See also* Arlington, Lord

Bennet, Robert, 39

Bennett, William, 173

Berkeley, John Lord, 116

Berkshire: Newbury, 125–26; Reading, 130, 137, 140of; other refs., 130, 135, 233

Berry, Maj.-Gen. James, 128, 235

Berwicksire, 118

Best, Capt., 12

Bethel, Slingsby, 26

Beuningen, Conrad van, 28

Biddle, John, 179

Billeting, 61, 63, 64, 71, 80, 240

Billing, Edward, 232

Bill of Explanation (1665), 104

Bincks, Joseph, 216

Birch, Col. John, 144

Biscoe, Col. John, 14, 26, 28

Blackader, John, 63, 89, 93f, 236f, 271

Blackborne, Robert, 5
Blackett, Henry, 200
Blackmore, Col. John, 41
Blagrave, Daniel, 26
Blair, Alexander, 52, 90
Blaire, Robert, 51
Blakeston, Sir William, 6, 8
Blenkinsop, Cornet, 200
Blood, Jr., Thomas, 204–7 *passim*, 214
Blood, Sr., Thomas: plotting of during
   Second Dutch War, 11, 29, 39–44
   passim, 104–7 *passim*; and possible
   involvement in the Galloway rebel-
   lion, 75, 274; and rescue of Mason,
   193–94; and Ormond kidnapping,
   204–11, 299f; and theft of crown jew-
   els, 209–13; and Battersea plot,
   211–12; as a royal agent, 214–23 *pas-
   sim*, 233, 301; other refs., 57, 220, 228,
   245, 247, 291, 299, 303
Booker, John, 173
Book of Common Prayer, 6, 126, 145,
   150, 179
Boteler, Maj.-Gen. William, 290
Boyd, Thomas, 113
Boyle, Michael, Lord Chancellor of
   Ireland, 109
Bradshaigh, Sir Roger, 21
Bradshaw, Edward, 134
Braithwaite, W.C., 139
Breda, Declaration of, 12, 225
Brewster, Anna, 175
Brewster, Thomas, 168
Bridge, William, 150, 180, 295
Bridgeman, Sir Orlando, 144
Briggs, Capt., 107
Bristol: militant activity at, 6, 47, 191,
   258f, 262; and radical plotting, 12, 15,
   33, 41f, 264; Quakers in, 137, 139, 160;
   other nonconformists in, 132, 153, 160,
   234–35; diocese of, 152; and radical
   press, 174, 182
Brookes, Nathan, 168, 183
Brooks, Thomas, 127, 148, 203, 291
Broughton, Sir Brian, 7–8, 11, 19, 147
Brown, John, 51, 58, 185–86, 188, 297

Browne, Capt., 39
Browne, John, 201, 297
Browne, Joseph, 234
Browne, Sir Richard, 34
Bruce, Michael, 57, 88–89, 242
Buchanan, George, 184
Buckingham, duke of: and ties to non-
   conformists, 44–45, 192–95, 198, 214,
   216, 232, 267, 298; and the Shaftes-
   bury circle, 230, 233; other refs., 7,
   109, 116, 208, 213, 266
Buckinghamshire: Winslow, 170; other
   refs., 12, 130, 151, 170, 233
Buckroyd, Julia, 65, 221, 277
Buffett, Col. Francis, 33, 41, 264
Buffett, Col. Richard, 33, 41, 223, 264
Bulkley, Stephen, 172
Bunyan, John, 121f, 124, 130, 133, 165, 216,
   234, 295
Burnet, Alexander, archbishop of Glas-
   gow: and Second Dutch War, 56, 58f;
   and attitude toward nonconformists,
   62, 86, 97, 100, 111, 239, 277; and Gal-
   loway rebellion, 64, 86; and radical
   press, 184
Burnet, Gilbert, 80, 95f, 100
Burnett, Robert, 118
Burnyeat, John, 159
Burrough, Edward, 173, 294
Burroughs, Jeremiah, 180
Burton, Maj. William, 26, 105, 162, 199,
   222, 263, 298
Bute, 99
Butler, Dr. Nicholas, 216–21 *passim*, 292
Butler, Simon, 107, 172
Butler, Timothy, 11, 107, 193f, 208, 291
Buxton, John, 212

Calamy, Edmund, 244
Calvert, Elizabeth, 168, 174–82 *passim*,
   228, 294
Cambridgeshire, 139
Campbell, Archibald, 184
Campbell, John, 238
Campbell, Patrick, 60
Campbell, Sir Hugh, 58, 265

Campsie, John, 117
Cannon of Mondrogat, 99
Cant, Alexander, 51
Capp, Bernard S., 5, 208
Carey, Cornet Daniel, 222
Cargill, Donald, 52, 238–39, 268
Carlisle, earl of, 41
Carmichael, Alexander, 94, 278
Carr, Col. Gilby: in exile, 15, 20, 27, 38, 62; in Ireland, 40, 75; in Scotland, 57, 68, 76, 102–3, 274; other refs., 50, 245
Carr, William, 229
Carrickfergus mutiny, 110–11
Carse, Margaret, 278
Carstares, John, 52f, 74, 81, 188
Carstares, William, 229, 237, 278
Carter, Capt. (William?), 12
Carter, Nathaniel, 162
Carteret, Sir George, 109
Cary (alias Carew), Capt. Edward, 11f, 209, 300
Cary, Dr. Nicholas, 234
Caryl, Joseph, 127
Case, Thomas, 180
Cassillis, earl of, 38, 111
Catholicism, hostility to, 4, 6, 43, 46, 105, 109, 142, 174, 182–83, 192, 231, 235, 297
Cavan, 111
Cawley, William, 24, 28
Chambers, John (alias Thomas Mills), 39
Chambers, Robert, 281
Chapman, Hannah, 168
Chapman, Livewell, 168
Charles II: hostility toward, 4f, 21, 34, 44, 190, 191–92; militia policy of, 8–9; and policy toward Scottish non-conformists, 50, 80, 83, 91, 93, 100, 235–40 *passim*; and policy toward Scottish radicals, 69, 99, 103; Irish policy of, 115ff, 241; and policy toward English nonconformists, 129, 148, 158, 165, 203, 245, 248; and the radical press, 183, 188; and Thomas Blood, Sr., 219–15 *passim*; and search

for an accommodation, 215–27 *passim*, 234; other refs., 3, 16, 110
Charlton, Sir Edward, 41
Cheshire: Bosley, 147; Chester, 43f, 127, 132, 148–49, 163, 182f; Congleton, 149; Middlewich, 163; other refs., 34, 36f, 42, 138, 151, 153, 157, 201f, 300
Chiesley, Sir John, 58, 62, 102
Church, royal agent, 216–20 *passim*
Church Commission (Scotland), 53, 62
Clanking Act, 93–94, 100, 277
Clare, 105
Clare, Henry, 34
Clare, Quartermaster, 107
Clare, Timothy, 34
Clarendon, earl of, 14, 16, 19, 26, 35, 44, 111, 130, 140
Clark, J.C.D., viif
Clarke, John, 234
Clydesdale, 56, 69, 89, 93, 99
Cockburn, J.S., 130
Cokayne, George, 42, 127f, 302
Coke, Sir Edward, 146
Colbourne, Maj., 33, 258
Cole, Thomas, 13, 25, 27
Colgwen, Humphrey, 79
Collins (alias Cullen), Thomas, 40, 266
Comprehension, English debate on, 142, 144, 215
Congregationalists: radical activity of before and during Second Dutch War, 2, 42, 107; in Ireland, 103, 109, 115; conventicles of in England, 125–29 *passim*, 134, 148ff, 155–59 *passim*, 227, 282, 284, 291; and views on toleration, 142ff; adherents of, 152; and licenses, 166, 215; and radical press, 170; other refs., 168, 203, 205, 222, 245ff, 302. *See also individual Congregationalists by name*
Connaught, 112
Conventicle Acts, English (1664), 6f, 8, 129–34, 137, 145, 169; (1670), 154, 182f, 189, 216, 250, 290
Conventicle Acts, Scottish (1662), 52; (1670), 95, 202

Conventicles, English: as a challenge to the government, 120–29, 282, 284; and the 1664 Conventicle Act, 129–34; and the toleration dispute, 142–51, 288–89; and the 1670 Conventicle Act, 153–64, 291; other refs., 101, 182, 195–204 *passim*, 218, 220, 226, 235

Conventicles, Irish, 111–19 *passim*

Conventicles, Scottish, 52f, 57–64 *passim*, 83, 85–96, 185, 189, 235–41 *passim*, 276f

Conway, Viscount, 45, 75, 115, 194

Corbet, Miles, 24, 29

Cordy, Capt. Nicholas, 9

Cork: Cork (town), 103, 118, 140f; Kinsale, 8, 118, 279; Youghal, 118; other refs., 105

Corney, Thomas, 27

Cornwall: Falmouth, 142; other refs., 33, 152f, 161

Cosin, John, 152

Costellogh, Dudley, 111

Cotes, Elizabeth, 169, 293

Cottrell, James, 179, 295

Courtney, Hugh, 38, 199, 208

Coven, Stephen, 180

Coventry, Sir William, 33, 237, 242, 264

Cowborne, John, 27

Cowborne plot (alleged), 26–27

Cox, Capt. Owen, 19

Cox, Nehemiah, 156

Cox, Nicholas, 155–56, 290

Cox, (Samuel?), 115

Crabb, Peter, 6, 41

Craven, earl of, 211

Crawford, Janet Chalmers, 99

Creed, Richard, 199

Cressey plot, 41

Crisp, Stephen, 135

Croft, Herbert, 231

Crofton, Zachary, 43

Cromwell, Dorothy, 26

Cromwell, Oliver, 5, 21, 227

Cromwell, Richard, 14, 26f, 40, 223, 233, 266

Crookshanks, John, 57, 60, 63, 65, 71, 76f, 81f, 114, 117, 184

Crouch (alias Cross), Robert, 228f

Crowder, Joseph, 37

Crown jewels, theft of, 209–12

Croxton, Col. Thomas, 34, 264

Cullen, Capt. Thomas, 108

Cumberland: Carlisle, 101f, 135, 148, 174; other refs., 5, 71, 99, 138f, 150

Cuningham of Bedland, John, 76, 82, 275

Cunningham, Sir William, 58

Curry, James, 90

Curtis, Langly, 172

Dale (alias White), Maj. (Daniel?), 33, 264

Dale-Buffett plot (1665), 33

Dalrymple, Sir John, 241

Dalziel, Lt.-Gen. Thomas, 68–80 *passim*, 86, 273

Daniel, Col. William, 55

Danvers, Anne, 18

Danvers, Charles, 32

Danvers, Col. Henry, 9, 32, 34, 127f, 209, 235, 245, 299

Danvers (alias Villiers), Robert, 8

Darby, John, 168, 175, 179, 182

Darley, Henry, 172

Davidson, Sir William, 15

Davies, Richard, 138

Davis, Colin, vii

Davis, John, 125

Dawson, Christopher, 11

De Brill, Apolonia, 46

Declaration of Indulgence (1672), 165–66, 250

Dempster, Andrew, 66

Denbigh: Wrexham, 127f, 133f

Dendy, Mrs. Edward, 25

Derby, earl of, 37, 266

Derbyshire, 13, 34, 37, 42, 44, 163

De Ruyter, Adm. Michiel, 21–22

Desborough, Maj. John, 107

Desborough, Maj.-Gen. John: in exile, 13, 26ff, 35, 39f, 150; surrenders, 15–16, 23, 199; a conventicler, 128, 199, 235

Devonshire: Devon, 148; Exeter, 125, 161, 283; Plymouth, 148, 258; Tavistock, 258; Totnes, 148; other refs., 19, 23, 33, 152f, 285

De Witt, Jan, 3, 13, 16f, 22–30 *passim*, 38

Dewsbury, William, 137, 173

Dickson, John, 93f

Doleman, Col. Thomas, 22, 30f, 202, 261, 298

Donaldson, Andrew, 60

Donegal: Letterkenny, 114; Taughboyne, 114; other refs., 242

"Dons," 218, 220

Doolittle, Thomas, 157, 160, 203, 218, 290

Dorset: Dorchester, 198; Poole, 26; Weymouth, 132, 138; other refs., 9f, 153

Douglas, Robert, 89

Dover, Joan, 169

Dover, Simon, 168, 172

Dover plot (alleged), 26, 40

Down, 104

Downing, Sir George, 14, 38

Drumlanrig, Lord, 70, 76

Drummond, Lt.-Gen. William, 64, 73, 78, 86, 273

Drumond, Thomas, 116

Dublin, 39f, 103–8, 112–17 *passim*, 280f

Dublin Castle, plans to attack, 104, 108

Dublin plot (1663), 103

Duckenfield, Col. Robert, 34, 43, 199, 264

"Ducklings," 218ff

Dumfries: Dumfries (town), 54, 64, 80, 97, 100; Closeburn, 188; Glendinning, 95; other refs., 63, 83, 99

Dumfries, Synod of, 52

Du Moulin, Peter, 229

Dunbarton: Kirkintilloch, 92f; other refs., 58, 92, 99

Duncan, Anna Ker, 99

Dundas, William, 50

Durant, William, 150

Durham: Raby Castle, 18, 200f; Shields, 200; other refs., 2, 7, 10, 35, 132, 152, 201, 258

Durham, Bishopric of, 259

Dyer, William, 175

Dysart, countess of, 221

East Lothian, 237

Eckly, Edward, 170

Edinburgh: control of nonconformity in, 53, 87–92 *passim*; and nonconformist activity before the Galloway rebellion, 54–58 *passim*; Quakers in, 57, 118–19; and the Galloway rebellion, 65–79 *passim*, 83, 273; and attacks on clergy, 97ff; other refs., 235f, 277

Edmondson, William, 117

Edwards, Richard, 33

Ejections of Scottish clergy, 51–52

Elliott, George, 173

Ellison, Lt.-Col. Jeffrey, 128

Ellwood, Thomas, 154

Elton, George, 8, 258

English, Francis, 162

Escapes, 10, 32, 41, 102, 147, 192–95, 203, 238, 297

Essex: Colchester, 140, 293; Rumford, 204; other refs., 38, 152f, 199

Essex, Arthur Capel, earl of, 108f, 116f, 236, 241f, 281, 305

Estates, concern for security of, 103, 114

Evans, John, 152

Exeter, countess of, 128

Exile community: on the eve of the Second Dutch War, 12–15, 260, 268; in the Second Dutch War, 23–32, 58–59, 62, 105, 298; and Scotland, 25, 66, 91; after the Second Dutch War, 150, 199, 242; and the radical press, 167, 184–88 *passim*

Eyon, Christopher, 17, 41, 266

Faber, Dr. Albertus, 44

Farnworth, Richard, 169

Faron, Thomas, 156

Faucett, Reginald, 11

Feake, Christopher, 123, 303

Fell, Margaret, 137, 147, 149

Fenn, Samuel, 124
Ferguson, Robert (plotter), 245
Ferguson, William, 67
Ferguson of Buittle, Robert, 60
Fife: Anstruther, 88; Culross, 92; Dunfermline, 92, 237; Hill of Beath, 92–93; Inverkeithing, 92; Kirkcaldy, 92; Largo, 88; St. Andrews, 236; other refs., 88f, 236f, 240
Fife, synod of, 52
Fifth Monarchists: radical activity of before the Second Dutch War, 7, 11, 19, 123; and the Second Dutch War, 20, 38–44 *passim*, 193, 266; and conventicles, 124f, 127, 133f, 148f, 159, 288–92 *passim*, 302; radical activity of after the Second Dutch War, 199, 204f, 208f, 222, 229, 247; other refs., 122, 143, 198, 240, 303. *See also individual Fifth Monarchists by name*
Finch, Sir Heneage, 47
Finch, Sir Henry, 146
Fire of London, 45–47, 174, 176
Fisher, James, 193
Five-Mile Act, 35, 230, 299
Flather, Joseph, 37
Fleetwood, Gen. Charles, 128
Fleetwood, George, 8
Fleming, Daniel, 135, 147, 164, 166, 192, 201
Fletcher, Anthony, 132
Fletcher, John, 72
Flint, Thomas, 264f
Forbes, George, 89
Forbes, James, 170–71, 178, 295
Forbes, Sir Arthur, 107, 117, 236, 242
Ford, Philip, 118
Ford, Thomas, 177
Fox, George, 118, 134, 136f, 149, 159, 282
Foxey, John, 199–200
Fryer, William, 194, 216
Fulthorp, Col., 12
Furly, Benjamin, 31, 169
Furly, John, 141

Gadgirth, laird of, 74, 184
Gaines, John, 168, 293

Galloway, 63, 66, 92, 97, 99
Galloway, diocese of, 60
Galloway, synod of, 51–52
Galloway (Pentland) rising, 64–76, 186f, 271–75 *passim*
Galway: Galway (town), 140
Garland, Augustine, 8
Garner, James, 52
Gartside, John, 147
Gataker, Thomas, 184
Giffen, Capt. William, 50
Gillespie, Patrick, 50
Gilpin, Richard, 149
Gladman, Maj. John, 221
Glasgow, 56, 59, 62, 68ff, 79f, 90–94 *passim*, 99, 236, 275
Glasgow, province of, 95
Glasgow and Ayr, synod of, 52
Glasse, Thomas, 7, 125, 127, 133
Glen, James, 184
Glencairn, earl of, 70
Gloucester, diocese of, 152
Gloucestershire: Marshfield, 127; other refs., 152, 170f, 182, 292. *See also* Bristol
Goffe, William, 262
Goodall, Robert, 36
Goodenough, Richard, 229
Goodgroom, Richard, 159, 198, 208
Goodman, Abraham, 198
Goodman, Christopher, viii, 122, 189
Goodwin, John, 168
Goodwin, Thomas, 155
Gordon, Cornet Robert, 66, 78
Gordon, John, 78
Gosfright, George, 199
Goslin, Elizabeth, 173
Gowen, Thomas, 113
Gower, Capt. Thomas, 11, 35, 200
Gower, Mrs. Thomas, 17
Gower, Sir Thomas, 7, 27, 164, 297
Goznold, John, 234
Graham, John, 38
Graves, Cornet, 259
Gray, Capt. George, 259
Gray, Robert, 98f

Greathead, Maj. Joshua, 37, 193
Green Ribbon Club, 233
Greenwood, John, 171f
Grey, Capt. Andrew, 65–67 *passim*, 272
Griffin, Sarah, 169, 293
Griffith, George, 245, 302
Grocer, Martin, 172
Groome, Capt. (Benjamin?), 26, 105
Grove, John, 263
Grumball, Capt., 107
Gryce, Capt. John, 45, 107, 216, 265, 280
Guilford, Francis North, Baron, viii
Guthry, James, 12, 50, 184ff
Guthry, John, 69, 71, 81f

Haggett, William, 216
Hague, Anthony, 57
Hale, Sir Matthew, 144
Haley, K.H.D., 229
Halket, Col. Robert, 58
Hall, Thomas, 113
Hallet, Thomas, 123
Halliday, Samuel, 242
Halliwell, Richard, 204, 206–9 *passim*, 247
Ham, English dissident, 107
Hamilton, Archibald, 61, 242
Hamilton, duke of, 68ff, 92f, 96, 239f, 277
Hamilton, Gilbert, 90
Hamilton, James, 90, 92, 94
Hammond, Robert, 262
Hampden, Richard, 128
Hampshire: Portsmouth, 148; Southampton, 148; other refs., 9
Hampton, William, 117
Hardcastle, Thomas, 284
Harrington, James, 27
Harrington, John, 233–34
Harris, Capt., 12, 38
Harris, Tim, 195
Harrison, Dr. Thomas, 134
Harrison, Edward, 155, 159f
Harrison, John, 211
Harrison, Joseph, 173
Hart, John, 116

Hartopp, Sir John, 128
Hase, John, 44
Hely, Capt. James, 263
Hendry, Archibald, 185
Hendry, William, 242f
Henry, Philip, 35, 156, 215, 300
Hereford, diocese of, 152
Herefordshire: Hereford, 191; Ross-on-Wye, 132; other refs., 152
Hertfordshire: Hertford, 124f, 139; other refs., 12, 38, 153
Heveningham, William, 198
Heydon, John, 44
Hickes, James, 54
Hickes, Margaret, 173
Hill, Col., 99
Hill, Joseph, 12, 259
Hobson, Paul, 8
Hodgkinson, Richard, 168
Hodson, Capt. John, 37
Hogg, Thomas, 89
Holburn, Maj.-Gen., 58
Holles, Denzil Lord, 217, 234
Holmes, Lt.-Col. Abraham, 10, 259
Holmes, Nathaniel, 222
Holt, Ralph, 234
Home, David, 89
Home, Robert, 89
Honeyman, Dr. Andrew, bishop of Orkney, 98, 187
Honeywood, Jr., Robert, 263
Hooker, Thomas, 180
Hope, Capt. Robert, 34, 264
Hopkins, Lt., 40
Horrockes, Thomas, 124
How, Samuel, 178
Howard, William, 229
Howgill, Francis, 137
Hubberthorne, Richard, 169
Hume, Capt. John, 50, 101
Humfrey, John, 143–44
Huntingdonshire: Huntingdon, 283; other refs., 152
Hutcheson, Robert, 107
Hutton, Capt. Robert, 10, 12, 259

Ince, Peter, 123
Indemnity to Scottish rebels, 82–83
Indulgence, Declaration of (1672), 95, 224; implications of, 224–35
Indulgence, English debate on, 142, 144, 215, 223
Indulgence, Irish policy of, 116
Indulgence, Scottish policy of, 90–91, 95–96, 235–40 *passim*
Informers and spies: quality of information from, 1, 247, 249–50; work of among English dissidents before Second Dutch War, 7, 11f, 18f; work of in exile community, 13–17 *passim*, 26f, 30f, 260, 303; reports on activity in England during Second Dutch War, 36–43 *passim*, 267; in Ireland, 104–8 *passim*; on conventicles, 147, 152–59 *passim*, 226, 289; and the radical press, 183; on radical activity in England after Second Dutch War, 194–200 *passim*, 216, 220–21, 298; other refs., 265, 301. *See also individual spies by name*
Ingoldsby, Col. Richard, 266
Ingoldsby, Sir Henry, 8, 280
Innes, James, 217–21 *passim*
Inverness: Craggie, 63
Ireland: radical schemes in, 7–11 *passim*, 33, 35, 39ff, 44, 103–9; as refuge for Scottish dissidents, 58, 77, 237; and the Galloway rebellion, 65, 68, 71, 76; security in, 68, 71, 109–12, 237, 242; nonconformists in, 84, 112–19, 140–41, 241–43, 282; and the radical press, 169; other refs., 217, 219
Ireton, John, 128
Ironmonger, John, 12, 15, 18
Isle of Ely, 36, 259, 262
Isle of Wight, 43, 139

Jackson, Arthur, 128
Jackson, Henry, 136
Jacomb, Thomas, 128, 217f
Jaffray, Alexander, 118
Janeway, James, 218
Jenkins, William, 124

Jenks, Francis, 231ff
Jennans, Mrs., bookseller, 170
Johnson, Francis, 205
Johnson, Katherine, 21
Johnson, Thomas, 168, 174
Johnston, Capt. Robert, 56, 101
Johnston of Wariston, Sir Archibald, 50, 184ff
Jolly, Maj. James, 134
Jones (alias Rogers), Capt. Roger: plotting of, 11–12, 17f, 107, 205, 211f; imprisoned, 35, 45; other refs., 171, 217, 221
Jones, John, 159
Joplin, John, 11, 45, 259
Joplin, Robert, 259
Jordan, Maj., 10
Jordan, Tobias, 17, 293
Jordan, William, 170
Joyce, Cornet George, 199

Keach, Benjamin, 170, 175
Keith, George, 118
Kello, Margaret Dury, 99
Kelsey, Maj.-Gen. Thomas, 24, 27, 222, 235, 298
Kennedy (alias Weir), Andrew, 188, 297
Kennedy, Gilbert, 242
Kennedy, Thomas, 65, 274
Kent: Canterbury, 125, 139, 150; Cranbrook, 170; Deal, 291; Dover, 6, 127, 147, 150, 156, 162, 266; Margate, 227; Sandwich, 150; other refs., 132, 150, 152, 170
Ker of Kersland, Robert, 82, 275
Keyes, William, 113
Kiffin, William, 148, 159
Kilgour, Maj., 72
Kincardine, 99
Kincardine, earl of, 90f, 187f, 236–37
King, Col. Edward, 35
King's County, 104, 237
Kirby, Richard, 134
Kirkcudbright: Anwoth, 61; Balmaclellan, 61, 66, 100; Borgue, 97; Carsphairn, 61; Dalry, 66; Irongray, 61,

66; Kirkcudbright (town), 60–61, 64, 100; stewartry of, 80, 83, 89, 97

Kirkcudbright, Lord, 61

Kirkton, James, 238

Knollys, Hanserd, 148, 159

Knowles, John, 127

Knox, John, viii, 122, 185, 187, 189

Lacey, Douglas, 194

Lambert, Maj.-Gen. John, 19, 21, 25, 30, 248, 261

Lanarkshire: Boghall, 95; Cambusnethan, 89; Carmunnock, 100; Carnwath, 92f; Glassford, 100; Hamilton, 90; Kirk of Shotts, 100; Lanark, 70ff, 102; Lesmahagow, 70; other refs., 80, 83, 88–94 *passim*, 99, 118

Lancashire: Bolton, 126; Lancaster, 286; Liverpool, 39, 21, 33, 36f, 44, 105; Manchester, 44, 163; Warrington, 44; other refs., 130, 132, 152f, 286, 300

Langley, Sir Roger, 10

Larkin, George, 178f, 295

Lascelles, Capt. Thomas, 12, 33, 265

Lascelles, Darcy, 201

Lauderdale, earl of: policy of toward nonconformists, 61, 86–89 *passim*, 93–96 *passim*, 221, 236–40 *passim*, 277f; and relations with Thomas Blood, Sr., 219f; other refs., 82, 101, 305

Laurence, Capt. Richard, 198

Lawrence, Anthony, 234

Leach, Thomas, 168, 174, 179f, 295

Learmont, Maj. Joseph, 69, 81f, 98ff

Lee, Maj., 11

Lee, Peter, 134

Lee, Samuel, 128

Leeving, Capt. William, 45, 108, 193f, 216, 267

Leighton, Robert, archbishop of Glasgow, 95, 239

Leicestershire: Leicester, 126; Lutterworth, 47; other refs., 11, 19, 34, 44, 193

Leinster, 118

Lerie, John, 154

L'Estrange, Roger, 167ff, 176ff, 182f, 231f, 249

Lever, Henry, 150

Levington, English dissident, 107

Levinton, Peter, 168, 228

Lilly, William, 34, 46

Limerick: Limerick (town), 8, 75, 103, 108, 279; other refs., 105, 107

Lincoln, diocese of, 152

Lincolnshire: Bytham, 128–29; Lincoln, 148; other refs., 13, 42, 152f

Lindsay, John, 79

Linlithgow (West Lothian): Bathgate, 238; other refs., 92f, 237

Linlithgow, earl of, 71, 78, 87

Linlithgow, presbytery of, 55

Linton, John or Robert, 200

Lisle, John, 14

Littleton, James, 212

Littleton, Sir Thomas, 212f

Liverpool plot (alleged), 26, 39–40, 104–6, 205

Livesey, Sir Michael, 26

Livingston, Alexander, 61

Livingston, John, 52, 188, 261

Lloyd, Griffith, 128

Lockhart, Capt. Robert, 70, 237

Lockhart, William, 38

Lockyer, Capt. John, 18, 193f, 208f, 221, 259, 291

Lockyer, Nicholas, 29, 42, 145–46, 178, 182, 221

London: revolutionary councils in, 2, 7–10 *passim*, 34, 201, 284; ex-Cromwellian officers ordered to leave, 11, 158, 203; and radical activity in Second Dutch War, 17, 19, 25–34 *passim*, 42, 259; conventicles in, 121–42 *passim*, 147–63 *passim*, 220ff, 278, 288, 291, 302; and the radical press, 167–74 *passim*, 178, 182f, 189; and apprentices' riot (1668), 195–97; and radical activity after Second

Dutch War, 198–211 *passim*, 229, 232ff; other refs., 12, 267, 283, 293f, 299
Londonderry: Coleraine, 113f; Londonderry (formerly Derry), 110, 112, 116f, 242; other refs., 114
Long, Col. James, 42
Longford: Castle Forbes, 111
Lord, Thomas, 40
Lothian, synod of, 52
Loudon, Lord, 184
Louis XIV, 28f, 110
Lowe, Maj. William, 222
Lowe, Roger, 130
Lucke, William, 149
Ludlow, Lt.-Gen. Edmund: and the Second Dutch War, 3, 13–17 *passim*, 23–32 *passim*, 199, 247f, 262; association of his name with plots, 8, 39f, 105, 202, 223; views of, 45, 144, 214, 247, 267, 298, 300; other refs., 109, 260
Lumbey, David, 37, 172
Lunn, radical agent, 13, 42
Lyons, Capt., 264

McArmick, William, 102
McCormack, Andrew, 69f, 76
McCulloch, James, 113
McCulloch, Maj. John, 69, 78, 113
McKell, Hugh, 55, 79, 81, 186
McKell, Matthew, 61
Maclellan of Balmagechan, Robert, 68
Maclellan of Barscobe, John, 65ff, 81f, 93, 99f
MacWard, Robert, 51, 58, 184, 188, 268
Magna Carta, 109, 145f, 230
Maitland, William, 60
Manchester, earl of, 35
Manley, John, 128
Mansell, Christopher, 202
Manton, Thomas, 128, 144, 155, 217f, 221, 292
Marlow, John, 232
Marsden, Jeremiah, 11f, 17, 193, 209

Marshal, George, 201–2
Marshall, William, 172
Marten, Henry, 198
Martindale, Adam, 154
Marvell, Andrew, 174–75, 229, 232
Mason, Capt. John: escapes of, 10, 193–94, 297, 300; plotting of, 11, 17, 208f, 245, 248; other refs., 46, 221f, 291
Mason, William, 193
Mather, Samuel, 115
Mawborne, Francis, 172
Maxwell, Gabriel, 74, 82, 114, 117, 277
Maxwell, Sir George, 58
Maxwell of Monreith, William, 65, 67f, 275
Mead, Capt., 13
Meade, William, 135
Medley, Samuel, 228
Medley, William, 229
Middlesex: Hillingdon, 289; other refs., 132, 139, 152f
Middleton, George, 45, 56, 216
Midlothian: East Calder, 97; Leith, 71; other refs., 237
Mildmay, Sir Henry, 8
Militia, need to settle, 8–9, 99, 112
Millar, William, 99–100
Millenarianism, 38, 199
Millington, Gilbert, 8
Milton, John, 122
Milton, William, 126
Mitchell, James, 69, 72, 81, 94, 97–100, 245, 279
Monck, Gen. George, 2, 4. *See also* Albemarle, duke of
Monckton, Sir Philip, 201, 232f
Monmouth, duke of, 195
Monmouthshire, 153
Monro, Maj.-Gen. Robert, 38
Montgomery, Maj.-Gen. Robert, 25, 38, 58, 74
Montgomery, Maj. Hugh, 112–13, 114, 237
Moone, Susanna, 174

Moray, 89, 119, 276
Moray, Sir Robert, 64, 86, 95, 187, 217, 220–21
More, Lt.-Col. (or Col.) William, 39, 104f, 205f, 209, 300
Morley, George, bishop of Winchester, 211
Morton, Andrew, 90
Mowatt, Matthew, 52
Moyer, Samuel, 198
Muddiman, Henry, 54, 68, 71, 131
Muir of Caldwell, William, 74, 82, 275
Muir of Rowallan, Sir William, 58, 265
Munro, Sir George, 58
Munster, 39, 103ff, 118
Musgrave, Sir Philip, 7, 41, 77, 135, 156, 164, 174, 201, 240, 262, 289

Naesmith, James, 52
Nangle rebellion, 111
Neave, John, 52
Nelson, Lt.-Col. John, 8, 280
Nelson of Corsock, John, 66, 68, 79, 81, 275
Nelthorpe, James, 222
Nelthorpe, Richard, 222
Nesbitt, James, 293
Netherlands: Amsterdam, 62, 230, 259; Arnhem, 13; Leyden, 26; Middelburg, 12, 259; Rotterdam, 13, 23–31 *passim*, 42, 81, 145, 199, 222
Netherlands: and the Second Dutch War, 3, 16–32 *passim*, 38, 261, 263; spies in, 13–17 *passim*, 26f, 30f, 260, 303; as source of weapons, 13, 102, 108; and radical press, 186, 188. *See also* Exile community
Nevay, John, 188
Newburgh, earl of, 60
Newcomb, Thomas, 294
Newman, Dorman, 234
Nicholas, Capt. John, 263, 302
Nicholson, John, 136
Nieupoort, William, 25, 28, 30, 262
Nithsdale, 64, 97, 99
Nithsdale, earl of, 70, 76

Nonconformist community, nature of, 1–2
Nonconformists in England: and the question of active resistance, 121–29; and the 1664 Conventicle Act, 129–34; and the toleration dispute, 142–51; and the geography of dissent, 151–53; and the 1670 Conventicle Act, 153–64; and the 1672 Declaration of Indulgence, 164–66
Norfolk: Great Yarmouth, 126–27, 133, 146, 150, 162, 226f; Norwich, 127, 138f, 226, 284; other refs., 44, 139
North, Henry, 44, 193, 195, 233, 267
Northamptonshire: Wollaston, 6; other refs., 147f, 152f
Northern insurrection (1663), 2
Northumberland: Berwick, 57, 77, 91, 101, 148, 237; Edlingham, 101; Newcastle on Tyne, 6, 18f, 25, 56, 67, 101, 125, 127, 147, 149–50, 182, 191; Norham, 101; other refs., 5, 240, 272, 305
Not, Capt., 40
Nottinghamshire: Nottingham, 141, 284; Nuthall, 12; other refs., 13, 42, 44, 200
Nunnes, Thomas, 173
Nye, Philip, 148

Oates, Titus, 235
Oaths of allegiance and supremacy, 43, 52, 59, 80ff, 112, 116, 123, 129, 133, 137, 141, 159, 200, 221
Obdam, Jacob van Wassenaer, Lord of, 16
Offaly: Banagher, 114
Okey, John, 24, 29
Oliver, Capt. Robert, 106
Ord, Edward, 133
Ormond, duke of: as object of radical hostility, 39f, 113; and security of Ireland, 30, 68, 71, 77, 106–10 *passim*, 115, 243, 274, 281; kidnapping of, 204–9, 211f, 299f; other refs., 116, 214
Orrery, earl of, 37, 39, 75, 106–12 *passim*, 243

Osborne, Sir Thomas, 7, 212f
Osland, Lieut., 35
Ossory, earl of, 208, 213
Oudart, Nicholas, 27
Overton, Col. Robert, 8, 199, 222
Owen, Dr. John, 128, 143f, 148–55 *passim*, 245
Oxford, diocese of, 152
Oxfordshire: Bicester, 147; Oxford, 6, 9, 21, 44; Stadhampton, 143

Palmer, Anthony, 7, 11, 107, 127, 159, 302
Palmer, Thomas (bookseller), 174, 179
Palmer, Thomas (minister), 11, 107, 126
Pardon, offer of royal, 221–22
Parker, Peter, 175
Parker, Samuel, 151, 232
Parkhurst, Thomas, 180f, 303
Parliament (England): Long Parliament, 6, 105, 109; Cavalier
Parliament, 23, 46, 130, 144ff, 150, 153, 191, 194f, 205, 208, 215, 223–34 *passim*, 290
Parliament (Scotland), 50, 52, 56, 93, 95
Partridge, Nathaniel, 156f, 290
Passive resistance, 121f, 124, 134, 136, 142, 189, 245, 285, 288
Paton, Capt. John, 81
Paton, Robert, 53
Patrick, James, 114
Patrick, Simon, bishop of Ely, 180f
Patshall, John, 41
Pattison, radical agent, 56
Peden, Alexander, 60, 63, 72, 81f, 114, 117
Peebles, Hugh, 94, 270
Penn, William, 118, 135, 159, 179, 232, 304
Penry, John, 171f
Pentland Hills, 73–74
Pepys, Samuel, 5, 54, 142, 196f
Perrott, Robert, 209f, 214, 247
Perth: Bridge of Earn, 95
Peterborough, countess of, 128
Peterborough, diocese of, 152
Peyton, Sir Robert, 232–33
Phaire, Col. Robert, 24, 26, 105
Phelps, Capt. John, 14, 26–31 *passim*, 263

Philpott, Thomas, 228
Plague, 32, 36
Ponder, Nathaniel, 232
Ponet, John, viii, 122, 189
Poole, Elizabeth, 179
Poole, Matthew, 128
Pooley, Christopher, 199–200
Popish Plot, 235
Porter, James, 94
Porterfield, George, 38
Porterfield of Quarrelton, William, 74
Portman, John, 198
Povey, Thomas, 4
Poveye (alias Thompson), Capt. William, 214
Powell, Vavasor, 20, 34, 148, 198
Presbyterians in England: and the Second Dutch War, 21, 35; and conventicles, 124–29 *passim*, 147–51 *passim*, 155–63 *passim*, 203, 218–20, 278, 284, 288, 290; views on toleration and indulgence, 142ff, 215, 217, 244, 246f; licensed, 166, 215; and radical press, 174–80 *passim*, 295; radical wing of, 204, 206, 245; other refs., 23, 133, 285, 298, 300. *See also individual Presbyterians by name*
Presbyterians in Ireland, 103–17 *passim*, 241–43, 247
Presbyterians in Scotland, 15, 49–103 *passim*, 184–89 *passim*, 235–48 *passim*, 271, 278. *See also individual Presbyterians by name*
Press, radical: in England, 32, 46, 166–84, 189–90, 227–34 *passim*, 292–96 *passim*, 303–304; in Scotland, 184–90, 296f; in the Netherlands, 62, 199, 228
Pringle, John, 150
Privy Council (England): on treatment of nonconformists, 130, 132, 141, 144, 148, 160, 226; and the radical press, 231, 234; other refs., 22, 43, 47, 201
Privy Council (Scotland), 50–76 *passim*, 80–83 *passim*, 87–103 *passim*, 118f,

184–88 *passim*, 235, 237, 240, 247, 250, 279, 282, 304
Proclamation for return of exile leaders, 26f
Proclamations ordering Cromwellian officers from London, 11, 158, 203
Protesters, 50, 58
Pym, Capt. John, 35
Pyne, Capt. (John?), 33

Quaker Act (1662), 137, 148
Quakers: in England, 7, 17, 31, 40ff, 130, 132, 134–42, 143–66 *passim*, 169, 172f, 177, 182, 190, 198, 203, 232, 245ff, 282–88 *passim*, 292, 296; in Ireland, 117–18, 282; in Scotland, 57f, 118–19, 189, 282. *See also individual Quakers by name*

Radden, Edward, 27, 33
Radicals, concept of, vii–viii, 1–2
Radwell, Maj., 31
Rae, John, 92
Rae, Richard, 57
Rae, Robert, 102
Ralston, laird of, 74
Ramsay, George, 74
Ramsay, Sir Andrew, 89
Rathbone, Col. John, 34
Rathbone plot (1665), 34–35, 39, 104, 264f
Raven, plotter in Netherlands, 31
Ravens, Capt. Thomas, 127
Rawdon, Sir George, 110, 113, 115
Reay, Barry, 138f
Recusancy statutes, 137
Redman, John, 169, 295
Regium donum, 117
Renfrewshire: Finlayston, 92; Kilmacolm, 100; Neilston, 100; other refs., 74, 80, 89–94 *passim*, 99, 239
Reresby, Sir John, 166
Revolutionary councils, 2, 7–8, 9, 34, 65ff, 104, 201, 284
Revolutionary manifestos, 2, 71, 208

Reynolds, William, 159
Richardson, Dr. Edward, 2, 13, 27, 31, 193, 199, 245, 259
Rigge, Ambrose, 137f
Riggs, Edward, 13
Riordan, Maj. Germaine, 14
Ritchie, John, 188
Robartes, John Lord, 116
Roberts, Timothy, 19
Robertson, Alexander, 61, 73, 75, 79, 81
Robertson, Sir John, 8
Robinson, Andrew, 57
Robinson, Sir John, 34, 43, 158–59, 217
Rochester, diocese of, 152
Roe, Mary, 4
Rolfe, Maj. Edmund, 262
Rolle, Samuel, 180–81, 295
Rood, Onesiphorus, 203
Roome, George, 66
Roscommon, 111
Rothes, earl of: and conventicles, 53, 62f, 92f; views of, 56, 64, 86, 97, 100; and the Galloway rebellion, 68, 76–80 *passim*, 274
Rowe, John, 127
Rowld, Capt., 266
Roxburgh: Ancrum, 55; other refs., 118
Royston, Richard, 179, 295
Ruatt, James, 52
Rudyard, Thomas, 232, 290
Rule, Dr. Gilbert, 115
Rule, Robert, 242
Rumford, George, 259
Russell, Henry, 159
Rutland, 152
Rye, John, 198
Rymer, Ralph, Jr., 46

Sacheverell, John, 123
Sadler, Theodore, 180
St. Andrews, province of, 94
St. John, Oliver, 27
Salisbury, earl of, 233
Salmon, Edward, 199
Salmon, Jr., Capt., 193

Saunders, Col. Thomas, 34
Say, William, 7, 14, 24f, 28, 248
Scot, John, 72
Scotland: radicals in, 11f, 15, 20, 25, 39; and search for a religious settlement, 48–54; radical ferment in (1662–66), 54–59; troubled southwest of, 59–64; and Galloway rising, 64–76, 186f, 271–75 *passim*; and flight of Galloway rebels, 76–84; conventicles in, 52f, 57–64 *passim*, 83, 85–96, 185, 189, 235–41 *passim*, 276f; and assaults on clergy, 96–100, 117, 236, 238, 278; radical activity in (1666–71), 101–3; Quakers in, 57f, 117–19, 189, 282
Scott, James, 55
Scott, Richard, 174
Scott, Walter, 118
Scott, William, 17, 26f, 30, 263
Second Dutch War, 15–32 *passim*, 58–59, 62, 104ff, 110, 174, 260ff
Security measures: in England, 8, 35–36, 43f, 47, 158, 202–4, 262, 266; in Scotland, 68, 76–77, 99–100; in Ireland, 71, 109–12, 242
Semple, Gabriel: Scottish conventicles, 53, 63, 236, 277; in Galloway rebellion, 65, 67, 71–74 *passim*, 81f, 271; in Ulster, 114, 117
Semple, William, 116
Shaftesbury, earl of, 229–30, 233. *See also* Ashley, Lord
Shakerley, Sir Geoffrey, 42f, 132, 134, 147, 149, 157, 163, 182
Shapcote, Col. Robert, 108
Sharp, James, archbishop of St. Andrews, 53, 63, 81, 86, 90, 93f, 97–98, 99, 277
Sharply, Ralph, 118
Shaw, John, 61, 114
Sheffield, Edward, 203–4
Sheldon, Gilbert, 130, 144, 151, 166, 291
Shepard, Thomas, 180
Shepperdson, Capt. Edward, 7, 259
Shiells, Ralph, 75
Siddenham, Francis, 182

Sidney, Algernon, 13–17 *passim*, 23–31 *passim*, 45, 247f, 262
Simmons, Mary, 169, 293
Simmons, Samuel, 169, 175, 293
Simon, Joan, 168
Simpson, James, 50, 261, 269
Skinner, John, 127
Smith, Aaron, 233
Smith, Francis, 46, 157, 174, 182
Smith, Henry, 199
Smith, John, 82
Smith, Nathaniel, 172
Smith, William (author), 170
Smith, William (conspirator), 205, 209, 222
Socinians, 179
Solemn League and Covenant, 47, 50f, 68, 71, 78f, 103f, 113f, 186f, 205, 238, 242f, 246
Somerset: Glastonbury, 33; Minehead, 133; Taunton, 7, 33, 39, 41, 134, 197–98, 258; other refs., 33, 122, 132, 151ff, 161f
Somerset plot (alleged), 38–39
Southampton, earl of, 35
Spanish Netherlands: Antwerp, 31
Speed, Samuel, 173
Spurway, Capt. Humphrey, 27, 33, 222, 237
Squibb, Arthur, 159
Staffordshire: Lichfield, 147; Moddershall, 32; Walsall, 147; Wolverhampton, 101, 147; other refs., 11, 34, 42, 132, 144, 147
Starkey, John, 234
States General (Netherlands), 24f, 29, 58, 228, 262
States of Holland, 263
Stationers' Company, 178, 183
Steele, William, 128
Sterne, Richard, 152
Sterry, Peter, 148
Steward (Stewart?), William, 101
Stewart, James, 72, 186f
Stewart, James, Jr., 237
Stewart, Maj., 67

Stewart, Sir James, 58, 102, 265
Stirling: Stirling (town), 58, 236; Torwood, 93; other refs., 92f, 240
Stirling, James, 186
Stoe, Thomas, 202
Stotesbury, William, 107
Stouppe, Brigadier, 28
Strange, Alexander, 94
Strange, Lt. Nathaniel, 7, 11, 19, 124, 127, 147, 245, 261
Strangways, Joseph, 216, 222–23
Streater, Col. John, 168, 182
Stubber, Col. Peter, 35
Stubbes, Henry, 124, 228
Stubbs, John, 118, 282
Succession concerns, 229–35 *passim*
Suffering, theology of, 121–23, 141
Suffolk: Ipswich, 170, 200; Pakefield, 285; Sudbury, 157; other refs., 130, 148, 200
Surrey: Dorking, 123; East Sheen, 128; Southwark, 41, 147, 152, 160, 179, 203, 206; other refs., 152
Sussex, 284
Swinton, George, 184
Swinton, John Swinton, laird of, 57, 118, 200f
Switzerland: Basle, 28; Bern, 24; Lausanne, 14, 29, 260; Vevey, 7, 14, 28
Sykes, Richard, 27
Sykes, William, 27
Sylvester, William, 40
Symmons, conspirator, 205

Tallidafe, William, 53
Tanner, John, 173
Taverner, Capt. Samuel, 40
Taxes, anger over, 4, 36, 109, 175, 191, 222
Taylor, Jeremy, bishop of Down, 65
Taylor, Robert, 106
Taylor, Timothy, 115
Temple, Capt. Sands, 30
Temple, James, 8
Test Act, 226, 229–30
Teviotdale, 118, 240
Thimbleton, Walter, 38, 199

Third Dutch War, 228–29
Thomas, Michael, 174
Thomas, William, 182
Thompson, Maurice, 20
Thompson, Nathaniel, 234
Thompson, William, 170
Thomson, Thomas, 53
Tichborne, Robert, 198, 222
Tiler, Evan, 234
Tillam, Thomas, 199–200
Tipperary: Clonmel, 103; other refs., 105, 107
Toleration dispute in England, 142–51
Tombes, John, 155
Tomlinson, Col. Matthew, 151
Tomlinson, Margaret, 9
Tompkins, Thomas, 144
Tong, Thomas, 40
Tong plot, 27
Tower of London, plans to attack, 11, 33f, 202
Trail, Robert, 50, 52, 58, 97, 188, 242
Travers, Capt. John, 149
Trenchard, John, 229
Trevor, Sir John, 158, 206
Triennial Act (1664), 6f
Troughton, William, 264
Tucker, Henry, 264f
Turner, Sir James, 52, 61–72 *passim*, 186, 273
Tweeddale, earl of, 86, 89, 92–99 *passim*
Twyn, John, 166–67
Tyler, Richard, 13

Ulster, 35, 39, 62, 85, 103–19 *passim*, 241f
Urquhart, Thomas, 89

Vancourt, Jean François de Briselone, Sieur de, 30
Vane, Lady Frances, 18
Veitch, James, 52, 90
Veitch, William, 67, 69, 72, 81f, 272
Venetian resident, reports of, 22, 55, 131
Venning, Ralph, 127
Vernon, George, 151
Vernon, John, 7, 124f, 127, 133

Vernour, Thomas, 100
Vincent, Nathaniel, 159, 203, 218, 220, 299
Vincent, Thomas, 156, 160, 218, 292
Voysey, Thomas, 125

Waite, Thomas, 8, 199
Walcott, Capt. Thomas, 105–9 *passim*, 280, 302
Wales, 9, 35, 152, 289
Walker, Richard, 172
Wallace, Lt.-Col. James, 58, 65–76 *passim*, 81f, 99, 245, 270, 274
Waller, Sir Hardress, 198
Waller, Sir William, 128
Walley, Joseph, 172
Wallis, Elizabeth, 170
Wallis, Ralph, 170–71, 177f, 293
Walsh, Ens. Benjamin, 6
Walton, Valentine, 16
Ward, John, 18, 200
Ward, Seth, bishop of Salisbury, 144, 285
Ward (alias Williams), William, 107
Warwick, William, 159, 169
Warwickshire: Coventry, 39, 147, 149, 163, 191, 226, 235, 288; Warwick, 101, 124, 133, 138, 141; other refs., 11, 124, 138, 151
Washington, James, 13, 42, 199, 298
Watchers, William, 170
Waterford: Waterford (town), 103
Waterhouse, Joshua, 228
Watson, Thomas, 124, 148, 156, 160, 180, 203, 218, 292, 295
Watts, Michael R., 152
Weapons and gunpowder, radical stocks of: in England, 8, 11, 18, 34, 42ff, 202; from Netherlands, 13, 102, 108; in Scotland, 58, 102; in Ireland, 105f
Weeden, Rebecca, 234
Wells, Capt. (Thomas?), 35
Welsh, John, of Cornley, 66, 99, 271
Welsh, John, of Irongray, 63, 67–73 *passim*, 81f, 89, 236f, 239
West, Edward, 218
Westmeath: Kilbride, 114

Westminster, 160, 174, 178f, 183
Westminster Confession of Faith, 234
Westmorland: Appleby, 138; Kendal, 150; other refs., 2, 7, 9, 71, 75, 99, 132, 139, 144, 150, 156, 164, 174, 192
Whalley, Col. Edward, 202, 262
Wharton, Philip Lord, 35, 128, 151, 153, 233, 297
Whitaker, William, 292
White, Adam, 116
White, John, 263
White, Maj. (or Col.) Thomas, 13, 26, 29, 31, 105, 222
Whitehall Palace, plans to attack, 11, 33, 44
Whitehead, George, 137
Wigtown, countess of, 95
Wigtownshire: Stranraer, 61; other refs., 80, 99
Wildman, John, 45, 195, 198, 213, 232, 298
Wilkins, Dr. John, 26, 144
Wilkinson, Edward, 44, 300
Wilkinson, Richard, 208, 291
William of Orange, 229, 250
Williams, Dr. John, 144
Williams, Leonard, 11, 17ff
Williamson, David, 55
Williamson, Joseph: and informers, 43, 211, 216–21 *passim*, 229, 233, 301; and radical press, 180, 232; and the post, 280
Wilson, John, 37, 179f
Wilson plot (1665), 36–37
Wiltshire: Chippenham, 42, 142; Malmesbury, 34; North Bradley, 161; Salisbury, 41, 282; Westbury, 161; Winkfield, 161; other refs., 42, 126, 137, 151ff, 157, 161f
Wincott, Thomas, 124
Winter, John, 180
Wise, Capt. Samuel, 259
Wither, George, 171–76 *passim*, 293
Wodrow, James, 238
Wodrow, Robert, 68, 70, 98
Wogan, Col. Thomas, 14, 26
Women: as radical couriers, 9, 11, 18, 25;

radical views of, 17, 21; and radical activity in Scotland, 60, 80f, 88, 97–102 *passim*, 236, 278; Quakers and, 119, 137, 140, 147, 286; and conventicles in England, 128, 132, 147; and the radical press, 168–79 *passim*, 182, 228, 234f, 293f, 304; other refs., 46

Wood, James, 53

Wood, Seth, 159f

Woodbridge, Benjamin, 126

Woodman, Capt. Thomas, 30

Worcestershire: Evesham, 125; Oldbury, 122; Worcester, 35, 157

Worden, Thomas, 282

Worsley, Dr. Benjamin, 221

Wren, Christopher, 160

Wright, John, 179

Yarrington, Capt. Andrew, 20, 35

Yeamans, Sir Robert, 160

York, James, duke of, 13, 33, 44, 47, 210, 231, 235, 241

Yorkshire: Cowton, 12; Doncaster, 193; Gildersome, 10; Halifax, 37; Hornsea, 136; Hull, 5, 43, 47, 127, 134, 147f, 163–64, 165, 222–23; Leeds, 36, 44, 266; Morley, 37; Northallerton, 10, 12; Shadwell, 127, 129, 164, 284; Whitby, 138, 142, 156f, 164; York, 77, 135, 149, 172, 227; other refs., 2, 7, 9, 19, 36f, 42, 138, 152, 157, 171f, 192f, 201f, 260, 264

Library of Congress Cataloging-in-Publication Data

Greaves, Richard L.
    Enemies under his feet : radicals and nonconformists in Britain,
1664–1677 / Richard L. Greaves.
        p.   cm.
    Includes bibliographical references.
    ISBN 0-8047-1775-3 (alk. paper):
    1. Great Britain—Politics and government—1660–1688.
2. Radicalism—Great Britain—History—17th century. 3. Dissenters,
Religious—Great Britain—History—17th century. 4. Subversive
activities—Great Britain—History—17th century.   I. Title.
DA448.G754   1990
941.06'6—dc20   89-21991
                                                                   CIP